SIMON AND SCHUSTER
New York   London   Toronto
Sydney   Tokyo

The
RAINY
SEASON

Haiti Since Duvalier

AMY WILENTZ

Simon and Schuster
Simon & Schuster Building
Rockefeller Center
1230 Avenue of the Americas
New York, New York 10020

Designed by Nina D'Amario/Levavi & Levavi
Manufactured in the United States of America

10   9   8   7   6   5   4   3   2   1

Library of Congress Cataloging in Publication Data
Wilentz, Amy.
   The rainy season: Haiti since Duvalier/Amy Wilentz.
      p.   cm.
   Bibliography: p.
   Includes index.
   1. Haiti—Politics and government—1986–   2. Haiti—Social
conditions—1971–   3. Haiti—Religious life and customs.
4. Wilentz, Amy.   I. Title.
F1928.2.W55   1989
972.94′07—dc19   89-31003
                                                          CIP

ISBN 0-671-64186-7

Acknowledgments

In the past few years, I have been fortunate to meet and get to know many people who have helped me to begin to understand Haiti, both *en gros* and *en détail*. I owe nonetheless a deep debt to a few who are in more distant ways associated with this book. My profound and affectionate thanks are due Victor Navasky, Ben Sonnenberg, Ed Epstein, Françoise Shein and Christopher Hitchens, without all of whom this book would not have been written.

Among the friends in New York who offered their advice and time were Kate Manning, Carol Gerstman, Jake Lamar and Ruth Liebmann. I'd also like to thank Gary Hoenig and Howard Schneider for the lessons they taught me at *Newsday*. And many, many thanks to Andrew Wylie, Alice Mayhew, David Shipley and Christine Morgan.

In Haiti, I was grateful for the guidance and shelter of Jacques Bartholy, Ira Lowenthal, Alexis Gardella and Carole Kraemer, for the inestimable assistance and wisdom of Bernard Diederich, and for the companionship and emotional support of the almost unflappable photographer Maggie Steber. I'd also like to express my gratitude to Don Guttenplan and Robert Friedman, both formerly of *The Village Voice,* and to my former colleagues Walter Isaacson,

Jason McManus and Henry Muller, at *Time* magazine, who were exceedingly liberal about my hours—and days and weeks.

Greg Chamberlain's and Josh DeWind's careful readings of parts of this manuscript were of great assistance in its preparation, as were those of Haitian friends. The Haitian collection at the Schomburg Center in Harlem and the support of the many people associated with the Schomburg who helped answer my historical and political questions were invaluable.

For the historical background used in this book, I am indebted to the following accounts: *Histoire d'Haïti,* by Thomas Madiou; *Description de la partie française de l'isle Saint-Domingue,* by Moreau de Saint-Méry; *Les Blancs débarquent,* by Roger Gaillard; *The Black Jacobins,* by C. L. R. James; *Written in Blood,* by Robert and Nancy Heinl; *From Dessalines to Duvalier,* by David Nicholls; and *Papa Doc and the Tonton Macoutes,* by Bernard Diederich and Al Burt.

With things as changeable as they are in Haiti today, it might be risky to list those without whose protection, counsel and friendship I would have been lost. Some I can mention, however. Among my mapreaders were the schoolteacher in Jean-Rabel who told me he would never vote in sham elections; the Belgian priest who ran a radio station in the north until he was summarily fired by the Archbishop there; Peter Welle, the CARE agroforester who was caught in the middle of the controversy over foreign aid; the kind priest then on Delmas who was so helpful to me in my early days in Port-au-Prince; friends at the Centre Karl Lévêque in Port-au-Prince; Alix, Milford and Wilson, three of my guides, as well as Ducé, Destouches, Hérold, Charlot and Martial at the Oloffson; Lucy and Abner in Duverger; Mimette, my friend with the kite in La Saline, and all the peasants and slum-dwellers who caught hold of my pad or my tape recorder and told me their tales of penury and injustice, and who fortified me—and themselves, their children and their country—with their open and revivifying spirit. I am grateful to Denise and Simone and Margot, as well.

Many thanks also to the wise man from Gonaïves, for all the hours of instruction and interpretation, to a certain young woman who knows who she is (and to two of her friends, B. and B.), to Marcus and Lyliane and Marcus, to a number of brave priests who know who they are and must go nameless; to the parishioners of St.-Jean-Bosco; to my friends among the November 1987 candidates; to the complicated memory of Charlemagne Péralte, and to his not yet

ACKNOWLEDGMENTS   7

vanquished héritiers: Ayiti and Waldeck and Johnny and Claude and
all the other street kids who were kind and generous to me, even if
they didn't know it, even if they didn't mean to be.

Of course, I cannot forget the patience and understanding of my
father and my two brothers.

And finally, special thanks to Nick Goldberg for his unflagging
support and tolerance throughout, as well as for his sympathetic yet
critical readings of this manuscript in its many stages.

New York   AMY WILENTZ
March 1989

To the memory of my mother, Jacqueline Wilentz,
to the memory of David Wilentz and Jerome Malino,
my grandfathers,
and to the memory of Michael Hooper.

And for R.C., L.P., L.V.
and, of course, B.

Contents

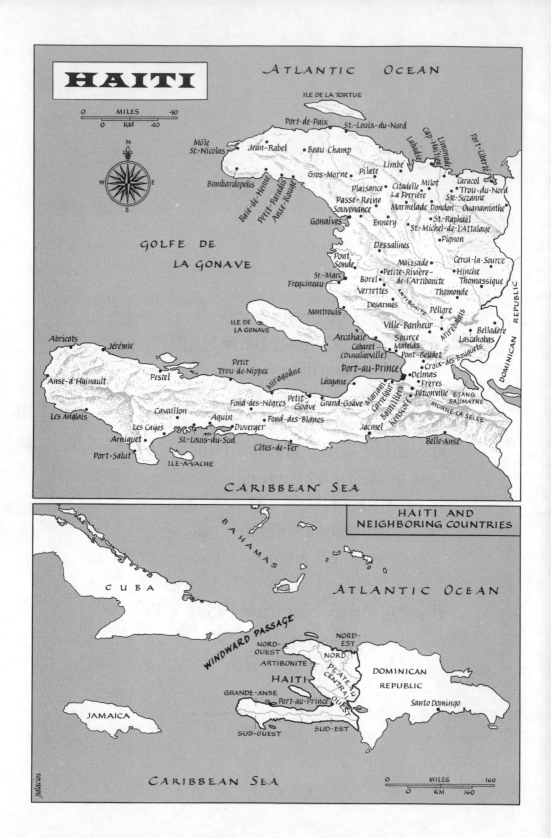

Se lè koulèv mouri, ou konn longè li.
Only when the serpent dies can you take his measure.
—HAITIAN PROVERB

Dreaming

It must have been a mistake. Certainly, no one in the village thought the packages were meant for them. More than a hundred had fallen from the sky late one afternoon—hard, compact squares wrapped in brown paper. The little plane that dropped them kept on going; it flew straight over the plain toward the mountains. The sound of something flying overhead woke a gravedigger, who saw the blocks in brown paper fall near the cemetery.

The villagers soon discovered that the packages were filled with a hard translucent substance, like rock but easily breakable. If you took the blocks and cracked them with a mortar and pestle, one villager found, you could pulverize them. He mixed the white powder with water and whitewashed his hut with it; the results were not white like the powder, but hard and shiny, like the crystalline block. Other villagers were envious of the one man's efforts, and from them he got a little money to do the same for their huts. Soon everyone who could get together the three-dollar fee had the job done. Others tried to use the powder as fertilizer, the way they had seen some white development workers do a few years before a few villages away, but it didn't seem to improve the soil. Some of the beans even died.

The village voodoo priest was at a loss to interpret the packages. He had a dream in which he built a new house out of the blocks, a great white structure bigger than the church in town. The next day at the lottery, or *borlette,* he bet ten gourdes, or two dollars, on the number 45, the numerological translation for a dreamed house, and he won. Elated, he had his acolytes, seven young girls, gather up the blocks and bring them to his temple, where he stored them. Occasionally, he substituted white powder made from the stuff for the flour he usually used to draw *vèvè,* intricate designs on the ground that help call the gods to a voodoo ceremony. Flour was expensive, and he preferred not to waste it. The gods didn't seem to mind the substitution.

Everywhere they went, the villagers talked about the strange blocks that had fallen from the sky. They wondered where the plane had been coming from, probably New York, because all the planes they knew of went to New York or came back from there. When they went to market south down the main road, toward the capital, village women would talk about the powder and how everyone was afraid to smoke it or taste it. They knew enough of their own powders—mixed by the priest to cure maladies or to inspire them—to fear that it was poison. In the market, the women told everyone how they had tried to use it as fertilizer. Eventually, some men who came through the market from the capital heard the talk of the odd powder in the village, and drove up in their jeep to see what the voodoo priest could show them.

He led them inside the concrete temple and back into one of the small rooms kept for individual gods, this one for Baron Samedi, Lord of the Dead, Keeper of the Cemetery, a spirit who dresses in black and often wears a top hat or a bowler and tails. The priest thought that Baron would keep the villagers away from his blocks. When the men from town got their eyes accustomed to the dark in the little chamber, they gasped and started to laugh. They turned to the priest and told him that he had here a product they needed very much in Port-au-Prince, and that they would be willing to pay him thirteen dollars for each package. That was a lot of money for something that had cost him nothing, and the priest said yes, although he was disturbed at getting so much for nothing, and thought that the packages must therefore be worth even more.

The next day, the street price of cocaine in Port-au-Prince went down 50 percent, to ten dollars a gram. Someone who said he was fronting for Freedom, the soccer team in the La Saline slum, bought fifteen grams. The Disco Doctor, a wealthy young physician who was addicted to the stuff, bought two hundred. He was the son of one of the doctors who had helped to save François Duvalier's life back in 1959, after the dictator, only recently come to power, lapsed into a coma. The Disco Doctor felt the burden of that family legacy: Duvalier woke from the coma and lived on for twelve years.

The Disco Doctor has a pretty stucco house up in Pacot, a neighborhood in decline but still chic, and he rents out all his extra rooms to foreign development workers and anthropologists, and to Haitian friends who have been kicked out of their houses by their wives, or who have walked out on them. The Disco Doctor himself lives in the top apartment, and he sleeps there when he has to, under a white mosquito net in a king-size bed that sits just in from the terrace, where he has a view of most of the capital. But the Disco Doctor doesn't dream, he says, and he doesn't like to sleep alone, when he can manage to sleep. Even now that he's off cocaine and has given up his crack habit, he needs someone nearby at night. Otherwise he gets panicky. Most people in Port-au-Prince feel that way even if they've never been addicted. The Disco Doctor is extreme, though. He'll drive all the way to the northernmost city of Cap-Haïtien to find someone to spend the night with, if he has to. He has a friend with a place up there, with another king-size bed.

Sometimes people from Pacot and the other, better parts of town run out of drugs and they can't find their usual dealers. Then, they have to go into the slums to get whatever they can find. A Mercedes will pull right up to a shabby concrete house on a main road in a slum, and a young mulatto will get out and start talking to the man sitting in front. That man turns and talks to a runner waiting in the road, and the runner talks to another runner, and in about fifteen or twenty minutes, after a few cups of very strong, very sweet coffee, the young mulatto has something like what he wants. He can go back to his house up in Pacot and stay up all night.

Sleeping habits vary in Port-au-Prince. They depend on where you live and what you do. The drug runners in the slums are poor, from among the poorest class in Haiti, the urban poor, often even worse off than their village counterparts, peasants like the ones who found the packages wrapped in brown paper. One runner I met, Djo, had too many people in his family to get a good night's sleep: his mother, his three brothers, their girlfriends, his girlfriend, a cousin who lives with them permanently, two cousins who came to Port-au-Prince three months earlier to find jobs that weren't there, and everyone's kids; it seemed like about a dozen.

Djo's house in Cité Soleil, the country's most populous slum, doesn't have the space for all these people, so usually when night falls they do a *relève,* or relay. First Djo and two brothers who have jobs that start early go to sleep; they sleep for four hours, maybe six, on the one bed in the one room of Djo's house. Meanwhile, the other men sit up outside, playing dominoes and drinking herb teas at tables lit by candles or illuminated by the spotlight of a single, bare bulb working on electricity siphoned off from Electricité d'Haïti's lines through cheap copper wires. When Djo and the two brothers get up, the other men go to sleep. The women crumple up on the floor in a corner with the children, almost on top of one another. Often one or two of them will stay up watching the men play dominoes, so that they can have more room when their turn comes, and maybe get some sleep. The relève gives visitors the impression that people in the slums never sleep, but in fact it's just that at least half of them are always awake.

Then there are people who live in even more crowded conditions: they sleep upright. One man leans against the wall with his head on his arms, and another leans up against him, and so on, sometimes as many as three or four deep. That is how they sleep. There is an expression for it in Creole, the slave language that grew out of a mix of seventeenth- and eighteenth-century French and African tongues: in Creole they call it *dòmi kanpe,* stand-up sleep. In this position, they dream the dreams that give them the inspiration for the numbers that they bet on in the borlette the next day.

Bringing Down Baby

When I went down to Haiti for the first time in the early days of 1986, I thought I knew what the place would be like: I would fly down and the Tontons Macoute, Duvalier's personal army of pampered thugs, would search my bags, confiscate my notebooks and my copy of *The Comedians,* Graham Greene's banned novel about Haiti in the 1960s. I'd walk through the cardboard slums in the daytime, shadowed by beggars. At night I would retire to the hotel veranda and drink ten-year-old rum. The Macoutes would spy on me, the rare foreign correspondent. On the walls I'd see cheerful, encouraging frescoes of Jean-Claude Duvalier, the young President-for-Life, and his beautiful wife, Michèle. A handsome voodoo priest would guide me to a temple in the hills, and I would watch as the peasants played the drums and Baron Samedi possessed his worshipers, his *serviteurs*. In shanties deep inside the slums, I would talk with Catholic priests pursued by the Macoutes; hunted and fearful, they would still refuse to accept exile, and would be hiding in a different hovel every night. Uzi-waving Macoutes would storm into my hotel and arrest the government official I was interviewing. The Venezuelan Embassy would be filled with dissenters fleeing Duvalier. After dark, government informers would sit on the hotel's ve-

randa, eavesdropping into the late evening while the bougainvillea
turned as black as the night sky. Eventually, the Duvaliers would
ask me to dinner. Champagne, cocaine, high heels.

I was wrong. By the time I landed in Port-au-Prince, the Catholic
priests were openly at the vanguard of an uprising, the Macoutes
were frightened, insecure, and the government informer was no
longer sure who was bankrolling him. The Duvaliers were on their
way out: no dinner. It seemed like a joke at my expense. I wanted
to study tyranny and bloody violence; instead, I had a popular
triumph on my hands. The Duvaliers fled, the Macoutes went into
hiding. It took me a little while to realize that if you wait long enough
in Haiti, and really not so long, the tyranny and violence is likely to
return, and that a people's victory is not always in the end what it
seems to be in the beginning. When I passed through customs that
first afternoon with a hundred journalists at François Duvalier International Airport, a three-man band was playing "Haïti Chérie," Dear
Haiti. The Macoutes barely searched my bags. I kept my copy of
The Comedians.

After a few visits, I began to learn about the different neighborhoods
of Port-au-Prince, but that first time, the taxi driver took me everywhere, I now know. In his big old Chevy he drove me through one
slum, and then another, and out along a stretch of shanties, and
down past the Palais-National and up past the cathedral, and then
round back behind another church through steep streets in what
seemed like another complicated, hilly slum. All along his labyrin-
thine route, my taxi driver aimed at dogs and swerved in front of
lazy jeeps with tinted windows and around tap-taps—small covered
pickup trucks filled with stifling passengers and painted with cheerful scenes and happy mottoes: Smile, God Loves You, Je Sais Qu'Il
Vit, Good Trip, Scoobydoo, Espérance, Sirop, Sans Problème,
Wonderful, Ce N'est Rien, Lovely . . . It was a dizzying tour de
force of evasion to get to a hotel that was just at the end of a quite
straight, quite major street. No slums. He charged me what I later
learned was an unthinkable fifteen dollars. Often these days, it
occurs to me that he wasn't just ripping me off. He didn't need to
take me so far off the main streets in order to charge me one-and-a-
half times the going rate. No, now I think he must have been making a political point. But at the time, all those slums were lost on
me.

Finally I arrived, exhausted by the shock of the heat, so many people, the dust, the dogs run down in the street, the children with kites on the roofs, and the screaming traffic, at the Grand Hotel Oloffson, the hotel Graham Greene wrote about in *The Comedians*. It was a more exotic choice than the Holiday Inn, where most American journalists stay if they can get a room. The Holiday Inn is a bland, efficient building a long way down the street from the Oloffson, right in the middle of things, not far at all from the National Palace. The Holiday Inn has a logo of a green palm tree and a bright-orange sun plastered across its stucco front. It also has telephones, and air conditioners that work.

But when I looked up through the palms at the Oloffson's white gingerbread veranda surrounded by overgrown bougainvillea, I thought I had made the right decision. The place, unlike the swarming, noisy Port-au-Prince I had seen on that ride, seemed to hold a promise of that tropical mystery I was expecting. The swimming pool off to the side reflected the moon in the palms and I recalled the scene in *The Comedians* where the narrator, a Mr. Brown, discovers the bloody body of the Minister of Public Works in the hotel's empty pool, a suicide in the moonlit shadow of the diving board. A statue of Henry Christophe—who had been a slave and a waiter before he became Emperor Henry I of Haiti seven years after the country declared its independence from France in 1804—guarded the Oloffson's door in a three-corner hat, and a dog slept next to him. I put down my bags at the Emperor's feet. Two slender women materialized to carry them away.

The veranda was crowded with journalists, evening was about to fall. Something sweet was in the air. The journalists were lounging around on the wicker and bamboo furniture, drinking rum. The whispered name Duvalier moved from table to table and back again, around the room, in French accents, in British accents, in Spanish accents, in American accents. If you weren't careful, you tripped over photographers' bags as you made your way to the bar, and their owners looked at you like the devil. I was disoriented after that taxi ride. It was hot out.

In spite of the reservations I had made months before, there was no room left for me. Everything was in chaos. Less than a week earlier, because of a slip-up on the part of the U.S. Embassy, everyone in the world had got the idea that Jean-Claude Duvalier was already on his way out of Haiti. The State Department had the story wrong, nothing new, announcing Duvalier's departure a week before

it actually was satisfactorily arranged. Perhaps the story helped encourage the President to leave. In any case, according to one account, the deal was almost done when the White House made its
first announcement. But then the Tontons Macoute, fearing for their
security if Duvalier left, backed out, Duvalier remained, and more
negotiations had to be undertaken, during which the Army promised
protection to the Macoute hierarchy. According to another story, a
member of Lieutenant Colonel Oliver North's National Security
Council team, in Haiti to collect Duvalier dollars for the Nicaraguan
contras, had been wandering around the National Palace late one
night when he noticed that all the lights were out in the living
quarters. Hastily presuming that Jean-Claude had fled, he tele-
phoned Washington to let them know the news. In the end, it turned
out that Jean-Claude, who had been known as Baskethead since his
schooldays, had been in the basement, playing Ping-Pong. But the
mistake wasn't rectified until too late.

After President Reagan's spokesman Larry Speakes made the premature announcement, Baskethead himself went on Haitian radio to
calm the ragged nerves. To say, uh, no, they were wrong. I'm right
here, in the palace, and, as he so memorably put it, "firm as a
monkey's tail."

By that time, however, the normally sluggish foreign press was
alerted to his possible ouster, and they had all managed to make
their way down to watch Duvalier crumble. They figured that even
if the United States had blown the story the first time, something
must be up. They knew that the United States was in on the deal.
And some of them even remembered stories from the end of 1985,
especially the incident in November in Gonaïves, in which three
schoolboys protesting the Duvalier regime had been killed by the
Army. Popular outcry over the killings had been the first concrete
sign that Duvalier was losing control.

And if Duvalier left, it would be big news. Family in power for
thirty years. Bloodthirsty dictatorship. Fall of the Tontons Macoute.
Beautiful wife flees with millions in jewels. Chaos in the streets. All
this, added to the regular Haitian features, made the editors back in
the world's capitals salivate: Plenty amid poverty. ("Great.") Voodoo's hold on the peasantry. Voodoo's hold on the elite? ("Maybe.
How do we illustrate it, though? That's my problem. You see?")
Voodoo and the Catholic Church. Just plain voodoo. ("Yeah, uh-
huh. Good idea. Great pictures.") Deforestation. ("Can we get art?
I mean, face it. Tree stumps. Do they read?") Drought? Boat people.

("Get me those bodies that washed up in Florida. Who took those pictures?") A refrigerated suite in the palace where wife and friends store their furs. ("Yeah, but has anyone ever *seen* it?") And now AIDS. The best. Even if Baskethead stayed on for another ten years, the journalists' time would not be wasted.

Keith, the Oloffson's manager, a Londoner, was the sort of opportunist who knew that at the Oloffson you had to take money wherever and whenever you could get it, and who experienced no qualms putting another American reporter—who had taken the same plane I took but not the same taxi, and had arrived at the Oloffson twenty minutes before I did—into the Chambre Mick Jagger, the room reserved for me. Keith knew he'd be able to juggle me in somewhere if I turned up in the end, and besides, I wasn't his responsibility: I was late, that was life. I begged him to find me a rental car, and he promised he would, but I wasn't convinced.

I had brought shorts to this place, and, looking around as the evening fell, I realized that everyone was dressed for dinner, in particular Heidi, a blond photographer in a black dress. She was wandering around the big bar room and swiveling to see who was there and whom to talk to. The man she had come down with, another photographer, followed pathetically in her wake, as reporters in their chairs toppled behind her. She would turn to her friend, occasionally introducing him or asking him to fetch a drink for her or whomever she was talking to. He obeyed. The Haitian waiters smiled at each other, nodding in her direction. Heidi was new to photography, and Haiti was a good place to photograph. She'd been in Guatemala already, with her boyfriend.

"I love the houses in Port-au-Prince," Heidi was saying to an Associated Press photographer, who looked around his table, crowded with other run-down-looking photographers, and smirked. They had all been down now for a couple of days, and so had Heidi. "They're so colorful," she said. "Isn't it amazing? You can get a lot into one picture, the houses are so close together, all those pinks and blues. So many people."

"That's because it's so crowded here," Associated Press said to her kindly, while the rest of the table went on smirking.

"I'd like to get a lot into her," muttered the Englishman I was standing behind. The table laughed.

"And the hats," she went on. "When they're sitting in the market, and you're on top of those hats, with the sun, and all the plastic stuff, you know, the buckets, and pails and everything, just fantastic."

"It's really great pictures," said a young American man. "The light in the morning, and the afternoon."

"I made a picture today of three boys in the market playing cards on the ground," said Heidi's boyfriend. "Great feature material."

I sat down by myself near the bar in the only empty chair at the Oloffson that night, and took out a notebook. I made some notes about Heidi. My "welcome" rum punch arrived. It was red, and too sweet, and, like a tourist, I wondered about the ice. Heidi was still declaiming, the boyfriend standing next to her and tapping a foot occasionally, looking around, his arms folded against his chest.

"The most picturesque little man, with a hat, you know, and those glasses," I heard her say.

A few tables down from me, a man with wild hair was scribbling on a brown envelope already full of scribbles. He was sitting by himself, too, but he did not look inviting. He glanced up once to see who was making a speech, and gave Heidi a long look. The nasty British photographer who was sitting at the table that Heidi was entertaining noticed him, and stood up and shouted, "Harry!" Hitching up his trousers, the photographer made his way across the room to the wild man's table.

"What?" said the wild man, still scribbling while the photographer attempted to engage him in the social niceties of two old colleagues who meet by chance in an odd corner of the world after many years.

"Haiti, eh?" the photographer said. "That's right. I heard it was your baby. How are you, man, still living abroad?"

"Look, mate," said Harry, "it's lovely to see you and all that, but I've got an interview in an hour. Perhaps we can chat tomorrow. I'm not staying here, though. Too bloody expensive. Look at that— ridiculous," he said, pointing to the menu with his pen. "Bloody avocadoes for five dollars. Run down to the corner and you can buy ten or more for that price. Bloody ridiculous." He turned back to his envelope. "I'm at the Palace." A hotel, I figured. He didn't look like the type to receive invitations from Michèle Duvalier.

I put down "Harry, Palace" in my notebook and went on sipping. I kept hearing what I thought were cars backfiring in the distance until I realized that it was gunfire. I ordered a second welcome rum punch.

"Excuse me, madame, but the second rum punch . . ." said the waiter, stopping politely.

"Oh, this one's not 'welcome,' " I said. "Is that what you mean?" He smiled.

Another round of shots, another round of drinks at the photographers' table. Then what sounded like machine-gun fire in the back of the hotel, over the sound of someone playing a wistful Haitian ballad on the untuned piano. I must have jumped, because the wild man looked up at me and smiled. He waved at me with his pen. I wasn't used to gunfire. I smiled back and would have raised my glass to him in a trite gesture, but I could tell that my hand would tremble. Now his pen was beckoning. I nodded.

"Who are you, then?" he asked me as I sat down at his table. Just beyond him, outside the veranda, the rain began to come down hard. The gunfire stopped for the rain.

"I thought I'd write a story about Haiti," I said to him.

He laughed. "What an odd thing. Me too," he said. He had been coming to Haiti for seventeen years. "No one here knows anything about the place, of course. Bunch of fools. One Frenchman hadn't even heard about the Cabinet reshuffle." What Cabinet reshuffle? I wondered. "Jesus. But I still always make it over to the Oloffson when I come down. You've got to. For the gossip. Here and the Holiday Inn—that's where you find out what the American Embassy is saying, because they'll talk to the American hacks." He took a gulp of what looked like rum punch.

"No fucking booze in this glass. This place is run by thieves," he said, looking at the three empty glasses lined up on his table. "Everyone here is on an expense account: they're all eating lobster, for Christ's sake."

"What's wrong with lobster?" I asked, because I wanted to hear his answer.

"It's bloody twenty dollars or something, mate. I can stay at my hotel for two nights on what they're spending on fucking crayfish in this place." Harry was disgusted. "Look, I come here, I go around quite nicely by tap-tap, which none of these fucking hacks has ever done, may I tell you, and I stay at the Palace for fifteen dollars a night, instead of bloody ninety or whatever that woman charges here, and I talk to Haitians, real, actual Haitians, there on this wonderful terrace, and I can see the whole bloody town in case it goes up in smoke, and the rooms are air-conditioned, or at least *my* room is air-conditioned and, what's more, the fucking air conditioner works. Wait," he said as I threatened to interrupt the flow. "And you can get a bloody line out, because even though there's only one phone, there aren't any bloody hacks, and the

Haitians don't use the phone that much. And they take bloody messages, and the management knows everyone in town, and you
feel like you're actually in Haiti," he said, smiling suddenly as if
in speaking he had rid himself of all his crankiness. He had been
coming to Haiti for seventeen years, he pointed out again, and
he knew what he was talking about. In fact, he always knew what
he was talking about, and he talked a lot. He worked for a British
daily.

"I hear Désinor is kicking up a fuss," he said after I ordered us
another two rums.

"Who's Désinor?" I asked. Please don't yell at me, I thought.

"Who's bloody Désinor?" he yelled. "Jesus, mate, how can you
expect to cover this story if you don't even know who bloody Désinor
is?"

"Well, then, who is he?"

"He's the old man's Finance Minister, big Duvalierist."

"Ah," I said. Now I knew. Later, I took a continuing straw poll
of the journalists there. "Who is Désinor?" I would ask them. "Dé-
siwho?" they would ask, and then fight among themselves as to who
he could possibly be. A few years later, Désinor would turn out to
be a name they all had come to know.

"I hope the fathead stays on another month," said Keith. "He's
bringing in the business. Good man." Keith laughed. "Good for
Avis, good for Hertz," he said, smiling at me. He had found me a
car.

"It would be good for us, that's for damn sure," said Suzanne, the
Oloffson's proprietor.

"I think what we need is more wine," said a French journalist.
Lights were going out around town. The rain had stopped for the
moment, and the guns were blazing again.

"Frank," said Suzanne to a waiter, "another bottle of white wine."
She drank with enthusiasm.

"I've been in this country too long," she said to the table. No one
objected. Harry, who had returned from his interview, came to sit
by my side with a look of self-satisfaction that made me think he was
stuffed with secrets.

"What's the name of the Papal Nuncio?" shouted the *Christian
Science Monitor* from across the table. Pen poised.

"Paolo Fucking Romeo," said the wild man. "And he will never talk to the press, not even to your paper. Forget it. Oh-ho, now here's a man who *will* talk to the press," he said, waving someone toward the table.

The man coming up the steps of the Oloffson, wearing white linen, was small, well formed, bald, handsome. "Dapper" was the word that you thought of. A medium-color Haitian. Intelligence lit his eyes. He oiled his way through the tables toward Harry. The rain hadn't touched him.

"This," said Harry like a tour guide as the little man reached us, "is Aubelin Jolicoeur." Jolicoeur swept the air with a bow for the table in general. "No other," said Harry. "How are you, Auby? Make yourself famous. Sit down."

"How are you, Harry?" Jolicoeur asked in English, with a French accent lightly laced with Haitian *w*s for *r*s. "It is *so* nice to see you again on these shores. No, I don't think I will," he said in response to several calls from the table for him to sit. He went on standing next to Harry, looking down, smiling and showing his remarkable teeth, pure white and sharp. "Whatever have you been up to, my dear fellow? It seems so long since we last met." He bowed again to Harry in particular, a smaller courtesy, and tapped the floor with his silver-tipped walking stick. His eyes were full of humor and calculation. They never rested.

"Madame," he said to Suzanne, bowing so slightly.

"Aubelin," she responded. "Frank, another bottle of white wine."

"Keith," Jolicoeur said, looking away.

Keith did not respond.

"Snake," Keith said to Heidi, loud enough so that Jolicoeur could hear.

"And who is Mademoiselle?" asked Jolicoeur in English, inserting himself between Keith's and Heidi's chairs and tapping the floor next to her with his stick. "You are so lovely, my dear," Jolicoeur said to her. He batted his eyelashes, turned his back on Keith.

"Poor Auby," said Harry to me." "He's getting on a bit for that act, don't you think? You do know who Auby is, don't you?"

"Yes," I said. "Doesn't everyone?"

"They ought to, not that he's worth it," he said. "Shameless. Look at him."

Jolicoeur had bent his head low over Heidi's hand and was kissing it with fervor. He turned it over, palm up, and kissed its center.

"So soft, my dear," he said. "You are like a poem to me. This

hand, so soft, so childlike, so lyrical. You are like poetry, a beautiful
sunset, children's laughter."

"Isn't he cute?" Heidi asked the table.

"Pas exactement," said Harry, laughing. "Are you *cute,* Aubelin?"

"Pas exactement, as you so accurately put it, my dear Harry."
Jolicoeur didn't really laugh, but he giggled.

"Your name, my dearest," he said to Heidi.

"It's Heidi."

"Heidi, my darling, I am yours," he said. "What a beautiful name,
so innocent, so Germanic. Heidi, Heidi. Aubelin Jolicoeur is at your
service. I worship the ground you walk on. I will never forget you.
Never." He kissed her hand again and saluted the table with a terse
wave of the walking stick. "We will meet again. It is fated." He
moved away.

"God, what an odious shit," said Keith.

"Oh, I thought he was dear," said Heidi. "I love that kissing hands
stuff. So old-fashioned."

"He's a rapist," said Keith. "He's always turning on women and
exposing himself."

"That's not rape. Anyway, your source, please," said Harry, pen
in hand, laughing.

Jolicoeur was the model for Petit Pierre in *The Comedians,* the ambiguous charmer and gadfly who gossips with the narrator, Mr.
Brown. Greene's description: "He was believed by some to have
connections with the Tontons, for how otherwise had he escaped a
beating-up or worse? And yet there were occasionally passages in his
gossip-column that showed an odd satirical courage—perhaps he
depended on the police not to read between the lines." In Greene's
day, Jolicoeur was in fact a gossip columnist, and, as Jolicoeur says
himself, the first Haitian public-relations man. He used to greet
celebrity tourists and famous Haitians at the airport and then write
up their stays in *Le Nouvelliste.*

His was a long career, and in many ways Greene had been too
kind to him. Jolicoeur fawned in whichever direction power lay, and
this made him a survivor. Under Papa Doc, he informed on foreign
journalists and academics if he felt that their work was critical of the
regime. This got him Brownie points. Any criticism of the powerful
which appeared in his columns—often he would suggest, in later

days, that Jean-Claude was not of the highest-caliber intelligence—was within the bounds of the acceptable. While denigrating Jean-Claude's intellectual abilities, for example, he would praise the First Lady for her good qualities. Jolicoeur knew who was in charge at the palace. "This woman and her generous heart," he wrote, "represent the only things before which I melt: beauty, intelligence, kindness in charity, as well as the children to whose well-being she devotes herself." With great fanfare, Michèle Bennett Duvalier had just set up a foundation in her own name for indigent mothers and children. It was used primarily as an account from which to siphon off millions of dollars in public funds.

After Jean-Claude left Haiti, Jolicoeur would become confused, trying to figure out where power was located in the shifting scene, and where he fit into the new political spectrum, if at all. "François Duvalier was my father," he kept saying to me one evening over champagne at his house, two years after this first meeting on the Oloffson veranda.

Frank leaned over the table and began pouring that third bottle of white wine.

"Look at that," said Harry, pointing with his elbow.

Behind Heidi's back, Aubelin was bowing deeply over the hand of another photographer, a dark-haired woman sitting at the photographers' table.

"At least that one's worth it," Harry said.

"Do you think it's really too dangerous to go up north?" Heidi asked Harry.

"Dangerous?" he said. "Why are you bloody in this business, mate? Of course it's dangerous. We wouldn't be here if it weren't dangerous, darlin'. Anyway, I was up there a couple of days ago," he said. "We were in the demos in the Cap, me and that girl over there, and a few others. It was bloody hard to file from there, bloody Téléco," he said, taking a ferocious sip of wine as he thought of the telephone company. "Then we had to rush back to town so that she could ship her pix." He pointed more openly at the photographer Aubelin was wooing. Frank was standing nearby, watching.

Heidi looked over her shoulder and frowned. The table of photographers burst into laughter, raised their glasses to Aubelin. The girl he was flirting with stood up and curtsied, and Aubelin put his arm around her. She danced a graceful little step to the music coming from the other room. Someone was playing that Haitian ballad again. I recognized it: "Yellow Bird."

"Well, Danny and I are going to go up tomorrow, I think," Heidi said. Her boyfriend looked up, startled. He was apparently not Danny.

"Well, you should be careful," said Harry, mellowing for a second. "It's wild up there, especially along the main road. On the way back down from the Cap we had to pass through maybe fifty barricades, all of the lads with machetes and ready to slit your bloody throat. We were lucky because we could speak Creole, so we just chatted them up—oh, thanks, yes," Harry said as Frank offered to fill his glass, "—made a little speech at every barricade about how the foreign press was helping the revolution, publicizing it, and saving lives and all that, and they'd cheer us through. At each stop we had to be more eloquent—night blacker, hour later, crowd more ominous, lots of tafia and clairin about," he said, naming the different kinds of raw Haitian rum. "Some of the lads wanted us to shout, 'Down with Duvalier,' but we couldn't, quite. You know, after all those years it takes a while to get used to them being on the way out, to realize the regime's had its balls chopped off and can't do anything much to you anymore. Some of the other hacks on the road were quite frightened—no Creole, you know. They handed out food, snacks, cigarettes, money—like the foreign TV crews who gave out hundred-dollar bills, anything except their film. *Look* at that man. Shameless."

Aubelin was dancing with the dark-haired photographer.

"He owes me hundreds of dollars if Jean-Claude leaves," said Suzanne. "He signs for his drinks, as if he still brings in business. Useless. But he still knows too many people for me to take him off the dole. Just wait until after the Duvaliers go." She looked darkly around the table and brushed some stray hair out of her eyes.

"Little shit," she said. She looked for Frank. I could see him in what seemed to be his habitual corner, watching the dark-haired photographer. Suzanne didn't notice. "One day, Aubelin is going to pay and pay. Where's Frank?"

"Hey, where's *he* going?" Heidi asked as United Press International came flying through the bar and went rushing down the front steps toward the parking lot. She stood up.

"What's he on about?" asked Harry.

"It's a fire," gasped UPI from below. "I saw it from the balcony." He was staying with four other journalists in the John Gielgud Suite, which looked out over the city. The photographers' table rose as one and began throwing on their cameras and running to find their car keys. Aubelin sat down and watched them leave. Obviously he felt that the dark-haired photographer had been ripped untimely from his arms. He had a small ironic smile on his face, and he shook his head once over at Frank, who shook his head back. The photographers and the reporters tumbled over one another getting to the parking lot, and took too much time finding dollar bills for the insistent hotel guides who had washed their cars for dollars twice already that day.

We all followed UPI, not that he seemed to know where he was going. Duvalier had declared a state of siege, and no one was much interested in venturing into the nightly gunfire. We were the only cars out, fortunately, because except for UPI, who had been setting up the mosquito net on the bed on the Gielgud Suite balcony when he noticed the fire, we had all had a little too much to drink. But it wasn't too hard to follow the only other cars in town. We zipped down the Rue Alerte and followed the cemetery wall until it ended. Then we headed right, about five cars full of the international press. The *Christian Science Monitor* was in my car, a memorable man with long legs and arms and a languorous voice. He kept his arm out the window.

"Watch the mud," he said to me after I drove over a pothole and splashed his elbow with gray water. Downtown, all the little green and red lights in the nighttime stores were out because of the curfew, and there were no lights at the corners, where there is usually a knot of bulky women throughout the night, frying up food called *fritay* for passersby, on small charcoal grills or over kerosene flames. Even the sign for My Dream Hotel on Grande Rue was off. The fire seemed to be burning behind Grande Rue, behind a huge old empty iron building filled with rickety wooden market stalls. The Iron Market, I later learned.

We drove around the building, and suddenly we could see the fire. It was a garbage fire. They were burning garbage. UPI stopped, and turned his car around. One by one, the others followed, reversing and turning back. "This is bullshit, man," UPI said to us from his window. "No pictures." Heidi nodded from the backseat.

"Shall we go on?" asked the *Monitor*. We were the only ones still facing forward. I looked at the fire not far away. There were no people around, but someone must have just put the garbage there and started burning it, because it would not have burned in that rain. Perhaps we should go investigate, but the place looked muddy, and that was putting it nicely. A child trying to run up to the burning pile and grab something back from its flames got caught in mud, ankle deep out where he stood. It looked deeper just up ahead of us, but I couldn't tell. Mud, like water, is deceptive. We decided to turn back. I started up the car, put it in reverse, and somehow, in seconds, we were stuck in mud. I hadn't seen what was in back of me.

"Jesus," said the *Monitor*. He looked warily out his window, down at the ground. "This stuff is disgusting." He pulled his head sharply in and leaned it back against his seat. "*Get* me out of here."

The car wouldn't go backward, but it went forward. I wheeled it around to the left.

"Skip the fire," said my passenger. "Let's go back to the hotel. I need a drink."

I had very little idea of how to get back. I headed right toward the waterfront and turned left. Still, no cars. There was no one to follow, even randomly, and no one to ask for directions. The boy in front of the fire was the only Haitian we had seen on the streets that night. I kept going, hoping I would somehow figure it out. The *Monitor* did not seem to know his way, either.

Up ahead in the distance, I thought I saw lights. We got to a circle, and suddenly there was a crowd. Their appearance was so abrupt I almost drove into them. About three hundred people, all dancing. In front of them, a squadron of soldiers, watching, awkward with their rifles at their sides.

"It must be for Carnival," said the *Monitor*. "Either that or we've stumbled on a demonstration. Let's call it a demonstration." He pulled his pad from his back pocket and started scribbling.

I stopped the car, and we got out. It was dark enough to mix with the crowd. Everyone was listening to music on the radio, it seemed as if every man in the crowd was carrying one. All tuned to the same station. A little boy came up to me and began dancing in front of me, swiveling his hips. The women lifted their skirts slightly as they danced, almost in place.

"Dance with me, baby," said a man in blue denim, grabbing my hand. He spoke in English, and pulled me close. I pulled back toward the *Monitor,* who loomed protectively. The man laughed and danced away. He had a red bandana around his neck, and a denim cap tilted back at a dizzy angle.

"Well, now you can say you've danced with the Tontons Macoute, my dear," said the *Monitor*. "An honor."

I was disappointed. I had expected sunglasses and a machete.

A flatbed truck pulled up slowly through the crowd, and the music it was transporting became louder and louder. The truck came to a halt in the middle of the circle. Two men were standing in front, playing guitars between two old amplifiers. A drummer was behind them. They were laughing down at my Tonton Macoute, who was dancing right below the truck. They watched him for a minute and then started singing a song about the Macoutes. He laughed and danced harder. I could distinguish the words *"macoute"* and *"ale."* *Ale* means go, or get out, get lost. The crowd danced and watched the Macoute dancing. He twirled in front of the circle that had formed around him and the truck, thrusting his pelvis toward each of the women until he came to a young girl standing with her arms folded. He grabbed her by the shoulders and tried to pull her into his dance, but she wouldn't move. She just stood there in front of him with her arms still folded and his hands on her shoulders. He began dancing more and more suggestively until he moved his hands down to her hips, and suddenly she ripped away from him and started running through the crowd.

His face changed. Automatically, his hand went for his stick, and he plunged into the crowd after her. The people scattered more quickly for him than they had for her, and she hadn't gotten very far before he reached her. The music stopped. He grabbed her arm, and this time she couldn't get free. He hit the side of her body with the stick, hit her again, over and over, until she was crouching in front of him with her captured arm pulled back and up behind her. The soldiers watched, we watched, the crowd watched.

"Macoute," said a man standing next to me. An observation.

The Macoute was getting bored. The girl had stopped screaming and had rolled herself into a protective ball. Finally he stopped beating her, and held her there, crouched in front of him, his stick resting on her back. He cast a mean glance over at the crowd, let go of her, and kicked her away. He turned and looked up at the musicians. They looked back. Their guitars were hanging loosely from their straps. The Macoute moved toward the crowd again, deliberately, and reached for another girl's hand. Slowly, he pulled her up toward the music truck, the stick raised in his other hand. He lay the stick across the girl's cheek, and looked at the musicians. They began to play. He began to dance. This girl danced. He smiled.

. . .

Even before Jean-Claude's father François became President in 1957, the Tontons Macoute began to make their appearance in Port-au-Prince. Back in those days, they were known as the Cagoulards, for the black, executioner-style hoods they wore over their faces while conducting their night raids on the homes and persons of Duvalier's enemies. The Cagoulards had French antecedents—a right-wing group called the Secret Committee of Revolutionary Action had worn black hoods and frightened the French from 1935 to 1940. The Haitian Cagoulards themselves had historical roots within Haiti, as well. In the mid-nineteenth century the Emperor Faustin Soulouque, the third and last self-styled Emperor of Haiti, organized a band of thugs called the Zinglins, whom he used to counteract the powerful and wealthy mulatto officers in the Army, and thus to remain Emperor.

In the cities, the Tontons Macoute were recruited from the slums; in the countryside, they were often members of voodoo's outlaw secret societies. The name Tonton Macoute, adopted by the Haitian people to describe Duvalier's henchmen, comes from a figure in Haitian nursery stories, a bogeyman who creeps up in the night and disappears naughty little children into his *macoute,* Creole for the straw shoulder satchel worn by many peasant men. *Tonton* means uncle, and is often used as a term of endearment, like *Papa,* as in Papa Doc.

In town, Papa Doc's Macoutes wore blue jeans, denim hats and sometimes sunglasses and red bandanas. More rarely, they wore suits, fedoras and sunglasses, and often they wore no uniform at all other than a pistol in their belt. In the provinces, the Macoutes sometimes topped the denim outfit with broad peasant hats. At voodoo pilgrimages in the countryside it was hard to tell the difference between the voodoo priests, who wore the blue denims, red scarves and broad peasant hat that represent the voodoo agricultural god Cousin Zaka, and the Tontons Macoute, similarly garbed. Often, the only difference was that the voodoo priest had a machete, and the Macoute had an old Enfield rifle. Often, the priest and the Macoute were one and the same.

Already in 1958, Duvalier was calling the Tontons Macoute the Civilian Militia, and a few years later they had officially become the Volunteers for National Security, or VSN. There were soon at least ten thousand of them, and they outnumbered the Haitian Army by at least two to one. As had the Zinglins for Soulouque, the VSN constituted Duvalier's bulwark against overthrow by the mulatto-

controlled (and in Papa Doc's day American-trained) Army. The
Army, Duvalier was well aware, had historically been the undoing
of one Haitian ruler and the maker of the next. In his own case this
was true: he had risen to power with help from the armed forces
after the previous President was hastily removed by the military.
Having watched the Army undo his predecessor, Duvalier was de-
termined not to be undone himself. He was a careful student of
Haitian history.

Less than twenty years after the slaves wrested power from the
French in 1804, he knew, the black former-slave leadership had been
replaced by a small mulatto and formerly free elite, which controlled
not only the reins of government and the armed forces but most of
the nation's wealth. This elite was virtually indomitable, and in
1957, finding that they could not prevent his rise to power, they
hoped that Duvalier would be their puppet; he seemed malleable,
and black puppet presidents manipulated by the mulatto elite were
by then a Haitian tradition. The Haitians call it *la politique de
doublure,* the politics of the understudy.

But Duvalier was different from his predecessors. He was not
about to understudy anyone. While building up the militia, he sys-
tematically undermined the Army, sowing discontent in its midst,
setting up militiamen to run some of its branches, assassinating an
important colonel and finally shutting the Military Academy, where
the elite of the Army were trained. He wanted no elite. From then
on, Duvalier alone was to be the elite—or, as he put it in 1964, "I
shall be lord and master"—and the VSN were his Gestapo, a state-
sanctioned secret-police force that operated with impunity. It was
no secret that Duvalier admired the tactics of the Nazis. When he
died in 1971, the Macoutes remained, and it was never quite clear
whether they and their military and political allies were leading Duvalier's son, the new President-for-Life, or whether Jean-Claude was
at least partially in charge.

My poor little Pony. It was a serviceable car, a Hyundai. It was
white, and cheap to rent. But now the muck from the market where
the fire had burned had gotten under the fenders and into the axles.
Even though the man who washed my car that night did a good job
cleaning off the stuff, it must have sunk into the Pony's depths. It
still stank every time I started the car up. The hotel staff was disgusted by it. They knew where smells like that came from: the

shantytowns. Smells like that breed bad diseases, like tuberculosis and *gwo chalè,* the big fever, malaria. You were not supposed to bring that smell up the hotel's driveway, not even during a coup.

"What you do?" said one guide the next day, reeling back from the car. "You visit La Saline yesterday? You be careful where you drive after the rain. Better change that car. Today is better."

The machine-gun fire the night before had found its target up the street from the hotel. He was lying in a corner of his driveway, wearing a white shirt, but by now it was red. His wife said that he had not been able to repay a loan from the Tontons Macoute. "It was some kind of a business deal," she said, "he never really told me, the way men are. He was scared, though, when he heard that Jean-Claude was leaving. He didn't want to go out. He knew they'd want to get him before their time was up. Terrible," she said. "What am I to do? But at least I have one thing to be grateful for. They left me the body."

No one was ready to interpret events in the days that followed. There was no definitive interpretation to be had. We couldn't even get the facts down, although when we got hold of the U.S. news-papers, the articles read as if the reporters knew something. They would give the daily death counts, but these were just figures the reporters had gotten from the morgue—no one knew how many people had been killed in the street, how many bodies had been disposed of in secret, how many were dying in the countryside. Things that normally a reporter knows were unknowable. How many had died. Where the gunfire was coming from. Who precisely was killing whom. Why. Where the President was. Where the Amer-ican ambassador was. Were they together. There seemed, for exam-ple, to be a general strike in town, but if you asked a merchant whether his store was open he would say, "Well, that depends on how you look at it." Or *when* you looked at it. Pairs of Tontons Macoute and soldiers walked along Grande Rue, forcing the busi-nesses to open each morning. Once the patrol was gone, the iron shutters came back down fast. Then the soldiers and the Macoutes returned.

On the television one night, late, a notice was broadcast assuring the shopkeepers that if they opened their stores their goods would be protected by the Army. The seeming strike continued. A few nights later, another announcement, after midnight. "You will soon receive an important message," it said. That was it. No follow-up. Everyone expected a coup d'état or Duvalier's departure, but instead we got nothing, a blank screen that we watched all night.

"I tried to get a session with Michèle," the dark-haired photographer told me, while the international press corps waited day in and day out at the Oloffson bar for Duvalier to leave. "I did her engagement photos, she liked them a lot. So I called the other afternoon and asked her if it would be possible to shoot some more, and she laughed and said, 'Oh, that's nice of you, but I don't think so. We're very busy.' And I said, 'Well, too bad.' And then she said, 'Bon voyage.' Imagine. When I got off the phone, I thought to myself, Hey, *I'm* not going anywhere, why'd she say that?"

Harry spent much of his time ostentatiously running off to important interviews, and the *Christian Science Monitor* spent most of his time watching Harry with affectionate loathing from his thronelike wicker chair on the veranda.

"I know he knows everything, but must he remind us so continually?" he asked. The *Monitor* knew a few things, too, and had connections with the Haitian bishops. "I'm off to a religious conference," he told the assembled press corps one morning when there was a rumor that the bishops had gathered in the capital for an emergency meeting. "No, dear, I'm afraid you can't come with me," he told Heidi as she began to clamor. "It's between me and my God."

My interviews were more secular. Grégoire Eugène, a self-proclaimed opponent of both Duvaliers, was someone who was often mentioned as a possible member of a future provisional government. It was easy to find him, because he lived two blocks from the hotel, a short walk through the hotel's palm and bougainvillea jungle into the hot sun, around two tap-taps picking up passengers, past the cigarette women with their packages of Comme Il Fauts, and down a short street. Eugène was popular with the journalists because he was close by, spoke English, and was always at home. In fact, he was supposedly under house arrest, but there were no signs of it, no black Macoute-mobiles near the house, no guards. A tall boy watched me carefully as I went to the door.

One story I'd heard about Eugène was that by trying to register his tiny political party under Jean-Claude, he had upheld the principle of the presidency-for-life—since any party legitimized under Jean-Claude had to subscribe to that concept—and had been given a jeep in return by the grateful dictator. The other story I heard was

that someone had come to interview him one day and found him
lying with his head on a table, and the fan going in the background;
he was using two copies of the Haitian Constitution, the latest in an
endless procession of such documents, for a pillow. Eugène was a
legal scholar.

He received me in his living room, a spry person with a wide
forehead and heavy-rimmed black glasses. "We'll talk in a moment,"
he said, leaning over his coffee table to inspect some papers there.
"Please, sit." The room was filled with Formica furniture, long tables piled with tumble-down stacks of half-collated documents, and
dozens of folded bridge chairs up against the walls. We sat in a wood-
veneer living-room set. The walls were bare, and the only decoration
was a bouquet of plastic flowers in the middle of the coffee table. In
this setting, they had considerable charm. There was a blue rose.

"So you're not under house arrest?" I asked. It was subject to
interpretation, of course. When a government makes no announce-
ments, everything is a rumor. Only execution with a body to show
for it is verifiable. If Eugène thought it would help his public image
to be under house arrest, he could be under house arrest even if he
was not. If he thought it would not be useful, he would say he was
not under house arrest even if he was. And there was no place to go
to confirm his story, either way. Even he himself might not really
know whether or not he was under house arrest.

"Well, they're not exactly guarding me," he said. "Sometimes they
watch the house, but it's on an ad-hoc basis, I would have to say."
He laughed to himself.

"There is a boy watching the door, though," I said.

"Oh, him," he said. "He watches the street and the house for *me*.
I like to know who's coming over. There are so many journalists
here now, you see. I don't know how many I've spoken to just
today." The phone rang. Each time he put it back down, it rang
again. Calls came in from New York, Paris, Montreal, Washington,
Miami and from all over town.

"We are forming a provisional junta, you see," Eugène told me.
"That is why there are all these calls. Yesterday the U.S. Embassy
called me and told me my name was on the list of junta members.
They want it to be part civilian, part Army. I can't tell if they're
calling to confirm a rumor they've heard or if they are starting the
rumor. They are talking to the palace every day, and to the Army,
of course. So they should know what's going on, but recently we've
seen that they're not always on top of things, are they?

"Anyway, here is the list I've got, but it could change, you see. These two are at the head of the Army," he said, pointing with a pen to the names Henri Namphy and Williams Régala. "These two here would be the civilians, you know, with human-rights records," he went on, pointing farther down the list to Gérard Gourgue's name and his own. "There I am," he noted with satisfaction. "But nothing is certain. Maybe he won't even go." Eugène recalled the crisis of 1963, when François Duvalier murdered countless enemies and managed to incur the wrath of Haiti's neighbor, the Dominican Republic, by harboring enemies of its new President. At the time, the United States was hinting at a possible military intervention to get rid of Papa Doc. "His father didn't go. Papa Doc, he packed his bags, let everyone know, called the airport, made a reservation, and then sat tight, just to see what would happen, who would remain loyal. That family has a way of changing its mind at the last minute. By the way, did you see the message last night?" Eugène gave a short laugh. "And then nothing."

That afternoon, a large crowd gathered around Duvalier's jeep downtown, and he stepped out, wearing khaki and surrounded by soldiers. He shook hands warily with a few people who looked surprised but acted friendly. Others, off in the distance, stared at him as though he were already a figure from history. He smiled, they smiled. Duvalier was trying to dispel rumors that he had already left the country. He was lighter-skinned than he had seemed in photographs I had seen of him, and not as fat as he had been. His voice was high-pitched, and he didn't seem to have much to say to the people who surrounded him. No jokes. He was awkward, a trait which, I had begun to notice, was rare among Haitians. Then he climbed back into the passenger seat, and the jeep drove off to the palace, with about fifteen cars following behind. Duvalier's chauffeur that day was his unsmiling wife. She was smoking.

The crowd moved off slowly. I began the long walk to meet my guide at the car, which we had parked earlier in the day up Grande Rue near the Iron Market. I made my slow way down the avenue, with a wooden dog in one hand and a statuette of a thin peasant under my arm. The seeming strike had been broken that morning by Macoutes and soldiers going door to door, opening up the stores downtown, but half the stores had already shut up again. A Macoute nudged his companion and pointed his chin in my direction. The thin peasant under my arm was poking me with his broad-brimmed hat. I was looking for my car or my guide or a place to buy a Pepsi. But all the little slivers of shacks, with their jaunty old red-and-blue Pepsi signs out front and a freezer in the back with a couple of cold Pepsis inside, were closed. They were not important enough to be forced open. I couldn't wipe the sweat out of my eyes, because my hands were full of dollar sculpture.

This will never end, I thought. My being white and hot, and carrying this sculpture, and needing a Pepsi while everyone watches: this will never end. Gray liquid in the gutter wafted up the same smell that was living in my car, refuse and sugarcane scrapings, rotten oranges and excrement. I looked woefully at a money changer who was sitting on the corner. "Dollars?" he suggested. The pink corrugated security gate behind him suddenly looked inviting in the shade, and I leaned up against it, staring out into the street over the money changer's head. A few dilapidated tap-taps passed by. I closed my eyes to shut out the late-morning glare.

When I looked again, the buses were gone, and out of the skinny brown shadows across the avenue emerged a pair of skinny brown shoulders, and then a whole boy, about twelve years old and naked. He loped and shambled in a zigzagging line out into the street. His lower half was powdered with something gray. His hair was reddish and matted. The flesh of his torso was almost translucent, a thin protective covering for his delicate rib cage. When he got to the middle of the street, he stopped and made a mangled sound. His leg started bouncing under him, and he hit at his knee to make it stop. Then he looked at me and at the money changer. His eyes were flat and gray. He put a hand up to his hair and pulled at it. I wanted to call to the boy to get out of the street, but I didn't want him to come any nearer. The honking of another rush of tap-taps sounded down the block. The boy's face panicked and his arms flapped back. Then the traffic descended, and my guide, a Pepsi in each hand, surfaced like a vision from among the herd of buses. When the street cleared again, the boy had disappeared.

"JEAN-CLAUDISME," read a big sign on a black-and-red background near the end of town. "PEACE, PROGRESS, DEVELOPMENT."

The painter Edouard Duval-Carrié did a portrait of Jean-Claude to commemorate the President's wedding in 1980. The painting shows the dictator—fashionably slenderized—standing at the edge of a path, wearing a lace wedding dress and holding a gun to his head. One of the popular theories about Jean-Claude's fall was that it was brought about by his marriage to Michèle Bennett, a redoubtable mulatto playgirl much feared by Jean-Claude's mother. Michèle came from a shady mulatto family, but once she married the President, her father's coffee-trading business began to boom, he bought Air Haïti, the "national" airline, and he obtained the Hertz car-rental concession in Port-au-Prince. All of Michèle's mulatto friends began to do better socially and economically.

What the Haitian people saw and resented as Michèle's family ascended was the renaissance of the mulatto elite, which had ruled the Haitian economy for a century before it was brought to its knees in the 1960s by Papa Doc through massacres and confiscation of property. Before his ascension to the presidency, Dr. Duvalier was merely a medical doctor who had attended the University of Michigan's School of Public Health on a one-year U.S government grant ("a simple country doctor," he called himself). He had been a minor intellectual as well, an ethnologist. In books written before 1957, you often find his name mentioned among those who were trying to establish voodoo, the religion of the black peasantry and slum-dwellers, as a system of belief no less legitimate than the Catholicism of the mulatto elite and the black middle class. Duvalier was one of a group of Haitians known as the Griots (old storytellers, from an African word), of whom the respected ethnologist Jean Price-Mars was the most famous.

The Griots espoused what former Senegalese President Léopold Senghor had invented in the 1930s as Négritude, which meant, as far as Price-Mars was concerned, a return among black nations to their black African roots and a rejection in Haiti of Frenchified academic and cultural pretensions. Once in power, however, Duvalier's Négritude turned into Noirisme, a political philosophy ostensibly aimed at taking power from the mulatto minority and giving it to the black majority.

The political ideology called Noirisme had emerged during the 1915–34 U.S. occupation of Haiti, when a pure racism not felt in the country since before Napoleon's army was defeated shocked Haitians into rethinking their racial identity. The American Marines practiced social racism; they kept to themselves and thought that Haitians, even those with degrees from the Sorbonne, were not good enough to come in their front doors. The occupation also practiced political racism, installing four successive mulattos as President.

Duvalier played on the inferiority that a whole generation of Haitians, especially black Haitians, had been made to feel and resent under the occupation. He used Noirisme to undermine the mulatto elite, in the early days a rival for his power, and to consolidate his hegemony among the disenfranchised. (Never stupid, however, Dr. Duvalier allowed many of the wealthy mulattos who were amenable to his presidency-for-life to continue about their business. It was a mutually satisfactory relationship: they profited from his power, and he became more powerful from their profits.)

The simple country doctor's son, however, grew up in a different world. He went to school with the children of the mulatto elite, went to their discos, they were his friends. He never applied Noirisme to his personal life, and when he dated women he often went out with mulatto girls. (His real preference, it was rumored, ran more toward men—and low-ranking soldiers were reportedly used to satisfy his whims when he was an adolescent.) For a dictator, Jean-Claude was never particularly aggressive on the social front. He would send a middleman to ask a pretty girl on a date, and if she said no he was always very courteous.

But Michèle went after him, and she got him. And, not surprisingly, she used him to further her own and her family's interests. This was acceptable behavior. What was unacceptable was her ostentation: the wedding reception, the ranch, the mountain retreat, the beachfront mansion, the alleged cocaine abuse, the million-dollar decorating binges, the million-dollar shopping trips to Paris and New York, the furs. Haitians in general were disgusted, and the black middle class and the rest of the mulatto elite were jealous. Michèle's male relatives quickly got into the drug business, and her brother was soon arrested in Puerto Rico, and later convicted on cocaine-trafficking charges. Her father used to boast that it didn't matter if he totaled the BMW he was driving; he had two more, and some other fancy cars.

No one approved of Michèle, not the Army, not the Duvalierists, not the Tontons Macoute, not the people. By allowing her and her family and their mulatto circle free rein to raid the national coffers, Jean-Claude had isolated himself from the old-fashioned, *noiriste* Duvalierists and made a laughingstock of what he called "Jean-Claudism," supposedly a liberalizing trend in Duvalierism. By the end, there were very few in power who actively supported his presidency (nor were there many who actively opposed it), and thus, having become a vestigial organ of the government, he was painlessly removed.

· · ·

The morning after Duvalier toured the town, I set out for Gonaïves against the advice of my guide, with some Pepsis clanking in the front seat and a couple of nervous photographers in the back. Two of them had children in New York, and they were more inclined to take pictures of the sun in the rice fields than of the house-to-house searches we saw the Army undertaking at several villages along the road. People kept emerging from their huts at gunpoint, carrying what looked like pieces of buildings, doors, parts of tin roofs, pipes, bathroom fixtures. The soldiers had them load the stuff into the Army trucks.

My photographers wanted to see what was happening in Gonaïves, where the movement against Duvalier had coalesced during the past four months, but they were scared, too. They didn't want anything much to be happening there. When I asked my guide the night before how long it would take us to get to Gonaïves, he looked at me as though I were mentally deficient. "I'm not going to Gonaïves," he said. "I have family." He reminded me of his wife, their three children, his mother, his mother-in-law, two brothers. So I left without him.

We took the highway that winds north next to the sea, Route Nationale No. 1. There is no other passable road. Only a thousand yards or so to the west, the blue green of Port-au-Prince Bay, the churning St.-Marc Channel. To the east, the bald hills and mountains of Haiti, stripped of their trees by peasants who have no other source of fuel, and turned into charcoal to supply the demanding Port-au-Prince market. Between the sea and the hills, thin villages, little patches of palm and banana and thatch where men throw big charcoal bags onto buses, and women squat in the market, and the children play with hoops and marbles. I switched on Radio Nationale, because Duvalier had shut down Radio Soleil, the Catholic news station. We listened to the broadcast. It seemed to consist of a lot of numbers, and soon we realized that we were listening to international soccer scores. There seemed to be a lot of soccer games played in this world. The scores went on all day, and we listened to them all day, except for a few minutes of merengue music from the Dominican Republic. I was hoping for news, but there was no news.

Near St.-Marc, four young men were making their way down the side of Route Nationale in a line, each one carrying a paintbrush. Behind them strolled two baby-faced Tontons Macoute, pistols in hand. One held a can of yellow paint. *"Aba Divalye,"* read some graffiti scrawled in big black letters, like a child's scribble, across a public fountain where the words "PAPA DOC" had been carved years before in bas-relief. Down with Duvalier. Below it, in a different hand, was written *"Tonton Makout Ale."* Tontons Macoute, get out. The Macoute put down his paint bucket, and gestured toward the fountain with his pistol. The young men were quick to respond. One after another, they dipped in their brushes, and slowly they covered over the message with a bar of sunny yellow. The paint ran out before they finished.

At noon, we stopped in St.-Marc, where the night before a big crowd had gathered in the streets. Because Mardi Gras was approaching, people were using the seasonal street celebrations, or *ra-ras,* as they are called in Creole, as pretexts and disguises for demonstrations against the government. Crowds would begin in ra-ra and end in protest. In St.-Marc the previous night, the crowd had carried a coffin stuffed with the effigies of Jean-Claude and Michèle through the torchlit streets. The authorities had quickly figured out what was going on, and four people had been killed. When we walked through the center of town the next day, past the Army headquarters, a few exhausted Macoutes lolled on the veranda, in the shadow of its shabby colonnades. There was no one out. The photographers decided to stay downtown to shoot graffiti. I turned right, aimlessly.

I had walked a block or so down a dusty street when a small boy grabbed my hand.

"You journalist?" he asked, in broken French. "I show you something. I am Edwin."

Edwin had a lot of friends. As we walked farther and farther away from the barracks, a ragged band of children began to join us. In a few minutes, there must have been thirty. Edwin kept tight hold of my hand. He led me down a dirt street lined with houses, down to the middle, where behind a broken wall stood something that looked as though it had been shelled. Crumbling white brick, shards of glass, pieces of wall. In front, the street itself seemed to be paved with rubble.

"This is where he lived," Edwin said. "He was a friend of the President's mother. This is how we treat the President's friends in St.-Marc." Edwin guided me through the ruins like a real-estate agent.

"This was the front wall, you know, to protect the garden," he said.

"This was the bathroom." Nothing remained. A hinge from a shower door. I was beginning to understand what the people had been carrying from their huts along the road.

"This was the dining room." Nothing. The light switches had been yanked from the walls.

"This was the storeroom. Lots of rice he had stored." We climbed gingerly up the jagged leftovers of staircase.

"These over here were the bedrooms.

"His office.

"Oh, and we also took the roof."

When we arrived at the Army roadblock at Gonaïves, we were arrested.

"Why?" we asked the young sublieutenant who escorted us to the barracks for questioning. He sat on my Pepsis in the front seat with his rifle poking out the window.

"Because you are journalists," he said. "Sorry, no journalists in Gonaïves this week. Here we are."

It was siesta time, around two, and the men in the barracks were having their nap. They slept on the floor with their heads in each other's laps.

Our sublieutenant took us upstairs. He told us to wait in an office down the hallway, across from a small room where a young man in nylon running shorts was sleeping spreadeagle on a cot, his feet practically in the hallway.

"Wait here for the commander," the sublieutenant said.

The photographers busied themselves with hiding their film. In these situations, they usually take your film, they told me. The photographers were in a frenzy of rewinding and pocketing, reloading "decoy" blank rolls when the commander appeared. He turned out to be the young man in the nylon running shorts. He had put on an orange tee shirt for the interrogation.

"Driver's licenses," he said, sitting down at his desk and setting to work. He didn't look up at us, but held out his hand.

"Passports.

"Car-rental contract.

"Press passes."

He wrote down all the information on the back of an envelope he found, after some searching, under the old black telephone on the desk. Finally, he looked up.

"But where are your authorization papers?" he asked.

"Our what?" I asked. The photographers did not speak French.

"Of course you may enter Gonaïves," said the commander. He smiled ironically. "You are perfectly free to come and go as you please in Gonaïves. We welcome foreign visitors in my city. But of course you must have your authorization papers." He waited expectantly for us to produce these. We looked at him blankly.

"But this is on the orders of the Minister of the Interior, just yesterday," he went on, switching to surprisingly good English. "You must be aware. No? All members of the press must have a pass from the ministry to travel outside Port-au-Prince. Now, I see you do not know about this. This is too bad. Let me explain it for you. Now, all you do is go back to Port-au-Prince, and you go to the ministry, and in three days you have the papers all fine and you come back, everything okay, no problem. Fine and good. Okay? But now you go back," he said, rising.

"No, no," I told him, with the photographers backing me up, saying, "No, no."

"We came all this way," I said, "and besides, there are no such things as authorization papers. You know that," I told him. "You must call your superior. We want to visit Gonaïves."

He picked up the phone, casting a look of despair at the ceiling.

"Yes, well, I was asleep," he said into the phone, in Creole. My Creole was sparse, since what little I knew came from language tapes, but still I got the gist. My French was carrying me. "I'm sorry. Okay, okay. I know, I know. I'll see you later, then, right?"

He looked over at us and smiled, and shook his head.

"Now, don't be angry," he said into the phone. "I'll be finished with this right away. It's nothing." He lowered his voice. "We'll have fun, *chérie*. Okay. *Bon. Ta lè*."

He turned back to us. "I am sorry, but my superior in Port-au-Prince says that you must have the papers."

I looked at him.

"That was your superior on the phone?" I asked.

"Yes." A long stare that said I dare you. He stood. "Look, let me explain it to you. It is to make sure of your safety." He registered our skeptical expressions. "And give me your film. Thanks. Now you go, and I see you in three days. Okay?" he said, ushering us out of the room. "Goodbye. No, there is no bathroom."

When I got back to Port-au-Prince, Christophe, a German tourist staying at the hotel, told me he had just come down from Cap-

Haïtien, the big town on the northern coast where there had been huge demonstrations.

"It was terrible," he said. "Awful. Imagine. I was sitting there, in a bungalow by the beach, and these three girls were painting my toenails." He pointed down at his feet: four toenails painted pink showed up demurely against the brown background of his sandals. The Haitian woman he was with looked down, too, and smiled. A little boy was sitting silently on her lap.

"There they were, all three bent over me, a lovely scene, that color of their skin, like charcoal, you know, beautiful, when suddenly a hoard of Tontons bursts in. Four or five. With machine guns, if you can believe that. Five machine guns and three whores, not a fair battle. Well, of course we all jumped up and ran. And now my feet are spoiled." He looked down wistfully.

"I hate history," he said, tapping the woman's knee with his cigarette pack. "And those girls, my Lord. You should have seen them. So beautiful.

"Oh, well." He lit a cigarette with matches made in Gonaïves. "Haïti Chérie, as they say." The little boy watched him.

"Champagne, Frank," said the *Christian Science Monitor*. The table was crowded. Dusty Gonaïves of the day before seemed a distant memory.

"I'll only drink it if you expense it," said Harry. "We don't shell out money for everything, like you bloody Americans."

"I'm getting sick of this story," said Heidi. "When is he going to leave?"

"Right," said Harry. "He's costing *Time* and *Newsweek* money, the bastard. Never have so many paid so much to wait for a man to take an airplane. Good for his country's economy, you might say. It's a fucking patriotic act, his staying on. Singlehandedly, the international press corps, that's us, in case you'd forgotten, is building Haiti's foreign currency. Great."

Frank poured champagne.

"I wonder where everyone else is," said the dark-haired photographer. "I get nervous when it's not crowded. I mean, maybe he's leaving right now and we just don't know it."

"No way," said the *Monitor*. "I have a friend who will call me when he's leaving. That's why I stay right here, drinking champagne." He leaned toward Harry. "It's my job."

48 THE RAINY SEASON

"Oh, I get it. Good thinking, mate. You've got logic working for you behind that thousand-dollar expense account."

"Thousand dollars," sniffed the *Monitor*. "I'm not the *Times,* you know."

Harry took out his manila envelope and scribbled. I snuck a look over his shoulder. Three initials and a phone number that he copied from what he had written earlier in the day on the palm of his hand.

"Isn't anyone looking for me?" Aubelin Jolicoeur came around the corner of the veranda. "Or perhaps I should say, Why isn't anyone looking for me? Have I offended? My dear," he said, bending over Heidi's hand. "You are looking more beautiful than ever." He turned to the dark-haired photographer. "And you, you are ravishing. I love you. No, I worship you."

She laughed. "Aubelin," she said, "I don't believe a word you say."

"But, my darling, I am completely sincere." He bowed to her. "Trust me. Everyone in Haiti trusts Aubelin Jolicoeur. I am more trustworthy than the morning star, and more faithful.

Harry laughed.

"Why doesn't Aubelin kiss *your* hand?" I asked him. "He'd get more out of it."

"He's not looking for information, mate," Harry said to me. "He's looking for love. This meal is a disaster. The fucking fish is inedible, but at least it's expensive."

"Champagne?" said the *Monitor,* looking over at us.

"Why not?" said Harry.

A car screeched up below in the parking lot, but we all ignored it.

"Hey, everybody," said an Italian journalist, running up the steps to the veranda. She was out of breath. "He's leaving. I just got the news. He's on his way to the airport."

"No," said the *Monitor*. He was crestfallen. "Where is my call?"

"Forget your stupid call," she told him. "Come on. We better get over there."

"But I was having so much fun," the *Monitor* said.

A hundred members of the international press corps and no Haitians waited for four hours that black night at the airport among the stinging ants to watch Jean-Claude Duvalier and his retinue drive out onto the runway and take off for France with truckloads of luggage, four children and three security guards. This time, for posterity, Jean-Claude was at the wheel. The President-for-Life sat impassively in his silver-gray BMW like a suburban father driving the family off for what would no doubt prove a tiresome voyage: wife, mother-in-law, somber-looking children and stepchildren. Michèle smoked. She took in the international press corps with one condescending glance, and exhaled.

After the plane took off, our thirty or forty cars followed a van filled with Duvalier's people and Aubelin Jolicoeur to the U.S. Embassy. Aubelin jumped out. At four in the morning, the embassy lights were on, but the gates were closed.

"Let me in," shouted Jolicoeur.

A small figure was making its way from the embassy to the gates.

"Let me in," Jolicoeur cried again. "It is I, Aubelin Jolicoeur."

"Not now, Auby," said the embassy official as he reached the gates. Now that the reporters could see him, we recognized this embassy official: it was Jeffrey Lite, the press liaison.

He didn't open the embassy gates. Instead, with a loyal assistant standing by, Lite gave an impromptu press conference. He spoke from behind the embassy fence, and the television crews shot from outside. His face was framed with shadowy bougainvillea.

"Jean-Claude Duvalier left Haiti this morning, February 7, 1986, on a U.S. cargo plane headed for Paris," he told us.

"We know that, for Christ's sake," said a television reporter. "We were there. Tell us something new."

"The country is being run by a six-man provisional government." Lite read off the names from a piece of paper. Grégoire Eugène's was not among them.

"Lieutenant General Henri Namphy, the head of the Armed Forces, is now the president of the provisional government," he said.

"How do you spell that?" shouted the reporters.

"Who was on the plane?" yelled some others.

"The President, his wife, their two children, her two children, her sister . . ."

"How about his mother?" shouted a reporter.

"Yes, his mother," said Lite, checking his paper.

"How about her mother?"

"Yes, I think so." He looked down. "Yes, her mother also."

"How about your mother, Jeff?" someone yelled.

"You keep my mother out of this," said Jeff.

. . .

I fell asleep at six in the morning with the sound of a twenty-one-gun salute in my ears, and woke up at seven to the Hallelujah Chorus being broadcast on Radio Soleil. My guide was waiting for me with a monstrous plastic jerrycan of raw rum. He didn't even ask me how was Gonaïves.

"The motherfucker is gone, right?" he said in English. "You saw him go? With your own eyes?" he asked me. "I can't believe it. My wife, she tells me not to believe it. She says wait." He looked at me for reassurance.

"Well, I saw him," I said. "With Michèle. In the car. I saw the airplane take off."

He unscrewed his rum.

"Now I can believe it's true," he said. "They will kill all the Macoutes in the street like chickens."

He was right. The morning began with crowds everywhere. People came out of their houses and lined the streets. They waved us down toward the palace, shouting, *"CBS News libere nou,"* and *"Viv lame, aba makout."* *CBS News* has liberated us. Long live the Army. Down with the Macoutes. A little girl ran down the street next to my car, waving an American flag. In front of the palace, thousands of people were waving green branches and singing "Auld Lang Syne." They shook hands with the soldiers behind the fence, lifted them up and out into the crowd, kissed them, poured rum on their heads, and hoisted them onto their shoulders. Foreign reporters had tears streaming down their faces.

The crowd ran to Radio Soleil. *"An ale libere Radio Soleil,"* they sang. Let's liberate Radio Soleil. They surged into tap-taps and trucks and jeeps driven by wealthier people who had come down from the hill to take part in the scene. They danced wildly in the station's parking lot. They overturned the eternal flame outside the palace, and smashed its urn. They peered into the hole beneath it, because they had heard that it was the end of a secret escape tunnel from the palace, or maybe Papa Doc's remains were stored there for safekeeping. They threw rocks into the hole, and laughed.

They found no remains there, and, without warning, they changed direction, like a school of fish. They ran down the long street to the National Cemetery—there was only crowd, no onlook-

ers, because all the onlookers joined in. In a few minutes, the crowd
came piling up by the hundreds against the graveyard gates, chanting, singing, clapping. Inside, surrounded by elegant plantings of
prickly cactus, the pristine, white-tiled tomb of the Duvalier family
sparkled in the early morning sun like a bathroom at a beach club.
Boys began piling over the cemetery walls, running along the tops of
the tombs, waving down at the crowd. The four soldiers guarding
the mausoleum shouted warnings, but resolutely kept their Uzis at
their sides. Clearly an order had been given not to shoot. The people, with one great heave, flung the cemetery gates apart and off
their hinges. The Haitians had come to pay their last respects to Dr.
Duvalier.

The destruction started slowly. A few men climbed to the top and
pulled down the proud Duvalier family plaque, to applause and
laughter. Brave boys pried loose a few tiles, and ran with their
souvenirs held high, under the soldiers' watchful eyes. Next came
demolition by hammer, wooden stick, battering ram. At the back,
meanwhile, a team was digging down into the crypt, looking for the
bodies.

By evening, the tomb was an empty shell. It looked like the house
in St.-Marc: four jagged columns and a piece of roof framing the
mountains in the distance. Just outside the graveyard's gates, the
charred bones and flesh of an embalmed corpse lay smoldering on
the ground. The people had found what they were looking for,
something that could be taken as the remains of the dictatorship. A
thigh bone jutted from the pile, and pieces of pickled flesh still clung
to one arm, which reached out from the heap in demonic salute. No
one could say for sure whether it was the spirit of the simple country
physician that had once inhabited the cadaver. But, like the famous
spidery hands of Dr. Duvalier, the fingers on the one remaining
hand were long and grasping. And, in a last gesture of defiance, the
middle finger was extended.

Rumors began to circulate about killings of the Tontons Macoute.
One charred body lay on the side of the road near the industrial
park, and another dead man was stretched out in the sun near the
CARE warehouse, where thousands of people were making off with
vegetable oil donated by the United States. The crowd burned down
the house and offices of the Macoute who ran the citizen identification program, and yellow citizen cards blew up and out of his home

and down on the street in front of it like leaves signaling the end of a season. By late afternoon, you would be driving down an empty street, thinking the wildness was finally over, when suddenly, out from a corner, a throng would emerge, running with a destination clearly in mind. Then someone would say, They must be going to get Edner Day, depending on their direction, or Paul Véricain, or some other notorious Macoute, and they would disappear down another street.

Up on Avenue John Brown in the hills of Pétionville, the wealthy suburb above the capital, the Army had surrounded the Macoute headquarters. Paul Véricain, better known as Tonton Paul, stood in front of the building with some of his men, his denims and red bandana worn with bravado. From within, the Hallelujah Chorus was playing on a radio. Behind the circle of soldiers, the angry crowd. They wanted Tonton Paul's skin. But Tonton Paul, a plumber by trade, was not just any Macoute. He was also the mayor of Pétionville. I asked him why he was still at his headquarters.

He gave a slow grin and twisted his armband. The crowd moved forward, trying to hear what he was saying to the foreign journalists who had been allowed through the Army line. The soldiers pushed the crowd back.

"We are observing the new President's curfew," he said, leaning on the locked cast-iron fence. "We are obeying the law." At first he seemed unworried, but when a call came in from the Army barracks down in Port-au-Prince, instructing him to move his men inside, he grew alarmed.

"We have been abandoned," he said. "Dr. Duvalier created the Tontons Macoute to enforce order. We were there to protect the people from the Army, to protect the people's President. Now we have become a symbol of what the people despise. The Army has to protect *us* from the people. Worse, the President has left us behind. *Our* President. A lot of us will die." Someone in the crowd was snapping pictures of the scene. ("This is for my children, so I can show them what the Macoutes were in Haiti," he said.) The next day, Véricain, looking robust in his civilian clothes, was driven away in an Army jeep—his Uzi close at hand—as soldiers held back a vengeful crowd.

"Where are you going?" I asked him.

"Someplace I can relax," he said. He would spend the next two years in the National Penitentiary, where his family brought him a good hot meal every midday, and fine cigars, and rum.

· · ·

That was the Dechoukaj. "Dechoukaj," like many other Haitian political slogans, is a word that comes straight out of Haiti's farm culture. It means to uproot a tree, to pull it out of the ground, roots and all, so that it will never grow back, and you do it when you are clearing a field to plant. It takes a lot of people: a picture of the word "dechoukaj" in the Catholic Church's Creole literacy textbook shows six people working together, straining to pull up a tree. "Dechoukaj" was the word used to describe the violent movement against the Tontons Macoute that followed Duvalier's downfall, and, more generally, to describe the necessity of ridding the country of Duvalierism. No one knows how many little Macoutes—and others who took advantage of the regime's lawlessness—were killed in the Dechoukaj in early 1986, perhaps more than a hundred. But the bigger fish, important mayors of towns, like Véricain, as well as chiefs of rural sections (*chefs de section*) and well-known Port-au-Prince swaggerers, were rescued from furious crowds and brought to prison under police protection. Some were later allowed to leave the country.

It was rumored that Madame Rosalie Adolphe, the head of the Tontons Macoute, left the country disguised as an ailing nun, on a stretcher. Though well-educated, articulate and sometimes even charming, Madame Adolphe did not have a good reputation with Haitians. Before she was named to head the Tontons Macoute militia, she had been the warden at Fort Dimanche, the notorious Duvalier death prison. Some say Madame Adolphe, who is familiarly known as Madame Max because her late husband's name was Max, is now living on Long Island, but others believe she is still in Haiti, three years after the Dechoukaj.

Madame Max's house on the Avenue Pan-Américaine in Pétionville was gutted during the Dechoukaj, and a few families of squatters moved in afterward and lived there for a while, peering out from behind walls ripped clean of all fixtures. As in other homes wrecked by the Dechoukaj, the toilets and bathtubs and sinks were ripped out and smashed, and all the tiles removed. But the squatters continued to use the bathrooms for traditional purposes, and there was a stink at the house. There was no water in Madame Max's swimming pool a year after the place had been torn apart, and the pool's cracked, dry bed still sat under the watchful eye of an odd sculpture:

a large pink shark with a smaller fish struggling in its mouth. You could almost imagine Greene's dead Duvalierist minister bleeding in a corner of the pool. Instead, the squatters sometimes used the empty basin as a kitchen, cooking bits of chicken on charcoal in the shallow end near the steps.

During that first week of the Dechoukaj, Henri Namphy changed the Haitian flag back from Dr. Duvalier's black and red to the old blue-and-red flag of the revolution, first created by Jean-Jacques Dessalines, the ruthless revolutionary general who worked alongside Henry Christophe during the war against Napoleon, and who masterminded the slaughter of the French planters and their families. Dessalines was the man who coined the phrase *Koupe tèt, boule kay,* to describe his strategy for defeating the colonials. It means "Cut off the heads, burn down the houses." According to legend, after Dessalines' blunt strategy had succeeded and he had won the revolution, he took the French tricolor in his hands, ripped from it its band of white and had the two remaining thirds sewn together. Thus was the white oppressor defeated and expunged. Later, Dessalines replaced the blue with black—a more obvious statement about who had been the victor in the revolution—but Alexandre Pétion, Haiti's first mulatto leader, reverted to the blue when he took power, in order to placate Haiti's lighter-skinned citizens. It was François Duvalier, a great admirer of Dessalines, who had changed the flag back to black and red.

In theory, the reversion to the original revolutionary banner put a symbolic end to the Duvalierists. Everywhere, the black version came down and the blue one went up. The dechoukeurs often carried the blue and red as they ran from place to place, uprooting Duvalierism. There was one small flag lying in the ruins of the Duvaliers' mountain mansion, up in the clouds above the city, where the dechoukeurs had found porno magazines and *Paris-Match* and *House & Garden* in the bathroom. In the cathedral, a makeshift red-and-blue banner hung at the side of the altar.

My guide took me over to St.-Jean-Bosco, a smaller church on Grande Rue where he told me I would be able to find someone with whom I could talk about the church's role in ousting Duvalier. Young men were lounging in the courtyard, and I asked one of them whether he could find me a priest to talk to. He looked at me and smiled.

"Which priest?" he asked.

"Oh, it doesn't matter," I said. "Whoever you think is best."

He smiled again, more broadly. "Wait here," he said.

I was soon joined by a man about whom I remembered little for a long time other than enormous glasses and a face like a bug, pop-eyed and watchful, a small, delicate man who looked even younger than the student I had sent off to find him. He had what appeared to be an eternal half-smile on his face. All the young men in the courtyard came and gathered around us, watching him intently.

"I'm Father Aristide," he said. "Can I help you?"

"Yes," I said. "That is, I think so. *You* seem happy."

"Well, I am, I am," he said smiling, showing crooked teeth. "We are all very happy here right now. We've been working on this for a long time, you know. All my life, in a way." He was thirty-two then.

"I don't know where to start," he said. "Where should I start?" He looked at the young men, who laughed. "Well, let's say this: We've been trying for a long time to figure out the best way to send away this government. Officially, my friends and I can't say that we've been organizing against the government, because we are in the Church. In other words, we are not doing politics, exactly, but what we *are* doing is trying to get a better life. We are not a political party, but our work is something like that. We are not neutral. We are doing politics without saying that's what we are doing." He laughed again, because he had said it.

"He's been preaching against Duvalier," said the young man who had brought Aristide over to me. "A lot. For a long time. They didn't like it much. About a week ago, a guy came into the church, this Macoute from the neighborhood, and he had a revolver, he had it out. He shot it. He thought he could just come in here and shoot Father Aristide. But we did not permit that," he said. "We disarmed him, fast."

"We're glad Duvalier is gone," said Aristide. "That's why we seem so happy. But this is not the end of the affair, by a long shot. The new government is perhaps a necessary evil, but it certainly is not the choice of the people who struggled and sacrificed to get rid of Duvalier. We have a warning to issue to this new government. If the people were willing to expose themselves to the regime's bullets to cry, 'Down with Duvalier,' they will surely do the same with the new government, which is, after all, the *same* government. What we have now is Duvalierism without Duvalier."

I looked at him skeptically.

He laughed. "Well, *you* may not be able to see it now. Now to *you* it may look like a new government, a new face, new symbols. But to us, we see Duvalier's face when we look at Namphy. We know Haiti better than you do."

"Well, that's true," I said. "No denying it."

He smiled again. "It's definitely true." He laughed. "Is this your first time in Haiti?"

"Yes," I said.

"Then you'll see. Jean-Claude is gone, and in a few days you and the other foreign journalists will leave. The news is over for you, but not for us. The people will be quiet for a while, but then they will rally, they will get together to continue organizing in order to break apart the system, which is still in place." His voice was gathering strength as he went along. I could imagine him preaching, even though right now he was sitting on a stoop in pants and a guayabera, with fat guinea fowls trundling around in the courtyard behind him.

"This last week has been only one instance of popular power," he said. "There will be others. We must sweep out the Duvalierists, wipe the slate clean. If this does not happen, there will be only more pain and misery, and violent death. There is no question." The young man who had brought the priest to see me was signaling him to finish. He tapped his watch significantly, but Aristide ignored him. "There is no question. No question." The young man took Aristide by the arm.

"Will you be coming back to Haiti?" Aristide asked me after we shook hands. He was being pulled away.

"Yes, I think so," I said.

"Then you will see," he said, over his shoulder. "What I have said will come to pass. But don't mistake me. I am not speaking pure prophecy. I know what will happen because I know what *has* happened, and I know the situation. The prophecy is true because it springs from the analysis. You understand?"

"PEPSI," reads the big sign near the end of town, now blue and red. "THE CHOICE OF THE NEW GENERATION." Jean-Claude's old sign was destroyed during the Dechoukaj.

Suzanne, the Oloffson's proprietor, went downtown to buy a gun a few days after Duvalier fled. She was afraid that the hotel had lost its protection, she was scared of the Dechoukaj. She knew she had a lot of discontented waiters and former waiters who wouldn't mind doing the place a little damage.

"Shit," said Harry when I told him about Suzanne's gun. "That could make dinner interesting."

An American dentist was distributing Valium on the veranda. Heidi took two and went off to pack. In the bar, a reporter from Radio Suisse-Romande improvised boogie-woogie on the untuned piano. Harry sat back in his chair.

"Well, I wouldn't have missed it for the world," he said. "Even if some loony with a gun walks up the steps right now and does me in here on the veranda of the Oloffson, I'd still be glad to have been here. For this." He held up his glass and motioned toward the piano, and the Swiss reporter nodded at him and started playing the Haitian national anthem. "For that." Harry gestured again, toward Frank, who was wearing a blue-and-red flag in his buttonhole. Frank bowed. "For Haiti," Harry said, clinking glasses with me. "May she rise from the shit she has so long been in." He took a long sip, emptying the glass. Then he narrowed his eyes and looked at me with a tight grin. "What do you think are the chances?"

From a song improvised by the reporter from Radio Suisse-Romande, February 7, 1986:

> *Pauvre Duvalier, allé, allé.*
> *Il a froid dans la neige*
> *Et Michèle va le quitter.*
>
> *Je suis un pauvre Tonton*
> *Dans un lit d'hôpital.*
> *J'ai perdu ma machète*
> *Et je ne suis plus un mâle. . . .*

> Poor Duvalier, he's gone, he's gone.
> He's cold in the snow
> And Michèle's going to leave him.
>
> I'm just a poor Tonton
> In a hospital bed.
> I've lost my machete
> And I'm no longer a man. . . .

. . .

Fires were burning in the three big garbage cans in a courtyard in the La Saline slum. Ten families were cooking their dinner over the

flames. Tonight they were cooking a big dinner, with meat, to celebrate the fall of Duvalier three days earlier. Three little girls came
walking into the courtyard among the shanties with white buckets of
water on their heads. They had come from the other end of the
slum, where the water truck had just made its daily delivery, late.
Marie-Hélène put the bits of pork she had been cleaning into the hot
oil over the flames, and turned to watch her three boys playing
marbles in the dirt.

"You think I can find a Pepsi?" I asked her, in my Frenchified
Creole. The day was still hot.

"Mimette," she said to one of her daughters who had brought in
the water. "Help the *blan* find a Pepsi, over at Bòs Jean-Jacques's."

Mimette picked up her cellophane kite and took me by the hand,
pulling. We walked a little way. The sun was setting over the port
across the Boulevard de La Saline, and I had almost gotten used to
the stinging smell of rotting oranges. Bòs Jean-Jacques's blue borlette was shut tight, but Mimette went around the back and I heard
her asking questions. A dog was sleeping peacefully out in front,
with flies making a meal off an open wound in his leg. A woman's
voice answered Mimette's questions.

She came back to me, and told me that Bòs Jean-Jacques was not
in, he had left La Saline for the countryside because he was too
scared. His wife said they were afraid they might get dechouked. He
had left the whole family here, except for the oldest boy, because the
oldest boy was in the business, too, and well known in the slum. But
I should come around the back, Mimette said, Madame Jean-
Jacques might have a Pepsi.

Madame Jean-Jacques was sitting in front of a grill. I couldn't see
her face behind the smoke, but her body was substantial in its bright
pink dress. A girl, a daughter, was standing behind her, combing
out her mother's hair and braiding it.

"I'm looking for a Pepsi," I said. Mimette stood next to me,
unsnarling the string of her kite. Another of Madame's daughters
was doing laundry with a washboard and a stone, singing to herself.
The smell of sawdust rose up from the nearby coffin workers'.

Madame Jean-Jacques did not reply. The first daughter kept
braiding. Mimette said something in Creole that I could not understand. Madame Jean-Jacques sat stonily.

"I think she wants money first," Mimette said, speaking slowly.
"They are afraid they will not have so much money now. Give her
some money."

I reached into my pocket and pulled out a dollar.

"More," Mimette said.

I pulled out another two.

"Good," she said. "I'll give it to them." She took the money and hopped over to the girl, who put out her hand, and I saw two dollars go into her hand and one dollar into the little front pocket of Mimette's white dress.

Madame Jean-Jacques's daughter motioned to me and turned brusquely, guiding me into a small cement house behind the boarded-up borlette. It was dark and hot inside; the cement holds the heat. In the back room stood an old-fashioned icebox, which the girl opened. There was one Pepsi, and seven or eight Sekola Oranges, a sweet, sticky Haitian drink. She looked up at me questioningly.

"Pepsi," I said. She opened it.

I took the Pepsi, and Mimette took my hand. We wandered back to the courtyard, where the smell of the cooking meat was beginning to cover up the stench of the rotting oranges. When she thought I wasn't looking, Mimette handed Marie-Hélène the dollar. Her mother patted her head. Three men were playing a fast game of dominoes, one of them keeping score with multicolored clothespins that he pinned to his beard. He was Marie-Hélène's boyfriend. They were listening to Radio Soleil, some song about the Tontons Macoute.

Mimette took her kite down to a bigger dirt path, a dry one a little distance from the courtyard, and started running. There was no wind. Her white dress flashed by among the shanties, and then the kite started rising above them, reflecting the setting sun like a rising moon. It skittered below the electric wires stretched across the path, among which the gray remains of other children's kites hung like ragged notes of music. The kite kept flying down the path, then stopped for a moment in thin air and started back toward us. Someone turned up the radio. Mimette's dress flashed by again in the other direction, and Father Aristide's voice came over loud, preaching about Duvalier's downfall and the Dechoukaj. The kite was approaching, flying higher and higher. The pork smelled like it was almost ready. Mimette's mother stopped stirring the pot and stood with a hand on her boyfriend's shoulder, watching the dominoes click and listening to the sermon. My Pepsi was sweet, and the sugary smell of the rum from the men's half-empty bottle filled the air. Mimette's kite flew high in front of us for a few sweet seconds before it got stuck in the wires like the rest of them. It bounced for a moment as she tried to pull it down, but it wouldn't come free.

A few minutes later, she reappeared in the courtyard with a kite frame and some new cellophane. Her mother laughed at her and said something about the wires. But Mimette was serious. She sat down on a small chair whose seat had long since fallen through, and began making a new kite. I leaned against the sharp tin of a shack and drank my soda. There were no Tontons Macoute in La Saline this evening. Aristide's voice was coming from radios all over the slum, and then the "Hallelujah Chorus," again. When I finished my Pepsi, I gave the bottle to Mimette, who had been watching my progress carefully while she reattached the old string to the skeleton of her kite. She put down her work, smoothed her white dress and ran off to get the deposit.

After Tonton Paul had been driven away, and the Army had left the area, and the people had wandered off, I went inside to inspect the Pétionville Macoute headquarters, deserted but undefiled. I opened some drawers, found dominoes, and looked upstairs, where there was a big room like a meeting hall. Downstairs, sitting on a desk in the main office, was a notebook. It looked like a child's workbook, its light-blue cover illustrated with a photograph of a palm tree in front of what looked like a resort. The notebook had been made in the Dominican Republic, and on its back cover was printed an exhortation to the youth of that country, *"Ser Justos."* Be Just.

"Third Watch, 6 P.M. to 12 A.M.," was penned inside the front cover. Inside were entries on notable events in Pétionville from December 5, 1985, through January 21, 1986, the period of the country's worst unrest, in longhand. The logbook of the Tontons Macoute. I took this little book. It's on my desk now, with its cheerful blue cover and shabby, torn pages. Every time I look at it, I feel I should turn it over to the appropriate authorities. It's an odious item to have around, with its subliterate entries and obsession with guns.

> Gun #2668351 [reads the first entry] has been released to a militia member for thirty minutes at the order of Company Commander Véricain. . . .
> The V.S.N. Pierre Jean has taken a gun in order to go home for half an hour. Okay. #4349383. . . .

For the good of the company, we acknowledge receipt of seven guns, two of them at the home of Commander P. Véricain. . . .

I have given guns to M. Gérard Raymond, sergeant on the Fourth Watch: six guns in the guardroom, one at the stairway, and one for the sentry box, none of which have been registered by number.

The little book also records denunciations of personal enemies of specific Macoutes:

This morning at 6:55 I left home wearing my athletic gear to go over to the Athleticlub across town to work out. I stopped by at my sister's on the way and she told me that a certain Aline, the girl with whom she has been quarreling, said that I was a crazy man and that only my death would cure me of this disease. This upset me very much. I am making this report for my sister.

Port-au-Prince, 2 January, 1986
W. Maître

And it mentions various arrests:

A certain Yvonne Valcin and a certain Exancia Valcin were arrested for having participated in a plot against the sister of a militiaman. . . .

We locked up Luckner Jérôme on the order of the Commander at about 12:20 A.M. I left in the guardroom his watch, one white shoe, his belt, keys, and a matchbox.

The name of one of the military members of the junta that came to power after Duvalier fell is scribbled thoughtlessly on the inside cover of the book: "Régala." Twenty-one pages of the book are missing, not ripped out but cut out, as though with scissors or a razor blade.

Maybe this logbook has historical importance. A tough-minded prosecutor, if there were one, might have been able to use it against certain members of the *ancien régime*. Paul Véricain, for example. The appropriate authorities might have used my little book to bring such men to justice. It contains clues and evidence about the Pétionville Tontons Macoute, who they were, what they did. There are plenty of names in my blue book, records of beatings and imprisonments. But I've got a problem. My problem is: Who are the appropriate authorities? I've been looking for them for three years now. I hold on to the book.

Boutilliers

    I kept coming back to Haiti after that first trip. There were demonstrations and conventions of opposition groups, there were shifts in the government, there were speeches and press conferences, arrests and shootings, and there was the feeling of a million people talking at once and all of a sudden. The press was free and the Army was firing into crowds of protesters. On the one hand, Christians were persecuting voodoo; on the other, progressive Catholics were being attacked by the Army and the remnants of the Tontons Macoute. Everything was at a boil, and I couldn't stay away. Finally, in the spring of 1987, I went down to Port-au-Prince to live.

    I thought I already knew my way around. I'd been to a lot of places in a series of rented cars, and then there was always that first taxi ride, which I thought of as my orientation. On my later trips, I kept rediscovering parts of town that I'd seen only once before, on that careening ride. But now I had names for the places I had passed through so fleetingly. Yes, I would remember, that hilly slum, or *bidonville,* as the slums are called in French. Now I knew its name: Bel-Air. Right, I would think, those shanties bordering the highway: La Saline. That street with my hotel at the end: Rue Capois. That steep and rocky road up behind the Oloffson: Rue Sapotille, the

street I lived on now. And on and on. Sometimes I thought the taxi
driver had covered the entire city. And for only fifteen dollars. I
came to think of the ripoff as a bargain.

One place my taxi driver didn't take me to, however, was Carrefour—too far out of the way, even for him, I suppose, and the traffic
jam on the Carrefour Road is unbearable at almost every hour. Of
all the areas of the capital, it was Carrefour that I had to get to know
on my own. No one can take you on a tour of this deteriorating red-
light district, or not on a tour that's worth taking. You have to do it
yourself. Every time I got taken to Carrefour, I ended up dancing
to Michael Jackson on an empty dance floor while the whores made
deals at tables in the darkness. But when I went alone, it worked
out. I'd broil in the late-afternoon sun through the loud, hot traffic
jam south of town, down the one road that goes in that direction,
listening to Radio Haïti-Inter, to Lyliane Pierre-Paul's news broadcast. *"Li fè katrè,"* Lyliane would say, signing on. "It's four o'clock."
Finally I'd get to a disco, or a club, or a whorehouse, or a restaurant,
usually all four.

One evening I went to El Caribeño. I'd been there before and I
knew a couple of the girls, Nina and Olga, and skinny Rosa. Most of
the girls were from Haiti's neighbor, the Dominican Republic; people told me that Haitian men preferred the Dominican girls' light
color—the color of mulattos. There was always someone new and
shocking there, like Marietta who wanted to use my lipstick in the
ladies' room and then tried to kiss me, but usually there was also the
same old crowd. I went into Room 11, Olga and Nina's room, one
of about thirty in two long low greenish buildings that face each
other like barracks across El Caribeño's long driveway. Sometimes,
when I visited earlier in the day, Nina and Olga and I would sit
outside on the long strip that ran like a porch in front of the barracks,
and drink Prestige, the Haitian beer that the girls said was not as
good as Presidente, from the Dominican Republic.

Tonight in their little green room, Olga and Nina wanted to put
on their red dresses. They were insistent and giggling. They wanted
to have their pictures taken. I laughed at them and told them I didn't
take pictures.

"But look," said Nina. "Come on, it's so pretty." She went over to
the white aluminum armoire and took a dress out. She smoothed the
red taffeta across the bed. "Good in pictures. Take my picture," she
said. She put her hand on my arm.

"I don't take pictures, Nina," I told her. She shook her head,
annoyed.

But someone else, some other foreigners, journalists, had been by the day before, she complained. They shot three, maybe four rolls, Olga said, for an American magazine. A handsome boy, the photographer, Nina said, part Haitian, she thought, but light-skinned. Very light. She shut her eyes to remember, and smiled at me when she opened them.

"They paid us," she said.

Olga made me stay while two men came in to talk business. When they went off again to buy rum, she shook her head.

"Haitians," was all she had to say. For the most part, the Dominican girls at El Caribeño thought that Haitian men were too dark, and barbaric, something to be tolerated for money's sake.

"Haitians," Nina said. "No rubbers." She turned away and began filing her nails. The girls were frightened of AIDS, and they had been told to use two condoms for every client. "Still, for some things," Nina had said to me earlier, "a rubber won't work." Nina looked appraisingly at the red dress on the bed. She was debating whether to put it on for the men.

Olga showed me a picture of her children in Santiago. I had seen it before. The smallest boy was standing in front of a Christmas tree glowing with lights. "That's Ernesto," she said.

I know, I said. She turned away and folded Nina's red dress back onto a hanger and hung it up next to her own, the only other item in the armoire. She left me holding her vinyl wallet, with Ernesto looking up at me, waiting for Christmas presents.

The men came back with a bottle of Barbancourt rum. They sat down on the bed.

"I'm going," I said.

"Stay," one of the men said, extending the bottle. "Drink it, it's Haitian. It's good."

The light was still on in Olga and Nina's room when I pulled away down the long driveway of El Caribeño. It was late, but everyone was still up, hoping for business. Other girls were drinking beer and putting on makeup along the stretch in front of their rooms. One waved goodbye to me with her lipstick, and then I turned left onto the Carrefour road, heading back to town. I drove fast, took advantage of a clearing, rare enough. It was almost cool at that hour. You could breathe for once. You could move. I had all the windows down, against convention. You're not supposed to roll down your windows at night in Carrefour. It's too wild. If you have to stop,

someone could stick a gun in your face, or pull you out of your car.
One man I know stopped for a child running across the road, and a
dead chicken landed on his lap. People use chickens in the ceremonies down here, he said, and sometimes they make charms out of
them and put them in the road to send bad luck away. But they
don't usually throw them around like that. It was a little messy, he
told me, but it wasn't too bad.

"I just picked it up where its head used to be and chucked it back
out," he said. A philosopher.

There were little lights behind closed doors as I drove, and the
road was empty. There were a few tap-taps parked by the side with
their names painted above their windshields, names like In God We
Trust, Oke Betty, Dallas, Lolita, La Théocratie, Belmondo. Next
to a pharmacy, I saw the dark hulk of a tap-tap called Chicago, with
its decorative swimming-tube swans and its beachball festoons looking in the night shadows like tropical birds flying head on into massive moons. Sometimes under a light a group of men were talking.
Otherwise nothing, another whore, a couple of drunks, two women
washing in the gutter.

And then there was a man. He didn't run out in front of me,
didn't jump into the street, didn't do any of the things people usually
do to get run down. He was lying there, instead, right in the middle
of the road. I didn't think about why. I thought: a pothole, a long,
dark pothole. I was used to the potholes, they came after the rains,
craters that looked as if they'd always been there just beneath the
asphalt. I positioned my tires to straddle this one, and I started to
slow down, when I realized, Hey, it's a guy. A man. I braked,
skidded, stopped just in time.

He didn't move. I didn't move. I was just breathing and I supposed he was doing the same, if he was alive. I hadn't touched him.
He still didn't move when I got out and tapped him with a toe. I
leaned over him. He was staring like a dead man, but breathing. I
grabbed his shoulders and shook him. He was an old man, and
drunk. Or he smelled drunk. I shook him hard, and he stumbled
up.

"You're in the middle of the road," I told him. He looked at me.
I must have seemed like a white phantom to him. I felt as if he
hadn't really seen me. He was still staring. Tears began to run down
his cheeks, but he wasn't crying.

"You're in the middle of the road," I said again. A truck piled to
the sky with shadows of green bananas swerved around us. The man

shook his head, shrugged. He lurched, suddenly, and then grabbed both my hands in a fierce grip. Suddenly I thought of my friend's dead chicken. The man stared at me and I tried to pull him out of the road, but he was immovable. He was in a trance; I still felt he couldn't see me. He didn't seem to mind standing here, in the middle of the road, in the dark, holding hands with a stranger. I did. My hands felt hot, and when they felt too hot to stand it anymore, which was fast, he dropped them, and turned his back on me. Then he turned around.

"Look," he said, the only word he said to me. And he pointed.

What I saw at the end of his fingertips were stars. Red and white stars, high up in a black sky. Red stars, I thought, amazing. The light down here plays tricks. But then I realized: It was Boutilliers.

Boutilliers is not on the maps I have, not on the two tourist maps, not on the detailed German road map. Still, it was meant to be a tourists' place, a high spot above the city, with satellite dishes and radio towers, warning lights for aircraft and a surprising lavender vista pavilion, a semicircular cement-and-glass structure that sweeps out over the mountainside, complete with a telescope for tourists. The telescope is not functioning.

Before they built the now abandoned vista center with its telescope for tourists, Boutilliers was already well known among Haitians. Remote, yet accessible from Pétionville, the capital's rich hilltop suburb where Tonton Paul had been mayor, Boutilliers had a view of all of Port-au-Prince, and it was dark at night up there, with the city glowing below like two handfuls of embers thrown into a pit. It was dark, quiet, and had everything the Pétionville kids needed for a make-out spot, a place to park.

Lovers could still go up there, but they don't. The place has developed a bad reputation. One Sunday night not long after Jean-Claude Duvalier married Michèle Bennett, a doctor and his fiancée, a former girlfriend of the President-for-Life, went up to Boutilliers, maybe for old times' sake. It was just before they were to be married. No one will say what happened, but they were parked, and then the car exploded, and the fiancée was burned to death, the doctor badly disfigured. The doctor told some story about two armed men, and explosives. Other people talk about an acid attack, and the First Lady's mad fits of jealousy. One of the doctor's friends said the lovers were freebasing cocaine and it got out of control. The doctor still practices in Port-au-Prince, and you can see that before the scars covered his face he was a handsome man. Not too many lovers have spent time on the peak since then.

AIDS and political unrest have scared tourists away from Haiti, and there isn't much traffic up to Boutilliers. The only people up there on a regular basis are three or four vendors who used to cater to the tourist trade, and who are still trying to sell guayaberas, bean necklaces, bad paintings, and wooden boxes to tourists who rarely show up. The vendors' stalls line the road that follows the mountain's curve, but from their perch behind the pavilion the vendors can't see down into the valley. They are there all the time, but they never go to the lookout terrace, they never look over the edge to see what's below. Either they're asleep in the afternoon heat or they're too busy trying to sell their stuff to some hapless passerby. Probably they already know more than they would care to know about the city upon which they could look from their vantage point on the side of the mountain, and they are not interested in the scenery.

I go up to Boutilliers regularly, alone. There the air is cool, even in the early afternoon, and you don't feel the hot, heavy animal of the tropics weighing down your shoulders. I don't do much up at Boutilliers. I'll buy a couple of necklaces. I'll buy a box, maybe, if I have to, if the man who's selling it starts to tremble, as he always does if he thinks you're going to leave without buying. But after dozens of visits, I stopped buying the paintings. Scenes of bright peasant life, or lovely little children in uniforms filing into school, pictures of grand bourgeois families dancing in a hall beneath towering hi-fi speakers, or of shocking voodoo ceremonies in blacks and reds with decapitated chickens flapping in blood and women writhing, panoramas of bustling, abundant markets, paintings of primeval forests, with lions, giraffes, panthers and other animals no Haitian has ever seen at home, where the wildest animal is the crocodile or the flamingo, or the tarantula. It's hard to keep looking at those paintings, but these Haitian artists paint them over and over again, as though they can't get the nightmare out of their system. For months, a vendor tried to sell me this one painting, of a church interior, because I made the mistake of looking at it. He started at thirty dollars, laughably high but negotiable. Still, for a long time I couldn't bring myself to buy it, no matter how badly the stooped and stuttering art dealer wanted to get rid of it, no matter how low he would go. I had promised myself no more paintings.

Instead, I'd string my beads around my neck and go stand next to the telescope. At least you can lean on it. The city always looks dead, unoccupied, Boutilliers is so high up. The only place that once sent signals of life to this lookout point was the sugar refinery, but that was closed for a while, because no one would pay the high prices it charged when you could get cheaper smuggled sugar from the Dominican Republic. So no more black smoke that used to churn out of the red-and-white smokestack and carry the smell of molasses and rum over Cité Soleil, covering up the slum's squalid stench for a minute here and there. When the sky was clear, you could see how the shantytowns—flat, irregular blotches from this far up, their corrugated roofs sparkling like cast-off bits of tinfoil—were the biggest residential areas of Port-au-Prince: Cité Soleil, St.-Martin, Fort-National, La Saline. Though there are now more than a million people living in the capital, fewer than half live outside the bidonvilles.

While I watched from up there on Boutilliers that day, a shadow as big as a mountain came edging up over the city, and I looked up to see the eternal black afternoon clouds descending behind me from the interior. Something called a tropical wave, *une onde tropicale,* a vengeful storm, a cyclone, had been predicted for today. Also coming down around the mountainside was the art merchant, who smiled a big smile in front of the black clouds and pointed to the painting that he carried like a shield across his chest. I shook my head and turned back to the city.

I always remembered too late that I had meant to bring my binoculars. Maybe from up here I could have seen whether the antiaircraft gun that the Duvaliers had installed on the lawn of the National Palace was still ready for action. I had heard that Namphy had removed it. Over the top of the telescope, I tried to site the radar receptor that sits on the top of one of the palace's three domes, another relic from the days when François Duvalier's enemies used to launch ludicrously abortive air attacks against him. Like the telescope, the radar receptor is not working.

I supposed I didn't look busy, standing there, leaning on the telescope. A tap on my arm, and I turned and saw a smiling face above a bright tableau.

"Fifteen dollars, now," the art vendor said to me in English. He pointed at the painting. Fifteen was a sizable reduction from the price he had quoted on my last visit. Still.

"Men, mwen pa vle-l," I told him in Creole. "I just don't want it."

He held the picture up in front of my face, pointing to its good

features. Look at the windows, he said. I obeyed: sunlight poured
into the church from those blue and green windows. I nodded. Yes,
the windows were quite nice.

"*Yo byen, wi,*" I told him. They were slatted.

"*Gade sa, gade,*" he said, pointing. Look at this, look. He pointed
to the priest, a small figure at the top of the picture, holding a chalice
in the air. The Haitian perspective. The priest was small, but his
great white robes cascaded down toward the altar as though the robes
themselves were more of a shelter than the church. The little people
of the congregation had their backs to us, and the artist had lavished
his brilliance of detail on the chalice, with the red wine licking its
gold walls. In spite of the sunlight shining through its windows,
outside the small, crowded church, in the corners of the picture, the
artist had painted a night full of the thick foliage of tropical trees:
palms, bananas, figs, breadfruit, and the calabash. Inside, the
priest's face was hidden.

"*Li wè Granmèt-la,*" the vendor told me. The priest sees God.
This sales tactic was hard to reject. But I did. Still, the picture was
very beautiful.

"*Mwen pa gen kòb. M pa vle-l, m pa renmen bagay-sa-a,*" I told
him. I have no money. I don't want it, I don't even like the thing.

"Fourteen dollars," he said. "I am a Haitian."

"*Li fè katrè.*" On a radio one of the sleeping vendors had left going
near his stall, I could hear Lyliane begin her broadcast. It was four,
and I didn't want to drive down from Boutilliers in the rain. The
mountainside is steep. I wanted to get home before dark, too, because it was July 1987 and the city that looked so peaceful from up
at Boutilliers was filled with demonstrations and barricades. Often,
the Army was out on patrol. There was at least an hour before the
storm would come in, which would give me half an hour to spend at
Barbancourt. Sometimes the reason I go to Boutilliers has less to do
with the view than with Barbancourt, a tourist rum-tasting outlet
opposite the Laboule sand mines, just below Boutilliers. I was thinking of the sweet spice-flavored rum as I started my car: the idea of it
was bad and the stuff itself was bad, but after the preliminary fruit
flavors, spice rum seemed an appropriate finale, even worse than the
others but more imaginative. Like magic at the sound of my engine,
the art merchant appeared.

"*Ou pa bliye sa-a?*" he asked. You haven't forgotten this?

"No, no. *Mwen pa vle sa-a,*" I said. *"Sa pa interese mwen."* It doesn't interest me.

"Twelve dollars," he said, pointing to the priest again. The chalice shone in the late Boutilliers light. The deep afternoon was closing in on us. "Twelve dollars," he repeated, in English. "Dirt cheap."

I started to pull away.

"Okay, ten," he said, running by the side of the car. "A bargain." He began pushing the picture through my window, a common last desperate sales ploy. There were tears in his eyes. "Seven. You can't say no."

"No," I said.

He pushed the painting in farther. The priest's robes were in my face. I stopped the car.

"Okay, okay," I said. "Put it back there. Here's the money. Thanks."

We threw the priest in the back. The art vendor carefully counted his money, pleased. When I looked at him in the rearview mirror as I started down the hill, he was crossing himself.

One problem at Barbancourt is that you have to walk through a crowd of vendors to get in, a sorry bunch of young men, almost kids, selling wooden figurines whose penises flap up when you lift the barrels that encircle the miniatures' bodies. I've gone through many approaches to get around these aggressive salesmen. First, I used to plow through them, but once I began to be able to speak to them in Creole, that method seemed impolite. Then I tried chatting with them, but this got no better results. "I have two sons," one young man told me. "The big one is in Cité Soleil and the little one is up here with me and my girlfriend. Look at this," and up it flaps. In the end, I ignored them, which worked best, since now they knew me and were convinced I would not buy. Eventually, the penis vendors' market would dry up, perhaps becauses penises are not a funny souvenir from a country where AIDS has done such damage. On a later trip I took up to Boutilliers, the penis vendors just weren't there. Instead, a less aggressive group of salesmen was selling a vast array of weeping Marys and native crucifixes done in hardwood.

The Barbancourt outlet is only that, though many tourists in the old days called it the factory. It has a giant still and sugar mill dating back to slavery, but neither has ever been in operation on the premises. People who work at the outlet up here call it the Castle. Like so many things in Haiti and other small, overcrowded countries, the Castle had its origins in a family feud. The plain rum that all Haitians drink, which is also called Barbancourt, has been made since the days of the colony at Croix-des-Missions, a town on the outskirts of Port-au-Prince, close enough so that you can see it from Boutilliers. The business was extremely successful, and then there was a row within the Barbancourt family. The loser got out with nothing but the name, and the Barbancourt Castle was the result, never anything other than a place where tourists can taste fruit-flavored rum and perhaps buy gift packages of it. The Castle is proud of itself: it has received the Haitian Rum Liqueur Gold Medal for Gift Packaging. When I asked the manager whether the cane for the liqueurs was grown nearby, he said, "Are you kidding? Look out there." He pointed through the open door to the trucks heading in and out of the sand mines across the dirt road. The tires stirred up the dry dust. It looked like a desert out there, from the cool interior of the Castle.

"The cane is grown down on the plain," the manager said. "In Cul-de-Sac and Croix-des-Missions. We built the Castle up here because it was on the way to Boutilliers. We thought we'd make money on the tourist trade." He shook his head.

Inside the Castle, the dark hallways lined with rum bottles lead to a central courtyard where a reed-thin employee in butler's blacks presents each visitor with thimbleful after thimbleful of sixty-proof fruit-flavored and other special types of rum. "Coconut," the butler announces, hands you your plastic cup with a puddle of liqueur at the bottom, and then withdraws. You finish that sip, and he shimmers back in from the blackness of the interior, saying, "Hibiscus." Like a tropical cliché, the orange bougainvillea casts shadows across the old slave mill. The sun is setting behind the sand mines. "Mango," the butler says. "Mint." Papaya, banana, licorice, chocolate, coffee, and by the time he says spice I'm feeling better about the priest in the picture, better about the penis boys, better about Boutilliers.

Boisterous laughter from the Castle's entrance. Through a spiced-rum haze, I see what looks like too many white people—that is, more than one at a time. One white person in Haiti, according to the received wisdom, is a tourist or a journalist; two are always Mormons; three are from the United States Agency for International Development or some other development project; four are from the American or French Embassy, heading out for lunch, and five or more are missionaries. These were missionaries, from the Christian Church Missions, in magenta tee shirts with blue crosses, from Texas, Oklahoma, Missouri. Some of the men carried penis statues; they loved the joke, whatever the joke was. The girls were giggling among themselves.

One of the girls was from Oklahoma, and she had read about Port-au-Prince in a newspaper back in Oklahoma City. Well, she told me, she always was interested in mission work and spreading the gospel, and she liked the sound of this place Port-au-Prince. She said it as though it were a new product for taking royalty with you: *Porta*prince. She knew she could help those people find the Lord, she just knew it. But then she had read about Haiti: six or eight million people, poorest country in the hemisphere, 50, 60 percent unemployment, 80 percent illiteracy, sick kids, malaria, TB, AIDS, voodoo. Haiti sounded like a good place, too. Lots of poor people, backward in their beliefs.

"I thought, How am I going to choose between *Porta*prince and Haiti?" She smiled. "I was devastated. Both places had so much mission potential. *Porta*prince maybe was smaller and more manageable, but Haiti, all those mountains, mountain people. Boy, was I glad when I found out the two places were the same. I guess it was the work of the Lord, trying to tell me something, you know?"

When I left, the other missionaries were leaning over the rail, joking about how many slaves it would take to make the sugar mill turn, but she was sitting over in a corner, talking to a handsome Haitian. She even managed a little Creole. I could tell that although the mission's two weeks in Haiti were up she would be coming back one day, soon.

"Two," said one of the missionaries, laughing. "One to run ahead with a watermelon, and the other to chase him and pull the mill."

I had my last sip, of Five-Star Special White Rum, and walked out past the butler and the phalanx of penises down to my car, which I drove down the mountain, past the sand mines, past the elegant houses, past McLaney's Casino in Pétionville, down Avenue John Brown, past the closed-up artisans' shops and above the minor shantytowns that tumble down the hillside, past Dr. Daniel C. Claude's sign that promises to cure AIDS ("AIDS is not an incurable disease," proclaims Dr. Claude's sign), down past the green Catholic school in Bourdon opposite the French ambassador's residence, formerly the Presidential Palace, past the barricades near the Esso station, with its burning tires and five kids who ask for my press card, each one with a rock in his hand, and who politely accept Marlboros before opening up a space for my car to pass through, and who wave me on, down through the traffic light at Avenue Martin Luther King, past two trucks of riot troops, past Ruelle Vaillant, with the beautiful wrought-iron school gates at the end of the short street, and then down and down and down, through more barricades, and then around the front of the palace, where two thousand people are demonstrating and waving branches at more riot troops on the lawn, past the National Cemetery and three skeletons of burned-out buses, right onto Harry Truman Boulevard, past the AIDS research center, past the U.S. Embassy, the stench of sewage in the bay filtering through the car's air-conditioning, over the wide stretch of potholes like mine explosions, and, finally, to the water, to Place Christophe Colomb, where the thin fence that separates the land from the sea is covered with bright paintings for sale.

The great white statue of Columbus that once stood here, looking out into the bay for other islands to possess, has been disappeared, pulled up by its roots and tossed unceremoniously into the water by a crowd a year or so ago. They weren't particularly impressed that Haiti, the western third of the island that Columbus named Hispaniola—after the domain of the King and Queen who were financing his search for gold and other riches—had been the great explorer's first major stop in the New World. (One of Columbus' ships, the *Santa María,* sank in the bay off Cap-Haïtien.)

According to the crowd's logic, they were getting rid of the white oppressor when they overthrew Columbus. It was he who had planted the Spanish flag on the soil of Hispaniola, and the Spaniards then went about the systematic exploitation and eventual extermination of the indigenous Arawak Indian population. By the mid-1500s, the colonials had to begin importing black Africans to the island to labor under Spanish masters in its gold mines and sugarcane fields, and later under the French, who began to dominate the colony in 1659.

The urgent need for a labor force created a volatile political situation in the colony and the tinder that would eventually be set off by the democratic ideas of the French Revolution. By 1681, there were 2,000 slaves in St.-Domingue, the French name for Haiti. A little more than a hundred years later, there were at least 500,000 Africans, and probably as many as 700,000, compared with 40,000 whites and 28,000 freemen of color, offspring of masters and slaves.

Many of the blacks were newly imported—because each year thousands of slaves died of overwork and undernourishment, negligence and beatings—and these Africans were understandably resentful of their new life. The masters were obviously outnumbered. Harsh measures were taken to keep the restive slaves in line. Their African religions were immediately recognized as a possible source of strength in resisting the French, and the colonials decreed that all slaves must be baptized into Catholicism, thereafter to worship in that faith only. The slaves' night ceremonies and dances were often forbidden, because they presented opportunities for slaves to associate with one another away from the eye of the master. Sometimes the planters' decrees were worded in unnuanced terms—for example, an ordinance in 1704 that forbade slaves from "gathering together at night under the pretext of holding collective dances."

Nonetheless, the ceremonies took place. The most famous of these meetings occurred at Bois-Cayman near Limbé, in the Plaine-du-Nord, over a long period during the summer of 1791. The gatherings were led by Boukman, a slave overseer and voodoo priest from one of the big nearby plantations, and other overseers from other plantations in the northern plains were invited. According to Robert and Nancy Heinl in *Written in Blood,* when Boukman held his final ceremony on the night of August 14, a pig was slaughtered, all present drank the blood and then swore allegiance on bended knee to Boukman's cause, which was death to all *blans,* the Creole word for a white man, or foreigner. Legend has it that as the slaves drank their potion a vengeful thunderstorm broke out above the meeting ground. Boukman ordered his followers to await a further sign from him on the twenty-second of that month. When the signal came forth from the drums that night, slaves from half a dozen plantations rose up, burned down their masters' homes and slaughtered the planters and their families. Boukman was later killed in battle, and the French put his severed head on display in Cap-Haïtien. "The Head of Boukman," read the motto below the appalling trophy, "Chief of the Rebels."

The revolt soon spread, and the massacre was brutal, repugnant, a mirror image of the hideous tortures that the masters had inflicted on the slaves over the past century. The masters had stuffed gunpowder into slaves' rectums, and exploded it. They had rolled their slaves in spiked barrels down hills, they had whipped them and tied them to boards and left them in the swamps to be eaten alive by ants and mosquitoes. The slaves repaid these favors in 1791 by decapitating the masters, raping their wives on top of their bloodied corpses, chopping off their arms and legs, sawing them in half, impaling their infants on proudly carried spikes. The entire northern plain was encircled by fire, and the slaves, certain that the gods of Africa would protect them and careless by now of their tormented lives, flung themselves heedlessly at the planters' oncoming cannon and musket fire. Each time the French shot down an approaching battalion of slaves, a new one seemed to rise up behind it, and kept coming. Among the black troops were *marrons,* or Maroons, slaves who had fled the hardships of the plantations many years before and lived far from the whites in mountain enclaves. (In French, *marron* means a domesticated animal that has returned to its savage state.) After two months of fighting, more than a thousand plantations had been destroyed. The revolution had begun.

During the thirteen years of its bloody and protracted battles, sackings and burnings, and periodic yellow-fever epidemics, the Haitian Revolution altered the course of world history. Using eighteenth-century-style guerrilla warfare as well as more formal tactics against the weary French troops, the indefatigable slaves exhausted Napoleon's energies, and the First Consul became disillusioned with his prospects in the New World. The Haitian engagement had been costly, both financially and in terms of human life. Napoleon had planned to make short shrift of the rebellious Haitians on his way to establishing New Orleans as a beachhead for the French Army. From there, he would continue his New World conquest until the French flag flew over all of North America, not just the enormous region of Louisiana and some parts of Canada. Instead, unable to keep Haiti, he turned his back on the Americas. As E. J. Hobsbawm writes in *The Age of Revolution: 1789–1848,* "The failure of Napoleonic France to recapture Haiti was one of the main reasons for liquidating the entire remaining American Empire, which was sold by the Louisiana Purchase (1803) to the USA. Thus, a further consequence . . . was to make the USA a continent-wide power." The Haitian Revolution was to become the world's only successful slave uprising, and in 1804 Haiti became the second independent nation in the Western Hemisphere, and history's first black republic.

It was not granted any favors because of that special status. The colonizers of the world—France, Spain, Portugal, England—feared the newly independent slaves, and the youthful United States, whose economy was still based on slavery, wanted nothing to do with the new republic. France hated the Haitians who had defeated

her—"gilded Negroes," Napoleon had called them—and refused to
recognize Haiti. The new nation remained for a long time an international pariah, and its leaders were obsessively concerned with a
possible invasion and return to slavery. In the mountains outside
Cap-Haïtien, Henry Christophe, the former slave and later Emperor
whose statue guarded the Oloffson's door, built La Citadelle, a fab-
ulous fortress that was constructed at the cost of hundreds of Haitian
lives. La Citadelle commanded a view of the valley and all surrounding mountain passageways, and even after several powerful earth-
quakes it still stands. But for more than a hundred years no white
man came to try to conquer the notorious land. When white men did
come, they were not the French whom the Emperor Henry had
feared, nor did they drop anchor at Cap-Häitien. They were American Marines, and they landed near Port-au-Prince in 1915.

By then, Haiti had become a place of considerable interest to the
growing world power to her north. The Môle St.-Nicolas, which
faces the eastern tip of Cuba on Haiti's northwestern coast, guarded
the Windward Passage to the Caribbean, an important access route
for maritime travel to Mexico and Latin America. The passage made
Haiti a crucial place to control in the days before air warfare became
commonplace. In the years leading up to the American intervention,
French, German and American agents were conspiring against one
another in Port-au-Prince. Everyone wanted dominion over the
Môle. By 1915, World War I had already begun, and the New World
was in a state of some anxiety. The United States, about to enter the
fray, wanted a stable Haiti friendly to American interests. It also
was concerned to protect U.S. business interests in Haiti, in particular those of the National City Bank.

But Haiti at the time was hardly stable. A succession of ill-fated
presidents, one of them supported by a peasant movement, the others by the mulatto elite, and all in cahoots with one or another
foreign power, had followed one another rapidly to power. On July
27, 1915, the last of these, President Vilbrun-Guillaume Sam, ordered his men to kill almost two hundred political enemies whom he
was holding prisoner in the National Penitentiary. The next day, he
was pulled, cowering, from the French Legation, hacked to death
by relatives of his victims, and then torn apart by an angry mob.
The Americans seized this opportune moment to do what they had
been considering doing for more than a year. They sent in the Marines, and began a controversial occupation that was to last nearly
two decades.

   The occupation was not forgotten by the boys at the barricades in the summer of 1987. Before condemning the statue of Columbus, the archtypical imperialist, to a burial at sea, someone scrawled *"Viv Chalmay Peralt"* along his side, a reference to Charlemagne Péralte, the Army officer turned guerrilla leader who was hunted down by the Americans, betrayed by one of his own men, and shot point-blank by an American Marine in blackface, four years after the Marines landed in Haiti. Shot, and then tied to a door near the Cap-Haïtien barracks, nearly naked, with a Haitian flag and crucifix propped up against his dead shoulder. Major J.J. Meade, the American commander of the north, had a photograph taken of the scene to prove that Péralte was dead. No matter Meade's reason for taking it, the photograph has served another purpose, not one Meade expected. The great Haitian painter Philomé Obin, founder of the Cap-Haïtien school, stood that photo up next to his canvas many years later and painted the famous *Crucifixion of Charlemagne Péralte in the Name of Liberty* that hangs in the Musée d'Art Haïtien. Whatever kind of hero Péralte may have been, the image of his martyrdom and humiliation has made him a deity in the pantheon of the endlessly ongoing, endlessly thwarted Haitian liberation. Place Christophe Colomb is now known, informally, as Place Charlemagne Péralte.

   Péralte is second only to Jean-Jacques Dessalines in the rankings of Haitian revolutionaries. After Toussaint L'Ouverture, the first military leader of the Haitian slave revolution, was betrayed, captured by the French and sent on June 7, 1802, to France, to die less than a year later in a prison in the Jura Mountains, Dessalines, one of Toussaint's generals, took on the task of winning the ongoing war against the French. Dessalines managed to bring two more generals, the black former slave Henry Christophe and the mulatto former freeman Alexandre Pétion, into a united front that eventually beat back Napoleon's navy, whose 55,000 troops in Haiti were led by the First Consul's twenty-nine-year-old brother-in-law Charles-Victor-Emmanuel Leclerc. In 1804, Haiti, in the person of Dessalines, declared her independence from France. Dessalines' secretary, Boisrond-Tonnerre, summed up the Haitians' triumph when he said that the Haitian Declaration of Independence should be written on parchment made of the skin of a white man, using his skull as an inkwell and his blood for ink. From 1804 until 1915, Haiti was a sovereign republic, and the people's distrust of foreign powers remained constant. Under the U.S. occupation, Haitian sentiment against the island's third wave of white invaders, the Americans, rose to heights similar to those expressed by Boisrond-Tonnerre, and when it did, Péralte was the first to exploit the resentment and patriotism in guerrilla warfare.

Péralte's face was everywhere in the summer of 1987, a statement of Haitian nationalism. You could find his likeness on a priest's office door. At a radio station in Cap-Haïtien. In the kitchen of a rich Haitian artist. Painted on a wall in the La Saline slum. On a door in an inner office of the Canadian Embassy. On flyers announcing demonstrations. Even on a new half-gourde coin minted by the provisional military junta that replaced Jean-Claude. The coin was decorated with a bust of Péralte based on a 1982 portrait by the painter Valcin II, which in turn was based on a triumphant medallion distributed in 1934 after the Marines went home. This was a Charlemagne who looked less like a martyr and more like a turn-of-the-century Port-au-Prince politician in his bow tie and formal jacket, or like an early abolitionist leader, with his fiery eyes and long moustache.

Even when the picture was not of Péralte, it was Péralte the people saw. When the junta finally issued a new one-gourde note—worth twenty cents—with a heroic portrait of Toussaint replacing the bust of a dreamy and bespectacled Dr. Duvalier, the little street boys who beg you for gourde notes and for fractions of gourdes would fight over the bills. They weren't satisfied with Duvalier gourdes; they wanted the crisp new Toussaint bills. "I want a new one," one boy said to me, looking down scornfully at the decrepit Duvalier bill I had given him. "The one with the picture of Péralte."

It's five, the hour when the smell of fried chicken from the red-and-white striped fried-chicken stand near the dock usually starts mingling with the smell of the port's sewage. But not today; today, there have been too many barricades for fried chicken. I sit there in my car, out in front of Columbus' deserted pedestal, switching back and forth from Radio Métropole to some station from the Dominican Republic. Mobile 15, one of Métropole's walkie-talkie reporters, comes on to announce that there has been shooting in Carrefour, and that the road is blocked after the Royal Haitian Hotel. Just before El Caribeño. Poor Nina, poor Olga. Bad for business. In my rearview mirror, I see an occasional ambulance go by, then a truckload of troops, a jeep filled with nuns, cars marked "PRESSE." No private cars: too many barricades, too many rock-throwers, too many troops. By five-thirty, the heat begins to break, but the city is still stifling under the smoke from the burning tires.

They are playing endless merengue in the D.R. A wind is coming down off the mountains; as it starts to blow away the smoke, the clouds I saw up over Boutilliers, blacker now, begin to descend. Just up the street, people in La Saline are trying to get ready for the storm, putting bananas back into their baskets, gathering up bagfuls of rags and plastic sandals, tying up their rickety stalls, calling out their children's names. Above the merengue, I hear a woman shouting, "Johnny, Johnny."

You can almost feel the cold rain when it begins to come in from behind the nearest mountains. You can see it approach. The slant of the sun's light is swallowed up in cloud, and one by one the shanty-towns, the yellow and pink cathedral, the white National Palace and the ochre Army barracks turn the same dark color of cinders, till only the blue cemetery, the National Cemetery, is still shining in the south, a shining city of the dead, with raised graves and huge mausoleums, each one capped with a cross.

If you drive into the cemetery just after sunrise you can see the *houngans,* or voodoo priests, throwing rum and coffee over a different kind of cross, a large black one, tall as a man, that stands off in a corner of the graveyard. They are feeding Baron Samedi. There is a black cross like this one, in his honor, in almost every Catholic graveyard in Haiti. Sometimes the houngan puts a bowler hat on the top of the cross and hangs a black morning coat across it, to signify Baron. The evangelical Protestants come to Baron's cross, too, to proselytize. A Protestant minister was there next to the cross one morning, in black suit and tie like all Haitian Protestant ministers and their sons, reciting the gospel in a loud voice. The voodoo people ignored him.

Carrying cups, beggars and starving people come to Baron's cross from all over town, sometimes a hundred of them, many of them teenaged girls with their children, many of them peasant men wearing rags and straw hats, many of them shantytown men who are over twenty now and have never had a job. Some of them make small offerings to Baron—lit candles, coffee-soaked bread—and knock on the cross for luck, but most just wait until the ceremony is over and the food distribution begins. The houngan hands out bread, and his attendants pour coffee into the empty cups. The Protestant minister also brings bread and coffee, gladly accepted by all. Afterward, everyone drifts away down the cemetery's broad white streets.

At the end of one street, near the gates of the graveyard, are the ruins of that tomb which only a few years ago bore the legend FA-MILLE DUVALIER and was guarded by an eternal flame and two soldiers in khaki. Now someone has planted a cornfield on the ruins, and the walls behind them are decorated with graffiti. "No Tontons Macoute in the next presidential elections," reads one. *"Sic suma gloria mundi Duvalier,"* reads another. During the rainy season, bodies tumble out of their graves, and the walls of the cemetery are destroyed by mud slides from the mountains, because there are so few trees left to retain the soil. In a sea of mud down on Rue Monseigneur Guilloux one day I saw a car that had plunged down Rue Cameau and crashed through the graveyard wall. It was resting now with its smashed bumper up against a broken grave. Crosses floated on the mud, and boys standing in mud up to their thighs were picking the car clean.

Last time there was a tropical wave, an onde tropicale, seventeen people died, most of them down in the slums near the water. Some richer people died, too, in their crashed cars. A schoolteacher who had just come back from Montreal. Her daughter. A lieutenant who got caught in his jeep and drowned. Sometimes the violence of the rains makes me panic when I'm out in them. The windshield wipers don't work, and then the tires start treading mud and pebbles, and then the car, the whole thing, begins to slide backward down the hill, even in first, and you see people behind you try to scatter. It gets scary, and along with scores of tap-taps I usually end up sitting out the storms inside my car at the Texaco station on Delmas, a main street that, like Avenue John Brown, goes from downtown up to Pétionville. Five minutes into the storm, all the lights in town go off, and you're left sitting nowhere in a steaming car, next to the tap-tap Chicago, with its soaked swans, listening to rain and to static from the unworking radio stations. A tropical wave tossed that car from Rue Cameau into the graveyard.

The rains usually come in toward nightfall, and they are dangerous not only for ground transportation but for aircraft as well. Planning around nature's timetable, the airlines have scheduled most of the flights arriving at Port-au-Prince for the afternoon and the early evening, just before the rains. If you are awake and out on the hot streets of Port-au-Prince in the height of the afternoon—and no one

who can manage not to be, is—you'll notice the planes coming in.
There are so few flights that they mark the time of day: Air France
at 1:15, American at 3:01, Eastern at 5:47 and Pan Am at 6:50.
These last two are the cocktail flights: every evening, all around
town, people who live in the hills sip rum-on-the-rocks on their
terraces and watch Eastern and Pan Am drift in, far away, over the
mountains and the bay and the coast as the lightning flashes above
the horizon and the sun goes down. In Cité Soleil these flights also
have a social role to play. Cité Soleil is under the pattern. Even
before the American flight is overhead, people in the shantytown
stop talking, nod their heads and point toward the sky. They are
waiting to be drowned out, and they are. The plane comes over low.

Up at Boutilliers, you can't even hear the planes. They drop silently into the airport—where the words "FRANÇOIS DUVALIER"
were gracefully deleted after Jean-Claude left—and unload their
usual cargo: returning exiles; sons and daughters with proud U.S.
resident status; shifty businessmen and Army officers all wearing the
successful man's uniform, a tight-fitting suit and a heavy gold Rolex
watch on the wrist; grandmothers and grandfathers coming back
from a brief visit to a son or daughter who is a doctor in Brooklyn,
or an accountant in Queens, or a schoolteacher in Manhattan, or a
student at Hunter College.

For a while after Jean-Claude fell, each plane from New York or
Miami or Paris carried home among the exiles at least one future
presidential candidate, who would be welcomed at the airport by his
party; usually this meant family and friends, all huddling together
under one banner painted with the party's initials, often unpro-
nounceable but always with a D for Démocratique, an N for Nationale or an H for Haïtien. The presidential candidates were all coming
back to a country they hadn't lived in for years, to an election they
hoped would take place, an election that Henri Namphy and his
provisional military junta had promised to schedule. Few of the exile
candidates knew much about where the country was headed or how
the people were feeling. They couldn't be sure of where they themselves fit in, either in the fabric of the society or even in the sheer
physical arena. Often, the presidential candidates had no house in
Haiti. They were coming home to their mother's house, or their
brother's house, or the house of a second cousin's second wife.

The home they aspired to, however, sits in the middle of the
tangle beneath Boutilliers: the National Palace, as white as icing.
In a big gray-and-white spangled room there, decorated at a cost of

hundreds of thousands of dollars by Jean-Claude's wife's close friend Johnny Sambour, the departing Duvaliers reportedly had a farewell party—champagne, cocaine—that kept a hundred members of the foreign press waiting until almost four in the morning at François Duvalier International Airport, among the stinging ants. I had ended up at the airport, not the party.

That party at the palace, if it took place, was a rare event. In general, Jean-Claude had spent little time there, preferring the seclusion of his beach house or his ranch or his mountain villa. The palace was more important under his black-clad father; it figured as an impressive backdrop. In 1963, years before Jean-Claude became President, his father François stepped onto a palace balcony in his black suit and black hat pointedly reminiscent of Baron Samedi, and told the crowd he had had shipped in from the countryside that he was "the personification of the Haitian fatherland." He had just masterminded a crackdown in which hundreds died.

He didn't stop there. "I am already," he told his audience, "an immaterial being." Drunk on the tafia provided for them by Duvalier's men, the crowd became delirious. In the summer of 1987, the general who was then the nominal head of the military government was said to be spending a lot of time drinking tafia at his suburban home, in the library he had had built behind the pigsty. General Namphy liked a good time, it was said. He spent whole days drinking, while more sober heads at the palace were dividing up the spoils of government service. François Duvalier was a quiet man, and did not drink.

In 1964, Dr. Duvalier issued the Catechism of the Revolution, in which was included this version of the Lord's Prayer: "Our Doc, who art in the National Palace for life, hallowed be Thy name by present and future generations. Thy will be done in Port-au-Prince and in the countryside. Give us this day our new Haiti, and never forgive the trespasses of those traitors who spit on our country each day. Lead them into temptation, and poisoned by their own venom, deliver them from no evil. . . ."

Toward the end of 1960, the Immaterial Being exiled the Archbishop of Port-au-Prince and several other Catholic clergymen. The Vatican responded quickly by excommunicating Duvalier. But by ridding himself of its leaders, Duvalier had effectively gained control over the Church, and he and his son appointed many of its future bishops. After all, both literally and figuratively the palace is not far from the cathedral, a pastel two-towered tropical fantasy. The cathedral is the tallest, and the biggest, building downtown, almost the biggest building in Haiti, except for some of the massive, astounding postcolonial symbols of Haitian independence, like the Citadelle, and now the new Téléco building near the Disco Doctor's house in Pacot. The cathedral has stained-glass windows, and plastic flowers hang in bunches from its columns. A big choir sings up front with an electric band. The sound system is good, except when a priest who meets with the regime's disapproval is scheduled to preach. Then, the electricity goes off. Otherwise, visiting priests get a warm welcome. They sit in thronelike chairs, and there is room for thousands of congregants.

When I'm downtown, I try to avoid the cathedral. Because of its size and centrality, this isn't easy, even though I was once unable to find it—once when I had first come to Haiti, and everything seemed to block my way and I was still orienting myself by that first taxi ride. I try to avoid the cathedral because it reminds me of unpleasant things: the hours I spent in the old slum behind it, Bel-Air, waiting for the riot troops from the palace to stop shooting, so I could go home. It reminds me of Radio Soleil, just a few blocks down, where soldiers open fire every once in a while, to let the priest who runs the station know who's in charge.

Before the altar of the cathedral in 1980, Jean-Claude married the divorcée Michèle Bennett (she wore a spangled headdress) in an extravagant ceremony officiated by her mother's cousin François-Wolff Ligondé, the Archbishop of Port-au-Prince, an appointee of the bridegroom's excommunicated father. The long road out to the wedding reception at Jean-Claude's ranch was lined with well-wishers rounded up by the Tontons Macoute, wearing palace-issued tee shirts printed with hearts and clouds and photos of the presidential couple and the motto "SOUVENIR D'UN GRAND JOUR"—souvenir of a big day. It was raining, and the Duvaliers' guests got wet. Under the huge party tent, the women's high heels sank deep in the mud. Michèle and Jean-Claude were two hours late for their own reception, and no one dared begin eating from the elaborate buffet until the happy couple had arrived. When they finally showed up, the sequined guests lunged at the food. Eventually, everyone calmed down, the women in their furs sipping champagne, the Army officers chatting, the head of the secret police off in a corner, and the witless, self-satisfied dictator looking on. For the occasion, special television sets were provided to the shantytowns so that the average Haitian could witness the marriage of the patriarch. The foreign press turned out en masse for the last time until Jean-Claude fell.

In spite of his endorsement of and participation in the wedding of Duvalier to a divorcée, Archbishop Ligondé lost little political standing among the greater part of the Haitian people. Certainly Ligondé, whose endlessly fawning sermons praising François Duvalier (and later, Jean-Claude) were infamous among Haitians, had little standing to lose. Among the hierarchy, Ligondé was the bishop the least liked by the people of his diocese. Although bishops as religious figures had traditionally commanded enormous respect among the Haitian peasantry, in the waning years of Jean-Claude's rule, this was becoming less true. A growing number of progressive priests and nuns on whom the Church hierarchy lavished little love had already begun to develop a large following among peasants and slum-dwellers, and the close contact these clergy people were forming with their parishioners created a familial bond that respectful fear of the bishop could not match. The people were beginning to see their bishops as authority figures, and beginning in some cases to associate that authority with the authority of the hated regime.

In the summer of 1987 many people believed that the fight going on in Haiti then and for the previous decade was not so much class warfare between the bourgeoisie and the proletariat or the peasantry, nor a contest pitting Port-au-Prince against the countryside, nor even a battle between the government and a number of political parties, but was rather a fight between certain strong segments of Haiti's only remaining institutions: the Church and the Army. They pointed to progressive clergymen like Father Aristide, on the one hand, and to Army strongmen like Colonel Williams Régala, Namphy's colleague in the junta, on the other. This seemed a plausible analysis until you considered the large and influential sector of the Church—including, in its latest permutation, Archbishop Ligondé and the Papal Nuncio—that was on the Army's side, and always had been.

The Army's barracks, the Casernes Dessalines, yellow and burnt sienna and ochre, are as wide and impressive as the cathedral is lofty. The Casernes, which means barracks in French and Creole, look like something built by the French foreign legion in a desert country, low and sprawling, with an open courtyard and shadowy rust-colored overhangs covering all the windows in the old wing. The cathedral, for all its soaring loftiness, is just one room. But the Casernes Dessalines, named after the revolutionary hero, is not just a barracks. It houses a hospital, a prison, even a movie theater. Legend has it that the Casernes houses *ma belle* also. Ma belle is a pillar in the middle of a room somewhere in the sprawl. If you are arrested and taken to the Casernes Dessalines and if someone wants to teach you a lesson, they take you into this room, they tell you to put your arms around ma belle—my beauty—and then they beat you.

No matter how many times a day you drive past, you never see soldiers leaving the Casernes. But whenever there is trouble in the streets, especially, it seemed to me, whenever I was in Bel-Air, and especially on the narrow Rue Montalais, truckloads would suddenly appear and start shooting into the crowd. In Bel-Air, stuck between the boys from the barracks and the walls of the looming cathedral, you felt you were trapped in a sewer with no exit, probably how people in Bel-Air have felt for a good long time.

There is often that stifling feeling when Army meets Church on friendly ground, for instance a party in July 1987 at the Military Academy just outside town. To get there, everyone had to drive along a route lined for miles with men in uniform, holding Uzis and rifles, in the same line-the-streets concept as the tee shirts for the wedding. It made me tense, and it took some doing to get into the party mode once we arrived. The atmosphere was not very relaxed: dozens of officers and politicians mingling, trying to get into photographs with President Namphy. Hardly any women had been invited. The U.S. ambassador stood inside a circle of Haitian politicians, towering over them with his Edwardian profile, wire-rim glasses and white bucks. He was there with the American naval attaché and a Coast Guard officer. Most of the Haitian officers wore name tags. There were many whose faces I already knew well enough without the tags: Colonel Williams Régala, the tough junta member whose cool was marred by a disturbing shock of gray hair above his brow; Colonel Carl-Michel Nicolas, the chief of staff, a heavyset mulatto whose skin was the same pallid color as his khakis; Colonel Jean-Claude Paul, the head of the Casernes Dessalines, who kept one hand on his Uzi while he held his champagne with the other; Colonel Prosper Avril, a Duvalierist who had been kicked out of the original junta because of popular protest—silent, watchful, controlled; and, of course, President Namphy, wearing his gold ID bracelet that says "Henri."

Namphy was drinking his champagne, although an officer I was talking to smirked and looked away and mentioned that Namphy must miss his tafia. Tafia and the President: it was a constant joke. "Henri" was chatting with Marc Bazin, a presidential candidate who had recently left a job in Washington with the World Bank to return to Haiti and wage his campaign. Namphy's officers were also drinking champagne, big men in khaki uniforms with red-and-blue braid and heavy gold Rolex watches, holding delicate plastic champagne glasses in their big fists. Foreign reporters had called the President and his period in Haitian history "Ennui Namphy," but events in recent weeks had shown that Ennui was many things, but not boring.

I watched him smile and crinkle up his blue eyes for a few minutes, and then I walked into the next room and nearly spilled my champagne on the Papal Nuncio, a big balding Sicilian who represents the Vatican's interests in Haiti. He was standing next to the buffet table, chatting with Jean-Claude Paul, who was not long after indicted by a Miami grand jury on charges of cocaine trafficking. At the time, people were being shot by the soldiers from Paul's Casernes every day and every night, and the government was again, as in the days of the Duvaliers, contemplating the banishment of a number of outspoken priests. Colonel Paul had a file cabinet in the Casernes that was filled with dossiers on those priests' activities. There was even a provisional list of those who would be exiled—though in the end the Army decided that assassination might be a more effective solution, and more in line with the popular new Constitution, which, mindful of Duvalier's abuses, forbade exile. At the party that day, in fact, we were celebrating the passage, four months before, of the new Constitution; before the champagne was uncorked, the generals and the colonels had pledged allegiance to the document, after having in the previous weeks violated almost all of its most important sections.

Nonetheless, there at the Army celebration was the Nonce Apostolique, as the Papal Nuncio is called in French, in white soutane girded with magenta sash, clearly in a good mood among the colonels and the generals, munching away contentedly. Le Monstre Apostolique, as many progressive priests call him. He stood next to the buffet table with Colonel Paul, his head inclined to catch the Colonel's every word. Each time the Nuncio spoke—whispered, really—

in French heavily accented with Italian, he caressed the large gold cross that sat on his stomach. Colonel Paul nodded, and the Nuncio nodded back. They were eating bits of grilled pig. I expected Jean-Claude and Michèle to arrive at any minute.

These, then, are the battlements of power, and for years they have been the same, long before Duvalier: The palace, where the President rules. The Casernes, filled with the Army's agents. They can send them out anytime, anywhere, and they take you or your father or your lover, and that's that. Often, even the President doesn't have much say: it's just Colonel Paul or whichever Colonel Paul happens to be in charge that year, or that day. And then the cathedral, where the kindly priest tells you to believe in God and wait for a better world beyond—one with more food in it. (Haitians express this fatalism best when they say it in Creole, a motto with a ring of resignation: *Bondye Bon,* the Good Lord is Good.) And finally the cemetery, where all the rulers and their victims—those lucky enough to have their corpses returned to their families—end up.

Things are not much different now, and their victims can be anyone. It's easy to become a victim of the regime, and that is why it is hard to fall asleep in Port-au-Prince, why everyone in Haiti is always nervous: everyone is a potential victim. I could be a victim, driving down the side of the mountain with "PRESSE" written on my dashboard. One resentful soldier, one bored former Macoute in his gold BMW, one loaded gun, and I could easily be killed. An accident, they would say, the gun went off accidentally. If the investigation got that far. Or the art merchant: he could be a target, too, if he happened to go downtown to buy more canvas for his artists on a day when the soldiers happened to start shooting into the market. Or the priest in the painting, in his small church. Father Aristide, say, an easy mark. He clears the altar, the congregation is filing out of the doors singing songs against the junta, he closes his Bible, takes off his robes in the sacristy, he walks across the courtyard, and two men in civilian clothes who have waited a long time for this pull out their pistols and the priest could be a victim, too.

Haiti is not just Port-au-Prince. There are a lot of things you can't see from Boutilliers because the mountains block your view. If you head up north and then follow the Artibonite River down into the plain from its mouth, you pass canals and villages and before the mountains start, you get to Verrettes. I talked with a French nun there late one afternoon on a balcony, with a storm coming in. Soeur Hermine works up near the top of the mountains; she's the only one with a radio, and now a television. Every day, she has ten or so village children come in to watch Port-au-Prince on the television, but they don't really understand the Creole, it's too fast for them, and they watch the shows from the bordering Dominican Republic, in Spanish, with equal enthusiasm, wide-eyed. Before Soeur Hermine's radio, it took a long time for news to reach the village. Now she's been there for fourteen years, but not everyone has reaped the benefits of Soeur Hermine's communications technology.

For instance, the older people in the village. "When Jean-Claude left," Hermine told me, "I was crazy. The news came over my radio at five in the morning, and I went running around to every house, telling everyone. But this one old woman, she was sitting, sewing, and when I said, 'You know, Jean-Claude has fled Haiti,' she said, 'Now, why would Papa François let his son leave the country just like that? I don't understand that family.' " François Duvalier died in 1971, fifteen years earlier. Soeur Hermine laughed.

I took a tour through the peasant cooperatives that evening at Verrettes. My guide was a priest, and all the peasants who said good evening to us as the sun was setting among the black thunderclouds called me *Soeur,* Sister. The sharp, slant light through the clouds pulled everything out from the green background like cutouts: the two rice farmers with their long machetes hanging at their sides; the three women who had been sifting rice, and who carried their long, thin sifting baskets under their arms; the two thin burros hauling heavy burdens of rice; the extra load of green plantains one was bearing, greener than green in the falling light; a tall man with a hoe who was buying a ticket for the lottery at the local borlette; and the little blue borlette stand itself, set up outside its owner's house.

All the co-op workers had left for the day. The priest led me through the rice cooperative, with its bags of stacked rice, and the sewing cooperative, with its two sewing machines and its neatly arrayed tables. He showed me the ironworking cooperative, scraps of metal strewn across the floor, and a forge in the corner. Last, he showed me the pigsty, where the peasants were raising new American pigs in a long cement structure, a pig apartment building where each family had its own room.

"This is just like the rest of the cooperative," the priest told me while he played with a litter of grunting, excited piglets. "We're doing all this together so that we don't have to rely on the old ways of doing things, so we don't have to pay off the chef de section and the local Tonton Macoute authorities, and all the old bad people. You call it 'grass roots,' " he said, pronouncing the English words awkwardly.

"We call it 'uproot,' " he said, also in English. Then he translated into Creole: "Dechouke." It's the word peasants use when they talk about pulling up a tree, roots and all, he explained. "It has other meanings, too—now."

That night, I had dinner with dechoukeurs, bands of boys and young men who since Jean-Claude's departure had been trying to rid the towns and the countryside of Tontons Macoute and other figures from the *ancien régime*. While a silent woman brought us huge platters of rice and grilled pork, and bottles of boiled water, they talked in the candlelight about their machetes, and about how the police and the Army were after them, about finding a place to hide in the mountains. A guard whom the dechoukeurs had posted stood outside the door, nervously stroking his machete and peering off into the black distance.

"It's hard to hide these guys," someone told me, "because they're so proud they can't stop talking about what they've done. They're too dangerous to hide." One of the dechoukeurs, a man of about thirty, knew everything that had happened in the world in the past five years, from listening to the Catholic radio station, Radio Soleil. He was illiterate, but he knew the first names of all American presidential candidates from elections long finished. Even Walter Mondale. He knew how many helicopters broke down when Jimmy Carter tried to rescue American hostages from Iran. Carter was for *dwa moun,* human rights, the dechoukeur told me. Jimmy Carter was his hero, in spite of those helicopters.

Later, after the three streetlights in front of the local church came on, peasants in town for the annual parish festival danced in the market, singing dirty songs about the government and the Army, and songs about the gods of voodoo. The night had a red glow to it, the sky was low from that storm, which never broke, and people were burning thousands of candles for the Feast of the Nativity. They parked the fragile wicks in trees, on fences made of cactus, and on the steps of the church. The Chanpwel, secret voodoo societies from the mountains and from villages lower down, were out in force, too, dancing on doorsteps to songs in code. The leaders had long whips. "They can disappear," a friend of mine told me. He meant it, and he wasn't talking about *political* disappearances. We danced for a while to a song they were singing about snakes, and then came back to the house I was staying in and ate pink and white cake left over from a birthday party. Later, just before midnight, I left my room to find water, and found a friend in the kitchen. He was looking for water, too. We couldn't find water, though, so we drank Barbancourt and listened to Radio Soleil broadcast songs advising the people to be on their guard for the Tontons Macoute. I woke up early the next morning to a city of voices singing about Satan in Creole. The parish festival had begun. It was Sunday, and the room I was sleeping in faced the church.

The day I came down from Boutilliers with the painting I had sworn never to buy, Port-au-Prince was burning and the Dominican stations were playing merengue. On the long way down Avenue John Brown, I had seen clouds of black smoke coming up from barricades all over town, mostly from the St.-Martin slums and the Boulevard Jean-Jacques Dessalines, Port-au-Prince's main street, often less grandiloquently called Grande Rue. I wanted to see whether La Saline was burning, too, and I wanted to get there before the rain. I had friends in La Saline. I wondered how Mimette was, for example.

When she is not busy with her kite, Mimette likes to sit on my lap on a broken-down chair in front of her shack and ask me for presents. She knows that where I come from is called Nouyok, but she thinks it's somewhere just outside La Saline. She told me she was born in a place called Brooklyn in Cité Soleil, like her mother, but they moved to La Saline because someone got sick and her father lost his job and her mother needed to buy from a different middleman, and I couldn't really understand the whole story or even parts of it, but Mimette and her mother and a long list of brothers and sisters— each one lovingly mentioned by Mimette—ended up at the end of the whole long story very near the river of mud and sewage that runs right through the marketplace during the rainy season. The river of mud is clogged with orange peel and mango pits, with piles of rotten tobacco and decaying cattle skins, and rocks here and there to step on, steppingstones irregularly placed, and a lost yellow slipper over there, made of plastic, and another a few paces down. Mimette walks lightly through the whole thing like a thoughtless kitten, in her clean white dress, with me following awkwardly behind, splashing mud.

And on dry days she trips along with her kite trailing behind her, over the empty cans of Japanese sardines and concentrated milk, over the coconut shells, over all the human wastes of the whole sordid shantytown, past the red-and-blue shack where Bòs Jean-Jacques keeps the local borlette. Every few days, if her dreams seem fortunate, Mimette's mother, Marie-Hélène, will place a cheap bet, maybe a quarter, at the table outside Jean-Jacques's place. His borlette is called Mon Rêve. My Dream.

"If you love me," Mimette once said as she sat mending her kite, "you'll give me ten thousand dollars." She looked up at me and put a small hand on my face to move my hair out of my eyes. Maybe Marie-Hélène will find Mimette before the storm breaks.

Marie-Hélène sells cornmeal in the market at La Saline out in front of the church of St.-Joseph. When it rains, Marie-Hélène panics, because one of her children is always missing and the storms are too dangerous. Mimette is the worst of her kids, the youngest, seven years old, and always disappearing.

Marie-Hélène just got a new boyfriend. I had seen them together only a few days before, at a roadblock he was monitoring. He had a rock that he put politely into a pocket before he shook my hand. His name was Johnny. Marie-Hélène told me about Mimette. She couldn't find her. The other kids were locked in the shack a few paces from Marie-Hélène's post in the market. But Mimette was gone.

"She must have lost her kite," I suggested, offering Johnny a Marlboro. "She must be trying to find it."

"Maybe," said Marie-Hélène. Johnny looked as though he had never even heard of the child.

"He's new," Marie-Hélène said to me when Johnny walked off to talk strategy with another guy from the roadblock.

When the clouds start pressing down on the city, the beggars run from the docks to find shelter. Most of them cluster under the garish pink overhang of the Casino of the Port, next to the Roxy Bar. "WELCOME TO HAITI," says the sign over the gambling house that faces the port. Beneath the sign is the insignia of the Haitian flag: palm trees, cannons and drums. Lightning in the mountains interrupts my reception of merengue, but the wind is fresh. At the opening that leads to the market of La Saline, I switch off the static.

Inside the slum, everyone is running. Tin clangs against tin as doors are fastened shut with pieces of frayed cord and rag. Suddenly expelled from a shack, a little boy scrambles through the market's churning dust to grab a last forgotten basket with four green oranges left inside. He tries to balance it on his head as he runs back toward the shack. It falls, though, and the oranges roll into the dust. He stoops to pick them up, then squats, searching, but another boy, a little bigger and quicker, gathers up three of the oranges, stuffs them into deep pockets of ragged, baggy shorts, and runs away. In seconds, his fleeing back is obscured by dust.

All color begins to ebb from La Saline. The borlette's blue painted tin, the basket of bananas left standing in a stall, the bright aluminum pots abandoned by a vendor, the pale-green walls of the church —the dust saps the color out of all of them, fades what little life is in them, turns them white. In the center of the empty market, it churns and churns, knocking over the spindly stalls, pushing sallow dogs up against the walls of St.-Joseph's, lifting and swirling the thin shreds of newspaper that held sugar, salt and rice, turning them into a kind of confetti, with words like "chaos" and "strike" and "massacre" showering down on the market. The little boy, his basket flapping forgotten from a finger, holds his one remaining orange in the other hand, his feet planted firmly, as the dust sifts over him, turning first his hair, then his arms and legs, and finally his face, white. His mother is calling, "Johnny." At the second crack of thunder, Johnny jumps from his trance and starts to run. Tears make two black lines down his cheeks.

And then the clouds came down off Boutilliers, the low black sky hid all the mountaintops and the sea. I put my windshield wipers on high speed, but I still had to open the window to defog. In seconds, I was soaked. I drove through water and mud for a while, but I got stuck on Rue de l'Enterrement, Burial Road, which runs between the cathedral and the cemetery. We were in a traffic jam, three cars in a traffic jam, one pushed by the high water across the road, and the other two unable to move forward. The rum from the Castle was beginning to hurt my head. The water was rising, rocks were coming down the side streets, and we three were the only people in the world, making our own traffic jam. I put the car into reverse, turned around, and there was the priest, still looking at God in the backseat. My car jumped, seemed to stall, and then kept moving. In forward again, I slowed down the wipers and picked through the rock slide in first up the hill toward home.

As I rounded the corner up the steep slope of my street, I saw through the slapping wipers the only person out that night. Wrapped in plastic against the rain, standing pressed against a stone retaining wall, the figure seemed to shine. The little light left, almost red from the invisible sunset, made his plastic wrappings glitter. Above his head, the reddish light was shining through something like a crown. Rain shut out my view for a second. Then the wipers. The figure again—this time I could see that it was a man—gleamed in the twilight. Then the rain again. Then I am closer. A man wrapped in cellophane, and for his crown a bucket of water in the wild rain.

"Good evening," I hear him say. And then the rain, and I go on and on, not seeing anything, making a blind way up a dead-end street, while Haitians wrapped in winding sheets of cellophane slip slowly down the hill toward the graveyard.

Unrest: July 1987

After spending one day, one of many, with demonstrators in front of the palace, across the street from the police station, and up in the Bel-Air slum behind the cathedral, you get a little tired. One and a half years after Duvalier left, it's harder to be out in the streets. The people you're with are angrier and hungrier, and they want you to tell the President of the United States just what they think of him, which is never flattering, and you can't explain that he is not a personal acquaintance. "You just go to the White House and tell him. Tell him he is *ka-ka*." No one is laughing now the way they used to, out of happiness. Now the smiles are cynical, the jokes are cynical, and the streets are dangerous, more dangerous than they were during the Dechoukaj. More bullets from the Army. You start looking at each street corner in a new way, checking for posts and columns to hide behind, for open doors to escape into. Someone told me that the low concrete walls surrounding the lawns outside the palace are good cover, but that cars won't block automatic fire. Crouching behind cars the way they do on television? No good.

Automatic fire is what scares you. It doesn't seem to stop. It's like being caught inside a popcorn maker. Things are coming from everywhere, people running, gunfire, shouting, the heat reflecting off the white palace, and you can't get away. Everyone is running into things, walls, trees, someone tries to take your wallet in the melee, hundreds of plastic thongs and sandals are lost and scattered as the crowd flees. You never know when the gunfire will start or where it's coming from. There is an element of surprise. The Army is not on your side. Tear gas comes next. Then you have to run.

Running with the crowd is one thing. They don't stop, and they don't carry you on. If you can't keep up, you have to find yourself a little alcove or you'll be trampled. An indentation in a building, a side street, an alleyway, anything will do, and you let the crowd pass by. But then you'll never catch up, and you can't take a taxi or a tap-tap, because when the crowds are out the taxis and the tap-taps stay in. So you have to keep running if you want to see what's happening. After a while, it takes the wind out of you. It's all right, though, because once you're cornered by the Army there's a lot of time to sit tight. You see what's happening. You find a place to hide and you stay put. There is no way out of it. You have to remain for the duration.

We'd been waiting downtown outside the magistrate's office for an hour, waiting for something to happen. The crowd was packed at the intersection, facing a squad of soldiers in olive green and riot gear. I hid behind a post, which is where I like to be in tense situations. People were distributing limes in the streets, because limes are good for the skin after tear gas; they cool the stinging. People were laughing nervously and cutting limes, and then there were shots and everyone started running, and I had to leave my post, which was a nice, secure white post, and start running with the crowd. A woman took my hand as the firing continued, and pulled me off into a shed. It seemed, as I stopped panicking and began to refocus, to be a lumber shed. Three young men rushed in as the shooting sounded again from nearby, and picked up short sticks. They ran out again into the gunfire. At first, no one in my shed knew who was shooting. Across the street, the three boys with sticks were running with the crowd. As they went, they smashed the storefront windows in their path. One was a photo studio. People in the crowd grabbed framed magazine photos of movie stars from behind the broken windows.

By now, everyone in the shed had heard who it was who was doing the firing. One man, they said, an off-duty officer from Recherches Criminelles, one of the police branches. Some people had been hit, they didn't know whether anyone was dead. "Macoute!" the crowd was shouting. The gunfire had stopped, and I went out again, with the crowd. We were running, and the woman from the shed was still holding my hand. "We're going to his house," she told me. It was about a mile away, up a hill in Bel-Air. The house looked like every other house in the neighborhood, cinderblock with pink paint. The crowd began taking it apart, as though it were Duvalier's tomb. They ripped everything out of it, a mushroom of dust appeared at the site. Meanwhile, another team built a barricade in the road, to ward off the Army. A boy was running away from the house with a stereo, but someone from the barricade grabbed him and took it from him and smashed it into the ground. You were supposed to destroy, but not to steal; this was a political act, he told the boy. The boy looked unhappy. It turned out later that they did not have exactly the right house, it was the policeman's cousin's. That was good enough, the woman from the shed told me.

After they were done, the place looked like a scene from the days after Duvalier's fall. Wreckage everywhere. The boys and the men were surveying their work, the girls were standing there with dust on their dresses. They turned slowly away from the house; a rumbling of trucks in the distance. Through the dust, we could make out the shape and color of the approaching Army trucks—a bulldozer to clear the barricade, and two or three Army trucks. No one stayed to count. We ran into the slum's corridors. The woman from the shed dragged me down a winding path about a yard wide, between rows of cement and tin houses. We ran up another narrow dust path, but the soldiers were too fast for us, we could hear them shooting right behind us. A hand came out from a shack and grabbed my friend and she pulled me along with her into a little lean-to. An old woman, a *commerçante,* was inside, with a young girl. The place was the old woman's store, but there was room only for one person. I was sitting almost in the refrigerator, and my friend was crouched under a table stacked with cans of concentrated milk and aluminum tins full of *biswit,* a staple Haitian bread. The old woman was scared. A cat perched itself warily on top of the refrigerator next to the radio, which was playing Billy Joel's "New York State of Mind." Radios, the sound of soldiers' feet crunching, and then gunfire, and the cat crying. The old woman was about to give us Pepsis when my friend, who had been listening hard, said, "They've gone, we have to run farther." She was afraid they would come back and search each house.

We went down the path, along with other people from the demonstration, all of them emerging from shanties and shacks in the
slum and heading away from the main road. It looked like a refugee
caravan. Lost sandals and thongs littered the way. When the shooting started again, we went up a side path and crouched in front of a
tin shanty whose owner had barred the door with a piece of wood.
We couldn't get in. The soldiers were down the path from us, nearer
the main road. They seemed to be shooting left and right. I sat at
the edge of our alley—with the others farther inside—hoping that
my white face might surprise the soldiers into halting their fire if
they came up this far. But they didn't want to leave the security of
the road and truck too far behind, and they never reached us.

The tear gas and the tension left us exhausted. It took me an hour
to walk back to the Holiday Inn, where my car was parked. The
Oloffson had closed; Suzanne had sold off most of the furniture and
shut up the place. During the unrest of that summer, I would try to
stop by the Holiday Inn once a day, to check in with the foreign
press, and to find Harry if I could and hear what he had to say about
the day's events. He had returned to Haiti the minute the demonstrations began, of course. As usual, he was staying at the Palace
Hotel, but he frequented the Holiday Inn because, he now admitted,
the phones were better there.

In the glass-enclosed restaurant next to the Holiday Inn's pool, a
bunch of photographers, looking dilapidated, were having beers and
hardly talking. They were dusty. It looked as if they'd been somewhere near where I had been. They were almost lying on their
chairs, with their legs sticking out at all angles from under the table.
Harry wasn't there. At a nearby table, reporters from the *New York
Times,* the *Miami Herald* and the *Washington Post* were clean and
civilized and sitting together having club sandwiches with the *Times'*
obsequious Haitian translator, who was listening to the radio and
making notes.

"So what's going on out there?" the *New York Times* asked the
photographers, jovially. "You don't look so good."

"Shooting, demonstrations," said one photographer, looking into
his beer.

"Any bodies?" asked the *New York Times*.

"Not that I saw."

"Just the usual," said the *Times* to his table.

. . .

The people can be dangerous, too, when they are trying to enforce a strike, almost as dangerous as the Army. For days on end, during the summer protests, the streets were emptied by strikes. Only the young men—Harry calls them "the lads"—were out, building barricades to stop cars from breaking the strike, and throwing rocks and pipe bombs at whatever traffic trickled by. Delmas, John Brown, Grande Rue and Boulevard de La Saline were all blocked off by fiery barricades, mostly made of burning tires because Haiti has a big street-side trade in used tires and there are always huge piles of tires waiting to be mended at corners around the capital. In the midst of the troubles, the Army went out late at night and tried to collect all the used tires from the street, thinking to prevent the barricade building. But there were just too many tires; the soldiers didn't have enough trucks or enough time, or a place to put all those tires.

The lads also used firewood, because that is readily available here, too, people in the slums use it for fuel when they don't buy charcoal. And garbage dumpsters, cast-off bits of old cars from the Rue du Quai, where cars are fixed, and sometimes the entire carcass of a ruined automobile. The lads knocked down cement telephone poles too, and then organized *coumbites,* large work groups, to push the poles across the streets.

I bought a carton of cigarettes to hand out to the boys at the barricades. In the beginning, just after the first strike at the end of June, they were pretty friendly. They'd see your homemade sign saying "PRESSE" and let you pass. If you shouted *"jounalis,"* the boys with rocks in their hands would stop midthrow and come over, shake your hand, and take a couple of Marlboros. After a few days, however, the lads were less friendly. U.S. Embassy people and Haitian Army personnel had been using press signs to get through the roadblocks, and some armed men, masquerading as Haitian press, had fired at the lads from their cars. From then on, we had to show our press credentials. Most of the lads couldn't read, however, and some foreign reporters used to amuse themselves by showing them their press passes upside down. Harry and I always got through, even when it meant driving through fire up onto the sidewalk.

Each day, after bribing the lads or watching the Army shoot into demonstrations, I went over to the University Hospital on Rue Monseigneur Guilloux, the only public hospital in town. Inside its green emergency room, a boy on a cot with his skull blown off, dying, his brain half out of his head. A dead boy with a chest wound, two leg wounds, his eyes half open. A man gasping for air with a bullet in his neck, blood everywhere, nurses not even bothering. No blood left in the blood bank. Relatives hunting for blood for the victims. A woman on a straw mat in the corner, her side spilling blood all over the green floor. A twelve-year-old boy with his arm shot off, bandaged, looking around distractedly, as though he had lost something important. Some soldiers had cornered him that afternoon, by himself near the cemetery. They stood him up against the graveyard wall, made him put his hands above his head, and blew his arm off with their Uzis.

I went downtown, finally, to buy books and groceries on a rare day when no strikes had been called and no demonstrations were scheduled. Walking down Grande Rue, I saw black smoke from near the market, but it couldn't be a barricade today, and I didn't pay much attention until I noticed that everyone in the street was looking at it, stopped dead in their tracks. Then there were shots, and everyone started running. The market women packed up their stalls in a rush, the shoppers jumped into their cars. I got into my car and put my press signs up, but a friend I had run into said, "No, take the press signs off, it's the Army, they shoot at the press," and I took the signs down, and we headed toward the fire. My friend told me that some market people had seen two city garbage trucks leaving town, odd on a Saturday, when most government workers are not on the job, and then they noticed feet and arms sticking out of the backs of the trucks. Corpses—and the people presumed the government was carting away those killed by the Army in the previous day's demonstration, a very bloody one. The market people built a quick barricade, set it on fire, pulled the truck drivers out from behind the wheel and stoned them. Then soldiers arrived and started shooting into the market. The bloodied truck drivers fled.

We got to the site of the incident about ten minutes after it was over, and the square had already become a living museum of Haitian history. A man showed me around, my guide. Someone's intestines were piled at a corner, from one of the corpses in the truck, my guide said. Two red garbage trucks were stopped in front of City Hall, blood and shattered glass on the street beneath them. "Those are the trucks that had the bodies," my guide told me. "The Army took the bodies away." Over in a corner where the market begins, a dead man shot by the soldiers, his blue shirt spattered with his blood, his intestines climbing out from under his pants. His arms were covered with white dust, he was a cement seller. Next to him, an abandoned basket of green oranges.

We drove out to Titanyen, the paupers' cemetery—a mass dumping ground where the Tontons Macoute were rumored to have buried their victims—to see whether the bodies had been dropped there. But we couldn't get in. Dozens of policemen were guarding the path down to the seaside burial ground. Later, on the radio, the mayor of Port-au-Prince had an explanation. "We always take the bodies of the indigent out of town to be buried on Monday mornings," she said. "But because of the strikes, this time we did it on Saturday. We can't just have all these bodies piling up and putrefying. This is a civilized country."

Words of Deliverance: 1

I couldn't tell what was happening. I'd been back and forth to Haiti four or five times by now, but things were getting out of control, and I couldn't always understand what I saw. On the street outside St.-Jean-Bosco, Father Aristide's small yellow church, a crowd of five or six hundred had massed, carrying branches and beating on wooden blocks. I didn't see Aristide anywhere; this was unusual. Typically, the first thing you noticed when you came to St.-Jean-Bosco was Aristide—the priest who had lectured me after Duvalier fell—surrounded by a group of young people, talking. This time, Aristide didn't seem to be there. The crowd had just begun pouring into the churchyard through the gates. It was July 1987. Inside the churchyard, youths were chanting slogans and talking, shouting at one another. Everyone was looking around, they seemed to be trying to figure out what to do next. A man in a yellow tee shirt was carrying a long stick in his hand, hitting it hard over and over into his other palm, looking around. Three boys standing under a tree were rapping on blocks with short sticks, pounding out a loud, repetitive rhythm. They all seemed to be waiting for something, but they didn't have their bearings here. I didn't recognize any of them from my visits to the church. They weren't kids from St.-Jean-Bosco. They weren't Aristide's followers.

All at once, they began pressing into the hall that leads to the inner courtyard, a huge, urgent mass filing into a very narrow, dark hallway. The crush was hot and fast. If you didn't know the corridor, its small steps at the front and back, how smooth the surface of the dark floor, the twist near Aristide's office, you had little chance of making it those few feet without falling. A lot of people fell. When we emerged into the light of the courtyard, someone was already ringing the school bell. It was loud, insistent over the clattering of the wooden blocks, like an alarm. Something was happening farther on, but I couldn't see anything; I was lodged against a wall among the crowd. Suddenly they started surging back in the other direction, down toward the dark corridor from which we had just emerged.

I didn't want to go back down the black corridor with the huge hot crowd, but I went back. Once they started pushing, I had no choice. And then I saw the reason, which was a slight figure perched on the shoulders of some of the tallest young men in the crowd, looking precarious and fragile. It was Aristide, and he couldn't get his balance. They were trying to take him out into the street. The man with the stick was right beneath him, giving orders to the youths who were carrying him. Aristide was holding on to his glasses and hunching over, unhappy, uncomfortable, embarrassed. He was not in control, but there was nothing he could do about it. Each time he almost fell, the man with the stick raised it over the priest's head, and the others lifted him up again. He swayed up there on the youths' shoulders, and they swept forward. They were laughing, tossing him. He was like a puppet in their hands. They were throwing him among themselves like a little girl's floppy doll, paying no attention to his discomfort. Each time they came to a step, he had to crouch over at the last minute to avoid slamming his face into the ceiling.

"*Nou vle Titid,*" the boys chanted, calling Aristide by his nickname that has connotations of cute littleness, as in *petit*. In French, *titi* is slang for "street urchin." We want Titid, the boys said. They had him.

When they finally squeezed out with him into the open, the man with the stick turned toward him again, to get a look at his prize in the sun. But Aristide had disappeared. The youths looked confused, almost frightened, as though he had disappeared into thin air. It took them a few seconds to realize he had dismounted, their burden had been so light. The man with the stick was screaming at them. They searched among themselves for the priest, pushing one

another aside, but they couldn't find him. He had already escaped
into his office, and then into the sacristy. The little street boys who
lived under Aristide's protection in and around the churchyard had
seen him flee. They were just a little smaller than he was and could
see him better than the tall youths, but they weren't saying anything
to the man with the stick. Instead, they mixed with this strange new
crowd, possible targets for begging. Little, sinewy Waldeck, who
was usually too busy playing cards or marbles to pay attention to
comings and goings at the church, was working the crowd, asking
for pennies from them and dollars from me. I was white, he reasoned, and so I must be richer than the others. But the youths
weren't interested in Waldeck and his begging. They were after
Aristide.

"These guys are no good," Waldeck said, standing next to me and
fiddling with his ragged shirt. "Give me five dollars," he said to me.
I just looked at him.

The youths couldn't figure out where Aristide had gone. Angry,
they started swarming into the church. They packed the place, all
these young men with their angry faces and tee shirts with slogans
from the students' federation and the peasants' collectives. In a short
time, Aristide emerged. He had changed into his vestments. He was
absolutely cool.

When he got to the microphone, the raucous crowd immediately
quieted. He looked at them for a good long minute. They stayed
silent.

"*Granmèt-la avèk nou,*" he said. The Lord be with you.

"*E avèk oumenm tou,*" the boys gave the traditional response.
And also with you.

"*Granmèt-la,*" said Aristide for emphasis, "*avèk nou tout.*" The
Lord be with all of you. He grasped the side of the table he stood
behind. He still stared out into the crowd. He was trying to figure
out who they were.

"*E avèk oumenm tou,*" the youths responded, unsure.

"*Granmèt-la avèk nou tout.*" He seemed to be seeking reassurance
in their voices.

"*E avèk oumenm tou,*" they shouted, rising to their feet. "*E avèk
oumenm tou.*"

Still he was not satisfied. But he told them, in a short, passionate
sermon, to stand firm, to work against Duvalierism, that opposing
Namphy's provisional military junta was holy work, that they themselves were holy.

"That last," he said later, "was questionable."

At the end of his talk, he asked them to join him in singing the "Dessalinienne," the country's national anthem. They all rose, raising their hands, as is the custom, in an approximation of the fascist salute, and sang the song, a stirring cross between the "Marseillaise" and the "Internationale." Waldeck filtered among them, still looking for funds. The priest disappeared.

The youths flowed out into the streets, with Waldeck and his pals trailing after them, but although they went around town past the National Palace, where they taunted the soldiers who were on guard, and over to the police station, where they made faces at the policemen and blocked police cars from moving, the authorities did not shoot. The youths wanted shooting, but they didn't get it. Not that day, anyway.

Back at the church, Aristide had a nervous prostration, and then a migraine. It was a nightmare, he said. He didn't know who those boys were, or who had sent them. Anyone could have paid them to come and start trouble. He hadn't recognized their faces. Who were they, and why had they come? Would he be blamed for their actions? He took to his bed, and his headache got worse.

When I first came back to St.-Jean-Bosco to meet Aristide again for the first time since Duvalier had left, I hardly remembered his face from that time when I had come by during the Dechoukaj in February 1986, and we had sat and talked inside the church courtyard with the guinea fowl waddling in the background. Yet Aristide's was not a face to forget: hollow-cheeked, goggle-eyed, wide-mouthed. The foreign journalists called him diminutive, bespectacled. "His Holiness," was the nickname Harry and the others used, though not in print. It was hard to believe that this small person who took up virtually no room at all could bring thousands of people to their feet and lead Port-au-Prince's slums with a wave of his hand.

As one of the few prominent people in Port-au-Prince who had stuck their necks out in Jean-Claude's waning days, publicly expressing the growing discontent and disgust with Duvalierism, Aristide had helped to create in the capital the same climate of unrest and protest that already existed in the countryside, and that made the dictator's departure necessary. By the end of Jean-Claude's days, Aristide was the most visible of the many young progressive priests and nuns—together called Ti Legliz, the Little Church—who had been organizing peasants and slum-dwellers in Haiti since the late 1970s.

The first time I met him, everything was chaotic and you couldn't talk to anyone for more than ten minutes before the excited crowds swept by. A few days later, Aristide said a historic mass in Gonaïves, where the Dechoukaj had begun in the fall of 1985 after three school-children were shot dead by the Army. Some of the Haitian bishops were there in Gonaïves, lined up on their thrones inside the bizarre modern cathedral in the middle of the town square. The church was crammed and boiling hot, and Bishop Emmanuel Constant of Go-naïves was looking through his breviary, as though lost in study. No one in the noisy, excited church was paying attention to him, when silence suddenly began to fall over the jubilant crowd, first up front, and then slowly making its way over the congregants. Aristide in his white cassock had come to the pulpit, and he was simply standing there with his hands clasped, waiting for silence.

"It was the first time I had seen him," said a British journalist. "He looked just the way you would imagine a little black angel would look, you know, the one who is always left out of the paintings with all the little white angels. Transfixed, beatific. And childlike. I wouldn't have been surprised to see a halo form over that head, you would have thought it was just light and heat coming from his words. When he spoke, they all went wild."

Back in February 1986, Aristide had seemed like a radical partici-pant in Duvalier's overthrow. When I met him again, half a year later, he was modulating. There was more sweetness, more common humanity, less vitriol. The sweetness, however, was not entirely believable, even with his famous angelic childlikeness. After all, sitting in a corner of his office was the life-sized effigy of a Tonton Macoute, and, as Aristide pointed out, the clothes were real, had once belonged to a real member of Duvalier's militia.

"We dechouked him," he told me.

"We?" I said. It sounded like an admission, coming from a priest.

"We, the people, I mean," he said, smiling.

It was raining again that night when I went to pick up my friend Charles, a Haitian mulatto I had met early in my stay. We were going up the hill to Pétionville for dinner. "It will just be small," said Jeanne, a friend of Charles's, when she called me. "Bring a date. Maybe Charles? I'm fixing lobster." This meant that Marianne, the woman who works in her kitchen and has the same name as Haiti's most popular margarine, would be making lobster. In Pétionville, when your mulatto host asks you if you want something to drink, and you say a Coke, he says, "Well, I'll get it for you," and claps his hands. Then black Joseph or Marcel or Dieuseul appears in the doorway, and your host says, "A Coke for Mademoiselle."

Our car barely made it up the hill, twice we went backward when we meant to go forward, and Charles kept cursing the car and I kept hoping we wouldn't get a flat from all the tumbling rocks, because it was raining so hard. We couldn't see anything but our breath on the windows. Everything was black outside, probably the electricity had been cut. The only lights were our lights, until we got to the top of the hill, where everyone has his own generator, just in case. We drove down the residential streets of Pétionville. Even in the daytime, when it's not raining, you can see only the less expensive houses, because the rest of them sit behind high cement security walls. We honked out in front of Jeanne's gates (*la barrière,* Haitians call them, appropriately), and finally Joseph the *gardien* came and opened up, and we drove down the circular driveway to Jeanne and Sylvain's house. We parked under the dark, dripping bougainvillea. The spotlights were on above the terrace, and I could see Jeanne's three Dobermans pacing the top of the security wall.

"Pierrot, *encore du champagne pour ce côté de la table, non?*" says Jeanne. More champagne for this side of the table, and I look down at my lobster, its meat artistically removed from the shell, some delicate green beans arranged at its side, some delicately boiled potatoes nestled next to the beans, gold silverware. Pierrot is not in uniform—Haitian servants don't usually wear uniforms. He has on a dark polyester shirt with blue palm trees on it, and some old pants. Pierrot is the boyfriend of Marianne the cook, but Joseph the gardien is her real boyfriend. There are endless battles because of this, according to Jeanne. Someday soon, she will have to get rid of Pierrot. Jeanne likes to tell stories about the servants. Jeanne's servants like to tell stories about Jeanne. Jeanne told me she got Marianne from her mother ten years ago after her wedding, and now every time Jeanne has a man over during the day, Marianne reports back to Maman. *"Cela fait partie de la comédie, tu vois,"* Jeanne tells me. It's part of the game, you see.

The champagne that Pierrot pours is good, and it makes Jeanne more voluble than usual.

"But I don't understand," she says. "If the point of having elections is to elect someone who will continue the work of the junta, why have elections?" She points Pierrot to Charles's glass. "Why not just keep the junta? Besides," she says, laughing, "Sylvain knows Namphy." Her husband smiles.

"That wouldn't be democracy, my dear," Sylvain says. "Anyway, it's not what the Americans want. Besides, people need to think that they have elected their President. It will help the national spirit." He raises his eyebrows. Sylvain is always ironic. He learned it in France. He also drinks too much; he learned that in France, too.

"The Haitian people aren't that stupid, as you all know." This is Charles. Of course my date says the wrong thing. Everyone looks at everyone else except for Charles, and I look at my lobster.

"If they're not so stupid, why are they living the way they do?" This from a former government minister. His wife picks silently at her food. The former minister is having an affair with Jeanne, that's what Charles told me.

"Well, they seem to have figured *something* out," says Charles. "Look at the demonstrations. Look at Father Aristide." Charles spears a potato and eats it whole. I feel he is eating with too much enthusiasm. Jeanne is watching him.

"What do you mean, look at Aristide?" asks Sylvain. "There's not much to look at, really, is there?" He gazes around the table for approval, and gets some murmurs, but the guests seem to find the lobster more engrossing than the talk. Pierrot pours more champagne. During dinner, Charles and I keep one eye on Pierrot. He is our favorite this evening, dispelling tension wherever he goes. It's raining hard outside the patio where we are eating, a sheltered alcove in the garden. I can hear American voices on the cable television in the next room; the kids are probably watching *Dynasty*. Every so often, three little girls wearing white dresses come running into the dining room to ask Jeanne to settle a quarrel. Jeanne pats them. They speak half in English, half in French. They go to the Union School, with all the American Embassy kids, where Creole is forbidden.

Charles is still following the conversation. "What I mean is that Aristide is tapping the people's intelligence, and giving some kind of form to the ideas they have but can't really express." This is a long speech for Charles, who is also checking on Pierrot's whereabouts. His glass is empty.

"Aristide is a little dictator, in true Haitian style," says Sylvain. "A fascist in the making. Couldn't be plainer. And the only thing 'the people' know, the only 'idea' they have," he says, skewering a piece of lobster on the end of his gold fork and holding it in the air, "is that they'd like to be eating this." He waves the piece of pink meat around, pops it into his mouth, picks up his champagne, and takes a sip. "And with our bloody corpses at their feet, I might add."

"Sylvain," says Jeanne. She looks over at Pierrot, standing in the doorway. Pierrot speaks some French, as well as Creole.

"Sorry." Sylvain goes back to his plate. But he can't leave the subject alone. He looks up again at Charles. "But so, do you think that's the kind of 'idea' that Aristide is helping the people form? To kill us and eat our food? Clever little bastard, no? Kill them and eat their food."

"Right, and rape their wives and daughters and nationalize their businesses, and murder all white and light-skinned people," said my date. "I don't know, Sylvain, I think the guy is more moderate than that. I think he's talking about jobs and food, you're right about the food. But it doesn't seem that unreasonable. Anyway, he talks about forming alliances with the bourgeoisie."

"Not with *me,*" says Sylvain. "I think he's preaching revolution. That's how the Nicaraguans got their revolution, by forming alliances with the bourgeoisie. You see how far *that* got them." He looks happy, he's finally said what he meant to say all along. Jeanne excuses herself and leaves the room with the smallest daughter tucked under her arm. "Look, Charles, you want a revolution. You want to go live in La Saline with this priest? You want Aristide to decide where you eat and where you live? You are us, Charles. What this priest calls 'the parasites.' Aristide would say, 'I'll take Charles's business. I'll live in Charles's house. I will take his girlfriend, his bank account. I will put him in prison. I will put him in Fort Dimanche.' "

"Sylvain!" Charles laughs. "You're being too dramatic. Aristide is the one who wants to *shut* Fort Dimanche."

"Well, some other place, then," Sylvain says. "Or he'll take you and turn you into a houseboy."

"You're exaggerating, just like the Americans."

"I don't think so," says Sylvain. "You can't be too careful with these popular leaders, even if they are priests. I always remember how scared my father was of Fignolé and his steamroller." Daniel Fignolé was a politician who rose to prominence in the late 1940s. He was feared by the elite for his following among Port-au-Prince's proletariat, whom he could bring out onto the streets at will. They were his *rouleau compresseur,* his steamroller.

"These rabble-rousers like Fignolé or this new one, they always appeal to the people's worst instincts," Sylvain went on. "Aristide, he appeals to their racism. You don't see any light faces in his congregation, have you noticed? He says 'the elite,' and they know that what he means is 'the mulattos.' Every day he's getting worse and worse. He'll have to shut up soon. He'll have to. Or be shut up. Pierrot, where is the champagne?" Sylvain looks around the table. "I mean, it can't go on like this, can it?"

On Mother's Day, a huge mass inside St.-Jean-Bosco, with little girls dressed in layers of lace, and boys in suits, and mothers everywhere in elaborate hats. The sun shining against the blue walls gives the church interior an otherworldly atmosphere, and little Aristide in his white robes looks like an angel at the altar. He is Titid today, making the congregation laugh, reaching out to them with his arms extended. Over and over, he has the children shout, as loud as they can, *"Mamamn, cheri, mwen renmen w."* Mommy, darling, I love you. I feel uncomfortable in the heat and sentiment. It's like being inside a candy box. The kids are delighted, they shout and wave, and the mothers look sedate, pleased with themselves.

The text today is Jesus saying, "What is the Lord's, is mine, and what is mine is the Lord's." Since the Lord is Jesus' father and today is Mother's Day, Aristide extends the text to mothers as well. It seems trite, but he is happy, beaming down at his people, his face relaxed, talking as if he were simply in a room filled with friends.

Then, slowly, another Aristide emerges. Beads of sweat form on his high forehead, and his eyes focus on something farther away than the people in the front rows. His long fingers grasp the side of the altar table, and his body begins to sway. He stops talking, and begins preaching, prophesying. Mother's Day is a thing of the past. He takes the text and with some stunning leaps of logic and rhetorical twists, arrives at the conclusion that the only Christian way to run an economy is through communal property, since we are all, like Jesus, the children of the Lord, all brothers and sisters.

Once he is into his sermon, he is possessed, in part by the force of his own words, in part by the congregation's response. He hammers at the air, points his finger like a knife, solicits repetition first from one side of the church, then from the other, personally and by name attacks capitalism and with a brutal round of statistics shows what it does to the People of the Third World, lets fly with the words "communal," "in common," "community," without quite pronouncing that one similar word that the Well-Placed U.S. Embassy Official, an acquaintance of mine, is always waiting to hear from Aristide's lips. With a dismissive flick of one raised wrist, he tosses onto the heap of disposable Duvalierists the two men who lead the military junta. "Namphy." Flick. "Régala." Flick. The congregation roars, applauds, rises to its feet unbidden. He's on a real roll, repeating the adjectives that define an appropriate Haitian society: "Evangelical, popular, socialist." He says the three words again. The congregation says them. "Louder," he says. They say them louder. "Again," he says. They repeat the words.

He's like a little stick of dynamite, the energy of his gestures, his intense focus, his explosive bursts of eloquence, his devastating power. The congregation looks like a mirror of the priest: total concentration, rooted excitement. "Titid, Titid," the two young men next to me whisper in aroused unison. The girls watch the priest with their mouths open, their palms turned upward on their knees, their feet in and out of their too-tight high-heeled shoes. No one wants to miss a word. Scores of young men hold their tape recorders up toward the loudspeakers. Everyone wants to do exactly what Aristide tells them to do. When he asks them a question, you can almost hear them thinking, "What does he want us to say?" If, as they sometimes but rarely do, they give the wrong answer, he laughs, and says, "Wait, think," and explains better what the question means. Then he repeats it, and he gets the right answer. He always gets what he wants.

At the end of the sermon, the congregation crosses itself, Aristide looks down on them and pats his brow with a white handkerchief, and they begin to sing a St.-Jean-Bosco standard: "Satan Ale," or Satan, Get Lost. By Satan, in this context, they mean the regime. Aristide himself wrote the words. A few days later, when I go to visit the Well-Placed U.S. Embassy Official, I can hear Aristide's voice in the background, saying, "Evangelical, popular, socialist." It repeats the words over and over while I'm trying to do an interview. Afterward, I wander around the offices looking for that voice, which I can still hear. In a small room at the end of the hall, sitting at a small desk, I find an earnest-looking clerk, listening to a tape and translating. He tells me he translates Aristide's Sunday sermon every week.

Aristide preached a brand of liberation theology that pleased no one except his extended congregation: the poor in the slums, the peasants who heard him on Radio Haïti-Inter and Radio Soleil, a scattering of young jobless lower-middle class youths with no future in the country, and a few liberals among the Haitian bourgeoisie and the exile community. He had all the right enemies. The Army hated him, because he mentioned colonels and sergeants and lieutenants by name in his sermons, and excoriated them for the abuses they committed against the people in their regions. "Namphy," and a flick of the wrist: onto the garbage heap goes the President. "Régala." Another flick. The American Embassy hated him, because he held the United States and its economic system responsible for much of Haiti's economic woe, and thus for the misery of her people, his congregation. The Church hierarchy feared him because he did not often miss a chance to include them in his list of enemies of the people, and they were jealous of him, too, for the loyal following he had attracted, and for the attention he received from foreign journalists. The very wealthy few in Haiti despised him also, because he accused them of betraying their countrymen and stated baldly that the system by which they enriched themselves was corrupt and criminal, and an offense against their fellow Haitians. He frightened them all with the violent honesty of his sermons. And the worst part was that he had a reputation for being Haiti's foremost Biblical scholar, and was always ready with a quote from the gospels to support his message. His targets did not like to hear Christ quoted against them.

Aristide's message was doubly frightening, because, try as they might, his enemies could not properly accuse him of preaching Communism. He gave sermons in which he lauded the sanctity of private property. "The peasant's land," he said, "the land that he and his family have worked for generations, that is his private property; no one else has the right to take it. The shopkeeper's little store, that he bought fair and square with his little savings, and from which he makes a decent income, that is his private property. But the class of landowners and the bourgeoisie who live off the corrupt system we have in Haiti, who do nothing, who give nothing back to the country, who steal what little wealth we have and put it into banks in foreign countries, their private property is the property of the peasants. Their private property is Haitian property, it does not belong to them. It should be taken from them."

Like other liberation theologians in Latin America, who use Jesus' teachings to raise the political consciousness of the poor, Aristide tried to make connections between the struggle of the Haitian people for freedom and what liberation theologians see as the struggle of Jesus for the liberation of Jerusalem.

"What weds the movement within the Church to the movement within Haitian society as a whole," he said, "is liberation theology, which has filtered into the youth of our country, which invigorates them, which purifies their blood, which teaches these youths that either you are a Christian or you are not. And if you are a Christian, you cannot allow what you are seeing to happen without saying something, because if you say nothing, you will be sinning by your silence. You will be sinning by your complicity. So in order to avoid that sin, which is a mortal sin, we refuse to accept what is happening. We cast off corruption.

"If you're a Christian, you cannot accept to continue the Macoute corruption in this country. Well, then, you are obliged to take historic risks. You are obliged to participate in this historic movement of liberation theology. In other words, the resurrection of an entire people is occurring right now. It is liberation theology that is lifting our children up against a corrupt generation, against a mentality of the Church and the society which sees corruption as the comfortable norm, and which one cannot stomach if one is truly a Christian. It is the history of the Jews and Jesus Christ that we ourselves as Christians are living through now. We have become the subjects of our own history, we refuse from now on to be the objects of that history."

When Aristide begins to talk, he no longer seems small. He leans forward and fixes you with a look from behind those glasses that makes you squirm and wish you could escape it. Unlike many Haitian politicians, and unlike many Haitian men when they talk about politics, he doesn't shout in conversation. He seems to give thought to your questions. But the timbre of his voice is intense, and his imagery is arresting. "Port-au-Prince," he said to me, the day after Jean-Claude Duvalier left, "face it, for years, forever, it has been the headquarters of corruption. It was the regime's central nervous system: Port-au-Prince speaks, and the order goes out, and the provinces react. The extremities tremble, they twitch, and people, the Duvaliers' enemies, die. That's how Duvalier organized it, Papa Doc, I mean.

"But then, in the months before Jean-Claude left, you had a situation where, suddenly, Port-au-Prince isn't giving any orders. Where Jean-Claude and his people don't know what to do, and can't get anyone to follow orders. Where they don't even know what orders to

give. Where the extremities, the provinces, are suddenly not responding. Instead, they're turning against the cerebral cortex, eating
away at the nerve tissue, exploding. First the provinces revolted,
then, finally, after far too long, Port-au-Prince. When Port-au-
Prince started to move against Jean-Claude, that's when the Americans realized he had to go."

I always liked Aristide. Almost everyone did, if they had the
chance to meet him. He would say brutal things, and yet the most
decent Haitian matrons turned around and kissed him afterward.
His colleagues in the Ti Legliz ranted about his irresponsibility
behind his back, but then when they were with him their anger
dissolved into a kind of mushy affection, as though he were an
incredibly cute kid who had just broken a precious heirloom. You
wanted to kill him, sure, but he was too cute to kill.

There were those, however, who could not tolerate the little priest.
Max Beauvoir, a voodoo priest whose Continental smoothness made
him a favorite at American Embassy parties, flinched at the sound
of Aristide's name. Well connected to American reporters and embassy officials alike because he speaks fluent English and cultivates
such ties, Beauvoir has a large house on several acres south of
the capital, complete with a voodoo temple. When tourists were
still coming to Haiti, Beauvoir, who had been on good terms with
Papa Doc and on somewhat less cordial terms with the son, used
to give extravagant, touristic voodoo ceremonies, reportedly very
satisfying ones, if expensive, with fire and hot coals and animal
sacrifice, and colorful costumes. U.S. Embassy people often attended. After Duvalier left, Beauvoir closed the place for a while.
His sister, who lives in Paris, also does voodoo tourism. It's a family
business.

"Your friend Aristide has an army of boys, young men," Beauvoir
told me. "Those youths you see hanging out at his church. He gives
them crack and sends them out to kill his enemies. It is he who is a
Macoute." Every time Max told me some new story about Aristide,
I'd hear it a couple of days later from the Well-Placed Embassy
Official. I couldn't really tell where the stuff was originating. If I
didn't hear it first from Beauvoir, then I would hear it first from
Baptist minister Wallace Turnbull, a fixture on the Haitian scene
since the 1950s, who runs a large plantation-style mission up above
Boutilliers.

"Beauvoir?" said Aristide. He shrugged as though the name was not worth considering. "CIA. Turnbull? Same thing."

Whether or not the two men had affiliations to that agency, they were clearly only a small part of the wider disinformation campaign against Aristide that continued through the hot summer of 1987 and after. He was paying bands of boys to burn tires, one rumor said; he was teaching kids to make Molotov cocktails, another alleged. It was Aristide, and not the Duvalierists, who were paying to have people assassinated every night in the streets of Port-au-Prince, in order to heat up the tension in the capital; he had ordered this one killed, he was planning the murder of that one. As Namphy's regime became weaker and more violent, such groundless rumors against Aristide—which you could hear from the mouths of bishops and ambassadors, as well as from Sylvain and Jeanne and Beauvoir and Turnbull—grew wilder and more fantastic. Eventually, whisperers would accuse him of involvement in the attack on the presidential elections, would say that he had invented out of whole cloth various Church orders against himself, would even go so far as to claim that Aristide himself had paid a band of men to feign an assassination attempt against him. In other words, every action of the right-wing forces was accompanied by a rumor blaming Aristide for the thing. The campaign seemed organized—each rumor popped up whole and was reiterated each time by the same bunch of people. The disinformation campaign was accompanied by persistent rumors among Aristide's people in Haiti, New York, Montreal and Paris of his imprisonment, torture, deportation or death. "If he is dead," said one of his friends, responding to a particularly persistent rumor out of Paris, "why didn't he tell me so this morning when I was having breakfast with him?"

In the sacristy one Sunday after mass, a year after Duvalier's downfall, Antoine, the blind beggar who comes by every week, puts out a hand in front of him and leans on his cane, a golf club, for support. A woman guides his searching hand toward Aristide's slight shoulder. The little girl whom Aristide is holding in his arms looks at Antoine over the priest's shoulder. "Five years old," Aristide is saying to her. It's her birthday, and already she is almost half his size. He kisses her lightly, and she pulls back her head to look into his eyes. The beggar's hand on Aristide's shoulder is becoming more insistent; without turning, the priest reaches back and takes Antoine's wrist in his hand, encircles it with his fingers. He puts the girl down and goes on talking to her mother. A knot of people is closing in on him. The small room is full, with people's heads sticking in at the two doors and others looking in through the windows.

Watching the circle of people from a few yards away, you wouldn't know that the priest is at its center; you have to push through to see him. A young man saunters forward and through the crowd, nudging the girl and her mother away. He puts a heavy arm around Aristide's shoulders and another over the priest's head, holding Aristide in a lock grip and cupping his ear. He starts whispering into it, and Aristide nods, and nods, smiles, shakes his head, says, "No, no, no," a small staccato sound full of disapproval, puts his free arm around the young man's neck and whispers something back to him that makes the young man tremble with laughter for a moment and give the priest an affectionate shove on the back of the head.

A young, smiling woman is waiting at the edge of the circle to talk to Aristide, watching this performance with her arms folded. He notices her suddenly and lifts his chin toward the young man, half in acknowledgment, half dismissal. He moves toward the girl, she takes him by the lapels of his shirt, he puts an arm around her waist, and they start whispering. A French reporter tries to interrupt, but Aristide, without looking up, puts out his palm to ward off the interruption. "In a moment," the young man, who is still standing by, says to the French reporter. The room is hot with bodies. Three Ti-Legliz priests are waiting in the doorway for the ritual to end: there is a meeting scheduled for noon.

A commotion begins, it seems to erupt right beneath the feet of the three priests in the doorway. Half naked, Waldeck and four more urchins burst into the room, tumbling through the door in a comic fistfight. They scramble through the circle and then around and through Aristide's legs, looking for protection. The girl moves away, laughing. Antoine the beggar leans into the priest, unsure of what is happening. The boys keep dodging in among the crowd, and Aristide swats at them absently while he talks to Antoine. The boys use Aristide's legs as a shield. Waldeck holds on to a thigh and peers out from between the priest's legs, daring his enemies to attack him in that well-defended position.

In the midst of the tumult, Aristide reaches into his pocket and takes out a few bills that he always has ready for Antoine each Sunday. He says a few more words to the beggar as he hands him the money—"Do you have enough to eat?" "How is your health?"

"Is someone taking care of you?"—and then grasps Antoine's shoulders with both hands, making a final connection and at the same time redirecting him toward the door. Aristide turns away to find a small boy hurtling toward him, the edge of a razor blade flashing in a little angry fist. He grabs the boy's arm as the razor is about to come down across Waldeck's face, takes the blade out of the fist, breaks it in two, throws it out the window.

"I didn't realize you were armed," he says. The boy laughs, all the boys laugh, the whole room repeats the phrase over and over, until the priests in the doorway seem to be saying it, too, and laughing in spite of their increasing impatience. The story of the razor blade will become an anecdote. But Aristide has already forgotten it. He puts his hand on Waldeck's head and starts up a conversation in Spanish with two nuns, liberation theologians on a visit from somewhere in Central America. Waldeck stands there, silent for once and smiling, the priest patting his head. He puts an arm around Aristide's leg and listens to the conversation. The other boys stop hitting each other for a few minutes. They want to hear Aristide speaking the funny language. He goes on and on, the nuns listen and reply and listen, the three Haitian priests linger in the doorway, shifting from foot to foot.

Waldeck, bored, gets out from under Aristide's hand, scoots around the feet of the French reporter and taps at his legs, punches his thighs. *"Fè foto m,"* he says, punching. Take my picture. The French reporter looks at the priest for help, but Aristide responds by raising both his hands in a gesture of humorous helplessness. Behind him, his white robe, hanging now from a rack in front of the slatted-glass window, shakes slightly in the infrequent breeze. A simple white cassock, swaying in the background, with "Parol Delivrans" embroidered down one side of the chasuble, meaning Words of Deliverance, and down the other, "Haiti."

Aristide supported the Dechoukaj, but the Church, some of whose clergymen used to carry guns beneath their cassocks under François Duvalier and were known as *prêtres macoutes,* decided soon after the Dechoukaj had begun that the people's movement against Duvalierism had gone far enough. Their reaction was understandable. They didn't like those few weeks in February 1986 when former Macoutes were burned alive in the streets of the capital or beheaded or castrated or all three, and perhaps they feared that once the phys-

ical dechoukaj was finished, a different and more dangerous dechoukaj might begin, a political dechoukaj. In their sermons and statements, the bishops asked point-blank for an end to the violence.

John Paul II, on his 1983 visit, had said that "things must change
in Haiti," and had firmly denounced all methods of violence. But it
was unclear how real change was to be achieved *with* the Dechoukaj,
much less without it. Though Duvalier was gone, the people remained dissatisfied. The mere departure of the dictator had done
nothing to improve their situation. Only the symbol of their degra-
dation had been removed. Unemployment, a malady affecting at
least 60 percent of Haitians, was on the rise. On the advice of the
new, Chicago University-trained Finance Minister, the government
had closed several quasi-national enterprises, because they were mo-
nopolistic and unprofitable, and thousands of jobs had been lost. No
new housing or health programs had been initiated. People were sick
and hungry, and unable to see how they could effect change within
the old, corrupt system and under the same bunch of corrupt leaders. The junta wasn't interested in reforming the nation's elitist
structure of government. And it was certainly unlikely that those
who had held power under Duvalier would be willing to relinquish
it without financial or physical coercion. These were not people
susceptible to moral suasion.

In fact, once the Dechoukaj stopped, the provisional junta's pros-
ecution of those who committed human rights abuses and just plain
murder under the Duvaliers ceased. After all, the junta itself had
been appointed by the Duvalier regime with counsel from the U.S.
Embassy; it was always improbable that its members would turn
around and slap their own people in the face. Nor were practical
steps taken to disarm the Tontons Macoutes, the least that could
have been attempted. In fact, the popular Dechoukaj, or the threat
of dechoukaj, was the only weapon that was used effectively against
the Duvalierists. Although its justice was often arbitrary, and certainly the charred corpses hanging from poles were appalling, the
Dechoukaj had major if temporary results: the Macoutes either fled
or went into retreat. It was a less violent, less extensive revenge than
was taken against Nazi collaborators in France at the end of World
War II.

Still, less than two months after Duvalier left Haiti, the Dechoukaj was over. Partly, this was in response to the Church's pleas, but
it was also a response from the people to the junta's continuation of
Duvalier-style violence. Haitians are in a ceaseless death dance with

the regime, always seeing how far they can go before stepping on the state's toes and receiving a punishing blow from the dance master. Once they see the limit of their freedom—for example, one month after Duvalier left, five unarmed protesters were killed by soldiers in Martissant near the capital—they will withdraw for a while and come up with a new tactic. Again, with the new tactic, they will push it to an extreme in order to test its usefulness. This is normal behavior under military dictatorship, especially under one that is theoretically both provisional and benign. Since no laws are valid under these conditions, the only way to find out what rights you have is to exercise them until you get a reaction.

After the Martissant killings, the next step was a march on Fort Dimanche, Madame Max's former enclave that stands on the salt flats opposite the La Saline slum. There thousands of the Duvaliers' enemies had languished, starved and died, if they were not simply tortured and executed. Aristide, among others, was instrumental in organizing the April 26, 1986, march. He had a petition circulated that was signed by eleven thousand people, demanding that the junta dismantle Fort Dimanche as a prison and turn it into a museum honoring those who had died within its walls. But the junta was not interested, as events would show. The marchers, unarmed, made their way toward the little embankment behind which the asymmetrical ochre fortress stands, and for a moment all was calm. Then, after a shouting match with some in the crowd, the soldiers raised their guns and fired into the air, severing a power line, which fell and killed a number of protesters. Others were slain by direct gunfire.

Aristide was there with a reporter in the Radio Soleil jeep, and he broadcast the incident live, with the bullets flying around their heads. Waldeck, who enjoys attending all public events, remembers a heroic version of the event. "I was lying down, hiding from the bullets, like everyone else," he says. "And there was Titid, with a microphone in one hand and his other hand on the Bible. He never even ducked. He's crazy." Six people were killed and more than fifty were wounded in the attack, which turned Aristide into a national hero. His voice was heard all over the country. Even today, young men in La Saline and Cité Soleil and Raboteau, the big slum in Gonaïves, talk about Fort Dimanche when they talk about Aristide, and tell you how they could hear the bullets while he was on the air.

(Aristide laughs when he hears this. "I'm not sure you could hear the bullets," he says.)

The regime claimed that the violence began when agitators in the crowd fired shots and threw stones. Beauvoir, the voodoo priest, was more specific. "Aristide was there in his little white car, directing the whole thing. He gave the order to his little boys to start throwing rocks. Why does he do these things? Using young children for violence. It's unthinkable. And then so many have to die, while he remains untouched." Everyone in Haiti knew Aristide's little white car, a Daihatsu Charade. *"La petite Charade,"* Aristide always called it. (Haitians always know your car, because there are still so few cars in the country.) During the summer of 1987, more than a year after the incident at Fort Dimanche, the Well-Placed Embassy Official was still telling me about the little Charade and Aristide's boys. But I knew that Aristide had been riding in Radio Soleil's jeep, and that Waldeck—who rarely obeyed even Aristide's slightest command—loves to watch violence, but has a healthy fear of soldiers and guns.

In September 1986, a few months after the Fort Dimanche killings, Charlot Jacquelin, who worked in the Cité Soleil slum for the Catholic literacy program Mission Alpha, was arrested by the police and the Army; he was never seen again. In response to repeated inquiries into Jacquelin's case by international and Haitian human-rights groups, the junta stated: "Charlot Jacquelin was never arrested by the police." At the time, all of Mission Alpha's literacy workers were endangered. The junta did not approve of the alphabetization program or its textbook, in which the word *dechouke* was prominently illustrated.

Members of the armed forces claimed that Mission Alpha was a Communist front that taught illiterate peasants and slum-dwellers to oppose the government. It was not a good time to go into the slums if you didn't live there, or even if you came from another neighborhood in that slum. It was not a good time to go into Cité Soleil or La Saline if you were white, or carried a camera or any kind of book, notebook or pad. Clearly, people were being told that any outsider, any teacher, any journalist was a Communist. In La Saline, a foreign photographer who was used to hanging out there was almost torn apart by a crowd of young men screaming "Communist!" Her guide told her that the youths had been paid to frighten off all journalists and Mission Alpha workers.

Neither Charlot Jacquelin nor his body ever turned up. Eventually, he became the best known of the junta's "disappeared." Many people told many stories about Charlot. The head of Mission Alpha, who said he had never heard of Jacquelin before he disappeared, was taking care of the literacy worker's pregnant wife. He told me Charlot had just been a simple Cité Soleil resident who was making very little money working for Mission Alpha in his neighborhood. For some reason, he said, the military had decided to use Jacquelin as an example to other Mission Alpha workers.

Pastor Wallace Turnbull had another story. As usual, Turnbull said, it was all Aristide's fault. Jacquelin was one of Aristide's boys, Turnbull said, and he had been ordered by Aristide to assassinate a sergeant in Cité Soleil. This time the pastor's story was particularly fantastical, but then again, he was accustomed to stretching things in order to make his stories turn out right. After the sergeant was killed, Pastor Wally said, of course the sergeant's friends wanted to take their revenge on his murderer. "So they arrested this Jacquelin, a common criminal, probably paid by Aristide to do his dirty work, and who knows what they did with him? Who cares?"

Many people did care. On November 7, 1986, a demonstration of about 200,000 took to the streets of Port-au-Prince. Jacquelin's disappearance was its theme. At least one protester was killed when the Army opened fire on the crowd near Radio Soleil. On the demonstrators' banners was written, *"Ba nou Chalo vivan, jan nou te pran-l."* Give us Charlot alive, the way you took him.

"Where do the planes go?" Waldeck asks. He points into the sky. "That one. Where is it going?"

I say Miami.

"Where is Miami? Is it north?"

"It's north of Cap-Haïtien," I tell Waldeck. He can understand this. He's from the Cap, the coastal capital of the northern province.

"North of the Cap," he repeats. "Oh. So it's on the other side of the water?"

"Right." In Creole, *lòt bò dlo,* or the other side of the water, means abroad.

"Hey, hey," says Ti Bernard, catching at my hair to get my attention. "When you go in the airplane, is there a lot of wind in your face? How do you hold on?"

"No, there's no wind. It's not like a car. It's all closed up, like a little room," I tell him.

"They put a little table in front of your seat, right?" asks Ronny. He's older than the other boys.

"Uh-huh," I say. Ronny nods at the rest of the boys.

"Avyon," says Waldeck. "That's 'airplane' in English." He is very proud of his English. He looks at me and pushes my hair out of my face. Haitians are fascinated by long hair and can't stand to see it around your eyes or near your mouth. "Where is that one going?"

It is sunset and the sunset planes are taking off from the airport, which is not so far away from St.-Jean-Bosco.

"Maybe that one is going to Paris, in France," I say. They all watch it, high in the air.

"Paris, in France," says Ayiti. In Creole, his name means Haiti. "France is on the other side of the water, too, right? That's where they speak French. *Je parle français,"* Ayiti tells me. Ayiti is beautiful, and mean. He's always threatening to slash my tires if I don't give him money. I've known Ayiti for years—he was one of the first boys I met when I came to Aristide's church the first time in 1986— and he is still threatening. He never does it, though. He's afraid of Aristide.

"You have a boyfriend on the other side of the water, right?" Waldeck asks. He asks me this question all the time.

"Yes, that's right," I say.

"But no children," Ayiti says. *"Fanm blan-yo pa gen timoun."* Foreign women don't have children. He smiles at me again. Ayiti likes me right now because I have promised to buy him a Walkman.

"Have you ever seen a *loup-garou?"* Ayiti asks. A loup-garou is a sort of Haitian werewolf, and Ayiti thinks of the bloodsucking monster because usually it is childless women who turn into loup-garous at night, shooting out of their houses on a tail of fire, and sucking the blood out of babies. When a child is sick, people commonly think that a loup-garou has been sucking its blood. Most Haitian kids think they have seen a loup-garou. A woman in Pétionville was macheted to death a few weeks before by a crowd that claimed she was a loup-garou. It's not a rare occurrence.

"One came to our house one night," Ayiti tells me. "I think the old houngan sent it."

"Did you see it?" I ask.

"No," he says, "but we heard it crying. Didn't we?"

They all nod their heads. They still look scared.

"It stayed all night, but it never came into the house," Ayiti says. "We started burning candles, and I think the light frightened it away."

"Where is that one going?" asks Waldeck, looking into the sky.

"Maybe New York," I say.

"That's your place," says Ayiti. "When will you take me there?"

"I'm going, too," says Waldeck.

"Me too, me too," say the others.

"We'll have to rent our own plane," I say.

"Our own plane," says Ti Bernard. "Can we sleep in it?"

"Will we have to speak English?" asks Waldeck.

"*I speak English,*" says Ayiti. Some of them picked up some English back when there were tourists, from begging and offering certain services.

"*You fuck you, I make you,*" Waldeck shouts, in a lowered, man's voice.

"Do you know what that means?" I ask.

He smiles and shuts his eyes. Nods.

"*Kiss me mister,*" says Ayiti.

"*I make you cheap,*" says Ronny.

"Who do you say that to?" I ask Ronny.

"To tourists," he says. He looks shy. "You know, Canadians, Americans."

"Oh," I say.

"*I am going in school,*" says Waldeck. "What does that mean?"

"*M pral lekol,*" I say. He nods.

"*Ow iss,*" says Chef.

"What?" I say.

"*Ow iss,*" he repeats. "That's how you say 'house' in English."

"*I love you,*" Waldeck says. "*Church,*" he says, pointing to the yellow church.

"*School,*" he adds, pointing to the school on the church grounds, l'Ecole Nationale des Arts et Métiers. The boys don't go there. It costs money to attend, and you have to be able to read.

"*House,*" Waldeck says, waving his hand in the general direction of the building Aristide lives in.

"You can take me to your house in New York, yes?" he asks. "*Please,*" he adds in English.

"When you learn to read," I say. "After you learn to read, okay? Where is your house?"

"At the Cap," Waldeck says.

"No, that's your mother's house," I say. "Where is your house here? Where do you sleep at night?"

"The street," he says. "Sometimes on Grande Rue."

"In the church, sometimes," says Ayiti. "If Titid lets us."

"In the tap-taps," says Chef. "When it rains at night, we sleep in the tap-taps." There is a big intersection near the church where tap-taps park for the night, across from the military airport.

"We had a house," says Waldeck.

"I know," I say. "In Tokio." Tokio is the bidonville across the street from the church.

"The Macoutes dechouked it," says Ayiti. Aristide bought the boys' Tokio house, a former voodoo *peristyle,* or temple, from a voodoo priest who had connections to the Tontons Macoute and who was too scared to stay there during the Dechoukaj. Max Beauvoir's interpretation: Aristide took advantage of the Dechoukaj to intimidate the voodoo priest, then took over the house. In any case, a year later, with the Macoutes out in the open again, Aristide's position in Tokio was no longer firm, and the neighborhood heavies forced the boys out, back into the street. It was like gang wars.

"Why did they dechouk it?" I ask.

"Because they don't like Titid," says Ayiti. "They don't like us either." The house hadn't been anything special, just a big empty space with straw mats, and sometimes a light bulb. One night when I went there, the bulb had been out for a week. The kids were using burning shreds of wood and paper to light their card games. I asked why the light was out, and they told me it was because they didn't have enough money for electricity, so the guy around the corner who sells electricity stolen from the state's power lines decided to cut off their connection.

I offered to pay the two dollars it would cost for light for the month, and Ayiti, Waldeck and some others trooped off in the night with me to the electricity man's house. He took my money and came to the temple with a stool to reconnect the wiring. I asked the kids why they didn't watch him do it and then do it themselves when the money ran out, and they said that he would kill them if they did that. It did not seem as though they were exaggerating. Of course, if they had pooled their money they could have bought the electricity, but they didn't want to. Cooperation was not their style.

"Are you going to get a new house?" I ask.

"Maybe," says Ayiti. "Titid says maybe. If he can find one."

"Is New York near Africa?" Chef asks. He has been putting this question together for a long time. "We come from Africa."

"No," I say. "Africa is across a lot of water on the other side of the Dominican Republic. To the east of Haiti."

Chef nods. "Can the Americans kill all the Africans?" he wants to know.

"How do you mean?" I ask.

"I heard something about how the Americans have a big gun that can kill whole countries," he says. "Is that true?"

"They have a bomb that can destroy big cities," I say.

"One bomb, all of Port-au-Prince?" Ti Bernard asks.

"Yes," I say. "They used it once in Japan, in World War Two."

"What's Japan?" Chef asks.

"That's the country where they make my car, far, far away from Haiti."

They all look at my car, admiring the work of the Japanese.

"I heard something about World War Two," says Ti Bernard. "The Americans conquered the whole world, right?"

"Sort of," I say.

"And they had Hitler on the other side, he had Tontons Macoute, right?" he asks. "I heard that on the radio." On the radio, news announcers describe Klaus Barbie as "*youn ansyen Tonton Makout Hitler*," a former Tonton Macoute of Hitler's.

"Yes, that's right," I say. The other kids look at Ti Bernard with respect.

"Where is England?" asks Ronny. "I heard that Sister Elizabeth is from England." Sister Elizabeth is one of the nuns who visits the boys.

"No, Sister Elizabeth is not from England," I tell Ronny. He looks disappointed. "It's Queen Elizabeth who is from there. She is the Queen, like the way General Namphy is the President here. But she has never come to Haiti."

"Queen Elizabeth," says Ronny. "Like Papa Doc?"

"Sort of," I say.

"Is Ronny smart?" I ask the boys.

"Yes," they all say, except Waldeck, who is jealous because he doesn't know as much.

"Is Titid smart?" I ask.

"Yes, yes," they all shout, even Waldeck.

"Who is the smartest man in Haiti?" I ask them.

No response. They look puzzled.

"Who is smarter," I ask them, "General Namphy or Titid?"

"The General," says Waldeck, quickly.

"Why?"

"Because he has the power," says Waldeck.

"He lives in the palace," says Ayiti. "He runs the Army."

"Now look at Titid," says Waldeck, giving the question some consideration. "He lives here."

"And he only has us," says Ayiti.

While he was studying abroad in the late 1970s, Aristide wrote articles for the Haitian Catholic newspaper *Bon Nouvel* that irritated Jean-Claude Duvalier's regime. When he returned to Haiti, he remained outspoken. On September 12, 1982, after having just been ordained, Aristide preached a sermon at St.-Joseph in the center of La Saline, in which he denounced the Duvalier regime and spoke of the misery of the people in the slum surrounding the church. "The other day," he said, "I was walking through La Saline, and it was raining. In the rain, in a flood of mud, the cart haulers, sodden with the waters from above and covered in muddy sweat, continued to pull their heavy loads without respite, as usual, doing the work of black slaves. Cart haulers, tragic, Sisyphean figures, condemned to carry eternally the creaking load of the pain of oppression. . . . Can we continue to find this situation of violence that is imposed on the poor normal? No. We must end this regime where the donkeys do all the work and the horses prance in the sunshine, a regime of misery imposed on us by the people in charge. They are," he said, paraphrasing Isaiah, "voracious and insatiable dogs, who go their own way, each one looking out for himself."

This message was not well received. Immediately, there were threats against Aristide's life. The regime stated that he was preaching violence, and the provincial delegate of Aristide's order was brought in to meet with members of Duvalier's Cabinet. Soon after, Aristide was sent by the Church into exile in Montreal. From the moment of that sermon, Aristide was considered more or less an enemy of the state. When he returned to Haiti in January 1985, he behaved as though his role were foreordained—unsurprised by his own ascent, the rise of a fatherless infant from the south come to Port-au-Prince with his mother and sister to make a new life.

Aristide's father was Joseph Aristide, a small farmer from the town of Port-Salut. When Joseph died, his wife decided to leave the countryside and bring her two-year-old daughter and three-month-old son to the city so that they could get a proper education and make something of themselves. She became a commerçante, buying up produce in the countryside and selling it in town. The household

Aristide grew up in in Port-au-Prince was staunchly Catholic, and there was always one priest or another at the dinner table. The young boy soon began his religious studies, with his mother's blessing. His mentor was Father Gabriel Désir, a Salesian priest who welcomed Aristide into that religious order, and who was a frequent guest at the Aristides' family table. The order, the Society of Saint Francis de Sales, was founded by Saint John Bosco, a nineteenth-century Italian priest canonized for his work with the homeless boys of Turin.

Throughout his religious and secular schooling, Aristide was always a model student. Indeed, he was a favorite of the Haitian bishops for a time, because he was so bright. By the time he finished his studies in Haiti, where he received his master's in psychology, and in Rome, Jerusalem, Britain and Canada, he spoke Spanish, Italian, English and Hebrew, and the Archbishop of Port-au-Prince liked to show him off as a brilliant scholar with a photographic memory for chapter and verse.

Aristide's place in Haitian history was not an unprecedented one, as Sylvain had pointed out at that dinner party Charles and I attended up in Pétionville. In the late 1940s and the 1950s, Pierre-Eustache-Daniel Fignolé, who like Aristide was born in the south and came to Port-au-Prince with his mother after his father's death, started a political party called MOP, Mouvement Ouvriers-Paysans (Workers' and Peasants' Movement) and became the leader of Port-au-Prince's discarded multitude. Fignolé was the man Sylvain's father had feared. A vituperative Creole orator with autocratic tendencies, Fignolé was appointed provisional President of Haiti in 1957. But it was a trick. His popular legitimacy was too much for the Army to tolerate, and they had put him in in order to take him out, permanently. Nineteen days after Fignolé's installation, top officers of the Army barged into a Cabinet meeting he was leading, kidnapped the young President, and sent him packing into a lonely New York exile that ended only after Jean-Claude left Haiti. (Fignolé died soon after his return to Haiti, a broken, useless old figure.) The leader of MOP was succeeded in the presidency by a former member of his party who had struck better, though duplicitous, deals with the armed forces and the Haitian elite: François Duvalier.

Unlike Aristide, however, Fignolé was a politician, not a priest. Aristide's vestments endowed him with a popular legitimacy he might not otherwise have had, but they also constricted his political movements. Fignolé, for example, could openly order "his people" into the streets, and did so with a frequency alarming to the Army. When angered by a government action or anxious to prove his continuing political clout, he could with a word call the people of Bel-Air and La Saline out of their lean-tos, and they would take over the capital, terrifying other residents—though never killing or pillaging —and smashing all of the city's streetlights, plunging the place into darkness. With another word, he could call them home. Because Aristide was a priest, he could not do this, although he had the requisite popularity. In the summer of 1987, the Well-Placed Embassy Official suggested, Aristide did it anyway, but covertly.

"It is not so easy as your friend in the embassy thinks," Aristide told me. Then he acknowledged what others had described as his strategic weakness. His power base at the time was not very wide. In fact, it was like Fignolé's base: the lumpenproletariat, *le lumpen.* And the lumpen are traditionally fickle. At moments of great historical change they may support you for your ideas, for your words. But many among them can be bought. In times of plenty they are loyal, but when was the last time Haiti had experienced a time of plenty? And in times of penury their support can be and often is purchased by the highest bidder—and for very little. For a dollar they'll demonstrate. For twenty, maybe less, they'll torture, they'll burn, they'll kill, they'll assassinate.

"Remember that time they carried me around the courtyard?" Aristide asked me. "When I almost cracked my head against the ceiling? Those people were bought, I think. And I still don't know by whom, though I have ideas." Recognizing the fragility of his base, he began courting the bourgeoisie a few months after the bloody march on Fort Dimanche. His success was limited, though his preachings against poverty and his later sufferings aroused sympathy among those less conservative than Sylvain.

Although he said that preaching against the regime was easier under Duvalier because it was more dangerous and therefore it aroused a deeper response in the congregation, Aristide's political powers rose to new heights during the summer of 1987, more than a year after Duvalier had fled. At the time, General Namphy, head of the military-dominated provisional junta, the National Council of Government (CNG), was under attack from all sides. No longer did Haitians consider him genial, affable, a Haitian version of Ronald Reagan. He was vicious in putting down dissent, and seemed cruel, authoritarian, distant, brutal, small-minded. In the few press conferences he held after Duvalier left on the seventh of February, Namphy let fall the mask of the cheerful, twinkly fellow—hate this presidency thing, can't wait to get back to the pig farm—and exposed the tight-lipped military dictator beneath. He and the military were clearly interested in elections only insofar as their results were manipulable.

Namphy and his men were worse than what the Well-Placed Embassy Official called them: "reluctant democrats." They were dictators in search of puppets. And the United States government, in backing elections held under such a group, must also have been looking for an acceptable tool. Part of the deal made in arranging Duvalier's departure with the U.S. State Department included an implicit promise from the Haitian armed forces that they would accept and implement a timetable for "free and fair" presidential elections.

Whenever change is effected without bloodshed in Haiti, it means that an equitable deal has been struck among all interested parties. When Duvalier fell, the parties involved in the deal were the Army, the Tontons Macoute, the Duvalierists, the economic elite and the U.S. Embassy—all of the interested parties, that is, except the people, who had risked their lives all over the country to bring Duvalier down. Of course, the problem was that eventually elections would (at least theoretically) require the participation of this excluded party.

From the first, however, it was unclear whether Namphy intended to honor his commitment to elections. What the junta never seemed to realize was that the change that had brought about Duvalier's departure was a profound one, and that it had not occurred merely —or even primarily—within the elite strata of the society. The political climate in Haiti had changed; the Haitian people could not be as easily disappointed as they had been in the past. Eventually, the junta would be forced to play the electoral game. Even before Duvalier's fall, with the beginnings of the Dechoukaj movement in the fall of 1985, a loosely organized, grass-roots movement against the dictatorship of Port-au-Prince and the Duvalierists had sprung up among the peasantry and the slum-dwellers—helped into being in large measure by the progressive, "liberation" Church—a movement that would prove itself powerful and not readily destroyed or controlled. This was not a movement inspired by the desire for electoral democracy, but rather one whose goal was to change the system that had exploited the peasantry for centuries. If elections were a step on the path toward popular democracy, the people would participate, but elections alone were never their goal. The peasants weren't particularly interested in a new President; they wanted a better way of life. The older ones had seen presidents come and go, and their lives had only gotten worse.

The democratic movement that began when the Dechoukaj ended a month after Duvalier fell was based on political alliances with the movement in the countryside; the political class in Port-au-Prince—potential presidential and senatorial candidates, former deputies, senators and mayors, returned exiles with ambitions—latched onto the organizations that had been created over the past decade by priests and lay workers and peasant organizers in the countryside and the provincial cities. They compromised with and manipulated this constituency and sometimes simply paid for support. The alliance grew rapidly. In some cases, it was helped along by American encouragement of certain moderate-right presidential candidates. The Port-au-Prince political class—*la politicaille,* it is called derisively in French—needed the support of the grass-roots movements in its quest for elections. Without massive popular support for elections, it was feared, the Army could never be forced into accepting a vote.

All along, the people were suspicious of the very concept of elections. As Evans Paul, a leader of the Confederation of Democratic Unity, an opposition group, said later, "If you have a barnyard filled with pigs, you can't very well hold a reception there." Although Jean-Claude Duvalier was gone, the system he and his father had put in place remained. Evans Paul and others like him felt that an election held in such circumstances would be a sham imposed by the United States in order to cut off the impetus for a revolutionary movement in Haiti. A revolution in which the Tonton Macoute structure within the Army as well as in civilian society was toppled, Paul felt, was a solution more responsive to the actual Haitian situation than elections. Peasants and shanty-dwellers agreed, when they had the time to think about the question.

When the junta finally realized that the United States was not going to give up on the idea of elections and that the game was going to be played whether or not they wanted to play it, they quickly tried to get control of the electoral deck of cards. No one was going to deal them a hand they didn't want.

They had a few bad moments. A constituent assembly largely

appointed by Namphy and his men came up with a surprising new Constitution whose Article 291 specifically prohibited "notorious" and "zealous" Duvalierists from participating in elections for ten years. The Constitution also called for an independent electoral council to organize and oversee elections in the fall of 1987. The Army and the ruling class were threatened: they saw a changeable but potentially victorious alliance forming among the United States, moderate Haitian politicians acceptable to "international opinion," and the popular movements.

A lame propaganda campaign against the Constitution was begun (*"Aba Konstitisyon Kominis,"* read graffiti around town), but on March 29, 1987, the new Constitution was resoundingly approved by 99.81 percent of the voters in an atmosphere of joy reminiscent of the day of Duvalier's departure. Among the voters, only Namphy cast his ballot with reluctance and refused to say how he had voted.

Just as they had responded to verbal assaults on the Constitution and physical assaults upon its authors by supporting it, the Haitian people rallied to the electoral process when the junta began to attack it. Haitians love a victim, because corruption in the country is so widespread that only victimization proves purity. Only one of the presidential candidates had ever been seriously victimized by the regime: Sylvio Claude, a Protestant pastor whom Jean-Claude Duvalier had imprisoned. He was immediately the most popular of the candidates; the others, more or less unscathed, must be corrupt. Thus the electoral process, unscathed, must be corrupt. When the Army started firing on electoral offices in the weeks before the elections were to take place, the people began rallying to the call to vote. Before that, they had been interested, but not enthusiastic.

From the beginning, Aristide was skeptical about the electoral process and the Constitution which enforced it. He could not bring himself to believe that any meaningful democratic initiative would be permitted under this regime, which was fully as vicious, he believed, as the one it had followed. He believed that the much touted Article 291 was a bait to lure the people to vote for a constitution whose passage in a referendum would then be seen internationally as a popular endorsement of the junta and of its ostensible democratic goals. By voting en masse for the new Constitution, the Haitian people, Aristide felt, had fallen into a trap that would lead them into sham elections directed by the U.S. government and the Haitian

Army, and into a continuation of the downward political spiral begun when the United States supported François Duvalier's rise to power. This put Aristide oddly enough close to the camp of Namphy's National Council of Government and the Army, both of which feared the erosion of their powers that even moderately free elections would ineluctably bring about.

Namphy was a singularly inept politician. Having started in power with popular opinion squarely behind him, he had quickly wasted his mandate through acts of brutality and authoritarianism. As his popularity waned, he was given the opportunity to make a really wrong move, and he rose to it. On June 22, the country's most radical union, the Centrale Autonome des Travailleurs Haïtiens (CATH), called a general strike and threatened to punish strike-breakers. Factions within the democratic sector—including the presidential candidates—failed to endorse and even condemned the strike as premature and strategically ill-considered. But although the strike itself was only moderately successful, Namphy's reaction to it established the anti-democratic, violent tenor of the season to come. On the day of the strike, in direct contravention of numerous articles of the new Constitution, the Army raided and ransacked CATH headquarters and beat and arrested three of the union leaders. The following day, Namphy issued a decree that attempted to wrest power from the constitutionally mandated electoral council.

The two actions, taken in concert, were of incalculable political stupidity. Namphy had underestimated his unpopularity and the strength of the building movement against him. By attacking the union and the independent electoral process at the same time, he gave his opponents an opportunity they could not ignore. The strike, which before had been destined to fizzle into nothingness, took hold. "We were surprised by history," said a friend of mine from the democratic sector, a man who would later become a senatorial candidate. "We had been willing to go along and just keep our eye on the situation, on the CNG, but once Namphy blundered so badly in dealing with CATH, we seized the moment. Really, we had no choice. It seemed the politically apt thing to do." With the entire democratic sector now fully behind the strike, the capital—and many towns in the countryside—shut down. Young boys built barricades out of tires all over town, and no one but the press and the Red Cross ventured out. You risked getting your windshield broken by rock-throwing youths. As the strikes and street disorders continued into the summer, the car-rental companies upped renters' dam-

age liability each week, until by midsummer it had risen from zero
to five hundred dollars, whether or not you bought insurance. Some
of the demonstrations that accompanied the strikes were carefully
planned and large; others were smaller and seemed to begin sponta-
neously. The Army reacted to demonstrators with bullets and tear
gas. Namphy was soon forced to rescind his electoral decree, but he
was unable to regain the trust of the people, and he did not even try.
The strikes continued to be surprisingly successful; strategic roadblocks manned by bands of youths with rocks at the ready helped
ensure their triumph.

Even the tap-tap Chicago went on strike: the most important
factor in getting together a strike in Haiti is whether you can convince the tap-tap drivers to go along with you. At the beginning they
went along, but it was never easy to keep them off the streets. They
took a big loss when they struck. The tap-tap drivers were not
strangers to Aristide. Once, during the summer, I ran into their
leader coming out of Aristide's little office next to the sacristy; following behind him were the three progressive priests who had waited
for Aristide that other day for so long in the sacristy doorway. The
Well-Placed Embassy Official told me that if you paid off the tap-tap
drivers, and paid them off handsomely, they would do what you
asked. I asked Aristide whether people from the democratic sector
were paying off the tap-tap drivers.

"Well," he said. He got that dismissive look on his face and re-
arranged his glasses. "Now, who do you think has more money to
pay off the tap-tap drivers? The opposition or the government? If it
were for money, they would go with the junta. It's not for money.
It's for honor." It annoyed him when there was any implication of
venality. "The reason the junta and Reagan can never understand
what we are doing, the reason they always talk about money, money,
all the time, well, that's because money is the only thing they understand. After all, Reagan's country was built on the idea that making
money is the greatest act of patriotism."

The junta tried to break the electoral council. The people demonstrated. The junta gave in. The junta tried to close down the
union. The people demonstrated, the junta gave in. It seemed that
at every step Namphy was defeated. With his tactical errors, he had
managed a miracle: he had forced the radical left, the democratic
sector and even Haiti's small and diffident Communist Party to unite
for a brief period. The democratic sector had a demonstration. The
Communist Party had a demonstration. The union had a demonstra-

tion. Women demonstrated. Students demonstrated. Many of the demonstrations were organized with help from the young people who made up the core of Aristide's followers at St.-Jean-Bosco. But even a tiny *groupuscule* connected to the radical New York-based newspaper *Haïti Progrès* had a tiny demonstration, in which twenty protesters were faced down in front of the monolithic U.S. Embassy by four truckloads of riot police, armed with the latest in U.S.- and French-issue shields and helmets, and looking more like the snappy South Korean police than the normally ill-equipped Haitian Army.

The protests did not come without a price. Frequently, the Army shot into crowds of unarmed demonstrators, and two or three times they burst into the slums by night and shot into the shanties. Cardboard and tin walls do not put up much resistance. Many people died sleeping on their straw mats, and others were pulled from their homes and beaten or killed. This only served further to unite Namphy's opposition.

The slum sieges were direct attacks on Aristide's power base. Concerned about the violent turn the Army was taking, he urged his people not to demonstrate in front of police headquarters or the National Palace. They did anyway. One day in July 1987, Waldeck and I spent four hours in a demonstration that swelled to perhaps five thousand at one point. We went to the National Palace, where they sprayed us with gunfire and tear gas.

Waldeck was in a good mood. He had on a new shirt and pants that he had bought with money from the church. The priests at St.-Jean-Bosco wanted him to leave town. Everyone was worried about Aristide's little boys. The most articulate kids had been interviewed on the radio, and sometimes when they were washing windshields at the intersections, on the few days when there were no strikes, soldiers from Fort Dimanche would come and pick them up and beat them and hold them overnight. Waldeck and Ayiti were pretty well known around Port-au-Prince, and Aristide had asked them to lie low. Another priest at St.-Jean-Bosco had given Waldeck ten dollars that day to buy a bus ticket and get out of town, visit his mother at the Cap. But in his new shirt and pants Waldeck wanted to do anything but lie low. He was out on the town in this demonstration, his shoulders carried with a little more swagger than usual, his new green pants clearly on display. He even bought me a fresco, a flavored ice that vendors sell from little carts. It was my first fresco; I had always known that the ice was made from unpurified water, and I'd seen the vendors dragging their large chunks of ice in the early mornings through the mud in the middle of La Saline; there were wasps hovering over their ice carts, and flies. But I was thirsty and grateful, and I took my little ice cup gladly from Waldeck. How could I do otherwise? The sun had been too hot for too long to worry about whether the ice was clean, and then, of course, it was the first and only time Waldeck had ever spent money on me. I had to say yes, and I had to eat the ice with obvious pleasure. After all, I had an audience. Waldeck brought the fresco over to me in front of a mass of his little friends from the church. They watched the transfer of fresco with studied nonchalance. The red syrup in the cup was already beginning to melt the shaved ice. Waldeck looked over at his friends, who were standing against the background of the stunning white palace like a frozen memorial to child warriors, and clinked fresco cups with me. He said, "I love demonstrations."

That day, he was my bodyguard, held my hand the whole time, yelled when he saw soldiers about to fire. When I told him to go home and stay away, he looked at me as though I were crazy, and bought another fresco. He spent most of the time when we were not in direct danger begging small change from foreign journalists, although because of the new shirt and pants he was not a very convincing beggar. The priests wanted Waldeck out of town, and by four, an hour after the demonstration faded away, he was at the bus stop for Cap-Haïtien, ready for his twelve-hour tap-tap trip. In fact there was no reason for Waldeck to stay in town. The strikes Aristide's people supported were bad for Waldeck and the boys, because when traffic stopped, so did their windshield-washing business. In this way the boys were just like the shopkeepers on Grande Rue.

At the end of July, Namphy decided to clamp down. No public demonstrations of more than twenty persons, the Army decreed, would henceforth be permitted. A few days later, about 120 priests and nuns gathered at a Catholic seminary up in Bourdon, on the way to Pétionville. There Ti Legliz decided to challenge the decree. They put on their vestments and, carrying their Bibles, marched off by twos in the hot sun, down John Brown and across town to the Church of Notre-Dame de Perpétuel Secours in the old Bel-Air slum. The blue-and-white line snaked slowly through the streets. On the broader boulevards of the capital, traffic stopped to watch the priests and the nuns pass by. In Bel-Air, they were cheered by people watching from their balconies. William Smarth and Antoine Adrien, two priests returned from exile in Brooklyn, were there, and so were the priests from Verrettes, the priest who had been run out of his village in the Northwest province by the reinvigorated Tontons Macoute, and in among them, small and unremarkable, Aristide. The Army did not touch the marchers. They didn't even come out to watch the priests and the nuns go by.

By now, more than fifty had died in Army attacks on demonstrations. Disgusted with local Army persecutions of his parishioners, Bishop Willy Romélus of Jérémie, capital of the province of Grande-Anse on the tip of the southern peninsula, called in July for the junta to hand over power to a popular provisional government, one that would uphold the Constitution rather than trample upon it. *Rache manyòk,* "Pull up your manioc," was the slogan coined by Bishop Romélus, a distant cousin of Aristide's and the only Haitian bishop with real ties to Ti Legliz. *Ba-nou tè-a blanch,* "Give us a clear field." Like dechoukaj, Romélus' slogan was another uprooting metaphor from the countryside, with *blanch* meaning cleared or empty or blank. When one farmer buys land from another in Haiti, it is customary for the original owner to pull up his manioc harvest before he vacates the field. Traditionally, the new owner cannot take over until the old one pulls up the manioc.

In a chapel in his church complex, Romélus spent whole nights praying with people from the community. The old women told stories about their sons being taken from their houses by soldiers during the night, and then they prayed in the blue light while the dignified gray-haired bishop sat up front, straight-backed, with his eyes closed. Young men gave speeches against the junta, ending with a cry of *"Rache manyòk!"* and again a prayer. Small children slept outside the chapel on mats their mothers had brought.

The opposition in the capital latched on to Romélus' phrase. On Aristide's lips, in particular, the bishop's slogan became a ceaseless attack on the junta, and the congregation at St.-Jean-Bosco repeated his cries of *"Rache manyòk!"* with fervor. By the time Aristide had preached *rache manyòk* a few times, and had been broadcast, like Romélus, on the radio, the slogan was a national byword. Aristide made continual use of it, transforming it, as he often does with plain phrases, into something far more complicated and far-reaching. When he went to speak at the reopening of CATH, the union that had been closed by the government in June after it called for the strike, he threatened the junta and strikebreakers. He started out by talking about the effectiveness of *"ti dife wouj nan kaotchou-yo,"* little red bonfires in tires, like the fires the press had been trying to drive around for weeks at the strike barricades. Such a little weapon compared to Uzis, he said. And so effective, so effective. The crowd laughed.

"We have asked you to *rache manyòk,"* he continued, addressing the junta. "Give us a blank slate. If you do not, then we will keep striking. We will give you blank streets, and if people do not clear the streets, then we will turn the streets red." (*Si nou pa gen lari-a blanch, nap fè lari-a wouj.* He was playing on the colors: *blanch* and *wouj.*) This little phrase stuck in the Well-Placed Embassy Official's mind the next day. *Wouj,* or red: there was something about that color, and Aristide. The combination got to the Well-Placed Embassy Official.

"That little priest is talking violence again," the Well-Placed Official told me at Le Corail, a restaurant in Pétionville to which we had driven in his new bulletproof van.

"When?" I asked.

"In front of the CATH's headquarters the other day," he said. "You must have heard it: 'We'll turn the streets red,' he said."

Only the day before, Leslie Manigat, one of the presidential candidates, had told me the same thing. "Aristide is a Communist," Manigat told me. "Priests should preach faith, not politics."

"Oh, come on," I said to the Well-Placed Embassy Official. "Aristide was talking about the red from the fires in the tires they burn. He's talking about enforcing the strikes."

"You must be kidding," said the Well-Placed Official. "He's talking about blood. He said the streets will run red with blood." Although this was not true, it was not surprising. The little man at the little desk at the end of the hall often does not translate Aristide's allusive Creole very well. In any case, the embassy hears what it wants to hear. Aristide knew this. He knew that his talk of red fires was not just literally incendiary.

"And when he says red, by the way, he's also threatening us with Communism." The Embassy Official looked grim. "He's a maniac. A Marxist maniac."

"A firebrand?" I asked.

He laughed. "Right. A radical firebrand." He scooped up another forkful of rice. "So what's the guy really like?" he asked.

I shrugged. "Who knows?" I said.

. . .

He was driving alone through Bel-Air in the little Charade one day during the strikes and the disruptions. It seemed like a peaceful day. He took the circuitous route that is actually a shortcut through the slums, because it circumvents the hysterical tap-tap traffic along Grande Rue, and the day was wild with traffic, a day of *ravitaillement* between strikes, during which everyone was supposed to get supplies and food and to make money for the coming strike days. When you are calling for strikes in the poorest country in the hemisphere, where people live on the pennies they make each day, you have to allow them a breather or they can't sustain the protest.

But as he turned down the Rue St.-Martin, there was a sudden commotion. He couldn't tell what it was, and kept driving. There was a crowd of young men, and some smoke. He recognized the beginnings of a barricade, but thought he could make it through. Sometimes if the timing is right you can make it. But his timing was off, and the young men, seeing a car approach, turned. In each hand was a rock.

He couldn't go any farther without running them down, and the crowd was growing. He stopped, helpless. People on the sides of the street turned to watch the scene: some rich guy in a car trying to make it through their melee. The rocks started coming.

"No, no," he heard a voice cry, from the sidewalk. *"Se ti Charadla. Se Titid."* It's the little Charade. It's Titid. The rock-throwers' arms stayed raised, but a curious look came over their faces, and they approached the car to see if what they heard was true. As they recognized the driver—or at least the car—they started to smile, and slowly their arms came down and they began to laugh.

"Get out of the car," one youth yelled at him, because the street lower down was still thronged with angry kids with rocks. The barricade was bigger, and burning.

"Park it over here and get out." He did as they told him. "Lock it," they said. Dozens gathered around to try to shake his hand. "We'll watch it until it's safe for you to come back. Come on."

The street was crazy now, and there was no telling when the Army, or the police, whose headquarters was nearby on Grande Rue, would be coming. Six or seven of the young men surrounded him. As usual, he was invisible at their center. They guided him down toward the end of St.-Martin, where it meets Grande Rue, a few blocks from his church. Rocks were flying, and the smoke was heavy.

"Wait here," they told him when they reached the corner. Several stayed to protect him while one went on down Grande Rue as a scout, to make sure that the way was safe. The priest crouched up against a building. There were shots coming from Grande Rue, and the sound of heavy trucks. It seemed like an hour before the scout returned.

"Okay," the scout said, "let's go." And the band of youths, with the priest among them, made it down one block, waited, and then the next and another, until he was returned, safe among the tear gas, to the confines of the church. Inside for the rest of the day, he had to keep all the fans going because of the gas.

When he returned to the Rue St.-Martin the next day, he found the remains of the disruption: black ashes of tires, broken market stalls, and parked cars with their windshields shattered. Except for the little white Charade, which stood locked, intact and shining like an icon.

"Their car was coming down the street near Aristide's church," the Well-Placed Embassy Official told me. "Anyway that's the story I heard from Turnbull. A couple from Turnbull's Baptist mission, and two of their kids. All of a sudden, you know the way these things happen, a group of guys surrounded them, near the Portail St.-Joseph." The Portail St.-Joseph is the crowded intersection near Aristide's church where the outskirts of the La Saline slum meet a massive Traffic Police headquarters and the walls of the military airport.

"They were sitting ducks, with their two kids in the back. Stupid, of course. They shouldn't have been out at all. But they didn't realize. This was their first time in Haiti, and really they had just arrived, Turnbull says.

"Well, there was this little guy on the corner near all the commotion, just a little way down from the church, in shorts, with a straw hat on, like the peasants wear? He was carrying a knapsack, Turnbull says, and the youths kept running up to him to take rocks out of it. He was sort of directing them. They kept saying, 'Whites, Americans, whites,' and throwing stones. They broke all the car's windows, and when I saw the family it was a shame, really, some of them even had to have stitches. Their faces were cut by the glass. Luckily, they didn't get hit by the rocks.

"Anyway, once the attack had petered out, and they were finally pulling away, a Haitian came up to them and said, 'That little guy with the rocks in his bag, you know who he was?' And they said no. They don't know anything about Haiti, of course. And he said, 'Father Aristide.' Father Aristide." The Well-Placed Embassy Official looked at me. "Can you believe it?"

The streets of Port-au-Prince were in chaos. The Army had already killed dozens during demonstrations, and now, on July 23, in the northwest near the dusty town of Jean-Rabel, hundreds of peasants who were organizing land-reform actions throughout the area were ambushed and macheted to death by others underwritten by local landholders. Their hacked bodies were left alongside mountain trails or thrown into the deep ravines that ring Jean-Rabel. The news from the Far West, as Haitians call the Northwest province, of which Jean-Rabel is the seat, increased the depth of anxiety and unrest throughout the country. An undeclared civil war, people were calling it. The massacre was seen as a new phase in the junta's crackdown on popular organizations. Namphy had only recently visited the town to reaffirm his bonds with the ruling families, the region's largest landholders. A visit by Namphy often signaled the beginning of a repressive wave. The old Tontons Macoute had been unleashed in the Far West; the junta had given the green light to those who wanted to preserve the status quo, by whatever means. The Army in Jean-Rabel participated in the massacre.

Everyone in Port-au-Prince was horrified by the attack, even the Well-Placed Embassy Official. The papers were filled with gruesome pictures of mangled corpses. When you looked at them, you had to do some hard imagining to identify all the body parts. Aristide, perceiving what he took to be a new and tougher line among the junta and its supporters, was talking and preaching about Jean-Rabel, day after day. You couldn't listen to the radio without hearing his voice. While others in the opposition had gone into informal hiding after receiving multiple death threats, he remained adamantly visible. His prominence had its drawbacks. He was used, he was attacked, and, worse, he was not always in control. One day, when they recognized him out in a demonstration, the crowd went crazy with excitement, pushing toward him, asking questions, fighting with one another to get to him. His bodyguards, a cluster of tough women from the slums, pulled him out of the commotion and into an open store, which promptly barred its doors. That night, he had another migraine, and decided not to go into the streets again.

. . .

"Poor Titid," said a friend of mine, a Haitian journalist. "He is always having these nervous prostrations. He's so sensitive. He stops eating, too, ends up looking like a skeleton. I remember last year interviewing him after there had been some commotion at the church, an assassination attempt or something. He's lying in his bed in his little room, looking like he's already dead, he's too neurotic to eat during a crisis, and all these church people are running around, taking care of him. They fan him, they try to convince him to take aspirin and Valium, they put cold compresses on his fevered brow, you know, and whisper warm words of comfort to him. Half of it is drama, but half of it or more is real. His cheeks sink in, and you can see his ribs against his shirt. And then the next day he's giving a sermon. A brilliant sermon. The breakdown makes his people love him more, and it gains him a lot of sympathy from Haitians who don't even know him. His frailty isn't perceived as weakness, the way it would be in your country. In a way, these crises are perceived as a kind of solidarity with the poor. He's starving himself, and they're starving. I'm a Haitian, and I find his behavior peculiar, but I almost admire him for his sensitivity. To me, to us, it's temperamental, but it's not an abnormal reaction to the kind of stress he has to deal with; I mean, it's not like the guy lives a normal life. He's a priest working for a church that basically hates him. He's living inside a family that won't tolerate him. They're always trying to get rid of him. He's like an abused child, and he exhibits the kinds of psychological reactions those children have. It's not an easy life, and it could make a man have breakdowns. So he does."

Sometimes, watching Aristide, you felt that you were watching an ectoplasmic organism under a microscope. It slithered inexorably on, subsuming everything in its path. It didn't even notice what it was doing. He seemed to move through life controlling others, often not even by calculation but symbiotically, because they wanted to be controlled by him. The youths in the church, the parishioners who ran his errands, his family, the younger priests who worked with him—everyone liked to say, "I did such and such for Titid." It was a minor cult of personality, and it was the personality that kept his followers faithful. They believed in his ideas, but, equally important, they loved the man.

He loved to be loved, wanted swirls of affection around him. Each
Sunday in the sacristy was like a love fest. He cared deeply about
the little street boys, but he was not always equally concerned when
it came to the problems of the youths around him. "He will have a
nervous prostration if one of the boys gets a cold," said one youth,
laughing at the exaggeration, "but if you come to him with a real-life
problem, usually he doesn't have time. He doesn't even listen." This
was because the little boys were his project, part of his identity, his
public persona, but the church youths were his team, they were
there to serve the cause.

It was a complicated organization, built up by Aristide but not
always responsive to his command. The structure of the team was
democratic, and often Aristide was overridden. "He's too conservative," one young man said. "Sometimes he puts the sanctity of the
Church above the sanctity of the cause. He worries too much about
offending his superiors. The suck-ups among the kids always go
along with him, but he knows they are suck-ups, so he doesn't respect them. He respects *us,* but he can't always control us. We don't
care about his superiors. They can all go to hell, as far as we're
concerned. But Titid, he gets nervous. He tries to calm us down. It
doesn't always work, poor guy."

It turned out that Aristide had good reason to fear the Church
hierarchy; he understood that as long as he and other young priests
like him remained within the Church, the Vatican—and in his case,
his superiors within the Salesian order—had the ability to pull
strings that could impede the procession of Ti Legliz toward "liberation," that could undermine the cause. They could silence him,
remove him to the countryside, exile him. Eventually, in fact, they
would try each of these strategies, and for a long time each one would
be unsuccessful in the face of protest from the young people affiliated
with St.-Jean-Bosco and other Ti Legliz churches in Port-au-Prince
and in the countryside. Any action against Aristide, the youths felt,
would be detrimental to the cause.

What was the cause? Aristide would say, "The liberation of the
Haitian people." He would say, "Food on the table for all Haitians."
Sometimes, though, it seemed as if the cause were Aristide himself,
his apotheosis. Because of his endless energy and unfailing courage,
he became such an important figure among the militant opposition
that he was for a time constantly at center stage. He used his powers
of attraction to further the cause—giving interviews to dozens of
foreign journalists about the regime and the people, appearing on

television to talk about the corrupt system, speaking on radio about solidarity among the oppressed—but he was so prominent and enjoyed his prominence so thoroughly that it often seemed that he was encouraging the development of a cult of personality. One day, I accused him of wanting to be a saint. He shook his head, didn't even laugh, and said, "To desire to be a saint or a martyr is a sin."

Talking to him once in his office, I noticed a newspaper with the front page headline "QUI ETES-VOUS, PÈRE ARISTIDE?" Who Are You, Father Aristide? I pointed to it and said, "So? Who are you, anyway?" This time he did laugh, and he said, "You'll see, you'll see. Over the years, that's the only way to prove my sincerity. That's the only way in Haiti." It became a running joke whenever we talked. "Who are you, Father Aristide?" I would ask. He always said the same thing: "You'll see." Eventually I did see, but it took a long time. As the years wore on, his courage and integrity were challenged again and again, by the regime, by the hierarchy and by the political situation. He was attacked with guns and machetes and sticks and rocks. Sometimes, I didn't know whether he was dead or alive. And then he would reemerge, sometimes in a state of nervous prostration—thin, frail and wavering—and sometimes strengthened by the trauma, but always with his faith in himself and in his cause unshaken. In those days, he seemed unconquerable, but in the end he too would be brought down by the hard facts of Haiti.

The Beast
of the Haitian Hills

I was always making plans to get out of town that summer, but it wasn't easy. Every time I reserved a jeep to go out into the unpaved countryside, something would happen to hold me back in Port-au-Prince. I was afraid of missing history in order to go sightseeing. What I didn't quite understand was that history was being made that summer in the provinces as well as in town—which has in any case always been true in Haiti. I had mistakenly assumed that the politicians and generals and businessmen and priests of Port-au-Prince were the only political actors in the country; after all, they are the Haitians whom American journalists always talk to, the only Haitians you see quoted in the American newspapers, the only ones who carry any authority with the U.S. State Department. They are the only ones who speak English. You don't need a jeep to go see them.

But in large numbers, the Creole-speaking peasants can wield greater political power than the polyglot Port-au-Prince politicians. Most of the time, it is true, the peasants act for themselves only; it is not easy to keep a family alive out in the dry countryside, and the competition for what little there is is fierce. Often, peasants don't know who is President; the big news from Port-au-Prince is just a lot of meaningless names to the farmer. He is more concerned with the lack of rain, the indifference of the gods, the rising or falling price of rice in the market. He wonders how much it will cost to send his four children to school next year, and how much it will cost to get the houngan to make a cure for his wife's headaches. Port-au-Prince politics—to him it's just *bla-bla-bla,* as Haitians say. But if it comes to his right to the land he farms, or how much higher a tax his wife will have to pay when she brings their produce to market, or whether or not he is going to get his free piglet from the foreign development project, the Haitian farmer becomes as politically involved and motivated as any politician in the capital.

Everyone in the countryside makes his various contributions to Haitian politics—not just the farmer on his little plot of land, but the village houngan and the princely provincial bishop and the progressive Catholic priest; the local sheriff and the gentleman farmer and the former Tonton Macoute with his rifle tucked away beneath his bed; the market woman with her overpacked burro and the coffee trader and his son; the sublieutenant and the foreign development workers in Gonaïves, Jean-Rabel, Verrettes. Not always, but often, their actions filter down to Port-au-Prince, and affect what happens there. If the provincial towns and the peasantry are not involved, nothing really changes in Haiti. Of course, a new general may become President in Port-au-Prince or a new political party may take to the streets, but real change comes only when the peasantry participates. Thus, the most important events in Haitian history have been preceded by organization and unrest in the provinces and on the mountainsides: the Revolution of 1791–1804, the end of the U.S. occupation in 1934; the fall of Jean-Claude Duvalier in 1986 and the subsequent popular movements.

In the spring and early summer of 1987, peasant organizations like the one that was later attacked at Jean-Rabel were strong. They were watching the march toward elections down in Port-au-Prince, and wondering whether those elections would be worth participating in. Presidential and senatorial candidates were traveling from village to village on flatbed trucks, with their bodyguards and megaphones, trying to convince the peasantry. Instead of talking about human rights and relations with the United States, as they did in Port-au-Prince, they had to talk about pig repopulation, contraband rice, and land reform. Meanwhile, all the candidates were courting the masters of voodoo. Some provincial houngans were powerful enough to throw the votes of two or three thousand people a candidate's way.

The Port-au-Prince politicians had to enter into another universe when they left the city, and so did I.

We finished our coffee at the Three Roses Bar opposite the coffin makers on the main road in Gonaïves. Night was beginning to fall, heavy and dark. Two men in white tee shirts played a violent game of dominoes under the Three Roses' fluorescent light. The hammering of the coffin makers and the rapid clicking of the dominoes hurt my head. Philippe, a friend of mine, a Haitian journalist, was worried about my headache.

"Sometimes," he said, "it's the coffee."

I thought it was the storm, a storm that kept pressing down on us all day from behind the mountains, but never came. The towering clouds distorted the sharp blue light over the mountains, naked and aging in the sun, till it felt as if there were blue light piercing the backs of my eyes, and the wind came flying down from the interior over the tops of the rickety houses like a loup-garou. Only when the sun began to set did the clouds lift.

After dark, the dignified, slow-moving Senatorial Candidate took Philippe and me around town. We stopped at a friend's house. In the yard, a group of men were sitting in a circle, talking about money. In the middle, a table with a tray of ice on it and a bottle of scotch and plastic glasses. The light came from inside the house.

"I was coming from Miami," said a thin man who was born in Gonaïves, but who had spent twenty years of exile in Algeria and Brooklyn before returning home a few weeks earlier to watch democracy come to his native soil.

From Miami. The locals who had endured Duvalier and never left looked at their former classmate with awe, and distrust. The Senatorial Candidate smiled to himself. He sensed that boasting was sure to follow this introduction. He himself had lived in New York and Montreal. He poured another scotch and raised his glass in Philippe's direction. Scotch cures headaches, Philippe told me.

"I was coming in from Miami," said the thin man, putting his drink on the ground and his hands on his knees. "I had thirteen thousand dollars in my wallet in my back pocket. After all, I am an accountant." The others nodded, depressed by the mere mention of such an august sum.

"Well, you know what the airport is, the scene near the baggage drop, and then outside, all the taxi men and guides?"

A few of those gathered nodded. Not everyone had seen the airport in Port-au-Prince. The accountant knew this.

"My daughter-in-law was picking me up, and we hadn't gone half a mile beyond the Texaco station when I realized that my wallet was gone." The faces in the circle grew cheerful. The accountant had had the money, but now he had lost it. Their jealousy abated, though they still disapproved of his boasting. The accountant picked up his scotch and drank it down. "Ruin. I was ruined. Ruined. My first day back. Thirteen thousand dollars. Ruin and ruination."

One man near me turned to another and said, "But how can you fit thirteen thousand dollars into a wallet?" He sat back, pleased. He felt he had gotten to the false heart of the accountant's boast.

"That's a lot of dollars," the other man agreed.

The rest of the group began to consider the question.

"Well, what if they were tens, or twenties?" said a plump landowner.

"That's thirteen hundred bills there, or at least six hundred fifty," said another man. "Too many to fit in a wallet. And to put in his back pocket? His ass must have looked like a sow's."

Everyone laughed. Except the accountant. He stood. His pride was wounded.

"Perhaps you all think that a twenty-dollar bill is the biggest kind you can get," he said. "Maybe that's the most money any of you has ever seen. Well, that's your problem. Dollars come in hundreds, and five hundreds and thousands. I had thousands, thank you. Thirteen thousand-dollar bills."

They regarded him incredulously. Someone sent a servant girl out into the night for more ice.

"A thousand-dollar bill," continued the accountant, leaning over and refilling his glass. "For most of you, that's like a crazy vision, a lie. It's impossible, right? A thousand-dollar bill. You've never seen it? It must be a lie. That's how you think: if you've never seen it, it doesn't exist. There are plenty of things you've never seen. The people of Gonaïves, my God. Where do you think you're living? This is Haiti, my friends, Gonaïves is a place no white man has ever heard of. You are nowhere.

"Oh-oh, you say to yourselves. He's a big talker, you're thinking. Now he's poor, back in Haiti. He's poor like us. He wants to find some excuse, he tells us he lost it all because some Haitian stole his thirteen thousand-dollar bills. As though he could ever have had thirteen thousand-dollar bills. Why, he's just a Haitian, you are thinking. A boasting, lying Haitian. No Haitian can have money like that, no black Haitian, no real Haitian. *Nèg sòt,* you are saying to yourselves, stupid guy, you're saying, don't deny it." He sat back down again, glaring at them.

"Thousand-dollar bills? No, thanks, *mon cher,* you say, we never heard of such a thing. The Eiffel Tower? A lie. The Empire State Building? A lie. Subways, computers, elevators, stores filled with furs and jewelry and toys? Lies. For you, it's all lies—all progress is lies. You don't want to believe it, a thousand-dollar bill. Just the idea of it makes you all sick, it makes you sick with hunger, look at you, your jealous, hungry faces. It makes me laugh.

"This suit cost three hundred fifty dollars. What do you think about that?" He stood up to show off his pinstripe suit, pirouetted, and laughed at them, their astonished faces, most of them shocked at his lack of manners.

"I bought these *shoes* fifteen years ago for fifteen dollars," replied the Senatorial Candidate, with a dry smile, pointing down at his broken black shoes. "They've served me well. What do you say to that, Thousand-Dollar Man?"

"I say you cannot have walked very far in those fifteen years, my friend," said Thousand-Dollar Man.

"*Li pale tankou dyas,*" said the man next to me. He's talking just like a man from the diaspora. The Haitians call those who went into exile under the Duvaliers the "diaspora," about a million worldwide.

"But look how far *you've* walked, my friend, in your stylish three-hundred-and-fifty-dollar suit," said the Senatorial Candidate. He took the pail of ice from the servant girl and poured short drinks for himself and the accountant. "Through Africa and the United States, all those long miles, my poor Thousand-Dollar Man." He handed the accountant his glass. "Sit down, you must be tired," he said to him. "And look where all that walking has gotten you, lucky Thousand-Dollar Man. Such a long and tiring journey, valiant accountant. Why, you've gone so far you're right back where you started from, broke and boasting in Gonaïves, the land no white man has ever heard of. Poor Gonaïves, what a fate."

The sky was white with stars now. No moon. We drove along down a dirt road away from Route Nationale, between fences made of the thick cactus that grows with its spiny branches extended toward the sky. Candelabra, the cactus is called. It's good protection against scavenging goats. The candelabra looked like moon creatures in the white beam of our headlights, ghostly and distorted. They seemed to dance in the light each time we hit a rock or a deep hole in the road, every few seconds. The bushes were dancing, and when we stopped to consider our next turn we could hear drums, not too distant.

"You turn right at the two mapous," said the Senatorial Candidate authoritatively.

"Fine," I said, "but where are they?" Mapous are huge trees, one of the tallest species that grows in Haiti. In their branches and at their base dwell the spirits. Worshipers hang macoutes, or straw bags, in mapous, filled with offerings for Legba, the greatest of the spirits, the keeper of the gates of the gods, the master of the crossroads, commander of language, and the one who allows man to communicate with the other spirits. Papa Legba is saluted first at any voodoo ceremony. His mapous grow high and spread wide, and their roots twist up from the ground as though they were the earth's viscera. The mapou is sacred. If you are near a mapou, you are not likely to miss it. It's like the cathedral in town, the most impressive thing around. I didn't see a mapou near where we were. We were lost.

"Let's follow the drums," said the Senatorial Candidate. "That must be where it is. Anyway, I've been here before, a hundred times. I think it's off somewhere to the right."

We backed up down the ruined road we had followed, through puddles of water like lakes and around great pools of mud, until we arrived back at the crossroads where we had taken a wrong turn. This time we chose the other road, and the Senatorial Candidate said this one was better. He could hear the drums playing more loudly now, closer. I couldn't tell any difference. Soon, though, we came to a small cement bridge over what must have once been a stream, a dry bed now in spite of the week's rains, and guarding the bridge like two colossi were the mapous, their branches filling the sky. Once we crossed the little bridge, even I could hear where the drums were coming from. Right down the road. In a minute we came upon the place, Souvenance, with twenty cars and jeeps parked outside the *habitation,* the family cluster where the Eastertime Souvenance festival takes place each year.

Inside, at the entryway to the habitation, women were selling small votive candles—called *baleines,* or whales, after the whale fat from which they used to be made—fried pork, and clairin, the almost hallucinogenic raw rum favored by Haitian peasants. Some reddish bulbs were burning, but mostly, the habitation was lit with baleines and charcoal fires for the *fritay,* or fried foods. I wondered where the electricity came from, way out here. Baleines burned in the candelabra, on the women's stands, in the trees, on the hoods of cars parked inside. Hundreds of people had gathered, most of them hanging out and talking under the trees and outside the houses of the habitation. Many of them were from the habitation, either they lived there or in the vicinity or their parents or grandparents or ancestors had been born there, and they had come up from Port-au-Prince for the week.

Souvenance is an important festival, it attracts *notables.* I recognized Aboudja, the huge voodoo drummer who lives in town, Compère Filo, a Port-au-Prince radio announcer, and Gérard Pierre-Charles, a Haitian historian. Aboudja was showing a crowd of young boys how to vary a certain beat on the big voodoo drum, and Filo was lying on the ground while girls from the habitation braided his hair. Pierre-Charles watched the dancing, leaning on his cane. The Senatorial Candidate made the rounds. Everyone knew him.

"Souvenance is the most democratic of the voodoo festivals," the Senatorial Candidate told me. "It's the closest to African ritual, but also the most 'advanced,' as your people would say." In Souvenance, he told me, the houngan is not called a houngan, but a *serviteur,* a distinction that implies that the leader of the habitation is not above his people, but one of them. But the Senatorial Candidate agreed that the festival's location was at the heart of an area where Haiti's black-magic secret societies predominate. "Souvenance," he said, "is not touched by them. This is because of Bienaimé's power." Bienaimé is the serviteur of Souvenance.

What the Senatorial Candidate did not tell me was that François Duvalier had reportedly been a member of the Souvenance habitation, and that one of his Macoute chieftains, Zacharie Delva, was once as powerful among the worshipers here as Bienaimé is today. Delva, probably an official of one of the local secret societies, was feared throughout the Haitian countryside, although friends and acquaintances knew him as a lonely bachelor who loved to invite them over and cook for them, a rare ability among Haitian men. Under Dr. Duvalier, Delva used to take his big black car with its mad siren on tours of the provinces, sowing horror and rumor wherever he went. According to Bernard Diederich and Al Burt in their book *Papa Doc and the Tonton Macoutes,* it was said that in order to make a point in backwoods villages Delva was not above sacrificing infants. In the early 1960s, Delva and his people got rid of the Bishop of Gonaïves, a Frenchman named Jean-Marie-Paul Robert, by arousing the populace against him. Robert fled to Port-au-Prince and was expelled by Papa Doc in 1962. Soon after making his local rule complete, Delva led a ceremony on the steps of the cathedral of Gonaïves, in which pigs were sacrificed to the spirits. Souvenance has a more complicated history than most of its followers would like to let on. But one thing is certain: the habitation rides the crest of the current political mood. In the spring and summer of 1987, the mood was democratic. Souvenance was democratic that year.

Like most voodoo, the ritual and celebration at Souvenance is wild but unthreatening, pleasant, expressive, open. Voodoo—*vaudou* or *vodoun* in its French orthographies—is in general hardly what it has been made out to be in most Western writing: writhing savages in mad orgies killing animals and children in a collective burst of blood sacrifice to their cruel and pagan gods. No white man knows, for example, whether the stories of Delva's infant sacrifice—and other stories like them—are true. For the most part, what you see of voodoo consists of drums and dancing and possession by the spirits. There is frequent animal sacrifice, and certainly the dancing used to look like writhing to Westerners until black dancing entered the white Western culture in the 1960s. Now much of the dancing looks only somewhat more exotic than a 1968 prom at an American high school. Animal sacrifice is most often of chickens, but also of goats, bulls and pigs. The great Legba, however, likes flowers, fruits and vegetables, as well as chicken.

The peristyle, or temple, at Souvenance is a large cement-block building, testimony to the wealth of the community. Most peristyles in the countryside are built of slender poles and covered over by palm or banana thatch roofs. A central pole, or *poteau mitan,* stands in the middle, down which the spirits descend like firemen from the heavens. Voodoo practices affect the spoken language in Haiti. In Creole, the word *poteau mitan* has come to mean leader, or central figure or idea. But at Souvenance there is no poteau mitan in the temple (although the central pole is symbolized by a bottle hanging from the middle of the ceiling), another metaphor for the decentralized form of voodoo practiced there.

Over the entryway to the peristyle at Souvenance is written "Mystique" in blue and red letters, and a five-pointed star sits above this. The five-pointed star is not just any star, not a meaningless design.

It started with the letter *A*, for Africa. If you cross the *A* with a line that exceeds the margins of the inverted *V*, and then connect all the lines, you'll get a five-pointed star. The star is the symbol of Africa, or Guinée, as *vaudouisants* call their continent of origin: Guinea. The five-pointed star is also a Masonic symbol, one that is used by voodoo's secret societies.

A huge dance is taking place inside the peristyle, about three hundred people, all of them dancing solo. Many of the young men carry tape machines over their heads to record Aboudja's drumming. The dancers' feet stir up dust from the dirt floor. The Senatorial Candidate looks in on the crowd for a few minutes, shakes hands with some political cronies from Port-au-Prince, and leaves to talk to friends outside. He's not too interested in dancing—after all, he has politics to attend to. And he likes to talk. It's hard to talk with the drumming.

While the young people dance, most of the older ones sit around on a ledge that encircles the peristyle, gossiping directly into their neighbor's ear. Blue-and-red banners hang from the ceiling, and the whole place is illuminated with naked light bulbs. Tonight is a *bamboche,* a party, not a ceremony. Troupes of young girls affiliated with the temple sing songs to Aboudja's drumming, dancing together in a crowd of white dresses, pushing back the young men, flirting, and then receding again to where Aboudja is playing with two other drummers.

Aboudja is a big man with knotty hair and a big beard, wearing shorts and a tropical shirt that is spread open over his vast, powerful chest. The thighs between which he holds the drum steady are like mapou trunks. Every few beats, he lets go of the drum and almost leaps onto it from above, pounding with the flat of his broad palms. The whole peristyle shakes. When Aboudja plays the big drum, its vibrations are as loud as the amplified bass at a rock concert, but there is no amplification here, only huge human energy. The girls in white dresses bounce off the ground each time Aboudja hits that hard beat. The drumming comes up from the floor, up through the soles of your feet, and goes right up your spine to your head. It dislodges whatever else was on your mind, and you can see how it helps people to get possessed. In fact, if the drumming isn't good, the spirits will not come down the poteau mitan to possess their worshipers, or, in Creole, to *monte chwal-yo,* to mount their horses. If the drumming is no good, there will be no possession. The drums call the gods, and the rhythm must please them. A drummer whose playing is off is the subject of derision at voodoo ceremonies, and if his streak of bad playing lasts too long and no spirits come, he will be replaced by someone whose drumming may be more acceptable to the gods. *Li bat tambou* (literally, he plays the drums) loosely means he worships the spirits. Aboudja is a good drummer. If you were a spirit, you'd arrive the minute he started to play. His sweat waters the ground.

At eleven sharp, a clear, high noise pierces the peristyle, like a policeman's whistle. The drumming stops. Bienaimé enters the temple, an old man, older than the Senatorial Candidate, tall and thin, rigid, straight-backed. A beautiful old face, cheekbones high with cavernous cheeks beneath them, and no expression. The dancers, exhilarated, part to make way for the old man. He is wearing a red shirt and blue jeans, new ones, another mark of Souvenance's prosperity. Bienaimé greets the older guests with a long handshake, but no words. He looks each one in the eye, but he doesn't seem to see anything. The latest gossip is that Bienaimé has a new girlfriend, seventeen years old. And she is satisfied, Philippe tells me, looking at Bienaimé and nodding. Bienaimé's initiates, or *hounsis,* follow him, carrying calabashes filled with rice and beans. A man who is Bienaimé's *houngenikon,* or chief hounsi and choirmaster, holds a long whip in his right hand and a whistle in his mouth. He brings up the rear.

A hounsi spreads a white sheet on the ground and places calabashes around its edges. Others put down long mounds of grilled peanuts, called *pistaches,* and popcorn. When they are finished setting the "table," the houngenikon goes to the peristyle's entryway and blows his whistle. Suddenly, a flood of children rushes into the temple, screaming with excitement. Each one holds a small hollowed-out gourd. The houngenikon, standing by the table, smacks the ground with his whip to stop the children from grabbing the food. The adults watch the chaos good-naturedly. Bienaimé stares off into space. When the whip comes down, everyone jumps except Bienaimé.

The kids gather around the table, screaming and hitting one another, jockeying for a good place. The hounsis protect the food against this crowd with their bodies. Bienaimé moves through the children, not noticing how much more difficult his passage is among them than it was among the adults. He glides up to the table, and bends, lifts a calabash of rice and beans and holds it out in front of him. The houngenikon scoops out a portion with a smaller gourd and fills a boy's bowl with it. The child scampers into a corner with his food. There is no line, and fighting erupts regularly among the children as the food distribution continues. They are all over the place. They seem ravenous, waiting for the handout, but when they get their food they eat a scoop, and then after a hundred or so have been served they begin a wild food fight.

Never before have I seen Haitians waste food, except for the people in Pétionville. In Port-au-Prince, the boys from Aristide's church hide from one another when they've managed to get their hands on something good to eat. Schoolchildren lucky enough to attend schools where lunch is given out crouch facing the wall to protect their rice, beans and milk while they eat. Not here, though, not tonight. Maybe these children have already had dinner. If that's so, it's odd. Haitian parents don't feed their children when they know a free meal is on its way. They can't afford to throw away the money. No one has money to waste in the Haitian countryside. But Souvenance is different, as the Senatorial Candidate has told me over and over. More advanced, he says. Maybe it's just richer.

Sometimes Bienaimé nods in the direction of a particularly noisy racket, and the houngenikon flicks at those kids with his whip. But no one tries seriously to stop the fighting. The air is filled with flying clumps of rice and beans. Only one young man out of all the hundreds of children and adults in the peristyle tries to pick up the bits of food that hit the floor in the fighting. He is in rags and has a disease that has brought out small bumps and discolorations all over his face and chest, maybe AIDS. A bunch of boys, turning from one side of the fight to the other, notice this boy scooping up the tossed food from the floor and eating it. Their faces register disgust. They descend on him, opening his fist and emptying its pathetic contents. He stoops to try to pick up the filthy stuff again, but the boys push him and shove him, edging him toward the exit. They kick him right out of the peristyle, pushing him down the steps, all the while shouting insults at him and warning him not to try coming back.

"Li se yon san manman," one boy tells me. At first I translate this literally: he doesn't have a mother. That makes sense, he was acting like a person who had no one to care for him. Later, the Senatorial Candidate corrects my Creole. He tells me that *san manman* means a vagabond, someone with no respect for anything or anyone, a brigand, a person capable of any transgression. He explains its derivation: someone without a mother has no reason to

respect rules and customs, because in breaking them he will shame no one. People use the word to mean outlaw.

In spite of the drums that chased everything else out of my brain, my headache was still with me, and the crowded place aggravated the pain. I had to get out of the sweaty peristyle. I pushed through the dancers. On the steps, a girl going in pinched my arm and laughed. She ran inside and disappeared among the crowd. Out in the open, the cool of midnight washed over me. Young men and women were standing around in groups, chatting and touching each other in polite flirtation, as though they were at a church social. I looked for Philippe and the Senatorial Candidate, but they seemed to have disappeared. The market women were dozing amid their wares. Filo, finished with his taping for tomorrow's broadcast on Souvenance, was once again reclining among the women at the foot of the habitation's central tree, a huge tamarind, a tree in which the warrior god Ogoun dwells. You could hear Aboudja's loud drumming coming from the temple. Two of the girls who sat next to Filo were singing a song to the drummer's rhythms, a song they had made up about voodoo and women, women's strength in voodoo, women in the new Haiti. They stroked Filo's bare chest as they sang, and wound his long, Rasta-style hair around their fingers. Finally, Filo arose from his half-slumber to add their song to his tape.

A steady, whirring noise that I hadn't noticed before was coming from behind one of the houses, a pink house with *vèvè* painted on it, the delicate designs of the gods. Back behind the house I came upon a big white *delco*, Creole for "generator" because Delco is the brand name of the first generators that were imported into Haiti. It was Bienaimé's delco, making light for the peristyle and the night-time market. In front of a nearby house, I found the Senatorial Candidate. He and Philippe and a group of returned exiles were talking politics and drinking clairin. How could those two drink clairin after all the scotch? But when they offered me a sip, I accepted. My headache left me. I listened to them. A Haitian woman who was getting her master's degree at New York University was talking about Marxism and tribalism.

I left the group and lay down across the hood of a white car parked next to them. Up in the dome of the black Haitian sky, the white stars were shining. They had moved a long way since I had looked up at them a few hours before on the road to Souvenance. The Big Dipper was all the way on the other side of the sky, hanging down over the peristyle where Aboudja was drumming. Like a seductive

veil, the leaves of Ogoun's tamarind trembled delicately over the face
of the heavens. Long after Filo had finished taping, the girls were
still singing their song, and I heard the NYU woman's voice, talking
on and on, in her native Creole.

"It's possible to arrive at a socialist state with a tribal base," she
said. *"Vaudou, strikti vaudou-yo, yo tribal, wi, men yo kolektif tou."*
Voodoo, the structures of voodoo, they're tribal, it's true, but they
are also collective. The Senatorial Candidate's low voice whispered
agreement, and I heard the clairin go around again. The opening
and closing of the bottle, the liquid pouring, the sound of plastic
glasses being passed. The stinging sweet smell of the clairin reached
me, a few yards away. The delco was whirring. I looked up at the
stars with the clairin still dancing in my head, and felt Aboudja's
drums coming up through the hood of the car, up through its tires,
reverberating along the axles, making the metal tremble, sending
tremors across my back and then up into my head through the spine.
The stars were as watchful as I was, looking down on us at Souvenance. Ogoun's leaves responded to the rhythm.

If voodoo were always practiced the way it was at Souvenance
tonight, with drums and food and talk, perhaps some valid social
system could be translated, as the woman was saying, into voodoo.
Voodoo, after all, had played some part in the slave revolution;
perhaps it could adopt a similar role in contemporary Haiti. But I
had also seen villages where voodoo simply upheld whatever system
was in place, and, even in the smallest villages, that was usually a
system of gross exploitation, with the houngan often leading the
way. Papa Doc's voodoo did not leave much room for socialism,
either. For the moment, Aboudja's drums made such political debate
irrelevant. How could Marxism or any other philosophy matter in a
country where drums could do so much? I let Aboudja take control,
and, like the candelabra along the road, the stars too began to dance.

Dieumerci lives about five miles down a dirt path from the Bassin
St.-Jacques in the Plaine-du-Nord. The bassin is a large mud pond,
sacred in voodoo. Dieumerci's *jadin,* Creole for "garden" or "farm,"
is a little patch separated from his neighbor's by a row of candelabra.
He has corn growing there, beans, manioc. The corn has been sparse
for the past few years, it never rains, Dieumerci tells me, and the
earth is used up. Not too many beans come up, either. Dieumerci
walked to the bassin in the Plaine-du-Nord this year with his wife,

who is a *dòktè-fèy,* or leaf doctor, and their four children. Every day, he tells me, he tends his small farm, and his wife walks five or ten miles, depending on the rains, to the nearest water source, and sometimes the children go with her, but more often they sit in back of the shack and watch the two chickens.

Now Dieumerci has only chickens and some beans. Before, he had two black pigs, not fat, but worth some money, and the sow was ready to have her litter. But a man came from town and took the pigs away; he told Dieumerci that it was a government program. He promised that he would pay Dieumerci for the pigs, or bring him another, new kind of pig, an American pig. This was five or six years ago, Dieumerci says. The man who took away Dieumerci's pig was working for the Haitian government, which at the request of the United States and other governments in the region wiped out the native pig population by 1983 because there had been reports of an outbreak of African swine fever, and the Americans were afraid the disease would spread to U.S. herds. Dieumerci says the government never paid him for his pigs the way the man promised.

He seems to think that maybe I will be able to pay him back—I am an American, after all. He looks hopeful. He can't afford to buy a new pig, he tells me, because the big white American pigs that he could get at Cap-Haïtien cost too much, they eat too much, they eat fancy feed, not garbage and mango skins like the little Haitian pigs, they need lots of water, and who has lots of water? And then you'd have to find a sty to house them in, because the American pigs aren't used to Haitian soil, Dieumerci says. They get sick. They die, and you've wasted all your money. His neighbor was smart, he hid a couple of his pigs when the man came with the big truck, and now his neighbor is richer than anyone else in Dieumerci's little village. Dieumerci had to cut down all the trees in his field last year to sell to the charcoal makers and put the kind of cash into his pocket that he would have gotten from selling piglets. But it still wasn't enough cash.

Dieumerci comes every year with his family to the Plaine-du-Nord, to the big voodoo festival there. He doesn't go in much for the ceremonies, though. Last year a Protestant pastor in the village recruited Dieumerci into his congregation, and Dieumerci hopes that the Protestant god will do better by him than the spirits have done. There are white people, missionaries, at the Protestant church in Dieumerci's village, and he thinks maybe their familiarity with the Protestant god will help him get enough money to buy a white

American piglet—fifty dollars. He tells me he's going to wait for two years, and if his luck gets better he'll stay with the Protestants, otherwise he's going back to the spirits.

Dieumerci's wife looks at him scornfully as he tells me about the Protestants. His "conversion" has caused many fights between them, she says. She blames it for the family's most recent string of bad luck, the little boy's fever, the hen that won't lay, a bad bean crop. She and Dieumerci fight all the time now. She's got a chicken under her arm, somehow she managed to get together some money, she says, and bought a chicken to be sacrificed at the Plaine-du-Nord. She hopes that the gift will placate the spirits, but she's not optimistic. She can tell that they are very angry with her husband. Even her most reliable cures won't work on her son's fever.

This is the feast of Saint Jacques (Saint James) for Catholics, but of Ogoun Feraille, god of war, for vaudouisants. The voodoo worshipers call Saint Jacques Ogoun, they call Ogoun Saint Jacques; after two centuries of hiding African beliefs behind Catholic ritual, certain saints and Christian figures have come to stand for specific voodoo spirits. Ogoun is a rough-talking spirit, a soldier who wears pinned-on epaulets, loves clairin, fire and knives. He lives in the Bassin St.-Jacques, a large mud hole, and comes out frequently to possess the faithful during his week-long feast, attended by thousands.

The mood at the Plaine-du-Nord is dark, darker than at Souvenance. Perhaps this has to do with the poverty of the worshippers, most of them poor peasants from the plain who have little connection with cities and city people, neither those in Cap-Haïtien to the north nor those in Gonaïves or Port-au-Prince to the south. These people know voodoo. They know farming. They know about market prices. They know history, some, but it's more hearsay than history. The blacks in Haiti came from Africa, this they know, they came from La Guinée, or, in Creole, *nan ginen*. In voodoo, death means a return to *ginen*, a return to Africa. They know that the ancestors were slaves, that they had a revolution. They know the name of Dessalines, and his story. Dessalines is their hero. After Dessalines the white masters left, now there are only Protestants. There is a place called Miami, a place called New York. Far away. There is money there. Someone's son once went to a place called Montreal, now he sends back money. In Port-au-Prince there are no jobs, but still you have a chance there. Here you have no chance.

That is what they know about the larger world, unless someone in the village has a radio. Then they know that Jean-Claude left, and they have heard about the Dechoukaj. They know that the Tontons Macoute are out of power, but they aren't sure how to interpret that fact. Does that mean that they should no longer obey the houngan? After all, they know he was a Macoute. Does it mean that the chef de section need no longer be obeyed? He was appointed by Jean-Claude, they remember. Now Jean-Claude lives in another country far away, with the French and his mulatto wife. Jean-Claude is gone. Do the peasants still need to obey the houngan? *Houngan Macoute*.

The houngan was a Macoute. This is true all over Haiti. François Duvalier was a genius at incorporating the structures of voodoo into the structures of his rural secret police. Once firmly ensconced in the palace, he called in houngans and *bokors,* or sorcerers, from all over the country. He paid for the little houngans from places like Bombardopolis in the Northwest province to come into Port-au-Prince, where he granted them an audience, convinced them that he was the Immaterial Being, the highest houngan, conscripted them into his vast spying network and conferred on them the privileges of the Tontons Macoute. Not all houngans fell prey to this ruse, of course. For those who were openly recalcitrant, Papa Doc had a solution. He closed their temples. Others pretended to accede, and then went about their business as usual. But Papa Doc scared them all, no doubt. He feigned closeness to black magic, and perhaps he really was a sorcerer, or fancied himself one. No one knows.

What people do know is that after his son fled Haiti, a virtual voodoo witch-hunt began. Houngans and *mambos* (priestesses) who had been Macoutes—and some who had not—were hunted down and killed. As many as a hundred may have died, and some less than disinterested reports go as high as five hundred. The voices and shelters of the spirits, drums and temples, were burned. But the people were selective in this dechoukaj. Just as they spared certain Macoutes who in that role had protected the community from Duvalier's wrath, they usually went after only the most notorious macoutes houngan. Protestant missionaries joined only too gladly in the attacks, which, spurred on by them, occasionally turned into small pogroms.

Toward the end of February 1986, just after Jean-Claude had left for France, a delegation of militant Protestants, led by an American, came to Father Kerveillant, the Catholic priest at the Plaine-du-Nord, another white man, and told him that they wanted to plug up Ogoun's mud hole before the festival began. With cement. "Strike while the iron is hot," they told him. "All over the country it is being done. This is our chance to rid ourselves and this country of this pestilence," they said. "This is the chance for progress to come to Haiti. Please support us."

"It was a good idea, I told them," says Father Kerveillant. "But it wasn't done soon enough. Either they had to do it immediately, before the people could suspect what was going on, or they had to wait longer, for the people to be psychologically prepared." As it happened, the people were not psychologically prepared for the destruction of one of Haitian voodoo's most sacred sites, and they turned out in force, armed with machetes and cocomacaques, hard peasant walking sticks, to rout the descending Christians. The battle went unwaged, the Christians retreated with their cement, and the hole remained unplugged, a source of unending irritation to the Protestants, whose leader refuses to talk about the failed attempt.

Although he consciously corrupted voodoo for his own aims, François Duvalier also performed a sort of service for the religion. By publicly granting it his allegiance, devotion and protection, and at the same time publicly scorning the Catholic Church, Duvalier removed voodoo from the arena of legitimate religious persecution. He himself was rumored to be a houngan or bokor, and to practice voodoo within the walls of the palace, but more sophisticated observers, who had watched Duvalier's rise to power, understood that he encouraged such rumors because they strengthened his political power with the people: the rumors about his conversations with the heads of his executed enemies, about blood rites, about sacrifices on the palace grounds worked in the people's imagination to transform Duvalier into a figure of awesome power, a magic terror who could be propitiated only by utter obedience. Duvalier was raised a Catholic; he knew voodoo mostly from his ethnological studies and his work as a simple country doctor. But he knew it well enough to make use of it. Perhaps Dr. Duvalier sometimes felt the power of voodoo in his gut; most Haitians do. More important, he understood the religion well on an intellectual level, could manipulate its imagery, was aware of its force, its potential uses.

It was hard to attack voodoo under Papa Doc; you never knew whether you might be attacking one of the President's men. By recruiting the rural secret police from among the voodoo network already in place, Duvalier effectively put an end to the hideous excesses of centuries of Catholic Church persecution of the voodoo faithful, an inquisition in many eras—including that of the U.S. occupation—almost as vicious and violent as the campaigns against heretics that Europe had known. In a sense, Dr. Duvalier turned the inquisition back against the Church, expelling scores of priests, often on the least grounds—for instance in 1962, when he expelled seven for refusing to include him in their public prayers.

He was slowly ridding himself of the foreign clergy, the French, the Belgians, the Jesuits. In the Church as in every other institution, Dr. Duvalier wanted control. He wanted a clergy that would do his bidding. Publicly he said that he was merely trying to replace the seditious foreigners in the clergy with patriotic Haitians. In fact he was eliminating his opposition. When the hierarchy complained, Duvalier did not hesitate to expel even the Bishop of Gonaïves. After a tussle with the Vatican, Duvalier replaced such men with Haitians, some of whom became his lackeys. A few of these are still on the scene, and still loyal to the memory of their patron.

By the time Dr. Duvalier's reign was in full swing, the Church in Haiti had enough on its hands protecting itself from Papa Doc and his people without going after the heathens. Dr. Duvalier had given voodoo an arm with which to defend itself from the Catholics. Unfortunately for voodoo, that arm was the apparatus of the Tontons Macoute.

The history of the persecution of voodoo in Haiti is a long one, beginning back in the days of the French colony, when slaves were first imported in large numbers. The French feared voodoo, and the famous 1791 voodoo ceremony at Bois-Cayman where the slave revolt began had proved that their fears were justified. When independence was won thirteen years later, Dessalines was fully aware of voodoo's continuing potential for subversion. (Probably without exception, all leaders of the revolution had firsthand knowledge of voodoo. Indeed, one legend has it that Toussaint himself, a former stableboy at the Bréda plantation in the Plaine-du-Nord, was present at the ceremony at Bois-Cayman.) Once in power, Dessalines calculatedly executed a number of voodoo leaders "as rebels against the new order," writes the distinguished Haitian historian Laënnec Hurbon in *Le Barbare imaginaire*. The new leader, soon to be crowned Jacques I, feared the reestablishment of voodoo power structures by the newly freed slaves, and was particularly perturbed by the continued attempts by Maroon chieftains to organize the peasants of the countryside. In order, writes Hurbon, to force the former slaves to continue working on the big plantations that he had handed over to generals in the Haitian Army, and to prevent further *marronage* (flight from the plantations), Dessalines began by executing voodoo chieftains, and then went further, proscribing voodoo practice altogether.

Along with the Catholic Church, Haitian political leaders continually accused rebels against the regime of cannibalism, the same accusations that had been mouthed by the French planters and all white visitors to Haiti during the slave uprisings. During a popular revolt in Jacmel in 1843, Hurbon writes, beggars with macoutes over their backs went through the town, recruiting the poor to the cause. Newspapers written by and targeted at the ruling mulatto elite said that these beggars were voodoo worshipers who carried human flesh in their sacks. Peasant leaders too were reported to be man-eaters. Yet along with the bands that fought them, Haitian leaders from Henry Christophe down through Duvalier have almost uniformly relied on some kind of voodoo adviser. The power of the spirits, especially their capacity for evil, is simply too strong to be ignored. Every one of these leaders knew that voodoo was a mighty political tool, but almost every one also believed in the spirits on some level, and wanted to be sure of his capacity to fight back against any magic his enemies might employ.

In other words, Hurbon continues,

> tolerance of voodoo was necessary to the general functioning of Haitian society, but its penalization, no less. Is this a contradiction? It seems rather that the outlawing of voodoo had a double objective: to deliver the country from networks of power uncontrollable by the political machinery, and to reduce to a state of outlawry the most exploited social groups: the slum-dwellers in the cities [most of whom had recently migrated from the provinces] and the peasants of the countryside. Merely by their position, one might say, these two groups bore the marks of sorcery. Sorcery of the poor versus sorcery of the powerful? In any case, at the time of the struggle for independence, sorcery was considered a part of a legitimate revolt; by the nineteenth century, this revolt having become illegitimate, nothing remained but outlaws.

. . .

In reaction to laws proscribing African ritual, such as the ordinance of 1704, which tried to forbid slaves from gathering together at night for dances, the slaves in Haiti soon began calling their own spirits by the names of the Catholic saints. They were trying to hide their African worship behind the mask of Christianity. Ogoun Feraille became Saint Jacques, Erzulie became the Virgin Mary. The voodoo priests among the slaves often learned pieces of the Catholic liturgy, and interspersed them among their African chants. This mixture of two differing systems of belief is called "syncretism" by theologians.

As generations passed in Haiti, the people became accustomed to the French as well as the African names for their gods, and accepted the saints into African rituals in much the same way they took French into their African languages and came up with Creole. As Maya Deren points out in *Divine Horsemen: The Living Gods of Haiti,*

> Voudoun would not have come into existence, nor would it still be flourishing so vigorously, if it had been governed by men rigidly dedicated to superficial sectarian distinctions. . . . Where at first, it might seem that Christianity had triumphed over Voudoun, it becomes clear, on closer study, that Voudoun has merely been receptive to compatible elements from a sister faith and has integrated these into its basic structure, subtly transfiguring and adjusting their meaning, where necessary, to the African tradition. The cross, for example, has been assimilated to the crossroads. Baptism was already a Negro tradition. The triple libation for "les Mysteres, les Morts et les Marassa" [the Spirits, the Ancestors, and the Twins], is applied to the Father, Son and Holy Ghost. . . . Against the serviteur who sincerely insists that he believes in the Trinity, who baptizes his children and his drums, places the saints on his private altar, and makes lavish use of the sign of the cross, the Catholic Church has been, in a sense, helpless. A religious system that opposed Catholicism would have been overcome. But in the face of such tolerance, the violent efforts to eradicate Voudoun have remained relatively ineffective.

Voodoo, in other words, is not an African religion; rather, it is a specific combination of Roman Catholic and African belief. As a religion, it has its roots in the peculiar cultural clashes that slavery brought about: you can find similar religions in Cuba and Brazil, and elsewhere in the Americas where African slavery was practiced. Voodoo is a slave religion, much as Creole is a slave language.

On the way out of Port-au-Prince, a small bridge built with U.S. aid marks the end of the city. Then you are in the neighborhood of Croix-des-Missions. There is voodoo in Croix-des-Missions, along with the big Catholic church and a number of smaller, Protestant missions. If you turn left just after passing over the dry riverbed beneath the bridge, just past the modern church with its slanting cross, you find yourself in a clearing surrounded by thatched huts— this is ten or fifteen minutes from the American Embassy and the Holiday Inn. You park the car and go into a house where you know they sell rum, even at seven in the morning. A bottle costs less than three dollars. This is your offering. A woman comes up to you, stepping around the chickens in the yard. She looks at your face to see what you want, a white person in her courtyard. Gangan Pierre, you say. She nods, and guides you to one of the small, mud-baked houses. There are two rooms in the house, separated by a hanging sheet. You are in the pink room; the other one is green. The woman seats you on an old wooden box and turns on the Panasonic radio, which as usual is playing merengue from the Dominican Republic. The walls in the pink room are covered with small, scrupulously detailed, obsessive paintings of voodoo spirits and ceremonies. Damballah the snake god and god of the universe, in his bejeweled throne. A citizen's spirit marriage to Erzulie Freda, goddess of love, wearing white lace, and white lace shoes. The turbulent blue sea in the rain, ridden by Agwe, god of the waters. Ogoun Feraille, god of war, astride the earth. Half a painting is waiting for completion on the artist's easel, another wedding to Erzulie, but the groom is unfinished.

When he peers around the sheet, you think he is an ancient. A slender rod of a human inside a shirt and pants, always (you discover later) the same shirt and pants. His hair is gray and black, and when he smiles hello there are few teeth. He approves of the rum, takes it from you. It is not his first rum of the day. He opens it and goes to the doorway, a slender silhouette in the hot early morning sun. He pours the rum out four times in the doorway, carefully, to the points of the compass, just enough to welcome and appease the spirits, before he takes a long pull himself and offers it to you. He settles into his chair in front of the easel and picks up his palette. Another swill of the rum, careful replacing of the cap, and he begins to paint. Brilliant reds and greens come from a palette that looks only brown. He taps his big toe to the rhythms of his speech.

"Religions are things created by man," he says, over his shoulder. He drinks more rum and begins to sing in *langage,* the ritual language of voodoo, an eerie sound, so close to Creole and French and Church Latin that you almost think you can understand it, like a foreign language in a dream. Langage is the special domain of voodoo priests, which is what André Pierre is, a *gangan,* or houngan, as well as an artist who sells his paintings to foreign collectors for thousands of dollars.

"Voodoo is the culture of my country," he says when he lapses back into Creole. "Why do they hate voodoo? Because it is with the help of this culture that we have won our battles of liberation. All of these priests, these pastors, they practice voodoo and preach that it is diabolical. Meanwhile, the faithful become poorer, they give all their little money to the pastor, and the pastor becomes rich. That is how the murderers of voodoo work. That is their method. Do you understand it? But though they may get rich, they will never destroy my culture. You cannot buy belief, though you may be fooled into thinking you have bought it. My culture cannot be defeated. The Spanish could not destroy it, Napoleon could not destroy it, Rome could not destroy it, the Americans could not destroy it, Dr. Duvalier could not destroy it, the Dechoukaj could not destroy it. No one will ever destroy it. Voodoo will survive. It will survive the guns of persecution. It will survive because it is good, and true." He shifts in his seat and begins to sing in langage. The gangan's eyes look flat, and he holds his brush in midair, half smiling as he sings.

"That is a song for Damballah." He turns and points vaguely to half a dozen paintings on the wall. "These are the spirits of voodoo. We have a king of magic, who was God, *Bondye,* who created the first magic of the world. The first magic of the world was done by God: man, who was created with the dust of the earth. The beautiful dust with spirit breathed into it. All men are magical, all men are voodoo. Voodoo is the only real religion, which respects all life. Voodoo is the religion of religions, it came before all other religions. It is the root of belief, all belief. The whole world is the work of voodoo, which will survive all religions. Voodoo is the cultural name for Haiti. Voodoo is Haiti.

"When times are good, Damballah has one foot on the land and one foot on the water. But when Damballah is angry, when the spirits are not fed, when the people have lost their way, the way of voodoo, he takes his left foot from the land and walks on water, and then the rain will fall only on the water and the land will become as dust, without spirit, while the mountains burn. The spirits will not listen to the drums. They will not come for the ceremonies. Then you will see faction set against faction, religion against religion."

Toward the end of 1811, Henry Christophe, then Emperor Henry I of the northern third of what is Haiti today, was battling with Alexandre Pétion, who ruled the south, including Port-au-Prince, for control of the country. Christophe was preparing to lay siege to the great city, and in order to accomplish that aim he bought off many voodoo priests and priestesses in the outlying areas of what was to become the capital of the nation. They fanned out across the area, according to the Haitian historian Thomas Madiou, and used voodoo ceremonies to warn the peasants there that all who opposed the will of Christophe would surely call down upon themselves the anger of the *loas,* or voodoo spirits. (In the north, Christophe, who had set up a fine court modeled on Versailles, had rigorously banned all voodoo celebrations. But he was not averse to using the religion for his own purposes when necessary.)

In the earliest days of 1812, the Virgin Mary (or the goddess Erzulie, in voodoo) suddenly appeared in the heights of a mapou in Pétion's territory. Not surprisingly, the bizarre vision was not the Virgin at all, but a spy of Christophe's, a fellow named Bosquette. After consulting with various mambos, Bosquette, a clever man, dressed himself up as a woman and, in the light of a full moon, climbed up into the mapou's highest branches, where he was then worshiped by the people, who had been alerted to the apparition by their priestesses. This apparition, connected in the minds of the peasants with priestesses loyal to Christophe, became further proof of the Emperor's ties to the saints and the loas. Christophe hoped by such means to pacify the enemy region and send his troops through without incident.

Although Christophe did not realize it, his strategy was weak: two could play at this game. When Pétion heard of the ruse, he sent the Catholic curate of Port-au-Prince, the Abbé Gaspard, up to the mapou, which had already become a sacred place frequented by pilgrims. Along with him, Gaspard brought a crowd of peasants

loyal to Pétion, whom he led in singing sacred songs at the foot of
the tree. Using tactics perfected during the Inquisition, Gaspard
told the crowd that if the tree was truly blessed and the apparition
of the Virgin legitimate, the tree itself would be invulnerable to fire,
but if the vision was false, the tree would burn. He splashed the tree
with holy water, lit a torch, and proceeded to set fire to the sacred
mapou. The mapou burned to the ground, and, according to Madiou, whose history appeared thirty-six years after the incident, "the
crowd departed, in some consternation at the sacrilege that had just
been committed, but nonetheless fairly well convinced that they had
been fooled by a false Virgin." Thereafter, the territory was securely
Pétion's.

"There is a revolutionary motor in voodoo, and the leaders of Haiti
have always known this," says Frank Etienne, a playwright, novelist,
educator and founder of the Comité pour la Défense de la Culture
Nationale. "During the Dechoukaj, some Haitians—old-fashioned
Catholics, some progressive priests, some politicians, the Protestant
missionaries and some of their flock—were arguing that voodoo
ought to be wiped out. They still called it superstition, just the way
the Catholics used to. They told me Christianity means progress,
liberation. Who wants such progress, such liberation?

"These people, they talk about poisoning, about how vaudouisants
use poison against their enemies," Etienne continues. " 'It's a crime,
poison,' they tell me. And I say, I support it. We used it against the
French, we used it against the Americans. If I must, I will take a
stand supporting poison. Because it serves a function. The Haitian
peasant has against him the notary, the justice of the peace, the chef
de section, the government employee, the surveyor, all in a complicated system of exploitation designed to strip him of what little he is
able to cultivate, what little land he owns. He has no access to
justice. The practice of sorcery is his courtroom, his justice. Poison
is his only advocate, his only weapon. I believe in the appropriate
uses of poison. I believe in voodoo. It is the soul of the Haitian
people. When you destroy voodoo, you destroy the people's souls.
And all that will remain are zombis."

Katylee came running up to me in the market at La Saline. Her hair
was done up in a white bandana, as usual, but she had something
new around her neck. It looked like a little bag with something in it.

Katylee worked as a housekeeper for the Disco Doctor in Pacot. Her baby was sick, she told me. Bad diarrhea.

"Are you boiling his water?" I asked. Haitian babies get sick and die because mothers give them infant formula that is mixed with bad water. They get gastroenteritis, with diarrhea. When their mothers see the diarrhea, they blame the sickness on water, and think they can cure the baby by giving him no more water. Eventually, these children die of dehydration.

Katylee didn't have much time to spend with her baby. She lived up in the bidonville above Pacot, where most of the people who work as domestics and gardiens in that neighborhood live. Her boyfriend was the gardien at the Disco Doctor's; he lived in a small house in the back, with his wife and three children, downstairs from the Disco Doctor's renters—the foreign anthropologists and Haitian divorcés. Chickens walked around Katylee's boyfriend's house, and around the back. The anthropologists' apartment looked out on the tops of trees that waved above the green ravine behind Katylee's boyfriend's house, full of mangoes and bright-green lizards and banana trees. The cock of the roost lived in that ravine, alongside Katylee's boyfriend's outhouse and the wide expanse where his family deposited its garbage. Sometimes, when the anthropologists looked out their window, they would see Katylee's boyfriend up in the high reaches of the mango tree, hitting down the ripe fruit with a stick.

"Yes, I always boil the water for the baby, like the doctor says," said Katylee. I knew it wasn't true. It costs too much to boil water, uses up too much charcoal if you boil it for the full fifteen minutes.

"But he's still sick?"

"Yes."

"Well, you should take him to a doctor."

"M te deja fè sa," said Katylee. I already did.

"So? What did he say?"

"He said it is the work of a loup-garou." Katylee looks at me to see how I will react. I remain serious. She has been to the houngan. "I heard the loup-garou, it came the other night, you could hear it screaming over our roof. My neighbor saw it, he says. It was burning up all red, and its hair was red from drinking blood." She is frightened by her own words.

"What does the doctor say to do?"

"He says he can help me. *Wanga sa-a, se pou gueri ti-moun mwen.*" This charm is to cure the baby. She fingers the bag hanging from her neck. "I bought it from the houngan."

"How much did he charge you for it?"

"De dola." Two dollars. *"Men li te di-m konsa, fòk nou paye-l anpil anpil pou change abitid lougawou-yo."* But he said that we would have to pay him a lot to change the habits of the loup-garou.

"What do you mean, a lot?" I asked her.

"He said a hundred dollars." Katylee twisted the wanga. "Can you help me?"

I gave her some money. Told her to buy Serom Oral, an over-the-counter cure for gastroenteritis, and to boil that water. The baby got better. I don't believe Katylee ever boiled the water.

On the reverse side of the Parol Delivrans chasuble that Father Aristide wears when he says mass, he had a seamstress from Les Cayes, where he used to be based, sew ten vèvès. They run down the left-hand side: Erzulie's is there, a heart with a crown, and Damballah's, two twisting snakes, and Ogoun Feraille's, a geometric mix of knives and flags, triangles and curlicues. On the right-hand are embroidered the vèvès of the drums.

Max Beauvoir's peristyle is out past El Caribeño, past all the clubs in Carrefour, just before Le Lambi (Creole for conch), a dance club where you can eat fresh conch brought in by the boatmen and drink Prestige beer while you watch street boys swim in the bay. Max's temple used to be like one of the clubs. In the old days, before Duvalier left, he used to hold his elaborate ceremonies there. I wanted to stop at Le Lambi before I went to Max's, but I had an appointment with Max, and Max does not take appointments lightly. I had left enough time, I thought, for one plastic cupful of spicy grilled conch, but I got stuck behind the tap-tap Chicago in the usual traffic jam that starts after El Caribeño, and the bottleneck suddenly turned the two-lane road into a four-lane road, and no one was moving. The people inside the tap-tap ahead of me peered out from beneath the swimming-tube swans that decorate its roof, men and women were stuffed in there, on top of one another. It was hot and I had the air conditioner on. When I noticed them watching me, I turned it off, and rolled down the windows. At the time it was considered politically incorrect to have air-conditioning in your car, it meant you were a rich Macoute. *"Makout!"* You could get sensitive to the charge, especially if that word was shouted at you by men carrying machetes.

Market women came up to the cars with fritay and Sekola Orange. No Pepsi. Chicago's driver was blasting "We Are the World" on his huge cassette player. I used a terry-cloth washrag I had bought in the market, made in the People's Republic of China, to wipe the sweat out of my eyes. Every ten minutes, we moved a foot or two. Finally the jam broke, a mile before Max's. I put the air-conditioning on full blast and sped by peasants walking their cattle in from the countryside.

Max's barrière is always closed. A silent gardien opens it for me. The houngan's jeep is parked inside the wide courtyard. Two big dogs, Weimaraners, patrol the tops of the building. They look down on me as I wait for Max, sitting in the shade. One of his daughters, a beautiful teenaged girl, mulatto with soft wild hair, greets me. She goes to tell her father I have arrived. She is barefoot. Ten minutes later, I hear the sound of two hand claps. His daughter reemerges to take me inside.

Max is standing behind his desk, a big man in a blue and white dashiki, heroically handsome. An IBM PC sits on the desk, and a cellular telephone. Behind Max are framed vèvès, and documents you can't really read. There is something on the wall about an ancestor who fought in the Haitian Revolution, something about the Digital Equipment Corporation, where Max used to work, "as a vice-president," he tells me, up in Massachusetts. Max is a man of the world, he has lived in Massachusetts, in New York, in Paris. He is a biochemist and a leaf doctor. He has the oily manner of a man whom you wouldn't want to leave alone with your money or your child. He claps his hands, and his daughter appears with Seven-Up on ice.

"You know they are killing us all," he tells me. The daughter leaves. "I have a list." He is referring to the attacks on voodoo worshipers that have started in the wake of Duvalier's downfall. He includes himself among the houngans who have been attacked. According to local lore, Max was one of Papa Doc's many voodoo "chaplains." He calls Papa Doc "Father Duvalier." Although he had little to do with Jean-Claude, Max was among the very few who admitted to preferring Duvalier to the new military junta, and Duvalier's justice to that of the Dechoukaj. "At least," he said a few days after Duvalier fell, "I knew what to expect of Jean-Claude. This Dechoukaj is the worst thing that has happened in the history of this country." That's saying a lot, in Haiti.

"They came here, you see, to attack me," he says. "A big crowd with machetes and stones. Why? I don't know. They had no reason.

It was the Church, the so-called 'progressive' Catholics, who sent this crowd, just a few months after the Dechoukaj began. They held my house under siege for days. It was just lucky that I have guns and men. For that time, I was a general. It is my only record of military service. I believe I acquitted myself rather well. We killed no one. Eventually, the crowd went away. That Aristide was here, too. He is jealous of my power, my property. I saw his little Charade, the white car. He is a san manman, a criminal. *Vakabon,*" Max says, using another word in Creole that is a strong insult.

As usual, there was another side of the story. After Jean-Claude Duvalier fell, Beauvoir had had to close his temple, because he was afraid of his neighbors, poor farmers and jobless shanty-dwellers who reportedly resented his bullying appropriation of the land behind his property as well as his associations with the Tontons Macoute. These people, newly empowered by the announced dissolution of the Macoutes, had soon laid siege to Max's house, hoping to recover property they thought of as their own. Like many of the battles waged in the days after Jean-Claude left, it was a land war. Aristide had had nothing to do with it. All over the country, people were trying to take back land they felt had been unfairly confiscated from them during the Duvalier dynasty. Though he warded off his neighbors' attacks, Max was appropriately nervous. He shut down the peristyle.

Max handed me a printout, a list of twenty-one voodoo priests and priestesses killed during the recent voodoo witch-hunt. Many of them, according to his report, were beaten and burned alive. He told me there were hundreds more killed by adherents of the Catholic and Protestant churches in a historic continuation of the antisuperstition campaigns of the 1800s, of the U.S. occupation and of the 1941–46 presidency of Elie Lescot. Beauvoir blamed Radio Soleil, the Catholic station, for the deaths, and said that Radio Cacique, another station, had gone so far as to tell the people to continue to "dechouke all those who had done wrong to the country, houngans as well as macoutes." In fact, Max's defense of the fallen voodoo leaders was reminiscent of his earlier defense of "the little Tontons Macoute," as he called them, who were killed in the wake of Duvalier's flight. "The junta should have officially asked the Tontons Macoute to come to the police stations and put them to trial, like Nuremberg. Instead, they left those people in the hands of the people, to be mass-murdered."

A sad assessment of the facts is this: that among the houngans and

mambos who died in the Dechoukaj, certainly many were guilty of
abusing their religious power for their own venal aims—to take the
land, women and money they desired, to imprison, torture and de-
fraud their enemies and their enemies' families—and were protected
in this criminal behavior by a criminal power structure that permitted any abuse as long as loyalty to the regime was unfailing. These
were the *houngans macoute,* and their fate was the logical outcome
of Papa Doc's successful attempt to fuse the voodoo and Tonton
Macoute networks. It is equally certain that some of those who died
were victims of a too zealous missionary clergy, who were anxious to
use the Dechoukaj to rid themselves of powerful local enemies. Some
may also have been victims of personal vendettas and feuds. During
political upheaval, many scores can be settled. Max was not happy
with the way in which the simmering hatred of the peasantry for the
rural chiefs and their voodoo accomplices was manifesting itself. He
knew his way of life was threatened.

Jean-Claude Paul was a serious man. He was built like a tank, wide
and strong, and if you got in his way he'd run you down. Unlike
other colonels in the Haitian Army, he didn't smile at girls, although
he was rumored to adore the romantic Julio Iglesias. He just grabbed
his Uzi more tightly, and walked right by you. This was the man
who reportedly ran Haiti's cocaine-transshipment business, used an
airstrip on his ranch for deliveries, worked with the explosive Me-
dellín cocaine cartel in Colombia. He also ran the Casernes Dessalines, which is located directly behind the palace, and commanded a
loyal force of about eight hundred men. He kept them very happy
and very loyal with fat cash bonuses from his own pocket, and managed to incorporate hundreds of the old Tontons Macoute into his
operation. After all, many of them had important connections, and,
even more to the point, many of them had arms. Brought into the
Army, former Tontons Macoute were called *attachés,* with typical
Haitian understatement. They carried identification cards signed by
Paul. These men with their Uzis and shotguns and pistols and revolvers could be useful, and, in the end, Colonel Paul would use
them.
    Paul's drug business expanded when the Duvaliers left. It was
understood that Ernest Bennett, Michèle Duvalier's father, had also
been involved with cocaine, and Duvalier himself had a useful airstrip on *his* ranch. When the Duvaliers left, a part of the drug

business was open to the next taker, though doubtless the old factions kept a hand in long-distance. Paul allegedly took some of the business over, though he never rivaled Bennett—with Bennett's bouquet of mulatto mistresses and his garage full of BMWs—for flash. Paul was more sensible. He believed an Uzi was a sufficient statement.

But not for him an unthinking reliance on temporal firepower. Like anyone with even a hint of superstitious belief, he wanted the spirits on his side, as well. He knew there were powerful forces at work against him, not only other men in other barracks who were jealous for a piece of the business, but, as well, the U.S. government, which decided in 1987 to target Paul as a major international drug trader. Scattered about the grounds of Paul's ranch were ritual objects that were intended to preserve him against evil.

And for a long time, Papa Paul—or Polo, as his friends call him —was well protected. But black magic, like U.S. foreign policy, is an unpredictable force. Almost always, it comes back to plague those who have used it. According to *Wall Street Journal* reports and rumors in Port-au-Prince, Paul reportedly had gone to powerful houngans to buy wangas, or charms, to protect him against enemies, but a Miami jury nonetheless indicted him on charges of conspiring to ship narcotics to the United States. And the wrath of the U.S. government was great: eventually the Americans let the Haitians know that a resumption of U.S. aid would be tied to Paul's permanent removal from power.

Black magic is a part of voodoo. For the past century, Haitian intellectuals eager to legitimize voodoo in the eyes of foreigners and to protect it from attacks by the Catholic Church have tried to establish an artificial divide between voodoo, which they claim is *white* magic, and black magic. A Haitian once lectured me on misinterpretations of voodoo. "Americans can't understand Haiti, and the thing they can't understand the most is voodoo," he said. "Even the name makes them have visions: crazy niggers in the mud, black dolls with pins, zombis running around attacking people. They can't understand that voodoo is voodoo, and black magic is black magic. *Magie noire.*" Voodoo is good, black magic is bad, he said. The decrees against voodoo written by Haitian governments, he told me, have mostly been directed against black magic.

But black magic has never been eradicated, and most of these laws and decrees were written by Port-au-Prince officials to show France and other civilized nations how far Haiti had come from its African roots. As Madiou wrote in 1848, "Haitians themselves would say that these pieces of paper [the laws against voodoo, which existed from the days of Christophe], were made for foreigners, so that foreigners would believe that we were like other civilized peoples. These laws were nothing but lies."

The ethnographer Alfred Métraux points out in *Voodoo in Haiti*, written in 1959, that magic is an ambiguous term, and that to separate "white magic," or magic used for good purposes, from "black magic" is a dubious and alien attempt at moral arbitration. No Haitian peasant would ever say, "Ah, that spell he cast is black magic; therefore, it is not voodoo." In somewhat the same way that Creole is a living language, without written rules, so is voodoo a living religion: it is the religion of the Haitian peasant, as the Haitian peasant practices it. And under the guidance of his houngan, the Haitian peasant practices black magic, magic intended to do evil, to cast spells, to wreak revenge, to assuage jealousy.

The most famous result of black magic is the zombi, someone presumably brought back from the dead by a bokor. The zombi is raised from death to do the bidding of his enemy. It is the most terrible of curses. Zombis are Haitians' living nightmare of their own history. After a person dies in voodoo, his soul goes back to Africa, to Guinée, that is, back to freedom. This belief sprang up among the first generation of black Haitians, slaves who had made the long middle passage and whose only happy moments were spent at proscribed voodoo dances and ceremonies in the woods behind the plantations, where they summoned up the better days in the land of their birth. These slaves dreamed of liberation after death, and the tradition of the return to Africa was passed down through the generations.

The flip side of this belief is the zombi, who dies free and rises into slavery. As slaves, the worst thing the blacks of St.-Domingue could imagine was a slavery that continued even after death. In postrevolutionary Haiti, where freedom from slavery was the most important aspect of a man's life, the worst that could happen, again, was slavery.

I may have seen two or three zombis in my travels throughout Haiti, in the small villages off Route Nationale and in the insane asylum near Jean-Claude Duvalier's ranch outside Port-au-Prince. The people presented to me as zombis were characterized by a lack

of speech and responsiveness that closely resembled the mental depradations brought on by starvation. Other Americans and Haitians
I know also believe they have seen zombis. When his jeep broke
down late one night along an abandoned road in the depths of the
countryside, an American who works for the CARE reforestation
program spent hours fixing it under the watchful eye of a peasant
who wouldn't talk to him, wouldn't come near him, wouldn't look at
him, wouldn't go for help, wouldn't acknowledge that the two were
on the same planet. But nighttime is in any case a bad time for
Haitians: the secret societies come out, bad spirits frequent the
roads, and anyone with any sense is at home with the doors and the
windows fastened tight. Only in those slums where there just isn't
enough room inside do people stay out at night. Either this peasant
was a zombi, said the CARE worker, or he thought that the white
man fixing the car in the middle of the night in the middle of the
road was an evil spirit, a vision sent to torment him.

It's not easy to return to life if you have become a zombi. It is said
that the bokor, after having made a deal with the corpse-washer,
usually a payment, steals the dead man's soul, and that is how the
corpse is turned into a zombi. People whose dead have enemies
resort to all sorts of tricks to stop their deceased relation from being
turned into a zombi. They build strong graves of stone; often the
construction begins long before the death—the costs are high, but
it's worth it to avoid becoming a zombi. The dead man's people
throw rice into his casket, so that the deceased will have to count
each grain, and because he is concentrating on the counting he will
not respond to the bokor's call to arise. They seal the corpse's nostrils
to stop his soul from escaping. But if, by some ruse, the bokor
manages to trap the dead man's soul, the game is up. The zombi
rises, and thenceforth he must serve the bokor, or whoever has
commissioned the zombification, as a virtual slave. The zombi does
not know what has happened to him, he has no consciousness, he is
not even human. His eyes are blank and he walks like a sleepwalker.
The Tontons Macoute took to wearing sunglasses in order to make
peasants think that they were zombis. If you couldn't see their eyes,
the theory went, they could be hiding the fact of their zombification.
A zombi will do anything he is told to do, and is therefore greatly to
be feared. Because Papa Doc, the Immaterial Being, was capable of
any abuse, his zombis reasonably would be monsters of cruelty.

The zombi works hard for his master, and if he should slacken he
is subject to severe beatings, which he never resists. He is the ideal

slave. Only if he tastes salt does he regain an awareness of his humanity, and his meals are carefully prepared. When a zombi tastes salt, his eyes reopen, and, in a frenzy, he will attack his master.

I met Clairvius Narcisse, a fabled zombi. His death had been duly recorded before he was found working as a zombi. He returned to normal life many years later—one supposes he partook of the curative salt—only to discover that in the wake of the publication of an American book about zombis, his own relatives had set up a speaking tour for him that included Brooklyn College. Clairvius looked like someone to whom something quite bad had happened, something worse than having to rise from the dead to talk at Brooklyn College. For a man on the lecture circuit, he was singularly unchatty when I tried to talk with him. But then, I met him back in Haiti, after his lecture tour. Perhaps he was tired. He is not a young man. He lives now in a small house at Passe-Reine, east of Gonaïves, at the Baptist mission, which in itself can be exhausting. His fatigue and silence are disturbing. He seems like a man who has been on Thorazine, or is in need of it.

All the worst fears of the slave are recalled in the various stories of zombis. A zombi called Ti Fanm, or Little Woman, who now lives along with Clairvius at the Baptist mission in Passe-Reine, was made to work her master's farm and serve him and his friends sexually, just like a slave girl. An older zombi story—recounted in *The Magic Island* (1929), written by William Seabrook at the height of the nineteen-year U.S. occupation of Haiti—tells of a band of zombis brought in from the countryside by a bokor who got them onto the payroll of HASCO, the Haitian-American Sugar Company, supervised their work in the canefields, and faithfully collected their pay each week.

But zombis, according to most legends, are not just innocent people whom some evil sorcerer wanted to enslave. Rather, those who become zombis are the victims of their own self-love; almost always, they have been hated in their own community, and their zombification is the punishment for a life of selfishness at the expense of others within the community. Among the sins that Wade Davis cites in *The Serpent and the Rainbow* (1985) as punishable by zombification are "excessive material advancement at the obvious expense of family and dependants . . . lack of respect for one's fellows . . . spreading talk that affects the well-being of others . . . land issues—any action that unjustly keeps another from working the land." It is true that in the Haitian countryside personal advancement is viewed with deep mistrust by the community. If a man does well, it is thought, his success must come at the expense of someone else's—or everyone else's—well-being. The Haitian peasant economy is so poor that this cruel perception is often true: a rich peasant can actually upset the fragile balance of the market economy and can actually make his neighbors' lives more miserable—merely by his own success. The fear of zombification helps to keep voodoo worshipers within the bounds of social norms. Zombification is more horrifying than the fear of death, because it is a death and enslavement that lasts forever. It is more effective a deterrent than the cramped cell at the local Army barracks, more effective than the torture of the Tontons Macoute. It means eternal slavery: you will work forever, and never profit by your labor.

The textbook of Mission Alpha, the Catholic Church's literacy campaign that grew active after Duvalier's fall, was called *Goute Sèl,* or A Taste of Salt. The implication was not lost on the people who were using the book to learn to read, according to Father Frantz Grandoit, who ran Mission Alpha for several years and who gave the book its title. The peasant understands that by learning to read, by "tasting salt," he will change from an abused zombi into someone able to understand the terms of his own enslavement.

Other implications of *Goute Sèl* were not lost on other factions of the population. After the zombi eats salt and becomes aware of what has been done to him, he turns on his master. None of the masters of Haiti supported the *Goute Sèl* program. They called the book and the literacy campaign Communist. Max Beauvoir has always argued against literacy programs and *Goute Sèl* in particular. He says that reading itself is evil and will destroy the peasants' faith in voodoo, will destroy their memory of the ancestors and the spirits. They'll start reading the Bible, Beauvoir says—that is one of the goals of the Catholic Church and Mission Alpha.

But, to Beauvoir's surprise, Haiti's Catholic bishops turned out to have views closer to his own than to Grandoit's. The bishops are masters, after all. Two years after Duvalier fell, they removed Grandoit and began dismantling the programs of *Goute Sèl.*

Joyce and her husband, Eldon, came to Haiti in 1952. It was a shock for Joyce, who grew up in Minnesota. But it was fate, she says. Joyce was a pretty girl, popular, and she was reborn in Christ right after high school. By 1958, she and Eldon had started the Baptist Mission for Haiti in Passe-Reine. Joyce is still beautiful, with cascading red hair and blue eyes, but time and Haiti have unhinged her. Hesitation and then headlong speech: those are Joyce's methods of communication. You get the feeling, as you sit watching her darting eyes, with the wooden masks of two Haitian peasants, a man and a woman, hanging on the wall behind her, that she is always thinking about something other than the subject at hand.

Joyce is in charge of a church that numbers some three hundred congregants, almost all of them peasants, including the former zombis Clairvius and Ti Fanm. Her mission runs a school, and every morning children come and sit in obedient rows, with the hot sun pouring through the cement slats, listening to the teacher talk about Dessalines in French, which they don't understand, and which he speaks poorly. Only the disciplinary measures are spoken in Creole. *"Fèmen bouch ou!"* (Shut your mouth!) the teacher will say, or *"Chita! Pa pale lè pwofesè-a ap pale!"* (Sit down! Don't talk when the teacher is talking!) But these remonstrances are rare. Most of the children don't eat enough, so they don't have the energy to misbehave.

It's hard for them to keep seated, because they are sitting on hard benches, but still, they listen patiently while the teacher tells them about the ambush of Dessalines on October 17, 1806, at Pont-Rouge by troops loyal to General Pétion in the south. They listen as he tells them that Haiti's greatest leader was shot, his fine regalia stripped from his body, his guns stolen, his fingers cut off so that the rings he wore could be taken, as well. Too bad the children can't understand, they would have been interested in the rings, and in the part about the kids who threw stones at Dessalines' dead body, which was dumped by his assassins in the middle of the government's administrative square. They would have liked the part about the madwoman Défilée, who came that night and gathered up in a bag what was left of the indomitable Dessalines, so that his heart and liver and brains would not be desecrated by his enemies. They would have been surprised by the courage of Madame Inginac, who erected a memorial to Dessalines soon after. "Here lies Dessalines," it read laconically, "Dead at 48."

For this education, the children's families pay a few dollars a month, always at least a little more than they can afford. The mission has a pigsty also, stocked with American pigs, and many mango trees and goats, and a CARE warehouse that is no longer used, because, since Duvalier left, CARE warehouses, filled with American food aid, have been the frequent target of peasant attacks. The peasants never liked the Food-for-Work program, in which they were given a meal a day, provided by CARE, for a day's work on whatever development project the distributor chose: building the new pigsty, digging a drainage system for the mission, cleaning out the animals' quarters. Food-for-Work: it sounded like slavery. The mission's warehouse was nearly dechouked after Duvalier left. Fortunately for Joyce and Eldon, it happened to be empty that day.

For a long time, Joyce thought that things were going well for her and Eldon in Haiti. They had a good conversion rate; even if the peasants didn't like Food-for-Work, they still wanted the Food part and that helped make converts for the Lord, though Joyce doesn't say so. And then Eldon preached a pretty good sermon about the torments awaiting non-Christians after death. Eldon could call up hellfire and brimstone, when he wanted to. Nobody went back to Africa in Eldon's sermons. They all went down to the fiery pit, and Eldon's Creole they could understand. Joyce was proud of Eldon's sermons, and proud of her clean home at the mission, with its linoleum floors and wood furniture from the 1950s, and *Time* and *Newsweek* on the coffee table. She even had someone to fold her sheets, Clairvius' wife of two years, a silent, stout mountain girl who did not accompany him on his speaking tours. "She's so talented," Joyce used to say. "You should see how she folds, even fitted sheets." Joyce was happy to have converted Ti Fanm and Clairvius to the Lord, happy to see Clairvius with a wife now. Two zombis for Christ, perhaps Joyce's signal achievement.

Then, in June 1983, something happened that changed Joyce's mind. Before, in the old days, Joyce used to think about converting the heathen, and bringing the Lord Jesus to Haiti. Her world seemed to be full of light. There were happy peasants, little black children, sweet mangoes, goats eating grass in the distance, and light. Things are different now.

There was this woman in the church, Joyce says, a clean, decent woman, who kept to herself. Joyce knew her, not too well, but at least to say hello to on Sunday, chat about the market, the weather. The woman raised eggplants in her field, the vegetables came up firm and plump. On market days, the woman would get up early, very early, about two in the morning, and wake her daughter, who would wrap a white bandana around her head and go out to gather up eggplants in baskets in the dark for the two women to carry to the market at Passe-Reine. Mother and daughter would get to market by four in the morning, well before sunrise, and set up their stall in the dark, spreading brown paper on the ground and lining up the purple, almost black eggplants. By the time their neighbors arrived at daybreak with more eggplants, the two women had sold off all their produce, and were getting ready to return to their field to care for the crop. So their neighbors had a hard time selling eggplants, and it seemed as though the two women might get a monopoly on the Passe-Reine eggplant market, just by getting up a few hours earlier than everyone else.

Their enterprise did not earn the women the admiration of their neighbors. People began to talk. The women's behavior was not normal, not acceptable. One neighbor said the older woman was a sorceress, that she called on evil spirits to wake her in the night, when no one else would think of rising, and that she paid her spirits with the hot blood of children. A child a few fields away had died not long before, and the neighbors suspected that the woman's child-less daughter was a loup-garou. The woman and her daughter knew there was talk about them, but they continued to keep to themselves, and went on taking their dark morning walks. One day in early June, when the sun was still down, a crowd of her neighbors confronted the woman and her daughter as they began their market walk. They shouted insults at her, and, enraged by her silence, they beat her and her daughter with sticks. Finally, they stoned them to death.

Joyce went down the road to see the bodies after the sun rose, and everyone was talking about the incident. There was a crowd around the bodies. "It was when I saw it that I just . . . well, her face. It wasn't there anymore. There was no face." Joyce looks very hard out the window, but the only things there are palms. She likes remembering the faceless body, and she doesn't like it. She has come to need it and fear it, like a fetish to which she keeps returning. "Hamburger, is what it was like, the place where her face would have been," Joyce says. Joyce hasn't forgotten her America even though she's been living outside the country for more than thirty years. "Her daughter," Joyce says, looking away from the palms, "she had a stick, you know, up . . . her . . . they say, anyway. I didn't see . . . that. At first, it wasn't so bad, although her face . . . I thought only four or five people were involved. Then, sort of slowly, over time, as I talked to more and more people, I realized that it was more, maybe twenty, then I realized, no, more like forty or fifty, and by now I really think it was a crowd of four or five hundred. I think it was everyone.

"They know I know. It's everyone, everyone who comes to my church. Everyone. They try to hide it, but they know I know they were in it. You know what one woman said to me? She said, 'She is lucky they smashed her face in. At least now no one can turn her into a zombi.' She was in it, too, that woman. When I put up a cross at the site on the anniversary of . . . the incident, I held a small ceremony, praising Jesus, and I could tell by the way they cried that some of them who came to this ceremony had participated. In the murder. They didn't mind coming to this ceremony to honor the souls of those two murdered women, the women they had killed. How could they come? How dare they? I asked them, you know, afterwards, if they went to market on that same day . . . the day of the . . . incident—that is, after. And they said yes. Yes." Joyce looks at me with great innocent blue eyes. "They went to market to sell their eggplants with blood on their hands. One or two even laughed when they told me."

But, I ask her, isn't it part of her faith to try to understand these people, and to forgive?

First, she says, they must repent. " 'Repent, sayeth the Lord,' " Joyce says. "They are unrepentant."

Maybe, I suggest, they don't think they did wrong. Maybe they think the eggplant woman was in the wrong.

But that's exactly what they do think, says Joyce. "That was my job," she says, "to teach them a new way to think, to teach them not to think like that. Why do they have to be so bloody-minded, so stupid and so bloody-minded? I taught them to love Jesus and every man, and to work hard and to better themselves through the Lord's teachings and their own hard work. They can say the Lord's Prayer in English. And what has come of all my teaching? What's come of it? This awful country with people pounding at your door, robbing you, they even stole a pig, old witch doctors in the hills, they'll do anything, and poor Ti Fanm wasting away, and this murder behind all of it, blood running everywhere for nothing, for a few eggplants. They'll kill you for nothing here, because nobody's got anything worth killing for, and man must kill. Man must kill. Twenty eggplants, that's something to do murder for? I guess. Twenty eggplants . . . how much is that? I don't know. I can't figure the way I once could. I used to be good at math. Eldon will tell you. And the other day, this young girl, black as coal, she comes up to me and she says, 'Madame,' and I look at her. She reaches up and takes my hair, you know, the way they do? Because they like to touch white women's hair? And she holds it in her hand, looking at it, sort of carefully, like she's studying it. Then she drops it and says to me, right in the face, 'Loup-garou.' Loup-garou . . ."

"Magic, both black and white, keeps the community together," says the Senatorial Candidate, sitting back in his rocking chair upstairs, in his green house in Gonaïves. The sun is going down behind the blue mountains, and the wind is rising. A woman is shouting *"Menti!"* outside the window. "Liar!" She's having a fight with a woman who is sleeping with her boyfriend, from what I can make out of the rapid-fire Creole. The Senatorial Candidate listens, smiles.

"As I was saying, this is really what voodoo is about, about the strength of the community, the *habitation,* in the old parlance. In a way, Haiti is a religious state, like Iran. The people live every moment by the laws of their religion. Of course, they are filled with beliefs that you and I could never subscribe to. Could you believe, really, in zombis? Really believe? I doubt it. Yet if you did, there would be no rule you would not abide by in order to be sure that when you died you would stay dead. You wouldn't steal land from your neighbor, you wouldn't sleep with her husband, like that girl down in the street, you would never think of violating certain basic standards of behavior.

"This works both for good and evil, naturally. If you thought that the local Tonton Macoute was a bokor, you would allow him to commit any atrocity rather than confront him and pay with your life. It's always the threat of punishment that keeps people in line. Here we have, say, zombis, or women who are turned into loup-garous because they have done some wrong. Instead of prison and hard labor, we have other, shall we say more spiritual, punishments. Then again, we also have prison and hard labor, and torture, if the spiritual chastisement should fail.

"And let's not forget, we also have hellfire and damnation, thanks to the Catholics and the Protestants. Thank God, I personally am an atheist," the Senatorial Candidate says, smiling at his joke. "I don't think you can be free to be reasonable in this country if you believe. I believed in politics at one point. Well, maybe I still do. After all, there are these elections. And I'm participating, so I suppose that's a form of belief. I guess what I meant to say was that I once believed in ideologies, the way the peasant believes in Ogoun, or a priest, even a good one, may believe in Christ.

"I was a Fignolist when I was young, and I even worked for Duvalier for a little while. I had little doubt that Noirisme was the one true path for Haiti. Then I discovered Marxism, that was a revelation, and I came to believe that class differences, not color differences, were at the root of Haiti's problems, that color was a useful tool demagogues wielded in order to manipulate the people and to hide from them the real path to their salvation—excuse the religious term. I won't say what I think that path is. Anyway, I had to drop Noirisme and Fignolé too. I began to see, also, that all the noiristes used voodoo, abused voodoo, to achieve their own personal ambitions. Duvalier was only the worst and the most successful.

"I mean, after all, you can see that the peasant doesn't have an easy life, to put it mildly. There are things he enjoys, and the countryside is still beautiful—isn't it?—but his is a pretty miserable existence, I'd have to say. Almost everything that happens to him is bad: his land is infertile, his children die, his pigs are taken away, the macoute steals his wife, the whole sorry litany, until he dies too young of tuberculosis or hunger—or AIDS now, what a dreadful disease. Voodoo provides a way for him to understand his wretched existence and to rise above it. He doesn't have to say to himself that it was because he could not raise enough food that his child is dead. He can say, It is because So-and-so put a spell on my child, or on my house. Or he can go to the houngan and say, Why did my child die? And the houngan will tell him, perhaps, that he has not been paying enough attention to this spirit or that one, and he will correct his behavior. Of course, all this stops him from grasping the root cause of his misery, which is exploitation.

"Still, he feels through voodoo that he can do something about his life. And where else, except in voodoo, can a poor farmer who all day has been pulling up manioc (just to take a random example) spend the night as a god, as Ogoun, respected and feared by all his neighbors? It's that transformation of possession that ignites people. I'm sure it was possession—the possibility of man becoming god— that made the slaves believe that they could defeat their masters. After all, the white man had guns, but he had never been Ogoun."

Sisi has a hundred voodoo nations dancing in her head, offspring of the gods of her ancestors. She is a skinny collection of old bones. She holds her chin in one hand and squinches up her lips while she watches the men of Duverger clean off a pig for the next day's market. Sisi is squatting near the fire in Duverger, a small village on Haiti's southern peninsula; the Protestant pastor's wife—who bought the pig from the chef de section and had it killed—is sitting on a low chair, in her pink dress, something most women would reserve for Sundays. She is directing the men. Most of the men are Sisi's family.

I had heard the pig go squealing down the road earlier, but didn't think much of it. I was washing carrots at Lucy's house. It was sometime after noon. It sounded as though someone was pulling the pig from the sty and taking him to a place he didn't want to go to. I could hear the chef de section up the road, directing the men who were taking the pig. Lucy was cooking out in front of her four-room house, skinning potatoes and manioc. She had her usual fever, and was sweating in the sun. She said it didn't make any difference if she sat in the shade or the sun, she was always hot. Her friend Jetta was draining coconut for the sauce, and Miss and Abner, Lucy's brother, were out in the kitchen, taking turns at pounding the beans under the banana-leaf roof. Ariole, Lucy's son, was trying to light the charcoal fire, and his pretty little cousin Adeline was helping him. Gustave, Miss's husband, was still out in the field, planting corn with his day workers.

I heard the pig squealing, and then, an hour or so later, I saw Sisi go walking down the road. Lucy was still cooking. Then Abner said, "I better go help them," and Lucy said, "Take the inside path." She looked up at him from her pile of potatoes, wiping a wave of sweat out of her huge eyes. She had a way of giving commands that sounded like pleading. Abner, a big, capable man with muscles like ropes, a man who could do anything, put up houses, plant fields, skin pigs, shuck beans, build outhouses and carry all manner of produce back from market—Abner could do anything, but he always listened to Lucy, his little sister.

She didn't want everyone to see her brother walking down the road to help the Protestant pastor's wife with the pig. Abner went behind the house. I followed him. Ariole had the charcoal fire burning by now, and he stood next to it, proud and still in his blue-and-white-checked school uniform. Next, Miss would kill the white chicken I had bought for Lucy's family from the market in Léogane on the way out from Port-au-Prince. The chicken had walked over me that morning while I was still asleep, and I wanted to miss its killing. I never got used to watching them flap around in their blood with their necks cut. I always find that it takes a chicken too long to die.

Over at the Protestant pastor's, the fire was going up and the sun was coming down, and the two different kinds of light met in the banana grove. The pig was good and dead, and the men were crowded around him, but he wouldn't take the fire. The pastor's wife presided over a bowl of the pig's blood. Then Abner came. He plugged up the pig's neck tight with a piece of corncob, so none of the leftover blood would escape, and then he began pounding the dead animal, to bring up the fat for the fire, and to loosen the skin. The other men helped him, and soon it sounded like drums. They moved the tinder under the pig and smoothed some of it over him, and he went up. You could see each coarse pig hair burn off the skin, and when Abner scraped away the ash the pig's flesh was done a golden brown. They did one side, and then the other. After he was brown all over, two of the men washed him, like a corpse. They were careful to use as little water as possible, taking handfuls of it from a tin bowl.

The pig looked beautiful. He started out gray, but now he was gold. They washed around his corncob wound, and took special pains to clean his snout. They wanted to make him pretty for market, and this cleaning and burning would show the meat to its best advantage. Then Abner took the pig by his hoofs and turned him on his back and cut him down the middle, each stretch of insides popping out as the machete traveled down his belly. Blood swam around the big heart, the great brown liver, the opalescent intestines. Abner scooped it out with a cup. He poured it into the bowl of blood. The pastor's wife smoothed her pink dress over broad knees.

Sisi watched. It was almost a year since she had presided over the killing of an animal. That time, it had been a bull, but the bull wasn't going to market. They had hung the head in the spirit room behind the peristyle. In spite of the sacrifice, it had taken the spirits too long to come the next night. The drums were no good, one of the drummers got too drunk, one of them didn't have the energy, and Sisi's favorite drummer, Café Amè, wouldn't come down from the mountains. Gustave's two day workers were wild that night, they argued about who planted better, who had a better rhythm with the hoe, and they drank more clairin than anyone at the ceremony, after a full day of drinking in the fields. They danced and danced, shuffling and grabbing girls off the bench where everyone sat, and then they bought more clairin with the two dollars they had earned between them that day, and then drank and laughed and had more screaming loud arguments.

Sisi was worried that night last year. ·She sat on a bench at the side of the peristyle and listened to the men arguing. Some of the hounsis got what they call tipsy, almost possessed. They twirled to the drums and reeled around, but so far, after five hours, no spirit had come. There had been no possession. Sisi toyed with a small bottle of clairin. She watched the dispirited gathering for a while and then shut her eyes. She shook her head. Abner was flirting in a corner; his wife was at home. Lucy was getting drunk with a young man. Ariole watched his mother from outside the temple. Little Adeline slept nearby, on a straw mat. Sisi lifted her eyelids finally, and regarded the proceedings with a cool eye.

"The peristyle is empty tonight," she said, even though we could both see that it was full of people. "No one is going to come."

She meant the spirits. It was the Protestant influence, she said. Too many people had gone over to the new religion, and now there were Mormons, she had heard, whatever that was, and a new school down the road, built by the Salvation Army. *Lame di sali,* in Creole.

"What if the spirits don't ever come?" I asked.

She smiled. "Then, soon, everyone will have to return to the drums. Oh, yes, everyone will come back, you can believe me. Even Madanm Pastè, the pastor's wife, in her pink dress. They'll be too scared, wondering what will happen here without the spirits. For now, it's okay. They have their Protestant pigs, they sell their meat in the market, the spirits go hungry, but they can buy a little something for their kids. They think it's all right. They buy a pink dress, and they think everything is fine, even when their neighbors have nothing. But after a while, when they see that their ancestors refuse their hospitality, they'll start to think again about this new God they've taken up. This Protestant God is foreign." She used the word *blan,* or white. "He's not like the saints—the saints let you dance. This new God doesn't want us to dance. None of my neighbors really believes in him, you see, it's just a way to get more money, more prestige. The Protestants will have a new church, they'll have a little pocket money to hand out, they'll have a white pastor who comes around every once in a while to make sure things are running smoothly." Sisi stopped suddenly, to watch something. I looked where she was looking.

Lucy was getting drunk, I could see what Sisi was seeing. Lucy, across the yard, leaning back against a big mapou and smiling drunkenly up at the sky. Everyone was drunk that night, but Lucy was drunker. I had never seen her drunk before. I had never seen her drink. It was nearly two in the morning, maybe three. The moon seemed to have set—I had missed its going down. Lucy had taken off the patent-leather sandals she had bought at last week's market, and she was trying to bury her toes in the cool night earth. The mapou's roots kept getting in her way. She stretched out her body against the tree. Her toes would dig a line, then stop, blocked. She batted her big eyes up at the sky, took a sip of clairin and then a sip of beer. She looked cool for once, as though the fever had abated. She let her head loll to one side, staring up at the sky through the mapou's leaves. Sisi pointed at her.

"She's lost," Sisi said.

Lucy turned her head away and was sick.

Sisi grabbed a girl by the arm and sent her in Lucy's direction. The girl looked disgusted.

"But each time the white pastor leaves and the people are back on their own, the same thing happens," Sisi said, keeping one eye on Lucy's progress. Lucy was standing now, leaning on the girl. The girl patted Lucy's forehead with a white rag. "They come to me with their problems, already they come to me. Why? Because they believe in the spirits of the ancestors. Soon, they'll start to worry. They'll see two more years without rain, and they'll begin to figure it out. They'll come back here, because this is how we live. Even the chef de section, you'll see him here, too, or at some other place like this. His pigs must have water, after all. He needs rain too. All those people you see at Madanm Pastè's, even those little nobody boys in their long-sleeve shirts and ties, they'll all be dancing and waiting for the drums to work. Because they will have to. In the end, there is no choice. We can't escape the will of the gods, even when we go around pretending to be Protestants. Haitians can't be Protestants, not for long. It doesn't work. Look at her, poor child."

The girl brought Lucy over to us, and Sisi sat Lucy down between her knees and held her hot head in her hands. The drums were still playing, they had become like background noise, you got so used to them. And then Lucy began to sing with the chorus, first, again and again, for Legba, then for Agwe, the water god. Miss appeared with a pot of sweet, sweet coffee to keep me awake. The two day workers had subsided, but some others were dancing. Ariole came over from Adeline's mat with his eyebrows tied into a knot of worry. He looked down at his mother, but Lucy was distracted by her fever. She didn't seem to see him. Sisi reached out to pat Ariole. He shook her hand away from his face. Lucy sang for Agwe, with the heat from her temples burning up against Sisi's knees, and Ariole went to the side of the peristyle and came back with a calabash filled with water. He washed his mother's face, her arms, her hands. He took scoops of water and poured them over her. The cool water revived her some. She kept on singing, but her fever wouldn't break. Lucy didn't seem to care. She smiled at her son and pulled herself up higher between Sisi's legs, resting her arms on Sisi's thighs. Ariole set aside the calabash, sat himself between Lucy's knees and fell asleep. She kissed the back of his head.

All along Route Nationale, everywhere you go, you see Protestant missions: Mission Possible, H.E.L.P., Mission to Haiti, Inc., Larry Jones Hands of God Ministries, hundreds of others. The most famous and perhaps the most grandiose of all is the Baptist Haiti Mission up above Boutilliers, at Fermathe. At the entryway, people are selling hats and guayaberas and bad paintings, just as they do at Boutilliers, although no one has ever dared to sell penis men at the Baptist mission. Pastor Wally wouldn't like that. Just inside, a crowded crafts boutique and a crowded cafeteria are open to the public, and American missionaries tired of rice and beans and cornmeal and cassava gather every weekend to feast on hamburgers, broccoli, raspberries, peanut butter cookies and other reminders of home.

Up at the Baptist mission, in the chill air of the mountains, there is enough water for all, as long as you agree to be baptized and to live by the rules of the Christians. Pastor Wally controls the water. "Anytime a country is in trouble, the church grows, because the church has the answer." This is the wisdom of Pastor Wallace Turnbull, the man many people claim is a CIA informant. Turnbull's family established the mission here in 1943, and it now has some 250 branches throughout Haiti, as well as a central office in Grand Rapids, Michigan. "They are sending for the Christians," Pastor Wally says, "and telling them they want to be converted. A vaudouisant who gets baptized thinks he is joining a more powerful religion to get protection from a more powerful God. We try to make sure they love Jesus too."

A big man with a Middle American accent who calls his wife

Grandma, Pastor Wally has a house at the top of the hill and, according to peasants who live at the mission, another sprawling mansion next door to the Duvaliers' former mountain retreat, a little farther down the road. Haiti has not done badly by Pastor Wally. At the mission, he presides over some two hundred fifty Haitians who call him "Bòs," and who rake and hoe and harvest and sew in return for clothing and religious schooling and care from the small but clean medical clinic. To work for the mission you must be baptized. In general, Pastor Wally doesn't pay his workers, he feeds them, usually with food from CARE's Food-for-Work program. The mission uses the food as pay, which saves the mission money. Here, Food-for-Work once again has all the earmarks of slavery, except that the peasants who work the mission land do not receive a parcel of that land for their own cultivation. Ask any Haitian, and he'll tell you he'd rather get paid. "What can I do with food but eat it?" a mission worker asked me, shrugging. "It saves me paying for my dinner, but that's all. I can't save a dinner of rice and beans and use it two months later to pay for my children's education. I'd rather make a dollar a day." But he has no choice.

If you don't look too hard at the ragged, stoop-shouldered farmers in the fields, the mission could be paradise, like a well-run plantation. The place where food is distributed is surrounded by scores of brimming greenhouses and blossoming gardens filled with flowers. Down by Wally's house is a pond covered with water lilies. Out near the driveway, the mission has a miniature zoo, with lizards and doves in cages, and two wizened monkeys that the missionaries' children love to watch. The monkeys fight over the food that the children throw at them. The bigger one always wins. He loves the cinnamon candy that they make at the mission.

"The biggest obstacle to progress in Haiti is the people's innate dishonesty," Pastor Wally tells me as his foremen distribute food behind him. The food distribution is unusually calm—elsewhere, I've watched the people scramble and fight over the cooking oil and rice that are handed out. But here it's well organized. Pastor Wally has the situation under control. "These people are taught to laugh at stealing and cheating," he says. "Their whole culture is based on that, all their nursery stories are like Amos and Andy, with the bad, naughty child always getting what he wants, and the slow good child left behind in the dust. Haitians like the bad child and laugh at the slow-witted one, with no pity.

"And voodoo. Voodoo is all about lying: the witch doctor tells

everybody lies and then makes them pay for his lying. They lie to
him, too, so that he won't put a spell on them. It's a deep well of
lying, this culture.

"We teach 'em to be honest. They can't get away with their lying
and cheating ways here, and they know it. In fact, we make 'em wait
six months before we'll baptize them, because we want to make sure
they understand. After a person has shown by his walk that he is a
proper Christian, he may be permitted baptism."

I point to a man with a hoe who is waiting patiently in line, his
eyes on the ground. "I wonder if that is the walk you are looking
for," I say to Pastor Wally.

He looks at me and laughs. "Look, they are starving and we give
them food. They're dying and we give them medicine. Medicine that
works. Isn't that Christian? This country is poor because of voodoo.
These people have no responsibility. The gods did it, they tell you.
They're so stupid. To us, it looks like utter stupidity, but that is the
African mind. They cut down a mango tree whose fruit earns them
ten dollars a year, in order to make charcoal that they'll be able to
sell for only forty cents, or a dollar. Stupid. They cut down all the
trees, and then the rain stops and then they moan and say that they
must have forgotten to feed the spirits properly. 'La pli pa tonbe,'
they whine. The rain doesn't fall. Hah."

One day in La Saline—a day so hot I had to wipe sweat out of my
eyes and pull my hair back from my face—a few minutes after I had
left Mimette wearing the lacy blue socks I had just given her, and
dancing in the dirt, I ran across a man in a dark suit and tie, someone
I had never seen before in La Saline. He was a Haitian, and he was
singing some song. He had a friend with him, in a suit and tie as
well, and his friend held leaflets in his hand. People were trudging
back and forth with their purchases and wares, women with cornmeal in wide bowls on their heads, women with baskets of bananas
on their heads, men carrying sacks of charcoal and flour across their
backs, most of them getting ready to take the scores of tap-taps
that leave each day from La Saline for the southern town of Les
Cayes.

The two men in the dark suits were Baptists. This is what they
were singing. They were reading it letter for letter in transliterated
English from the leaflets they were distributing to the illiterate commerçantes on their way to Les Cayes:

Ay don-no wat you fink, bat
Dji-zos iz may lay-f.
Ay bili in-n you
Evrudey in-n may lay-f.
Ay wan tou pliz you, lo.
You tek tou dey, you giv mi lay-v
So, ay lov you.

Ay don-no way-i lov-z mi.
Dji-zos Kouay-z iz may lay-f (bis). . . .

When I asked them to translate what they were singing, the two
men could not do it, but they pointed to the Creole written below
the transliterated English. Translated, the Creole, an approximation
of the above, reads:

I don't know what you think, but
Jesus is my life.
He takes my hand, he gives me life.
Every day of my life,
I must praise you, Lord.
You take death today, and you give me life.
So, I love your name.

I don't know why he loves me,
Why Jesus Christ loves
A sinner like me.

. . .

Before Duvalier fell, Benito was a Macoute. He is a bokor and a leaf
doctor, and he has the only mill in Beau Champ, a small village in
the Northwest province where water, money and food are scarce.
For a fee, he grinds the peasants' corn at his mill. It runs on electricity from his delco. Benito's habitation, made up of five or six houses,
is a few doors down from the Catholic priest's compound. Benito's
consulting day is Tuesday.

"*Gen maladi e maladi,*" Benito says. There are diseases and diseases. Benito is put together like a bantam cock. He has flesh on
him, a little too much around his middle, and strong bandy legs,
muscular arms. He has a face that looks as if good jokes would come
from him. There is humor in his eyes, with a little cruelty, and a
nasty, humorous curve to his mouth. For a Haitian peasant, his skin

is light. A French franc hangs from a ribbon around his neck. He is surrounded by his women, his wife and his hounsis, six of them, all his mistresses. Benito has an empire of his own.

As in other places in Haiti, the Dechoukaj that followed Duvalier's departure changed Beau Champ. "We had what we call a *nonviolent* Dechoukaj here," says one Church worker, smiling. "We chased away the big Macoutes or they fled from fear, and then we put the mid-level Macoutes on trial, in public. They had to restore what they had stolen from the people, and to swear that they would change their ways." That is what happened to Benito. He paid back some money, forgave some debts, and now he works alongside the Church-sponsored community pharmaceutical dispensary, instead of working against it. That way, said the Church worker, "Benito can earn his living and the people can continue in their beliefs, but at the same time they have a chance to get proper care—if Benito's cures don't work, or aren't applicable."

"Gen maladi mystè, gen maladi Bondye," Benito says. There are diseases that come from the spirits and there are diseases that come from the Good Lord. Benito treats the ones that come from the spirits. On Tuesday morning, his patients gather at the habitation, passing by the leafless tree hung with goat skulls that stands in front of the peristyle. Ragged peasants with fever, young women having problems getting pregnant, pregnant women with pains, old men whose heads never stop aching, children with fevers, women with rheumatism and hands hardened from working the fields, a crazy boy who Benito says has a zombi in his head. The boy with the zombi in his head looks like a zombi himself, blank and affectless. He is wearing red pants and a red tee shirt, in accordance with Benito's prescription, and he has bands of red rags tied around his stomach, his wrists, his ankles and his head. Benito says that an enemy of the boy's family sent a dead man's spirit to occupy his head. He looks into the boy's eyes. With a gentle finger, he traces the bruises where another bokor beat the boy to get the zombi out of him.

"Bad practice, bad practice," says Benito. "Beating him only makes him crazier. It makes the zombi mad." Dollar bills hang from Benito's ceiling as the peasants wait patiently on benches for the ceremony to begin. On a cross for Baron Samedi, Benito has glued new orange bills, Haitian gourdes, along with a rotting cock's head and a jumble of knives at the base. On the altar behind Baron's cross stands a white doll holding a small pocket mirror, and a plastic King Kong doll with a gourde on his head. Benito sits on a makeshift throne covered with red velvet. Bottles of clairin brought by the patients cover the altar table, and one special bottle has two padlocks tied to its neck. On the white walls of the peristyle are painted crude designs, red fish, hearts, turkeys, cars and scorpions. A piece of paper is glued to the wall with Legba's vèvè marked on it in blue. Benito's youngest son, a two-year-old with blank eyes and gray dust over his body, dances naked in the doorway, waiting for the drums.

The drummers wander in, swilling clairin, and take up their places next to the one window. A song of welcome and prayer begins among the peasants, high and sweet, and then the drums start in and the place begins to shake. Benito closes his eyes up on the throne. His houngenikon, or chief acolyte, sends the patients outside with clothing for the ritual. They return, dressed in red, and an old man steps forward for treatment. Benito takes a spool of blue thread and measures the man with it from head to toe. He rips the thread at the proper length, and gives one end of the measured thread to a hounsi, holding the other himself. They wax the thread with paraffin from a baleine, to make it strong, tying knots of prayer into it as they work. The old man stands by, watching the process, with the drums going in the background and Benito's little spirit boy dancing among the grown-ups' legs.

Once the sacred thread is prepared, the old man comes forward with a bottle and a piece of blank white paper. The week before, Benito had told him to bring both items along, for his cure. Benito takes the bottle and the paper, and sits down in his throne. All eyes are upon him. The little boy brings him a bottle of clairin, and he takes a swig. Benito holds the old man's bottle up and examines it, then takes the paper and wraps it around the bottle, securing it with the measured blue thread, winding the thread all around the bottle until the bottle is half blue and half white. He fashions a cross out of two pieces of light wood, and attaches it to the bottle's neck with the blue string. Then he searches around on the altar for a moment, finds a piece of blue chalk, and begins marking the bottle with indecipherable letters and designs.

Meanwhile, the houngenikon, pipe in mouth, is cooking something up in a white porcelain basin. Benito sets aside the bottle. The houngenikon nods to him: the mixture is ready.

Benito leans over it, and all the patients watch, sitting silent while the drums change rhythm. He strikes a match over the mix of clairin, water and medicinal herbs, and the liquid ignites, a blue fire. The spirit boy is close by, and Benito and a hounsi take him by the arms and legs and swing him over the fire, a blessing for the fire or the child, it's hard to say which. Benito washes his hands in the fire. The hounsis take the basin and commence washing the women patients with the gritty stuff, first making the sign of the cross on their patients' foreheads with it. They wash each woman's body without removing her clothes. Their hands travel beneath the red costumes. The male patients wash each other.

The drums pound harder, the chanting has stopped. The drummers are accompanied now by two men who hit pieces of scrap metal together, one with a high pitch, the other low. Benito is possessed, his eyes go out of focus. He takes a lit baleine and runs its flame slowly across his palms, his stomach, his face. His flesh does not burn. The chorus begins again, the women singing *"Ale, ale,"* to the evil spirits that have caused their illnesses. Depart, depart. The old man approaches Benito timidly, head bowed. He hands Benito a depleted pack of cards, and Benito toys with them thoughtfully, resuming his seat. He is still possessed, and from time to time he grabs the old man by the hand and looks searchingly, almost pleadingly, into his eyes. The man hates to look at Benito's face, but he does. He must. The little boy dances around them, drinking clairin from a bottle top.

Benito looks away from the old man and stares over at the assembled, as if he had just been recalled to his surroundings. He reaches over to the altar, picks up a packet of papers, and begins scribbling prescriptions, or what I take to be prescriptions, on them. Later I discover they are bills for Benito's services. He hands one to the old man, and the man begins sorting out a number of very old gourdes. It comes to ten dollars and some cents. Eventually, the old man will have paid Benito three hundred dollars for his cure. In addition to what they eat from their harvests, most peasants make about twenty to thirty dollars a year in cash from their crops. Everyone in the village is in hock to Benito, and everyone must pay up his year's debts at the New Year's voodoo celebration on January 25. The old man must bring 557 gourdes, or $110, to the January festival, and, Benito tells him, he must also bring a cock for sacrifice, hard candies, coffee, bread and sodas to help with the celebration. The old man looks lost.

He sits down and puts his hands on his knees. A hounsi comes flying in the door, sobbing, possessed. She is angry and crying and takes long drinks of clairin. With a baleine, she sweeps fire across her face and across her tongue. She takes a boy, another son of

Benito's, from the crowd and swings him up on her back, dancing and careening into the seated patients. "This boy is sick," Benito tells the crowd. "Every time my son is supposed to go to school at Port-de-Paix [the biggest city nearby], he falls ill," Benito says. Benito takes a stick and a knife, and winds a blue satin cloth around his own neck. He holds a candle over the boy's head and makes a few passes at him with the knife. With the knife, he makes the sign of the cross on the boy's bare stomach, and then jabs him lightly and not so lightly in the navel with the knife, not piercing the skin. He burns a cross in the boy's hair with the candle. Then he puts the fire to his own chin, which does not burn. He hits the boy's temple with his own, and makes the open-palmed gesture of helplessness. He jabs at his own stomach with the knife, and hits the boy's sides with it, makes the sign of the cross with it on the boy's forehead, kisses his son on the lips, spits clairin onto the boy's cheeks and rubs it into his face, makes crosses on the boy's palms with the lit baleine, and then, roughly, sends him away.

No one in Beau Champ who is not specifically connected to the habitation likes Benito. That's not the idea. Like other people elsewhere who resort to other kinds of medicine, they tolerate him, resent his exorbitant fees, and think that perhaps his cures may work. They believe in him as far as his treatments seem effective, and their belief is heightened by the religious aspect of his cures. Those who are not healed believe that the magic of the bokor who cast the spell of illness upon them was too strong for Benito's cure, just as in the late stages of the disease a cancer patient in a Western country may believe that the hand of fate was just too strong for technology to match. Both science and tradition support many of Benito's cures: many of the leaves and potions he uses have antibiotic or painkilling properties and, in the parlance of American medicine, have been shown to be effective in suppressing or curing the diseases for which they are used. The leaves used against tuberculosis, for example, are natural antibiotics and may help in the early stages of the disease, according to Haitian doctors schooled in the West.

However, sometimes time itself is the great healer, and Benito often leaves much of a cure in time's capable hands. I asked him for a treatment for the cold I had at the time I visited Beau Champ. Tropical colds are very hard to shake for people from temperate climates. I had had this one for two weeks, I told him. Benito smiled and told me he had once cured a white person from Miami of a similar problem; his fee was three thousand dollars, he seemed to recall. I said that I didn't have that kind of money. He asked me whether I could help him get a visa to the United States, visas being in high demand and difficult to secure because of the Reagan Administration's tough policies against Haitian immigration. I said I didn't know anyone in the embassy.

Benito looked me over. We were sitting in front of the rest of his patients, and he had already made many speeches to them, telling them I was an important white visitor who had come from far away —New York? Miami? Canada?—to pay homage to Benito's extensive medical knowledge. He was anxious to reveal his greatness before them. Relenting in the matter of the fee, he offered me my remedy "as a gift," for free. His patients were impressed, and Benito handed me the rolled leaves and the wrapped white twigs with ostentation.

Half of the treatment, it turned out, was a tea, and half what the French call an infusion, herbs to be soaked in water. I was to take the tea twice a day, once in the morning and once at night, two cups each time, the first with sugar, the second with salt. As for the infusion, I was to soak it in water in a half-filled bottle and drink as much of it as I could each day, but I was to empty the bottle each night, because it would spoil if left more than twelve hours. I was to repeat this procedure every day for six weeks. The tea was good, and I drank it as prescribed. I drank the infusion less enthusiastically— it didn't have much taste and it reminded me of weak peppermint. Unfortunately, fate was not to allow me to judge Benito's cure. After four days, the cold disappeared.

Or perhaps Benito's treatment was unusually efficacious. Hérard Simon, a cryptic, difficult houngan who lives near Souvenance, once explained the workings of leaf doctors to me. I had asked him about a boy I had seen taking a leaf cure for his tuberculosis. I wanted to know whether Simon thought that the cures were valid. After all, he was a sophisticated man, one of a number of houngans who had founded Zanfan Tradisyon Ayisyen (Children of the Haitian Tradition) to preserve and protect voodoo during the troubles after Duvalier left. I told him that the boy I had seen was dying, and asked him if the healing process would work.

Simon smiled at me. "It always works," he said. He waited a few beats. "But sometimes, it takes too long. . . . You see what I mean." He rocked back on his chair, still smiling, beaming at me, really, over his extensive belly. "This is why we houngans sometimes propose what we call an integrated medicine, you know, part penicillin, say, in the case of tuberculosis, and part healing. Let me explain: so that the children can be cured before they die, but so that the medicine remains in the hands of the healers. If you take penicillin and cure someone who believes in the spirits, he will believe that whoever gave him the pill has the magic of the spirits. In other words, antibiotics in the wrong hands can create social and cultural evils. They give American missionaries power they should not have in Haiti. They give Christians spiritual powers with the peasants, powers to undermine the peasants' belief. Give Haitians—Haitian peasants, Haitian leaf doctors—the medicines, and the country remains Haitian. Let the missionaries distribute the pills, and you have medical imperialism."

But, I wondered, if Benito could charge the starving peasants three hundred dollars for a questionable cure, what would he demand for something that really worked? Who was Simon really trying to protect with his argument, the peasant and his religion or the bokor—his pocketbook and his power?

Almost every week, and sometimes more often, one leaf doctor or another comes by to visit with the doctors at the National Research Institute and Laboratory on Harry Truman Boulevard. "The National Research Institute" is what the sign says on the side of the building. But for about five years the National Research Institute has housed Cornell University's research project on AIDS in Haiti. If you wander down its blue corridor on Tuesday, when the clinic is open, you can see healthy but worried people waiting for a test, and others in various stages of the disease waiting to see a doctor. Many of the patients are healthy-looking mothers with babies. Some are plump Dominican prostitutes, like the girls at El Caribeño. Many are young men who have spent a lot of time with Dominican prostitutes. Most of these people, whether or not they have tested positive for the disease, are in reasonably good condition. If you ran into them in other circumstances, the disease wouldn't cross your mind.

But just as frequently, a skinny shadow of a man will be lying along the bench breathing in gasps, with his mother sitting next to him, looking away. A pale baby will be half alseep, half dead in his mother's angular lap, his skin covered with a bumpy rash. A young woman with a rasping cough will be standing up against the blue wall, her dark skin ashen, her eyes closed. For these people, their first visit to the institute is also their last. They are tested, and sometimes, if their symptoms can be treated, they are given medicine or prescriptions for medicine, and sent away. There are no beds for AIDs patients at the institute; it's a research center. There are no beds specifically for AIDS patients anywhere else in Haiti. Mostly these people go back to the slums to die. Often they receive treatment for the disease, but not from the Cornell project.

Instead, they go to people like Daniel C. Claude, the healer; Matthieu, the houngan of Kenscoff; Madame François, a leaf doctor in the Cité Soleil slum; or J. D. Percy, a downtown astrologer and medicine man. All of these people claim they can cure AIDS. On John Brown on the way to Pétionville, Daniel C. Claude has replaced the old cardboard sign I used to pass on my way down from Boutilliers with a new red-and-blue one that still declares: "AIDS IS NOT AN INCURABLE DISEASE. DANIEL C. CLAUDE, HEALER." Claude, who lives down the side of the hill in a shabby two-room house with goats wandering in and out of the yard, says that he has a surefire cure for AIDS, but that its effectiveness depends on how advanced the disease is. "If the man can still walk," Claude says, "I can cure him." The cure consists of teas, infusions and baths. Within six days from the beginning of the treatment, Claude says, he stops the diarrhea, and his patients begin to gain weight.

"I regulate their blood and I use leaves to remove the lesions from their skin." After six weeks to two months, he says, "all the germs are gone." The price? From $4,000 to $10,000, depending on how sick you are. It was cheaper than AZT, the only treatment for AIDS then available in the United States. From the way he lives, however, it doesn't look as though anyone is paying Claude that kind of money for his cure.

Madame François has her own method. She bleeds her patients with leeches, gives them shots of antibiotics, and at night she says prayers over them to chase away their demons. She is what is known as a *picuriste* (shot doctor), one of hundreds of mambos, houngans and Protestant pastors who provide ambulatory folk medicine in the slums of Port-au-Prince and along country roads throughout Haiti. Like the others, she travels with a beat-up briefcase filled with vials and pills and needles. Picuristes buy their drugs cheap; they dispense dumped medicine from the United States—antibiotics, vitamins, sleeping pills. Most of the dumped oral medicines have expired and are no longer salable in the United States. Such expired drugs are sold by American drug companies and pharmacies to middlemen, who then ship them to Third World distributors. The traffic is not illegal. The medicines Madame François administers by hypodermic are so old you can't even read their labels. She has no refrigerator, so whatever requires refrigeration is spoiled. Hypodermics are the picuristes' biggest expense, so they try to get maximum use out of them, like drug addicts in the developed world. This combination of Western *remèd,* Creole for "medicine," and Haitian application is not exactly what Simon meant when he spoke of "integrated medicine." Madame François's hypodermics, like those of other picuristes, are reused without sterilization up to twenty, twenty-five times. Dr. Jean Pape, who runs the National Research Institute, says that there is indirect evidence that picuriste practice spreads AIDS, especially since most of the people who regularly use the services of the picuriste are being treated with antibiotics for tuberculosis, which in Haiti is often one of the first signs of AIDS.

The houngan Matthieu, a rugged old man who lives in a habitation above Boutilliers in the cool airs of Kenscoff, used to cure AIDS, and perhaps he still does. But he no longer advertises his abilities in this area. His daughter and son-in-law both died of the disease. "I can cure everything," he says. "Malaria, tuberculosis, any kind of fever, syphilis, cancers, whatever. But AIDS—that is beyond our powers." He calls AIDS by one of its common names here, *diare masisi:* faggot's diarrhea. It used to have another name in Haiti: *katrach,* or four H, for the four kinds of people who were originally thought to carry it—homosexuals, hemophiliacs, heroin users and Haitians.

Because their disease is incurable, AIDS patients are particularly susceptible to the depradations of bokors like Benito, who may or may not know that the cure they are attempting is impossible. At the Albert Schweitzer Hospital in the Artibonite Valley, an hour or so outside Gonaïves, doctors see only the last stages of the disease. "Usually," Pape says, "the houngan milks the patient of his last penny before sending him around to the white doctors. By the time they get to Schweitzer, there is no hope, and no money left in the family."

Not all the houngans and bokors who treat AIDS are uneducated people like Madame François or Daniel C. Claude. Max Beauvoir cures AIDS.

"People tell me you have a cure for AIDS. Is this true?" I ask him.

"Of course," he says. "My patients are coming along beautifully." I ask him whether I can interview one of them—anonymously, of course.

"Oh, no," he says, shaking his head and smiling. "They wouldn't want that. Of course you can understand their reticence. But I assure you, my success has been beautiful, just beautiful. It makes me so happy." He refuses to say what he charges.

"Will you share your discovery with the rest of the world?"

"In good time," he says. "All in good time. We wouldn't want to be premature, would we? I want to make sure that it is generally successful, you see."

I ask him whether he is aware that Western doctors have declared the disease incurable, and that all over the world scientists are trying to slow the disease, find a vaccine, find a cure.

"Of course I know this," he says, smiling the same smile Simon used when he spoke of integrated medicine. "But there are things, my dear, that Western doctors have not dreamed of in their philosophies. You don't suppose that Western doctors are our equal in medical learning, do you? After all, what Western doctor can make —or unmake—a zombi? The West does not know everything. We can do many things, and I assure you, my AIDS patients are coming along beautifully."

People like Beauvoir offer AIDS cures not to the poor of La Saline —who can't afford the steep fees—but to people from Pacot and Pétionville, to whites, and to Haitians from the diaspora. In most cases of disease, such people wouldn't dream of going near a houngan. When Jeanne and Sylvain's daughters get sick, Jeanne takes them to see a doctor on Rue Berne, downtown in Port-au-Prince, where the best Haitian doctors have their offices. Once, when she herself was ill with malaria, she checked into Canapé Vert, the fanciest hospital in Haiti, between Port-au-Prince and Pétionville. Sylvain and Jeanne have spent many years abroad, and they know all about CAT scans, X-rays, chemotherapy, angioplasty, penicillin and open-heart surgery.

But they weren't prepared for the diagnosis of Sylvain's brother. AIDS. The brother used to hang out with Canadian tourists and people from the Canadian Embassy, and they spent many nights in the early 1980s in Carrefour at places like El Caribeño. Sylvain thinks that that is where his brother picked up the virus.

"He always loved the Dominican girls," Sylvain says. "So did our father, and so did I. But I stopped at about the time I married Jeanne, thank God. My brother gave it up only after the AIDS scare, but by then it was too late." Sylvain's brother hadn't been feeling well for a long time when he was finally diagnosed. The family decided to send him to Paris, where the best AIDS treatment was thought to exist. He went, but the disease continued to progress. Finally he came home, so ill he could no longer walk. He was desperate.

"Look, he never believed in the stuff, you know," Sylvain says. "But when you are in the state he was in, you start to think that anything is worth a try. And you can't forget that we were all brought up—all Haitians are brought up—on stories of loup-garous and spells and magic. It's what our nursemaids teach us about in the crib, for Christ's sake. And when you are desperate, this stuff starts to come back to you, or maybe you start to come back to it. Whatever.

"Anyway, my brother wanted to see the houngan. He was insistent about it, it was the only thing he had the strength left to insist on, and even though Jeanne and I thought it was ridiculous, we couldn't refuse him. I think in the backs of our minds there was still the hope that, who knew, maybe it might work. No matter how you reject the mumbo-jumbo, you believed it as a child, and it's all still there, waiting for an emotional crisis. You know how these fancy women will go to the houngan if they're having trouble with their boyfriend. Michèle Duvalier used to do it, they say. Well, we did it, too."

They went to see Matthieu in Kenscoff, and brought him back to see the sick man. Matthieu had not yet decided that AIDS was the one incurable disease. He agreed to treat Sylvain's brother. He came to pray over him at night with candles and two hounsis. He made him a wanga, a charm like the one Katylee had worn around her neck, and he bathed him in special sharp-smelling leaves. Sometimes the treatment seemed to reduce the fever, Sylvain says. Sometimes the diarrhea stopped for a few days. But the skin diseases never went away, nor the cough. Sylvain says that now he thinks the lowered fever and better digestion were just a part of the natural course of the disease.

"But at the time, you have to understand, we were desperate to believe that Matthieu could do it. Every sign of improvement, no matter how slight—and believe me, they were slight—made us hope. And then he died." Sylvain shrugs. "Jeanne won't even talk about it now, as you can imagine. It's embarrassing, and we allowed Matthieu to come only in the dead of night. It's too ridiculous to have other people know, even though *they* probably do it, too. We never told my mother. She is a good Catholic and would have been outraged. She would have called in the priest, and my brother wasn't interested in the priest.

"Now I think of it as something we had to do. I think if I had AIDS, or Jeanne, we would do the same thing again, even though it didn't work for my brother. When something is really too horrible to bear, you resort to the spirits. Magic. It's funny, you know. People who really believe in voodoo—they go to the houngan until they are so sick that they figure, What the hell, I'll give the white doctors a try. We simply do it the other way around. With AIDS, both have the same result, it seems." He smiles. "Maybe Matthieu couldn't help us because we had rejected the spirits for so long." He smiles again.

The Beast of the Haitian Hills (La Bête de Musseau), a novel written in 1946 by the mulatto brothers Philippe Thoby-Marcelin and Pierre Marcelin, tells the story of a Haitian mulatto who, filled with remorse after the death of his much-beloved and much-betrayed wife, decides to leave Port-au-Prince and become a gentleman farmer in the hills above the city. The bucolic locale of Musseau to which the protagonist, Morin Dutilleul, repairs is today a wealthy suburb between Port-au-Prince and Pétionville, filled with the villas of mulattos and American diplomats. But in 1946 Musseau might just as well have been Duverger or Beau Champ for all it had in common with the metropolis.

Morin Dutilleul buys a tract of land and believes he will be able to enlighten the peasants of Musseau with his knowledge of modern planting techniques and his sophisticated but tolerant understanding of their ways. He makes many mistakes, the most basic of which is arrogance. He does not hesitate to lecture the local justice of the peace, nor does he hold his irreligious tongue in the presence of Bossuet, the powerful Musseau houngan who is able, so local legend has it, to transform himself into the fateful Cigouave, a beast that lives in a nearby grotto, half man, half ferocious, night-prowling devil-dog.

Dutilleul rapes his young housekeeper, drinks himself stupid every night and rebukes the peasants for their ignorance, with impunity. One day, when he sees the peasants leaving offerings at the foot of the mapou on his land, he decides that enough is enough. The next day, he and his hired man chop down the tree. The villagers are horrified:

"Oh, godmother! Master Morin has gone completely crazy, yes, ma'am! He has just cut down the mapou tree by the spring!"

"The altar of Almighty Legba!" groaned the shopkeeper, her eyes wide with terror. . . .

"Now all the women with child may well hold their bellies and scream, for evil days have fallen upon us. Mark my words!"

". . . He did it because this morning he found a food offering which Bossuet and I had just placed at the foot of the mapou tree in honor of Legba. He declared that the tree, growing on his side of the brook, was his property. Since it belonged to him, he could not tolerate such lawlessness on our part. He would make sure it could not happen again. . . ."

From then on, things do not go well for Master Morin. His servant girl becomes a loup-garou, enslaved to Baron Samedi. He himself gets more and more drunk each night, and hears the wild call of the Cigouave beneath his window. In his drunkenness, he rapes the girl again, and she, in her stupefied werewolf state, believes him to be Baron Samedi himself. Coming to her senses the next day, the girl flees Dutilleul's house. He himself, "overwhelmed by a profound lassitude," leaves Musseau, putting the hired man in charge of the farm. When the deteriorating hired man comes to him later, begging for advance wages so that he can pay a houngan to offer a sacrifice to Legba and appease the god for the uprooted mapou, Morin lectures him:

"I would like nothing better than to do such a service for you . . . but not so that you should squander your money on that houngan. . . . I am sure that the pains you feel come from that bad case of yaws you have on your back and legs. Now what you should really do is go to the hospital where they will take good care of you. . . . And I will foot the entire bill until you are well. But as for advancing you money to throw away on those superstitious ceremonies, that I will never do!"

Soon after, at his wife's grave, Morin runs into a friend of hers, who tells him that the reason his wife had decided to have the child

whose stillbirth killed her was to put an end to his continual philan-
derings. This is the final blow. In a guilt-ridden panic, Dutilleul
drinks himself blind for seven nights in a row, and awakens to find
himself back at Musseau, the Cigouave at his bedside, "its phospho-
rescent eyes upon him. It was panting like a dog, with dripping jowls
hanging loosely." The animal chases him relentlessly from his bed
and through the streets until he reaches the Pétionville highway and,
rushing blindly on, falls into the ravine.

The Beast of the Haitian Hills is a cautionary tale about sophisticated Haitians who choose to ignore the depth and meaning of voodoo. Written twelve years after the end of the U.S. occupation, it is
full of the intellectual lessons that the new wave of ethnology and
Negritude had taught the Haitian elite. The peasant is human, the
elite had learned, and his beliefs, however primitive they may seem,
have real significance in terms of the life he leads. The elite, the new
intellectuals said, must begin to understand the Haitian peasant.
They must begin to recognize the inextricable ties that bind not only
the peasant but the elite to the land and to the beliefs practiced upon
it.

Revile and ignore the peasant at your peril, the new philosophers
warned. Haiti could not exist as a sovereign nation, free of outside
control, without respect for its peasantry. The republic of Port-au-
Prince had never effectively stood alone against foreign intervention,
had never produced anything that could be called economically useful. Undeniably, it was the peasantry that gave the country what
meager economic standing it could claim, cutting the cane, harvesting the rice, planting and picking the coffee. They were the ones
who led and supported the Caco guerrilla war against the Marines.
To be strong and free, the elite and the peasant must stand together,
as they had under Dessalines, Christophe, and Pétion, when at last
Haitians of all colors and classes decisively routed the French.

But this new lesson was not easily learned. For more than a century, the elite had been trying to lengthen the distance between itself
and Haiti's backward peasantry. Painfully Frenchified, the elite was
desperate to win membership for Haiti in the exclusive club of civilized nations. The only way for a black nation to do that, the elite
understood, was to whiten its skin and act like Frenchmen. So the
elite married light, baptized their children, sent their sons to school
in Paris, spoke only French in public, said their catechism faithfully,
and rejected everything that pertained to peasant life, especially
manual labor and voodoo. The men let the nail on their pinky fingers

grow long. As Philippe Thoby-Marcelin wrote in his afterword to *The Beast of the Haitian Hills,* "Like all the people of the bourgeois milieu to which I belonged, I [had] considered the Vodoun cult a body of superstitious practices, grotesque as well as dangerous, probably including human sacrifice and even ritual cannibalism." By rejecting voodoo, the elite felt, it was making common cause with the civilized world, the world of the white man.

The U.S. occupation, and national resentment over the Americans' racist behavior and imperialist goals, fertilized the intellectual soil for the new, proto–Black Power movement. The occupation taught the elite that despite their best efforts, they were still unregenerate Negroes in the eyes of the civilized world—as represented no longer by the more tolerant French but by the new emerging white world power in the Western Hemisphere—hardly better than their coal-black brothers in the fields, and often equally unfit to enter the Americans' houses through the front door. Unwittingly, William Jennings Bryan, then Secretary of State, summed up American attitudes about the Haitian elite after he had his first briefing on the country in 1913, two years before the occupation began: "Dear me! Think of it!" he said. "Niggers speaking French!"

They did speak French, and that was just one sign of how little interest they had up to then in their country's Creole culture. The Négritude movement, with its literary rediscovery of voodoo folklore and its anthropological rediscovery of voodoo ritual, sparked the elite's intellectual curiosity, but did not move much farther than that. Not surprisingly, the religion of voodoo never moved back into public practice among the elite.

Nonetheless, patterns of thought and behavior that one can see in voodoo occasionally manifest themselves in Haitian political behavior. Old bokors in the hills of Haiti will look at a sick man, nod their heads and say, *"Nèg fè, nèg defè."* What one man does, another can undo. When a houngan says this, he means that he can counteract a spell cast by another houngan. But the proverb can be applied equally to practitioners of politics in Port-au-Prince, whose vision of political goals is often obscured or twisted by an intense personal rivalry with other *nèg politik.* Doing and undoing: this is what Haitian politics is about, and it is one of the reasons Haitians rarely describe political activity as a continual movement forward, but rather as a process of correcting the mistakes of the past.

Each political party, like each habitation in the countryside, has traditionally been the province of a single powerful man. The parties

have traditionally been based partly on ideology but mostly on personality—one of the reasons so many Haitians laughed when the
1987 Constitution, with Papa Doc in mind, forbade the "cult of
personality." Sylvio Claude's Haitian Christian Democratic Party
has little to do with Christian Democracy as it is meant elsewhere in
the world, and everything to do with Pastor Claude and the network
he has built up with his charismatic Creole preachings. Hubert de
Ronceray's party is a tool to advance his political ambitions, and the
same goes for Leslie Manigat and Grégoire Eugène, two other politicians who were to run for President in the upcoming elections.

Like the habitation, these parties consist usually of a core of about
twenty-five men—and a hundred or so hangers-on—whose own personal ambitions are tied to the success of their leader. Madiou, the
Haitian historian, calls this the *père de famille* problem, the head-
of-the-family problem, where the children, or followers, submit
themselves to the will of the father, or leader. A good mulatto,
educated in Paris in the early 1800s, Madiou writes that these political problems come down from Guinée, that they are distinctly African. Whatever their origins—and Madiou is often condescending
about black Haitians—the tightly knit *groupuscule* and the cult of
personality exist today much as they did in Madiou's Haiti, and in
the Haiti of the Emperor Henry.

In structure, there is hardly any difference between political parties of the democratic opposition and the groups that attached themselves to various Duvalierist figures like retired General Claude
Raymond or Franck Romain, the mayor of Port-au-Prince, or Clovis Désinor. All are based on attachment to the *gwo nèg,* the big
man. The rule of one houngan, however, is rarely threatened by the
actions of another. Each has his own circle of adherents within a dis-
tinct geographical and familial location, the habitation. In Port-au-
Prince politics, however, the "habitations," or parties, are vying with
one another for total control. Power sharing is not yet a received
concept in Haitian politics. Thus one gwo nèg will take possession
of the National Palace—the peristyle, if one takes the metaphor too
far, as Papa Doc did—leaving all the others without a habitation
whose spoils and offerings they can live off.

This feeds into a culture whose voraciousness is based on poverty
and rigid limitations. All of Haiti is like Joyce and Eldon's Passe-
Reine: there is so little to go around, and anyone who takes more
than his share is subject to suspicion, envy, recrimination, dechoukaj. The President is always perceived by others within the politi-

caille as someone who has taken more than his fair share, although the Haitian people are usually willing to give him the benefit of the doubt for a short time. Thus, the minute a man becomes president, he becomes a usurper of the habitation as far as his rivals are concerned and must be overthrown. The population in general eventually begins to mistrust and resent the President, while fearing him, much as the members of a habitation may fear and resent the houngan. The only people who continue to believe in the President are his own men, his hounsis, who participate in the spoils of his regime. Everyone else in the country is excluded.

François Duvalier took this method of governance to its extreme: not just Port-au-Prince, but all of Haiti, would be his habitation. He was cleverer than most politicians, and realized long before he took power that with only his political followers in Port-au-Prince to defend him, he like all other presidents before him would soon fall prey to the machinations of those he had excluded. He therefore looked to the hills for his salvation. In expanding his network to include thousands of lesser hounsis—the rural Tontons Macoute, who received a pittance from the palace for their services and were granted impunity in their own regions—he established a faithful cadre willing to terrorize an entire nation into submission to the supreme bokor.

Since the Revolution of 1804, groupuscule allegiances, cults of personality and a reliance on spoils and revenge have characterized Haitian politics. Westerners have long sought the underlying reasons for this inefficient and often violent tendency. Too often, it is dismissed, as Madiou dismissed it and as U.S. State Department employees dismiss it and as wealthy Haitians dismiss it, as an African trait, as though methods of conducting politics were carried in the blood and in the skin.

Haitian politics, however, has not been transmitted by the fact of race but rather by the facts of history. The Haitian Republic is still a unique phenomenon, born out of a successful slave revolt. Its freedom was not gained after a long transition to independence; the republic's was a bloody birth with no midwife present. No Raj was established on Haitian soil; the French did not take their slaves and educate them and give them positions of governmental responsibility. Instead, slaves were purposely denied education; without learning, it was believed, they would not know enough to revolt, and even if they should rebel they would not be able to work out a successful campaign against the slaveholders. Other wars of independence, like the American Revolution, were led by rebellious colonials or elite cadres of the colonized, who established governments that in many ways resembled those of their mother nations. The Haitian slaves had no such political roots; most of the colonials on the island joined with the French in opposing the slave revolt, and many of those who managed to live through the revolution were methodically exterminated as potential spies, enemies of the black man's freedom.

The slaves of Haiti had only two models on which to base an idea of governance: the plantation and the tribe. Though some of their leaders had learned to read and write, they could not, nor did they try to, impose a new form of order on the Haitian people. In Haiti the people rebelled against slavery and then replaced it with nothing. (Henry Christophe, indeed, established a new plantation society in the north, literally upon the ashes of the old; and Pétion in the south and the west allowed the former slaves to revert to subsistence.) These new Haitians defined themselves in a negative way: they were not slaves. They were freemen. Now they could eat everything they grew.

Slaves became peasants, and their descendents have remained peasants. In examining how the country has been run—or not run —it is useful to think of it as France was during the period of feudalism, even if the analogy is not exact. Some peasants, not only mulattos but blacks as well, have amassed wealth and power, and the rest, living on subsistence farms or doing day-work for the wealthy peasants, are ruled by these families. These families traditionally have control of their province's major town—Jean-Rabel, for example, or Fort-Liberté, or Hinche—as well as of large tracts of the land surrounding it. With their ample pocketbooks, they buy off the local military forces, who along with armed civilians—friends of the family—ensure the family's continuing domination of the peasantry. These feudal lords send their sons to France or the United States for their education, and the sons become government officials, Army officers, priests. The serfs remain on the land, illiterate. Slowly, with the help of peasant organizations, this is changing, but among the ruling families there is great resistance to such change. No vast, resentful bourgeoisie that would clamor for equal access to resources and for some kind of democracy has come into being in Haiti; the country's resources, concentrated and jealously held in the hands of a small elite, cannot support a vibrant bourgeoisie. Worse, the nation is divided into city-dwellers and peasants, and the Port-au-Prince shopkeeper, like the slaveholders before him, does not usually believe that his prosperity would be enhanced by uplifting the peasant masses.

François Duvalier did two things that have slightly accelerated change in Haiti. He gave tens of thousands of illiterate peasants and slum-dwellers a sense of empowerment by including them in the Tontons Macoute. He lifted up the *untermensch*, as so many fascists have done. And by unleashing this secret police—many of them often no better than hired thugs—on the less accommodating of the ruling families, by allowing and ordering the murder of all who opposed him, and by continuing the destruction of the country's economy through the corruption and graft that were already endemic, he created the huge Haitian diaspora. Once these displaced Haitians had seen what they were capable of achieving in adopted countries whose economies worked, many of them vowed to bring what they had learned in exile back to the land of their birth. In other words, with the Tontons Macoute, Duvalier created an underclass with a new sense of its potential power, while at the same time forcing the elite and his many enemies in the bourgeoisie into exile and into a new awareness of their potential for changing Haiti. During the years that followed Jean-Claude's downfall, the two new pseudoclasses often clashed. *"Li se yon dyas,"* a contemptuous street kid in Gonaïves would say of the well-intentioned Senatorial Candidate. He's from the diaspora. *"Limemn? Se ti makout li ye,"* a returned exile would similarly say of some young peasant who was now advocating the overthrow of the "petit-bourgeois, electoralist" elite. "Him? He's just a little Macoute."

The First National Congress of Democratic Movements took place outside Port-au-Prince during the last weekend of January 1987. At first, its organizers were nervous: Would the participants really turn up? Would they find the money to take tap-taps into town from as far away as Cap-Haïtien and Jérémie? And then, if people came and the Congress was a success, would the Army decide to attack this show of opposition strength? Most of their worries were unfounded. The Congress went off smoothly enough, an impressive event, with scores of small grass-roots organizations from all over the country converging on the capital to discuss what had happened since Duvalier's fall and what strategies would best serve the people as the nation advanced toward elections. The Congress—its organization, its breadth, and its openness—clearly demonstrated that in spite of the stubborn resistance of traditional elites, a grass-roots movement for democracy was gradually accelerating. The government kept its hands off the Congress. It sent spies.

The Congress was held in a huge meeting hall run by the Salesian order, and went on each day until deep into the night. Meetings began indoors, and afterward, workshops were held out on the grounds, under the stars. Famous Port-au-Prince lawyers listened as peasants spoke about how country people could inject their ideas into the new Constitution. Schoolteachers and priests who had left the Church railed against the human-rights abuses that had been committed by General Namphy and his army. Rich mulattos sat on the dais with choir girls from the slums. The diaspora was present in scores.

The leadership of the Congress took pains to emphasize its plural-ism. Not only peasant and worker movements but civic associations, youth groups, women's organizations, neighborhood committees, human-rights advocates and even the Catholic Church (both pro-gressive priests and hierarchy, the Congress organizers claimed) were participating, they pointed out. If you looked carefully at the participants, you could find, at one time or another, almost everyone who was involved in the opposition in Haiti: exiles returned from Paris, the Dominican Republic, Venezuela, New York, Montreal, Miami; future presidential candidates; priests, nuns and pastors; Duvalier's former political prisoners; houngans; musicians, agrono-mists, doctors, lawyers, engineers and radio broadcasters; and the Gonaïves students who had led the fiercest demonstrations against Jean-Claude in 1985—everybody was there. Aristide sent some of his people over, and if you looked hard you would see the future Senatorial Candidate holding a burned-down cigarette in his hand, looking bemused and listening to some long speech at a workshop on the peasant movement or whispering up against the meeting-hall doorway with a Congress organizer.

On the evening the Congress opened, a Christian blessing was invoked for its success, and then the speeches began. But the Chris-tians were a little late. The night before, the vaudouisants, with the houngan Hérard Simon at the helm, had held a ceremony to seek the spirits' approval for the Congress. I drove out to the peristyle with the leader of the League of Former Haitian Political Prisoners. He was handling a big Mitsubishi jeep with prideful mastery, and blasting American music on the elaborate sound system. The night was black, and the stars didn't show themselves until we had left the scattered lights of the city behind. As usual, we got lost and arrived late. The ceremony was over, and the party was in progress. The politicians from Port-au-Prince and the uncomfortable members of the diaspora stood in tight groups outside the open peristyle, gossiping, their backs turned to the drummers. Inside, the massive Simon was shaking up a dance with a little boy who certainly knew how to swivel his pelvis. Willowy girls from Croix-des-Bouquets shimmied up in front of Simon and took his attention momentarily. Otherwise, he fixed his small, vigilant eyes on the politicians; he stared at them straight over the little boy's head. The drummers were passing clairin among themselves. Simon didn't drink any.

"In addition to the Catholic Church," the leaders of the Congress had said, "the Protestant denominations as well as other cults, notably voodoo, will of course be invited to participate in the Congress because they play an important role in Haitian civil society." It was a valiant attempt to embrace voodoo, to give the houngans who had suffered through and survived the Dechoukaj a chance to make common cause with leaders and politicians who had at least gone along with the idea of the "uprooting," if they had not supported it. It was an attempt at reconciliation, and Simon went along, for the moment. The Congress' leaders were trying for something historic, a movement that would go beyond the traditional groupuscule of the gwo nèg and his followers, and expand to include all facets of the opposition.

The organizers of the Congress, however, made one mistake. They presumed that, along with peasant, worker and youth movements, voodoo could also be subsumed, as though it were just another political association. But the Duvalier decades, during which voodoo partook of institutionalized power, had strengthened the more prominent houngans, and they had a distaste for assimilation that was bred of a thorough realization of their own force, as events would prove. For now, Simon was with the opposition, because the opposition looked strong. At the Congress' opening ceremonies at the Salesians', he and his hounsis made a second appearance with the drums.

Within a year, however, Simon and others of his "cult" would show a different face, the distorted mask of voodoo allied to the palace. They danced for the Congress in early 1987, but no one in voodoo had forgotten the money-making powers that the Duvaliers'

Tontons Macoute had conferred upon practitioners and priests, nor had any of the influential vaudouisants forgotten the more recent desecrations of the Dechoukaj. Voodoo is an oral religion, and that means it has a long memory. Men like Simon and Beauvoir didn't need to refer to their newspaper clippings to remember who had salted their food during the preceding years. It was not to the opposition that they had looked then. The opposition had been, for the most part, in exile. The big houngans hardly remembered who the exiles were. They had a clear memory, however, of Papa Doc, his thick glasses, the hat, the gourdes they had gathered while others lapsed further and further into poverty. Today, perhaps, the opposition was powerful. Today, perhaps, they would give the opposition a try. But if the opposition should fail . . . Simon could dance for one master today, and dance for another tomorrow. Voodoo has no immutable master.

Words of Deliverance: 2

It was a small item in *Le Matin* toward the end of July 1987: "The Reverend Father Jean-Bertrand Aristide will soon be moving from St.-Jean-Bosco to the church at Croix-des-Missions, where he will be the pastor of the parish." Croix-des-Missions is a parish on the edge of Port-au-Prince. I heard about the item from the Well-Placed Embassy Official, who told me about it with ill-concealed glee. He didn't recall the new assignment precisely, however. "I think they're sending him somewhere in the Dominican Republic," he said.

Aristide was angry. He held his coffee cup tightly in his fist as he talked one morning about the move. "They're just trying to get rid of me," he said. "Typical, that the embassy would say the Dominican Republic. They'd like to get me out of the country. And the Church in collusion as usual." He was feeling victimized. The move would mean a complete change in his ability to reach his people and in the way he conducted his life.

Like everyone in the progressive church, Aristide had little affection for his employer; that included the Papal Nuncio, as well as the Haitian hierarchy and Archbishop Ligondé of Port-au-Prince, related by marriage to Jean-Claude Duvalier. The resentment was mutual. The regional director of his order had told him of the new assignment, Aristide said, and while he would resist it within the bounds permitted by the Salesians, he would eventually obey.

Aristide had been a subject of controversy at St.-Jean-Bosco for some time, and the controversy was not just about his brand of theology. His relations with his mentor, Father Désir, who was now nominally in charge of the church complex, had soured over the years since Aristide had come to St.-Jean-Bosco. Jealousy may have played a part in it; once Aristide started preaching, the congregation began to grow, and it was obvious whom they were coming to hear. His personal appeal and the strength of his preaching attracted a large and fiercely loyal group of young parishioners who had never shown such affection for Father Désir or for the other Salesians at St.-Jean-Bosco or Croix-des-Missions, although not a few of those priests were quietly progressive.

Rather than work within the bounds of the programs for the poor that had already been established in the slums by others among the Salesians, Aristide chose to initiate his own projects, most notably Lafanmi Selavi (C'est-la-vie Family, named after one of the street boys, Selavi). This organization, run by Aristide and a core group of involved young people, worked to find funding in order to provide housing, food and vocational and literacy training for boys like Waldeck and Ayiti and Ti Bernard, while allowing them complete freedom. Aristide did not hesitate to emphasize the political underpinnings of Lafanmi Selavi, pointing out in interview after interview that the condition of these children was the result of a society in which the rich were unutterably rich and the poor impossibly poor. He blamed the condition of the children on the state itself, and portrayed Lafanmi Selavi as one of the very few projects in Haiti that sought to raise the consciousness of the people it was intended to help, rather than simply to feed them. This did not endear him to those within the Church, and especially among the Salesians, who had been working modestly with Haiti's poor for decades.

The Salesians, who arrived in Haiti about fifty years earlier, had grown used to working quietly under tyranny. Dr. Duvalier had left the order essentially untouched; its members had abided strictly by the example of Saint John Bosco, who had selflessly served the poor. The Salesians worked with slum-dwellers in La Saline, Cité Soleil and the smaller bidonvilles in Pétionville. But for the most part they did not raise their voices against the Duvalier dictatorship. Only in the late 1970s, when U.S. President Jimmy Carter began to point to human rights as an issue in the Third World, did members of the order begin to speak out, and then only rarely. Even so, it was not clear what the hierarchy within the Salesian order thought about the propriety of such preachings.

The order transferring Aristide to Croix-des-Missions was a repeat performance of an episode from 1986, when the Salesians had enjoined him to silence. That time, he threatened to leave the country, because he could not obey the order in good conscience. But the youths from his congregation would not let him go. They blocked his way and held him and the other priests, including Father Désir, virtually hostage at St-Jean-Bosco for fifteen days until the Salesians rescinded the order. It was during those fifteen days that Aristide had had his first famous nervous prostration.

Croix-des-Missions, Aristide's new assignment, was known as a bastion of the Tontons Macoute, and many of the men Aristide excoriated every Sunday lived nearby, among them Isidor Pongnon, the young cigar-chomping commander of Fort Dimanche, and Henri Namphy, president of the military junta. The church there was tiny, about half the size of St.-Jean-Bosco, and about ten to twenty minutes out of town by car. It was longer by foot or tap-tap, the way most of Aristide's congregants would have to get there. Nor was it a safe place. Instead of being surrounded by his protectors from the slums, the priest would be encircled by his enemies, and the broken windows of the residence at Croix-des-Missions faced out onto the plain where most of them lived. He was being exiled to enemy turf, and, in fact, the Church had not offered him the pastorship: there was already a pastor in place, with whom they were satisfied. All the priests at Croix-des-Missions were *blans*, white foreigners, Belgian and Dutch. Even without its political overtones, Aristide's new assignment would have been an awkward one.

A few days before he was supposed to move out of St.-Jean-Bosco, Aristide packed his bags in the dead of night. He was anxious to avoid a repetition of the previous year's scene, when he had been held by his own people. He did not tell his congregation about the impending move, nor did he inform the young people who were his most loyal followers. Only a very few knew, those he needed to help him pack and move.

The Sunday before the move was scheduled, I went to mass at the church. But by ten-thirty, an hour after the mass usually began, Aristide had not shown up, and most of the congregants were standing around outside the church, wondering where he was.

"*Titid pa la,*" Waldeck said to me. Titid's not here.

"Where is he?" I asked.

"I don't know," he said. "No one knows. I'm scared."

"What if he leaves us here, by ourselves?" said Ayiti. "The soldiers from Fort Dimanche will come and pick us up."

"Titid left this morning," said Ti Bernard, running up to the group with a deflated soccer ball in his hands. "Early, it was still black out. He took the little Charade."

"You saw him?" I asked.

"With my own eyes," said Ti Bernard. "He was with a friend, he had his valises with him."

"Hey," said Waldeck, coming to join us. He grabbed my hand. "Give me some money. If Titid's gone, we won't have any money. And the strikes too. No money. Give me some money."

"No," I said. "They'll take care of you. Don't try to fool me." Under Aristide's supervision, the kids each had their own little safe-deposit box where they kept their valuables—things like sneakers and marbles and a couple of dollars. Waldeck already had twenty or thirty dollars in his account, Aristide had told me, laughing.

"Ou chich," said Waldeck. You're cheap.

Aristide disappeared into the countryside. For a week, no one knew quite where he was. Soldiers from Fort Dimanche started arresting the boys who were washing cars at the intersection near the church. Four were beaten and held overnight. Waldeck went on the radio to denounce the arrests and tell what he had seen: a truckload of grown men in uniform beating up boys, handcuffing them and carting them away to prison. The bruised children were released after a few days and proudly showed off the billy-club marks on their chests and backs, but the church people were worried about Waldeck again. No more interviews, he was told. Absolutely no television.

The young people from St.-Jean-Bosco organized meetings and press conferences to announce that they would not countenance Aristide's removal. There was a rumor that he would be called to Rome after a few weeks at the new church. The thought was intolerable to his followers. "It's not just Aristide we're concerned about," said one of the young organizers at a press conference. "The massacre at Jean-Rabel, that was one action taken against the progressive church, an attack on the church-organized peasant movement. This is the second step, and is not really just an attack on Aristide but on the urban population he represents and on the progressive church as a whole. If we don't stop this, if we don't say no, absolutely no, now, the tide will be irreversible."

Aristide did not remain silent for long. After a tour of the northern province for the festival of Ste.-Suzanne, he arrived in Cap-Haïtien, and gave a lengthy sermon about the importance of self-defense (in French the phrase has a different nuance: *légitime défense*). The mass, which had been planned as an outdoor meeting, was moved into a Catholic school to avoid violence. The Army in the Cap was restive. Thousands of students turned out for the mass, and the school was filled past capacity, with another thousand gathered outside. Even before the service started, Army jeeps began patrolling the street outside the school. Soldiers lined the roads, ostensibly to prevent violence.

Aristide was at the top of his form. The 1987 Constitution, he remarked to his listeners, gives the citizen the right to bear arms at home. He quoted from the Gospel of Saint Luke in which Jesus tells his followers: "And he that hath no sword, let him sell his garment, and buy one." He was not preaching armed struggle, Aristide said later, but merely advocating that the people not face the Army's Uzis empty-handed. "You know those little piles of stones that women here use to do their laundry?" he said. "Well, everyone has a pile like that at home, to beat the clothes clean. I was merely suggesting another use for those little stones." He smiled. "People have machetes at home here, too. Stones and machetes, of course, are not much of a defense against soldiers who come into the slums and the villages and open fire, but at least it's something. You don't want to tell your people to struggle against power and give them no means to defend themselves. If you do, you end up with what we've had so far, which is dead bodies."

While he was preaching, the Army began firing tear gas into the school, and soon after, as the sun set over the mountains behind the Cap, electricity to the city was cut. The students outside dispersed, but the Army kept firing into and over the school, filling it with tear gas. For hours, the priest and his congregation sat inside the darkened church, waiting for the tear-gas cartridges to stop raining down on the roof. All night there was gunfire in Cap-Haïtien.

The government was not impressed with the subtleties of Aristide's preaching, and was quick to attack him. Information Minister Gérard Noël issued a truncated tape of the Cap-Haïtien sermon to the radio stations. On it, Aristide quotes the verse from Saint Luke and then asks, rhetorically, "Does this mean that Jesus is advocating that we keep machine guns or rifles in our homes to protect ourselves from an army of terrorists?" He waits for the audience to respond, but they are confused. So he begins to take up the thread of his argument. "Okay," you hear him say, and then the tape is cut off. That was where he began the lecture about the little stones. In a government communiqué, Noël accused Aristide of preaching armed revolution, and warned him that this was dangerous. Aristide responded with a blunt message that was read over the radio. He called Noël a liar on several counts, and finished with the phrase *"M pa kwè nan Tonton Nwèl."* I don't believe in Father Christmas. The phrase *Tonton Nwèl—Nwèl* is Creole for Noël, the Information Minister's last name—had other meanings as well.

Back in Port-au-Prince, Aristide's followers were busy. The day after the Cap-Haïtien mass, about a hundred of them filed into the cathedral downtown and set up a sound system in front of the altar. They took over the first five rows and quietly sang the songs they were used to singing at St.-Jean-Bosco, for the most part religious hymns with political overtones. That evening, seven among them began a hunger strike, pitching their camp on blankets in front of the altar. It was an example of passive resistance unprecedented in Haitian history. They said they would not leave until certain of their demands were met by the Church hierarchy, highest among them that Aristide be allowed to remain in his parish. For the young people, taking over the cathedral itself was important: to them, the huge building where the Archbishop often says mass is the symbol of the Catholic hierarchy in Haiti.

The Church and the Army were taken aback. From their point of view, Aristide's followers had occupied the cathedral, although anyone is allowed into the cathedral to pray and worship, which is what the youth groups said they were doing. There was simply no way to remove them without resorting to brutal Duvalierist techniques. The Haitian Church was not yet ready to remove young people forcibly from a place of worship. The hunger strike also meant that the hierarchy could not simply wait until the protest petered out, because that might leave the Church responsible for a number of "dead bodies," as Aristide would say. The bishops were cornered. It looked as though what had begun as an attempt to undermine the progressive church was going to blow up in the hierarchy's face.

Every day, the crowds of curious in the cathedral grew larger. Late one afternoon, a solider in civilian clothes entered the church, armed. He was spotted, disarmed and thrown out by the leaders of the youth groups. Aristide's people felt that the man had been sent to disrupt the hunger strike, and perhaps to cause a panic that would empty the cathedral. Meanwhile, the young men and women lying before the altar were growing visibly thinner—though, like most of Aristide's followers, they had started out skinny—and weaker. A few were on intravenous. Waldeck and the rest of the street kids lounged among the strikers, and when they begged from the curious gathered in the cathedral, they didn't mention, as was their wont, how hungry they were. On occasion, even Waldeck had a sense of what was fitting.

Aristide was back in town, at his new parish, also visibly thinner. The little Charade was hidden away, in order to throw his enemies off his track. Death threats were phoned in and relayed to him almost daily. He was under strong pressure to ask the strikers to desist. It was a game of hot potato, in which the hierarchy and Aristide attempted to blame each other for the possible deaths of the strikers. But Aristide would not ask the young people to stop.

"How can I?" he asked. "I didn't ask them to start. It's their strike. I have always insisted that my relationship with these young people is not one of order and obedience. If I used my personal influence to stop it now, what would I be teaching them about struggle? What if because they did not stand firm and force the hierarchy to back down, because of a lack of that strong example, another Jean-Rabel should take place, or the power structure here in town should attack the youth here? What will these kids say to me then? 'Because you were afraid to let four of us die, hundreds have been slaughtered.' Responsibility is a complicated thing. If I asked them to stop, and they did (which is far from certain, by the way), they would have suffered to achieve nothing, and I would be perceived as giving in to the hierarchy's demands. The progressive church would be destroyed by such an action, and I could no longer respect myself, and those kids could no longer respect me." His argument was not illogical. But it could be and was interpreted as his way of using the strikers against the hierarchy and its attempt to remove him from his parish. In fact, many of his detractors claimed that Aristide had masterminded the entire cathedral siege. He denied the accusations, as did the strikers and others among the youth groups.

After six days, the hierarchy was finally forced to accede to the strikers' demands. It was a victory for what Aristide would later call "the People's Church," Legliz Popilè. In a humbling blow to the bishops, the strikers demanded that Aristide himself come to the cathedral to give them the news that he was to remain at St.-Jean-Bosco. They feared that otherwise they might be tricked into abandoning their strike without gaining the concessions they sought. After a long day of negotiations and worsening hunger for the strikers, three bishops, accompanied by almost every member of the progressive clergy, arrived at eight o'clock in the evening of August 19 to say a brief mass in the cathederal, and to read a statement that met with the strikers' broad demands. The night was hot, and even under the high vault of the lofty cathedral the crowd was sweltering.

Then Aristide appeared from the bishops' midst, a tiny figure in white, emerging from among their white cassocks like an actor taking a curtain call, and seeming even smaller than usual in the arc of the cathedral's high altar, surrounded by the entire Haitian press corps and hundreds of his own people. The three bishops were pushed into the background. When Aristide started to speak, the crowd of four or five thousand rose to its feet with one huge cry, and could not be stilled in spite of his repeated pleas. Every seat and all standing room in the cathedral was taken. The night outside was black, but the church was alive with lights and tree branches carried by the people. You couldn't move. Aristide came to the altar, and then left it to embrace each of the strikers, who were seated in various states of collapse behind him. He kissed each one to wild applause from the congregation, who could not see a thing.

And then he preached a short sermon, resonant with the imagery of luxurious food, powerful in a starving country, even more powerful after a hunger strike. "The happiness we feel tonight after this historic victory," he said, "is a slice of the cake of contentment we will one day share. . . . What these young people have achieved here tonight is just a beginning of the work we must do in order to make the regime *rache manyòk*.

"Let us return home calmly now, with happy hearts, with neither noise nor merriment. Let us return home calmly. But when we return home calmly, does that mean the battle is over? No! Let us return home calmly, with happy hearts, so that we may one day reap the rewards of what we have done within the Church and within our nation. So that we can continue our work, so that the struggle can advance, and evil diminish, and so that this battle will finally end, and we can turn that slice of happiness into a whole cake of contentment and sit down at God's table—at the table of brotherhood—and share it together as brothers and sisters. Amen."

That was Aristide's message of goodwill, much of its content—

except for the wildly applauded cry of *rache manyòk*—discussed with the three bishops before his arrival at the cathedral. A confidential U.S. Embassy cable later characterized that message as "highly inflammatory." Afterward, the town was taken over by careening cars and tap-taps honking their approval. The following day Aristide gave a press conference at the church during which he was less joyful and more passionate. During the conference, he could hardly remain in his chair, and kept jumping up and standing behind the table as though he were at the altar. The conference amounted to a restatement of his radical and deeply held belief in liberation theology, but he spoke in new and more profound tones of confidence and power. The victory at the cathedral had clearly emboldened him.

"The church," Aristide said, "no matter what country it is in, cannot remain totally outside what is happening in that country. Now, in Haiti, we are living through a critical situation, where it is not just two or three people who are going to fall into the ravine of death. No, the minute that elections come to pass under the junta, many will perish, many, many will disappear, many, many will die like flies, and the corrupt system in whose waters we are now drowning will be deepened, strengthened.

"We the nation of Haiti are a bicycle, and it is the youth of Haiti who are driving that bicycle. Now, the captains of corruption want us always to be steering that bicycle on a curve to the right, to the extreme, corrupt right, where the road will get worse and worse and we will fall off the cliff of death. But we the youth of Haiti, in the name of our faith, say no! to that right-hand turn. We say yes! to a turn toward the left, a historic turn to the left. Freely, voluntarily, and in the name of our faith, we refuse this right-wing curve of corruption. Instead, we shall advance toward the left, where our real faith, our unshakable belief, can build a socialist Haiti. For only in a socialist Haiti will people be able to eat, will *all* people be able to eat; will people be able to find justice, will *all* people be able to find justice; will people be able to live in liberty, will *all* people be able to live in liberty; will the lives of people be respected, will the lives of *all* people be respected."

"He'd better be careful," said a man who runs a car-rental agency on John Brown. "He's the biggest guy now, and they are definitely going to go after him. They can't just let him go on and on like this, he's too strong. Poison. They put one drop in his glass and he's dead in a minute. It's easy, Haitians are good with poison, we used it to kill the French during the days of the colony, you know. Or they send someone around to blow him away, some little nobody they pay for it, you see. Simple. No one ever knows who did it. I mean, they're not going to use the Army to get him. It would be too obvious. But it's just child's play. They'll do it, they won't hestitate."

Aristide stopped eating food prepared for him at the church. Every day, women parishioners would come into the churchyard with tin pots full of Creole conch, or chicken in red sauce, with rice, and salads. He ordered out from restaurants, something almost no one does in Haiti. All day and all night, young men guarded the church and the residence. The other St.-Jean-Bosco priests, fearing they might get caught in an attack on Aristide, or be manhandled by his followers, had temporarily abandoned the place. The gates to the street were locked. Aristide was alone with his people.

What good did all Aristide's preaching do? It kept certain issues in the public's mind: the military's complicity in violence against demonstrators and unarmed organizers, the resemblance of the junta to the Duvalierist regime, the possibility of a new Haitian society that the Haitian people could build together. It also kept Aristide's name and person at the top of the government's list of personae non gratae, which means in theory that others who believed as he did could go about their business quietly while he took the heat. He took a lot of heat. He was the only one in the midst of the bloody summer who never stopped speaking his mind. He didn't offer political solutions to the impasse at which the people and the regime had arrived. "I'm a priest," he said. "That's not my job." Instead, he offered inspiration to Haitians, inspiration in the form of his fearless example, and inspiration in the form of his brave words.

But Aristide's practice and preaching had a darker side, one he did not intend but was powerless to prevent. His proclamation of a "historic turn to the left," as well as later, even bolder statements, added fuel to the government's anti-Communist campaign. The junta were rounding up opposition cadres all over the country— some of them political organizers who were trying to establish a consensus among the people for an electoral step toward democracy, some of them Ti Legliz priests and nuns organizing peasant land-reform movements, some of them charismatic lay people who were working with peasants and young people, and some of them the peasants and young people themselves—and charging them with Communism. Aristide was protected by his growing fame—or so it seemed for a time—while those who worked in relative anonymity were subject to increasing harassment, detention, torture.

Haitians have a phrase for the useless, yammering histrionics of politicians: *bla-bla-bla*. If you asked kids in the slums about Aristide, they would say, "He speaks the truth." If you asked political observers and other players in the Haitian political game, they would say, "It's blah-blah-blah." Yet their own behind-the-scenes attempts to overthrow the regime failed, usually undermined by last-minute compromising with the regime—for example, the attempt, after all the summer's bloodshed and with the people in retreat, to expand the junta to include members of the opposition. This attempt at a political solution was essayed only when the opposition had lost all its momentum, and the junta easily avoided even responding to the suggestion. Those who criticized Aristide's hotheadedness and blah-blah-blah were stymied by their own hesitation, as well as by their need to organize scores of splinter groups into a unified whole. By the time they got their act together, literally, it was always too late. What was needed was a coalition between the hotheaded and the cool-minded. When that finally was about to happen in November 1987, on the eve of the elections, the Tontons Macoute erupted with their Uzis and machetes and the support of the Army and the elite to destroy that process.

   If, after the strike in the cathedral, Aristide had encouraged his people to work with the democratic sector—with one of the presidential candidates—he might even have been able to save the elections from their sorry fate, although, conversely, his support for a candidate might have aggravated the anger of the Duvalierists. But he remained adamant, again and again saying that elections were not the solution to Haiti's problems, and that they would merely provide a useful cover under which the Duvalierist system could remain virtually intact. Unlike others on the left, however, he did not support a boycott of the elections, because he felt that left-wing calls for a boycott would weaken the Left's credibility and strengthen the repressive hand of the regime. "I'm too smart for that," he told the U.S. Embassy's political officer, according to another confidential embassy cable. "I know that's just what you want me to do, and I won't play into your hands."

In the end, though an astute analyst of the political scene, Aristide was not a politician. He would not boycott, but neither would he compromise. If you were right, he felt, you were right, and there was therefore no need for compromise. He was a true believer, with all that that implies. In any case, he was not temperamentally or politically inclined to compromise, even among friends. The democratic sector was in fact as wary of Aristide and his goals as he was of them and theirs. "Working with a natural leader is hard enough if you're trying to organize anything," said one member of a leftist democratic group. "But working with Aristide—even though he is the most popular figure on the Haitian political scene since François Duvalier—is impossible because he doesn't want to hear what anyone else has to say, unless they agree with him. He listens to three voices only: his own, his youths' and Christ's."

In any case, Aristide's following, while larger and larger, was always volatile, changeable. His people were desperate, poor, unorganized. They faced a regime that was also desperate and disorganized, but armed, well financed by friendly foreign powers, and capable of ruthless repression. In such a situation, it is almost impossible to build a structure for change. The usual blueprints for constructing a revolution do not work.

In a country where the people are starving, the power of the general strike is limited, and the people's loyalties can be bought. In a country where the people are unarmed, the strength of the popular will is questionable. In a country where the Army is cruel and unpredictable, demonstrations cannot be sustained. After the initial outbursts of popular sentiment, you are left with only three choices. You can keep talking, but fail to achieve the goals you are talking about. Or you can organize your people, help them understand the system they are living under, cooperate with other groups, bide your time, and try eventually to make a revolution. Or you can compromise with the enemy, in this case the junta and the United States that backed it, and achieve an imperfect political compromise.

In the end, the Haitian opposition in the summer of 1987 was too fragmented to manage any but the first of these, a lot of talk, although they tried all three. The presidential candidates eventually took over the *rache manyòk* slogan and undercut it, saying they would pull up the junta's roots with the upcoming elections. It would not be so easy as that, they would soon learn. But the failure of the *rache manyòk* movement was not an important failure in the grand scheme of history. Haitian history is full of such failures. The work that Aristide did to raise the people's consciousness in the summer of 1987, the work that the opposition, politicians and priests alike, did to organize the people for change: these were the important successes, ones that began to transform the political understanding of a generation of Haitians.

Four days after the hunger strike ended, Aristide said a Sunday mass in the church courtyard, attended by thousands. As market women gathered around him and kissed his feet, he wept and said, "Today, I feel that I am preaching at my own funeral." Back in the heart of his own religious family, he could let his emotions out, and he did. His voice was subdued, he was allowing his physical frailty, his vulnerability, to show. "Jesus," he said, "had the courage to go to Jerusalem even though he knew that, as a prophet, he would be killed. It is this same courage that brought these young people to the cathedral, the courage of Jesus, in spite of his suffering, to move toward death." He wasn't one to play down the messianic analogies. Women fainted to the left and right from grief over Aristide's persecution. People sobbed throughout the sermon. Afterward they touched him as though the mere physical contact could work miracles for them. They held on to him as if he had been saved from death, or were about to be sacrificed. Old women patted his head until he looked like a wild man, disheveled, his hair pushed flat in places and pulled into puffs in others. "When I look at myself these days," he said, "I don't recognize the man in the mirror."

He had accepted an invitation from the youths of the parish at Pont-Sondé, a few hours up Route Nationale to the north, to speak at a big celebration that afternoon in honor of the murdered peasants of Jean-Rabel. One of the three priests who often visited him at St.-Jean-Bosco had warned him not to go, but he was set on it. "I'm not going to stop my work because some people are trying to scare me," he said. "If you let them frighten you, then they've already won the battle." At the last minute, three of the church youths who were to follow Aristide up to Pont-Sondé in the little Charade decided to stay behind because one of them was ill.

The Army in the Pont-Sondé area, a Tonton Macoute stronghold, had shown considerable interest in the upcoming celebration. During rehearsals for the mass, a corporal from the Army made an impromptu visit to the residence of some of the priests involved, according to the newspaper *Haïti en Marche*. The corporal asked

one of the priests for the names of the others who were organizing
and attending the celebration, for their nationalities, the dates of
their arrival in the area, and what activities they participated in that
were not strictly religious. On the day of the celebration, a sergeant
from nearby St.-Marc warned people he knew not to attend the
mass. Later, while the mass was in progress, soldiers in civilian
clothes recorded the license plates of the cars that had come up from
Port-au-Prince.

But the afternoon at Pont-Sondé seemed calm. In the shade of an
old tomato-processing plant near a canal of the Artibonite River,
parishioners were dancing peasant steps to the drums, and singing
songs about Jean-Rabel. The nearby church was too small to hold
the crowd. Aristide was standing off to the side, talking to the three
priests, relaxed. A French television crew, in Haiti to follow the
Aristide story, took one look at the pleasant proceedings and decided
to head back to Port-au-Prince for an evening off.

A man in peasant rags hovered outside the small circle of priests,
watching curiously. "Which one is Aristide?" he asked me.

"That one," I said, pointing.

He laughed. "That little one has made all the fuss?" he asked. He
smiled and went over to touch Aristide's hand. He kissed it.

It was nearing the time for Aristide to speak, and his arrival on
the podium was greeted, as usual, with pandemonium from the
audience. Huge applause and even wilder dancing gripped the congregation. He took the microphone and was about to speak when
four or five men with guns began shooting into the crowd. Panic
among the people. Some threw themselves to the ground, others
tried to flee over benches and rickety chairs. Aristide, shocked, remained immobile, facing the fire as the people flew out of the hall.
Bullets whizzed around him. He turned and found himself looking
straight into the face of a man who was shooting at him, from a
distance of about twenty yards. He stood there, watching the man
fire, and the man stood there, firing. But the bullets missed their
mark, and a group of French missionaries, realizing suddenly that
Aristide was still standing undefended on the podium, finally surrounded him and pulled him away.

Back at the priests' residence, the people who had come up from
Port-au-Prince debated their next step. Should they return in the
dark to the capital, knowing the dangers of night travel on that
deserted highway, or should they remain at Pont-Sondé, sitting targets for the next attack? Returning, even in the vicious rainstorm

that had just begun, they decided, was slightly less dangerous than staying through the night. Perhaps the rain would protect them. Fifteen minutes after the five cars with the priests, nuns and other invited lay people had gone, some friends from Port-au-Prince arrived at the Pont-Sondé residence and said that they had just come through a very tough barricade at Freycineau, south of Pont-Sondé. The barricade was surrounded by men in rags, carrying machetes and guns, and the people from Port-au-Prince feared it had been built to ambush and assassinate Aristide.

At St.-Marc, just before Freycineau, the five cars returning to Port-au-Prince were stopped at the Army's standing roadblock, and the passengers were ordered to get out. One officer checked the numbers of their license plates with a piece of paper while another searched each car, "for arms." There were other cars on the road, but theirs were the only ones stopped. They stood in the pouring rain for fifteen minutes during the fruitless search. Four priests, including Aristide, got back into one of the cars, along with their driver, Joe Burg, an English-speaking Canadian seminarian who had just arrived in Haiti. After the scare at the Army roadblock, the two priests in the back with Aristide made him lie down on the floor between them and covered him with a cassock.

About a hundred meters farther south, around a bend from the Army post, the caravan was stopped again at a more imposing barricade, made from felled trees, large pieces of concrete and a jack-knifed trailer. About fifty men, armed with machetes, sticks, rocks, pistols and a few Uzis, poured out of the bushes around the barrier. This was Freycineau. "Here's Aristide," some of the band shouted. "Communists!" They began stoning the priests' car, shattering all the windows but one. They knocked out the headlights. Glass was flying everywhere, the priests were hit in the head by flying rocks, and rain was pouring in through the broken windows. Aristide was praying under the cassock in the back, and up front Jean-Marie Vincent, a priest from Jean-Rabel and a leader of the peasant organizations there, was trying to get at his rosary, but he couldn't find it in the panic amid the flying glass and rocks. The men in the crowd were hitting the car with their sticks and machetes. "Get out!" one of them shouted at Father William Smarth, one of the priests in the backseat. A few of the band eyed little bald Joe Burg with suspicion. What was a white guy doing here?

Father Smarth emerged. As he stood next to the car, one of the men from the barricade approached him with his machete raised.

"But, brother, we are just four priests," Smarth said to him. The man lowered his machete, but another in the crowd hurled a large rock at Smarth, hitting him just below the hip. The priest let out a deep moan.

"Who is that in the back?" asked another man, pointing at Aristide, still lying beneath the cassock.

"He's wounded," responded the other priest in the backseat, blood dripping from a wound in his eye. "You want to finish him off?"

Smarth got back into the car while the search proceeded.

Now they were going through the other cars, looking for Aristide. They mistook Axel Martial, a young seminarian, for the priest, and they beat him, stoned him and pushed him up against one of the cars. He was wearing gold-rimmed glasses, like Aristide's, and he was thin as a rail. They had a gun to his head and were about to shoot, when their leader, a soldier in civilian clothes, came up to Martial, took his face in his hands and gave him one quick look. "That's not Aristide," said the soldier, pushing the young man's face away. "Aristide doesn't have a beard." Meanwhile, another group of thugs, mistaking a little green Charade that was part of the caravan for Aristide's white Charade, set it on fire. On the other side of the barricade, headed north, a tap-tap was stopped, blocking any exit.

The tap-tap began to move through the roadblock, but, with the rocks still flying and their headlights out, the priests didn't notice. In the front seat, Jean-Marie, the priest who had been searching for his rosary, finally gave up and commended himself to God. But before he shut his eyes for his final prayer, he noticed that the barricade had changed slightly. Yes, he thought he could see a hole in the left side of the barricade. With blood dripping into his eye, he tried to peer through the rain and the rocks. Definitely it was a space, it looked big enough to get through, even though there was a ditch on that side.

"*A gauche!*" he yelled at the Canadian driver, "*A gauche!*" But Burg just looked at him. "*Allez!*" Jean-Marie shouted.

Burg sat there, wondering why Jean-Marie was yelling at him at a moment like this, and in French, no less. After all, they were all about to die, anyway. What could be making Jean-Marie so angry? And then the priest understood the problem.

"Left!" Jean-Marie shouted, in English. "Come on, go!"

Burg looked to the left, saw a little hole, and out he went, slamming on the gas, through a wet ditch, with no windshield and no headlights, into the drenching rain.

· · ·

No one knew what had happened next. The people in the other cars who were finally allowed through the barricade and arrived in Port-au-Prince that evening had no idea what had become of the priests. Nor did those who had been riding in the ill-fated green Charade, who eventually found other means of transportation to bring them home. On the radio the next day, they said the priests had disappeared after an assassination attempt at Freycineau. No one knew if they had been followed or caught. Their car had simply vanished, and no one had heard from any of them.

"If they were alive, they would have called by now," said a colleague in town. "They would have called." Everyone kept talking about the nuns who had been murdered in El Salvador. At Aristide's church, hundreds of youths had gathered. The capital was tense, awaiting the news. If he was dead, what would happen? The kids at the church were crying. "They've killed him," one said. "Now we will kill them."

"Wait until you know for sure," said another. "Just wait. We don't want to do anything stupid."

A vigil began at the residence of Father Smarth, and everyone who had gotten through the barricade was there. Parishioners from Aristide's church walked around in a daze. They sat listening to the radio, which had no news, and every time the telephone rang they panicked. They wanted good news, but they didn't want bad news. No one wanted to be the one to answer the phone. No news came.

Finally, a car pulled up. Everyone ran outside to greet it. It was Gilles, a French priest from Verrettes, with another white man no one recognized. The girls from St.-Jean-Bosco held back, waiting to hear what Gilles would say.

He smiled at them. "It's okay, it's okay, sweethearts," he said. "He's all right. Everyone's hurt, but they're all all right." The girls started to laugh, and then to cry. "Adrien's eye is hurt, by a rock," Gilles said. "And Jean-Marie's head and his arm, and Smarth was hit in the side, and Titid is fine but he's having a nervous prostration." Gilles smiled at the girls again. "So you see, everything is as usual." He turned to the little white man next to him. "Oh," he said. "And this is your hero, Joe Burg. He was driving the car."

After they had gotten through the barricade, the priests had continued on until they got to a Protestant mission called the Church of God. There they told the people they had had an accident, and they introduced Aristide as Father Jean. They were afraid that they would not be welcomed if his identity were known. The Protestants were nervous right away, and more nervous when they saw the car, which didn't look as though it had been in an accident, exactly, but they let the priests remain and treated their wounds. By dawn, Gilles, who lived not far away, had heard the news and decided that the lost priests must be dead or at the Protestant mission or at the church nearby in the town of Montrouis. He drove over in his pickup truck and finally found them at the church, in various states of injury and agitation.

Later that day, the four came into town in an ambulance, escorted by Bishop Constant of Gonaïves for reasons of safety. They went directly to the hospital, and Aristide, who was hardly injured—a wound on the knee from flying glass required a few stitches—had to be supported on either side and could not talk. Two days later, however, still limping dramatically, he was ready for a press conference with French television. He sat down beforehand and had a cookie and a Sekola Orange.

Three bishops were present at the end of the hunger strike in the cathedral, and Bishop Constant accompanied Aristide home after the attack at Freycineau. It was beginning to look as though there had been a reconciliation between the hierarchy and the progressive church. Nothing could have been farther from the truth. In fact, the hunger strike and the attack at Freycineau had forced the bishops momentarily into the camp of the progressives: they could not afford to let the kids in the cathedral die, and they could not very well desert colleagues who were under threat of death. But in both cases, an essentially physical force had been brought to bear on the hierarchy that coerced it onto the side of the progressives.

These moments were not invigorating for the bishops. Rather, the hierarchy was worried that, along with Aristide, it might be perceived as making that "historic turn to the left." Now that the immediate danger of Freycineau was past, the hierarchy was intent on sending some sort of apology to the junta, on solidifying its alliance with those in power, on publicly severing its ties to the progressive wing. Throughout the unrest of July 1987, according to an August 1987 cable from the U.S. Embassy, then Bishop François Gayot of Cap-Haïtien, who was the president of the Haitian Bishops' Conference, had been meeting with Namphy to discuss the Church's role in what the cable calls "the transition," meaning, presumably, the transition to democracy.

Six days after the four progressive priests were nearly assassinated at Freycineau, the Haitian Bishops' Conference released a message concerning the People's Church in Haiti. It was signed by all ten bishops; even Bishop Romélus, who had invented the *rache manyòk* slogan, had felt compelled to sign the statement—his ties to Aristide, both political and personal, had severely strained his relations with the conference.

> The Church [the bishops' message read] is a body of which Christ is the head and we are the members. Thus, as in all bodies, there must be a relation between the head and the members. Now, if the so-called "People's Church" is going to say "We have no need for the head of this church," that is as much as to say that it is severing itself not only from the body of the Church, but, similarly, from the head, which is Christ. A people's church in opposition to a Church presided over by its legitimate pastors is—from a theological point of view—a deviation from Christ's will and his plans for our salvation.
>
> Consequently, the expression "People's Church," because of the reality and the content of which it is the vehicle, is unacceptable. The Church, following its preferential option for the poor, has struggled and will continue to struggle with the people for their eventual liberation and salvation through Jesus Christ. . . .

In a section discussing various ideologies and their compatibility, the bishops, referring implicitly to Aristide's "turn to the left," had this to say about socialism:

> In most of its forms, socialism is inspired by ideologies that are incompatible with faith. Between communism and capitalism, there is a place for an intermediary route. Could this be socialism? Not at all certain, since no country has had concrete success with socialism. We are calling for a creative effort in this country to find a system adapted to the cultural and spiritual values of our people.

The conference also outlined its own jurisdiction, making it clear that the bishops' hands were tied by Church law in the matter of

Aristide's removal to Croix-des-Missions, as well as his reinstate-
ment in his own parish. This was the responsibility of the Salesian
order, they implied. It was not our fault, they were saying. This was
not at all an apology to Aristide and his parishioners, but rather a
way of explaining to the government why the bishops on their own
had not been able to force Aristide out.

In fact, almost the entirety of the bishops' message was a tacit
response to the issues raised by Aristide himself, or by the People's
Church during the events that had become known as the "Affaire
Aristide." In response to Aristide's sermon on self-defense at Cap-
Haïtien, where he quoted from Saint Luke ("And he that hath no
sword, let him sell his garment, and buy one"), the bishops closed
with this less warlike quote from Saint Paul to the Ephesians:
"Stand, therefore, having your loins girt about with truth, and having on the breastplate of righteousness; And your feet shod with the
preparation of the gospel of peace; Above all, taking the shield of
faith . . . the helmet of salvation, and the sword of the Spirit which
is the word of God." The bishops' overwhelming concern with Aristide's ideology, his teachings, his statements and his comportment,
down to their apparent need to find a Scriptural rebuttal to his earlier
citation, was a measure of how much, during those hot and rainy
summer months, the priest had come to influence the thinking and
the politics of his nation.

"Whatever happened to the little Charade?" I asked Aristide a few
days after he was released from the hospital. I hadn't seen it anywhere.

He looked wistful. He had always liked driving around too fast in
his Charade. "Oh, I gave it away. To those people whose car was
burned at Freycineau. Since they really meant to burn *my* little
Charade. I thought it was only fair."

"I was talking with someone at the embassy the other day, about the
Aristide affair," said the Well-Placed Embassy Official. "And I said
to them, 'Isn't it terrible what happened the other day at Freycineau?' And you know what they said?"

"No, I have no idea," I said, although I could see it coming a mile
away. "What did they say?"

"They said, 'Yeah, too bad they missed him.' " He smiled, and
shook his head.

· · ·

The Affaire Aristide did not take place in a political vacuum. While Church and state were trying to eliminate the priest, the democratic sector had momentarily jumped on the *rache manyòk* bandwagon. Linked together in a loose organization called the Groupe des Cinquante-sept, or Group of Fifty-seven, a large number of grass-roots associations, sometimes as many as fifty-seven, sometimes fewer, sometimes more, were putting together successful general strikes and demonstrations against the junta, while the twenty or so presidential candidates, most of them largely ignored, tried to figure out how, or if, they should wage their campaigns during the troubles.

Campaigning was no easy matter. After the massacre at Jean-Rabel, everyone was wary of organizing in the countryside. And the candidates were right to be nervous. In early August, Louis-Eugène Athis, a prospective candidate, went to Léogane for a meeting, and was macheted and burned to death along with two campaign workers by a crowd of thugs shouting, "Communists!" The murder of Athis, in fact a well-known anti-Communist, stunned the political community, and the government's slow-moving, amateurish investigation did little to quell the candidates' fears that the vicious "enemies of democracy" were working with the tacit encouragement of the junta. After Athis' death, the electoral campaign came to a halt.

In early July, the biggest organization among the Fifty-seven, Konakom, the Coordinating Committee of the past winter's National Congress of Democratic Movements, held a press conference at the Holiday Inn, after a day of demonstrations. It was five o'clock, and an angry storm was brewing in the gray skies outside the windows. While Victor Benoit, the head of Konakom, was announcing that the organization would soon propose names of the people the group had selected as an alternative provisional government to replace the junta, the storm broke. Palm trees whipped in the rushing winds, and you could hardly hear Benoit's voice over the rain. Soon rain began to fall through a leak in the roof onto the papers in front of Benoit and onto his head. It was not a propitious sign for the proposed alternative government, whose members turned out to be uniformly competent and unknown, and whose selection was greeted by a torrent of boredom among the Haitian people.

The morning after the press conference, seven bodies were discovered in the cemetery, washed out of their crypts by the night's raging storm. All of Port-au-Prince was shocked. No one wanted to interpret the event, it was too horrible. The people in the slum that borders on the graveyard were furious. Why did bodies wash out, and not coffins? they wanted to know. A group of them, armed with machetes, hunted down the cemetery keeper, a man who, they said, waited until nightfall and then helped robbers steal coffins from the cemetery for resale. Hundreds of corpses, they said, were lying in their crypts without coffins, a sacrilege against the dead in a country where dead ancestors are living spirits among their descendants, and where zombis, the living dead, struggle to return to their tombs when they realize what they have become. According to newspaper reports, the people from the slum took the cemetery keeper and chopped off one of his arms.

"One good thing about all the assassination attempts," said Aristide, "is that I survived them. I know that sounds silly, or obvious, but think about it this way: Here you have a man, everyone is against him, the Macoutes, the hierarchy of the Church, the government, the Army. They go after him, with guns, machetes, stones. What happens? He survives. How do you think this makes people feel? I'll tell you. They think I'm protected. That I can't be hurt. That Jesus or the spirits are protecting me. That I am indestructible. This is great protection for me, because it makes a hired killer a little reluctant to take me on. Who wants to have on his hands the blood of someone the spirits protect? Worse, if he comes to kill me, the odds are, he thinks, that I will survive, and he will be punished. He thinks a powerful force is keeping me safe."

"Is it?" I asked him.

He smiled. "You be the judge."

Pass by the church at Croix-des-Missions where Aristide was to have moved, turn left after the bridge, and you find yourself back at the home of Gangan Pierre, the painter. It is nearing midday, and Gangan Pierre is trying to eat a mango. It's too ripe, and stringy. He doesn't have enough teeth. He rips out a hole in the mango's skin with his top tooth, and then he examines the fat fruit. A preliminary lick. A nibble, but the mango is too tough. He shrugs, holds it to his mouth, and sucks. A girl comes from the green room with coffee in porcelain cups. She balances the tray on a cardboard box in front of you. An empty bottle of rum sits on the floor next to Gangan Pierre's easel. From the bright courtyard, a chicken seeking shade wanders into the room. It pecks its way through the dirt over to the radio and looks up, turning its head to one side, listening. The radio is playing a commercial for Marianne margarine. When the jingle begins, the bird starts to sing. Its clucking disturbs the gangan into speech. He removes his mouth from the mango. "Stupid bird," he says. The mango is a deflated mess. He throws it toward the chicken, which flaps its wings and runs back through the doorway into the yard. Pierre wipes his mouth carefully with his sleeve. There is orange mango in his teeth.

He turns his back to you, faces the painting he is working on. The white lace of Erzulie's wedding gown is almost finished. Pierre hunts around beneath the easel for white, new white. The tube he comes up with is crusted, cracked, blackened with age. He looks at it with suspicion, but when he squeezes it against his brown palette the paint comes out white, a white squiggle. He picks up a skinny brush.

"This is a country in a drought," he says. "Look at angry Agwe." He points without looking to a painting on the wall, an angry colossus riding over the oceans. "Our people have no water to drink, everywhere they are thirsty. Women walk twenty miles in the countryside to find water to bring home to their babies. Agwe has abandoned Haiti. Last night, he returned. The spirits return now only to show us our sins. The bodies come out of their tombs in the rain. This rain was from Agwe. It is a sign."

He has painted in one of the groom's shoes, a fancy affair with green laces. He is painting white shadows under Erzulie's bosom. He picks up another brush and finishes her shoes. "Agwe says that Haitians have forgotten the spirits. These bodies, coming out of the mud—they are to remind us of our ancestors. Haiti has lost its harmony. For too many years, we have had murder and torture and hunger and the killing of children, and we have forgotten the spirits. We have forgotten nature, but now nature reminds us of our ancestors. Nature says, Do not forget your dead or they will come out of their tombs to remind you. The politicians and the priests must abandon their anger, the Army must put down its guns. We must celebrate the spirits and not lose ourselves in worldly interests. The leaders have lost sight of their goal.

"Their goal, Agwe says, should be to make a country where people can drink water. And the only way to do that is to feed the spirits. Today, Haitians have forgotten to feed the spirits. But we do not all forget. We do not all forget." He dips his brush into brown paint again, and sits back, silent. Minutes pass to the beat of merengue.

He dabs in another shoelace. Sits back. You wonder whether he will speak again. He takes up the rum, opens it and looks at his painting. Outside, there is the noise of a car stopping, and the sound of heavy footsteps.

The gangan's meditation is interrupted by visitors, six men in olive green with Uzis at their sides. As they enter, he motions you to hide your tape recorder. The men are too big and too many for the house, their heads nearly touch the ceiling. He welcomes them with rum and coffee. They use his telephone, the only one near the highway here except for the one at the church at Croix-des-Missions. As they depart, each soldier shakes the gangan's hand. He smiles ruefully when the last one leaves, and shrugs.

"They must put down their guns," he says again, and, turning to the easel, he paints in Army epaulets on Erzulie's groom.

They are dancing at the Roxy Bar, down by the port, two nights after the storm. The electricity is back on, although the air conditioner is still broken. The place is packed. Three Dominican girls are dancing to merengue on a dais in front of a wall of mirrors, and a disco ball sheds fragments of light over the clientele. The girls are wearing gold bikinis. Roxy regulars are performing perfect steps on the dance floor in their tight pants and flared dresses. One man is asleep on the floor. Everyone else is waiting for the floor show to begin.

At center stage is a cot, and on it a body under a sheet. The only thing you can see of this body is its hat, an Army hat with a brim, khaki-colored, like Namphy's. A woman in mourning is sobbing next to the bed, on her knees. A priest appears in a long white robe with a magenta sash. He is wearing a tall peaked hat, a miter. He looks at the body on the cot with concern, knitting his delicate brows and clasping his hands together. It looks as if this bishop is too late to say last rites for the general. Too bad. As the priest leans over to administer a farewell kiss to the dead man's temple, though, an important part of the otherwise inert body springs to life. As the too long kiss is bestowed, a huge caricature of an erection appears beneath the sheet, lifting it slowly like a mountain. The audience laughs and breaks into loud applause, the music starts up again, and seven male dancers, Haitians dressed in black body stockings, luminous white teeth painted on their lips, begin dancing around the two white figures at center stage. They could be the corpses from the cemetery. They embrace the bishop, who throws off his robes and hat to reveal that he is a woman in a gold bikini. She takes one of the black bodies in her arms and, with the rest of them, whirls in pirouettes around the general's deathbed, she and the rest pounding at his shrouded body until the huge erection subsides. When it has finally disappeared, the bishop in the bikini takes a bow, held aloft by the seven toothy corpses, and the man who was sleeping when the show began sits up on his elbows and asks the bishop for a date as she passes by on her way to the dressing room.

The actual General's erection, however, was made of sterner stuff, and in the end the junta stood tall amid the summer's carnage, and refused to *rache manyòk*. All the while, the U.S. government, though momentarily shaken by the strength of popular protest, remained steadfast at Namphy's side. The junta, said Elliott Abrams, then Assistant Secretary of State for Inter-American Affairs, represented "Haiti's best chance for democracy."

A few weeks later, as he stood holding the Constitution in his hand in front of the police headquarters that faces the National Palace, Yves Volel, another presidential candidate, was shot to death at point-blank range by plainclothes policemen who emerged from the headquarters. No one was ever charged with the murder, though there were many witnesses, and video and audio cassettes of the event exist, taped by Haitian television. Less than three weeks later, Abrams wrote that the junta had "contributed importantly to laying the groundwork for a new, more democratic Haiti."

"We got it backwards," said a priest from up near Jean-Rabel. "We should have started with *rache manyòk* and finished with Dechoukaj. With *rache manyòk,* we're the passive ones. We're saying, Please, sir, could you please pull up your manioc so we can move on to our new land? We're the supplicant. Of course, after a year, the junta is entrenched enough not to need to say yes. When we did the Dechoukaj, when we were the active party doing the uprooting, clearing our own field, we were not yet strong enough to pull up the tree. This summer, when we *were* strong enough, we stood around instead, begging these guys to leave on their own. And what did we get for all our pains? Nothing. But there will be another stage, another movement. This thing isn't over yet."

. . .

Waldeck was sitting in the passenger seat of my car. We were going on an ice-cream outing. "Put on the *friz*," he said, pointing to the air-conditioning. Anything cold was a treat for Waldeck and the boys. Except for the air-conditioning in cars, and a few trips to the beach in the dark-haired photographer's car, and the chills that accompany their fevers, they had never been cool. Waldeck pulled down his tee shirt, which he was wearing rolled up under his arms tropical style because of the heat.

"Turn on the radio," he commanded. "No, not that," he said, objecting to the news. "Music." Waldeck wanted only merengue or Haitian *compas*. He tapped his foot and looked out the window at the passing traffic, occasionally waving to someone he knew in the market crowd. A few minutes later, he was fast asleep.

At the ice-cream stand, he orders two vanilla cones.

"Two?" I say.

"Yes."

"But you'll make a mess in the car. You won't be able to eat them before they melt."

"Two," he says. "Yes, I will."

With a cone in each hand, laughing, he gets into the car, and starts licking like a puppy, but he can't do it fast enough, the white ice cream drips down his chin, and finally, with considerable ceremony and preening largess, he gives the second cone to a crippled beggar boy at a red light on Grande Rue.

One day, Aristide and I talked in his little office behind the church, and he tried to explain his personal beliefs. He wanted to show how his understanding of the Bible and Christianity fed into his political views. We sat on folding chairs and he leaned back in his chair, a rare relaxed gesture.

"I believe," he said, "that there are certain forces that motivate men and women: love, anger, justice, cruelty, greed, charity, morality; and those forces which are good, you can put them all together and call them God. The man with the beard in the sky, no, I don't believe in that.

"As for miracles, well, I believe in miracles. The Bible is a scientific book, but you have to have the keys to unlock the science in it. If you simply believe it literally, then you will never understand it.

Literal belief in the Bible is underdevelopment. Is Jesus the son of God? Perhaps not literally. But if you take Jesus as a person whose belief in justice, love, equality, and in man himself pushed him to the farthest limits of man's capabilities, then you can see that he is the son of God—that is, the offspring of all the forces for good that together make up what we think of as God. So are we all the children of God, and that is exactly what Jesus says.

"I believe the Resurrection is an ongoing process. The Apostles— you can see why they developed the idea of the Resurrection. There they were, with Jesus, and they expected him to become a king. There they were, waiting for a king, and instead he was killed. They expected a king and they got a martyr. Now in order to continue as a force they had to believe that Jesus, their leader, was still a force. If the Army here killed me, killed Sylvio Claude [the Protestant pastor and presidential candidate], there might at certain moments have been talk of resurrection.

"The story of Jesus' returning to eat with the Apostles—to me this is interesting in terms of resurrection, how resurrection happens on the human scale. It's as if you had a husband, and he died. Well, often, you would think about him, and he would be with you, and you would remember things and even have a continuing relationship with him, even though he was dead. He would be resurrected for you. That's the way it was for them. In order to survive the shock of Jesus' death, they imagined him coming and eating with them, the simplest thing, you know, the simplest human act, breaking bread together.

"And, of course, it was political as well, if you look at it outside its theological context. They were clever. They lost their king, and were given a martyr. Out of this martyr, through the Resurrection, they made Jesus into something more than a king. They said to the Roman imperialists, 'Look, you think you have taken away our leader? You think by destroying him, you have destroyed the movement? Think again.' And then, by the simple strength of their words and their belief—and we know that those two things combined are the strongest things on God's earth—they used the Resurrection to make him into what they had always said he was, the messiah: God.

"But I'm not saying Jesus was not resurrected. Everything in the Bible is true, you just have to be able to understand it. There are a lot of people, priests too, of course, who don't understand it, and they ruin a lot of people's lives. The Resurrection exists. It is more meaningful than if you could prove that Jesus had returned from death in the flesh. When he was alive, Jesus could reach and talk to and influence maybe, what?, ten thousand people together at the most. No loudspeakers, you know." He laughed. "No radio.

"Now, through books, the Church, his followers, he reaches more and more people every day, perhaps not always in the purest form, but at any rate, he reaches them. So that is certainly resurrection. The spreading of the word, and in our case, in the case of liberation theology, the use of that word in action. In a sense, we are all living Jesus' life every day. We have been living it all summer. It was a good life, even if it was short." Aristide laughed again.

"It's a present?" Aristide asked the girls. They said yes, giggling.

"Ah." He took the package, wrapped in pink and red paper, left over probably from some Valentine's Day. "Thank you," he said. They giggled some more, three young girls from the slums, standing in the church courtyard, each one slender, each smiling, one in a white dress, one in a gingham dress, one in a pink and yellow flowered skirt. There was singing and the sound of drums coming from the church. The singing in the church stopped. It was getting near evening.

The girls kissed Aristide and said goodbye. The minute they disappeared, he started unwrapping the present.

"Who knows what it will be?" he said. "When these people give me gifts, it's very important to them, they are poor people and can't afford much. I like this kind of present, usually it makes me smile." Inside the makeshift package was another makeshift package, in green paper. Aristide laughed. "Probably they spent as much on the paper as on the present." He looked up. The singing in the church had started again, louder.

"Hear that?" he asked me. "The kids are writing a song. It's about this year, the year of solidarity with the peasants. It's about Jean-Rabel, I think, and *rache manyòk*. They were telling me about it this morning. We're going to record it after they finish." The drums reverberated through the courtyard. He fiddled with the ribbons from the package, listening to the drums.

Yet a third wrapping, this one blue foil. "It's pretty, isn't it," he said, continuing to unwrap. Beneath it all, three white undershirts in a plastic bag.

He turned to me, laughing. "Now see?" he said. "That was definitely worth it, wasn't it?" He opened up one shirt and eyed it critically.

"Well," I said. "It might be a little long."

He held it against himself. It came almost to his knees. "Oh, well," he said, philosophically. He folded the shirt back up and put it into the bag. The sky was dark blue in the courtyard.

From the back of the church, through the doors of the sacristy, ten or so young people emerged, one boy carrying a big voodoo drum.

"So?" Aristide said to them.

They gathered around him, and the drummer started playing. The kids began to sing. The song was about the peasants, and the Jean-Rabel massacre, and the generals. They danced and clapped as they sang, and soon Aristide joined in. It was a little peasant dance, like voodoo in the countryside, and in fact very few of them there that night, including the priest, were more than a generation removed from the land.

Blind Antoine was sleeping in the corridor in the dark with his eyes open, and I almost tripped over his golf-club cane as I made my way out to the car.

"I'm cleaning up," said Aristide. He had a broom in hand. He was sweeping the hallway in front of his office. Waldeck ran by with a pail of water. The skinny old woman who worked as a maid in the church was picking up orange plastic chairs and stacking them. There had been a party there that morning, maybe it had been for Blind Antoine's birthday.

Aristide handed Waldeck the broom, and disappeared into a corner. When he returned, he was carrying something the likes of which I'd never seen before.

"Do you know what this is?" he asked me, holding it out in front of him. I backed away. The thing was gray and gnarled. It looked like some prehistoric relic of a mastodon, or a now extinct giant turnip, or a piece of unfortunate modern sculpture. I did not want to touch it.

"It's a manioc," he said, watching my reaction.

"It's so *big*," I said.

"That's right," he said, smiling at me. "It's big, and it grows very deep, and it's very hard to pull up." He looked at it fondly. "I think it's time to put it away now, don't you?"

I smiled at him.

"But just in storage, you see. Not forever. We won't forget where we put it, will we?" He looked over at Waldeck.

"No, we won't forget," Waldeck said, leaning on the broom.

They did not forget. But soon enough, the cabinet where they put that old manioc, and the building that housed that cabinet were burned down to the ground, not by an act of God but by an act of men, and the world Aristide had created for himself and his boys was torn apart and thrown onto the garbage heap where he had once hoped to toss the whole wretched regime. After Freycineau, it had seemed that Aristide had borne as much as it would be expected of a man to bear. But there would be worse, and when worse came, he was not surprised.

Cutting Down Trees

"We're all going to die," said the old woman. Plunging her hands into the dust, Délira Délivrance said, "We're all going to die. Animals, plants, every living soul. Oh, Jesus! Mary, Mother of God!"

The dust slipped through her fingers, the same dust that the dry wind scattered over the high hedge of cactus eaten by verdigris, over the blighted thorn acacias and the devastated fields of millet. The dust swirled up from the highway as the ancient Délira knelt before her hut, gently shaking her head covered with a gray frizz as though sprinkled with the same dust that ran through her dark fingers like a rosary of pain.

She repeated, "We're all going to die," and she called on the Lord.

But so many poor creatures call continually upon the Lord that it makes a big bothersome noise. When the Lord hears it, he yells, "What the hell's all that?" and stops up his ears. Yes, he does, leaving man to shift for himself. Thus thought Bienaimé, her husband, as he smoked his pipe, his chair propped up against a calabash tree. The smoke (or was it his white beard?) flew away with the wind.

"Yes," he said, "a black man's really bad off."

—Jacques Roumain,
Masters of the Dew, 1944

All farmers know that to grow crops you have to have trees. The roots of trees retain topsoil, the nutrient-filled layer of dirt that nourishes whatever you plant in it. Trees keep that good earth in place. And trees keep the cycle of rainfall going. They absorb the rain from the skies, and then the sun heats it back out of them, creating the humidity that again forms the clouds that will bring the rain once more, and water for the seed. Haitian peasants know this, too. *Si ou gen youn sous k ap ba-w dlo, ou pa koupe pye-bwa kote-l.* If you have a stream that gives you water, the proverb says, you don't cut down the trees around it. Peasants use this proverb all the time; it means "Don't bite the hand that feeds you."

In 1924, Dr. J. C. Dorsainvil began his *Haitian History Primer,* still used in Haitian schools today, with the following description:

> After Cuba, Haiti is the largest of the Antilles. Four mountain chains run along its length. Its plains, covered with plantations, are watered by numerous and abundant brooks, streams, and rivers. Forests, coffee bushes, banana trees, and corn cover its mountains, "their summits crowned with clouds."
>
> Because of its natural wealth, its fertility, the sweetness of its climate, and the incomparable beauty of its landscape, Haiti is worthy to be called "The Pearl of the Antilles."

I would like to take the late Dr. Dorsainvil on a plane over the Pearl of the Antilles today. As you fly toward Cap-Haïten from the north, you see clouds, clouds that float over the bit of forested area just south of the Cap. But once the plane has broken through this fluff, there is nothing but bare mountain—impressive, bald peaks and folds that look like the tan flanks of an overworked, abused beast of burden. (One of the smaller mountain chains, in fact, is called Dos d'Ane—Donkey's Back.) Then, farther south, the fertile Artibonite Valley, sitting like an enormous billiard table between the naked mountains and the sea. Here again there is a scatter of clouds, and then, behind the high peaks that back Port-au-Prince, other darker clouds are gathering, moving in from the green Dominican Republic. These are the terrors that bring the rains that burst forth over Boutilliers, sweeping away the streets of the capital and turning the corpses out of their tombs.

Once the richest and most fertile colony in the New World, the Pearl is today the poorest country in the Western Hemisphere. Only some 11 percent of its land is now considered arable, although 43 percent is currently under cultivation, and forest covers less than 7 percent. These facts are not unrelated. A map prepared for the United States Agency for International Development (USAID) shows the areas in Haiti where the land has a 60 percent or higher tree cover, enough trees to make dense forest cover. Of these, only six are larger than twenty square miles. You have to look long and hard at this map to find the other forty or so tiny spots, most of them near the Dominican border. Haiti's Northwest province doesn't have any. Aerial photographs of the Haitian coast show huge buildups of sediment at the mouths of every river, evidence of the loss of topsoil in the interior. Haiti's topsoil is in the sea.

When you travel through the country, you drive over dry riverbeds and through desert terrain—cactus, dust and bare jutting rock—in the oddest areas, up near the mountains, inland on the plains and next to the sea. "The very existence of widespread rocky outcrops in a tropical setting," wrote the authors of USAID's 1985 field study on Haiti,

> indicates the severity of the Haitian erosion problem. . . . Almost always, bedrock exposures reflect accelerated man-induced soil erosion in humid tropical areas. Generally, 90 percent of total nutrient supply is found in the upper 10 cm of tropical soils. Almost everywhere in Haiti, this rich topsoil is gone.

You can read about this problem in books and pamphlets put out by the hundreds by foreign aid organizations whose offices dot Port-au-Prince. Haiti's inexorable deforestation, and its concomitants, drought, famine and disease, have taken on the proportions of apocalypse in the eyes of foreign specialists. The end has long been foreseen. Since the 1940s, environmentalists and other observers have been predicting that Haiti would soon wash into the sea, its rivers become dust, and its mountains and plains deserts. Soon, they say, this land will be a place of scrub and sand incapable of supporting life, a moon country populated by cactus and cockroach alone.

Such dire forecasts for a country so small as to seem manageable —a test-tube nation, as Jean-Jacques Honorat, a Haitian agronomist, has called it—have attracted many experts from the other side of the water: meteorologists, agroforesters, botanists, sylvicultural-ists, anthropologists, zoologists, nutritionists, marine biologists, so-

ciologists, agronomists, epidemiologists and economists among
them. During the past half a century, backed by hundreds of millions of dollars from foreign governments, these specialists have
made their pilgrimage to the doomed land, all on the same quest: to
rescue Haiti from its fate, to water the dust and make the mountains
green again, to fit the country once more into the global scheme, to
mold an economy able to conform to accepted rules, to normalize
the God-damned place. Almost to a man or a woman, the foreign
saviors have been welcomed and ignored by the Haitian government,
and tolerated by the people.

They have done things. Here and there, a highway has been built.
Along that highway, a few water fountains have been constructed,
and some of them still work. At the roadside, windbreaking trees
and oleander bushes have been planted to shield the highway from
erosion. Hundreds of studies have been published explaining the
country's agricultural system. Diagrams and flow charts with arrows
and shading and dotted lines have been drawn to show how produce
gets to market, how money moves. In the capital, a drainage-system
project for rain runoff has been intermittently started and abandoned. Water has been pipelined to Gonaïves. Yaws has been nearly
eradicated. Baptists have built concrete schools in rural outbacks.
Mosquitoes have been bred and sprayed and sterilized and experi-
mented on, in an effort to eradicate malaria. It has been discovered
that mosquitoes breed in those oleander bushes. Reports and statistics on AIDS are being compiled. Here, up in the Northwest, is a
toilet at the residence of a priest. Over here, in Cité Soleil, is a
broken public fountain. Up over here, at Fort-Liberté in the north
near the Dominican border, twenty wood houses have been built for
the poor. Down here, in the south, is another toilet at the Salvation
Army, and a clinic that is open twice a week for four hours. For the
most part, the experts' efforts have been unavailing.

You can read about deforestation and its effects in the books and
pamphlets written by these experts, and then you can read about it
in the faces and bodies of Haitian peasants. The bloated bellies and
orange hair of the children of the Northwest are chapters in a long
book about the failed bean crop, the persistent drought, the pitiful
corn harvest, the lack of green pasture for livestock. The bony arms
and legs of the mountain women, and their skeletal babies, are passages about the lack of water in the countryside, and testimony to
drinking water that is stagnant, infested. The tough sinews and
concave stomachs of the day workers, and their meals and snacks

that consist of clairin and more clairin, are the summation of a story of dry earth, of the need for sustenance and comfort, of crops that are impossible to raise, even with the hardest and most grueling work, of rain that never falls, of food that just isn't there. The long journey to Port-au-Prince and the provincial capitals that some 25,000 starving peasants make every year, peasants who leave their dry fields behind to go live in slum shanties and work, if they are lucky, in poorly lit factories—this journey is an epilogue in the history of a land that no longer provides.

In November 1987, *National Geographic* published an article called "Haiti: Against All Odds," about democracy's imminent arrival in this difficult little land. The piece opens with a photograph of a small child sleeping naked on a sheet of cardboard in a Port-au-Prince slum. The stirring photographs continue: Aristide thrusting a hand into the air as he speaks before a crowd; the Army about to run demonstrators to ground, the body of a man whom troops killed at random in the slums; General Henri Namphy saluting in his impressive gold-buttoned uniform decorated with patriotic blue and red braid; AIDS patients, and the gleaming National Palace juxtaposed with the slums. *National Geographic* included all the requisite photographs in its profile of a troubled nation in transition, as well as a few regulation Haitian pictures: an art studio, a peasant in the mud at a voodoo ceremony.

One photograph, however, stands out. At the center of the piece is a two-page spread, an aerial view looking north along the border between Haiti and the Dominican Republic. On the right, the verdant foothills of the D.R. The greenery is thick and deep, velvety. And on the left, Haiti, bare and brown, sun-stroked, cursed. It looks as though a plague had come to the land, as though the Haitian trees, seeking shelter, had migrated to the D.R. A few trees remain on the Haitian side. You can almost count them.

The authors of the book of no trees were Alexandre Pétion and Jean-Pierre Boyer, the first mulatto leaders of free Haiti. After the assassination of Jean-Jacques Dessalines in 1806, Pétion ruled the south of Haiti and Henry Christophe the north. Christophe's kingdom was a prosperous one, but he maintained its prosperity only through enforced labor and the attachment of agricultural workers to state-run plantations—basically a new brand of slavery, this time managed by blacks. Pétion organized a more relaxed south. He abandoned the concept of large plantations and instead parceled out the land in small plots to pay off his large standing army. Productivity fell. His people loved him.

By 1820, Christophe, now Emperor Henry I, weakened by an attack of apoplexy and tormented by internecine feuds among his court, saw his rigid rule of the northern kingdom threatened by conspiracy. Beset by menaces from the south, and unwilling to fall into the hands of his enemies, Henry I, dramatic to the last, killed himself with a single bullet through the heart. According to legend the bullet was silver, and a single attendant, along with the Queen —deserted even by Henry's personal guard—dragged the stout King's body to the secret burial place within the stone confines of the Citadelle, the majestic mountaintop fortress Henry had had constructed outside Cap-Haïtien.

Boyer, who had served Pétion as secretary and who upon Pétion's death in 1818 succeeded him as chief of state of the south, marched on Cap-Haïtien almost immediately after hearing of Henry's death. He understood that Henry's reign had endured so long in the north only through the force of his character, and the spies Pétion had sent to infiltrate Henry's court had kept the southern leaders informed of the discontent within the Palace of Sans Souci, Henry's Versailles, as Henry's health began to fail. When Boyer arrived at the Cap, exultant crowds welcomed him with cries of *"Vive le Président!,"* and shortly, the new head of state reunified Christophe's north and Pétion's south. He ruled for twenty-five years.

Boyer continued the parceling of land that Pétion had begun, until by 1823 production had dropped in the north as it had continued to do in the south, to such an extent that the government's coffers were empty, even though at the time of its fall only three years before, Christophe's kingdom had provided some six million dollars (then a considerable sum) for the Boyer exchequer. The smallholders Pétion had created were former slaves and sons of former slaves, and they preferred to farm for themselves and their families rather than for the state. Their reaction to their former enslavement was to favor freedom, and they were willing to work hard—for themselves. In the north, the new landholders quickly moved into subsistence farming. When Boyer, alarmed, tried in 1826 to reverse this trend with an elaborate Code Rural, which sought in a somewhat more benevolent way to reinstate Christophe's enforced agricultural labor, he was met with complete, stubborn resistance by the new peasantry. The plan failed, and Haiti's system of land use—where small parcels became smaller and smaller as they were divided among numerous sons, where squatters took over government lands in the mountains and after generations gained "common-law" rights of ownership to them, where little large-scale agriculture was practiced but where local market systems and subsistence farming met the needs of each family—was established. The system still has not been specifically institutionalized, and the question of land rights continues to cause battles in the countryside.

For many decades, even, perhaps, for a century, the smallholdings seemed adequate. People lived in poverty, but they lived. Haiti had rich soil, large forests, plentiful water. But intensive farming on small plots sapped the land, and, with holdings so limited, it was rare that the Haitian farmer had enough land or money to allow a field to lie fallow. The population grew rapidly. Eventually, the depleted soil produced smaller and smaller crops for bigger and bigger populations, and the peasantry grew poorer and poorer. In desperation, new generations began chopping down the forests to provide more farming land. Because each smallholder had his own small property, there was little cooperation or planning involved in land use, only exploitation. The government paid little attention to agricultural development, except to exact exorbitant market and export taxes. Haiti's spectacular mahogany forests were soon destroyed through foreign commercial harvesting for export. A growing urban population, much of it fleeing the unremitting poverty of the countryside, turned to charcoal for fuel—the cheapest and most efficient available—and whole areas of timberland were felled to meet demand. No government policy could reverse the trends. In 1954, a century and a quarter after Boyer attempted to promulgate the Code Rural, less than 9 percent of Haiti remained forested; today, that percentage has dropped below seven. Before Columbus set foot on the island, forests had covered more than 75 percent of the land.

Near the end of the La Saline slum, right next to Boulevard de La Saline, the major thoroughfare that runs along the capital's port, is the bidonville's charcoal market. Hundreds of huge gray bags of charcoal stand side by side here on the red earth, some of them taller than a man, leaning up against each other like tired soldiers in the sun. It's not a big market. Only twenty or thirty shanties could be built in the space it occupies. It is busy, though, a hub of activity. Charcoal vendors come and go at all hours of the day. They buy in all quantities: handfuls, buckets, apronfuls, bags and scores of bags. Almost all of them are women, and you can recognize them even when they are not sitting amid the charcoal: they all wear black so that their clothes won't show the heavy charcoal dust. They seem to be in perpetual mourning.

Usually, they arrive with a man they have hired to transport the day's or the week's charcoal load. A bag costs an average of six dollars, and they pay the man 50 cents to haul it on his back to their market stall. If their stall is far away, not in La Saline but up on John Brown or over on Jean-Paul II (formerly Jean-Claude Duvalier), they may buy a spot for their bag on one of the two-wheeled wooden carts, or brouettes, that are hauled across town, each one under the power of a single man. Sometimes a cart hauler may carry as many as twenty bags on his cart, dropping each one off at a different spot in town. He is given his route orally, and remembers it by heart, since he cannot read. You can recognize a cart hauler, even without the cart. He wears no shirt, his pants are rolled up to just below his knees, and he has muscles that look as though they were made of wrought iron.

A richer charcoal vendor may transport her charcoal bags by tap-tap from La Saline to her market stall. Even more affluent charcoal distributors come with trucks to pick up deliveries they have ordered for their Port-au-Prince depots from the provinces, and they send them out to their subscribers; Sylvain and Jeanne subscribe to a service like this, and so does almost everyone in Pétionville. Even though Sylvain and Jeanne have a gas stove, their maid Mariane comes from the countryside via the Pétionville slums, and she likes to cook with charcoal. Ask any Haitian woman, and she will tell you she prefers food cooked in a pot over charcoal to food cooked in a pot over gas. Haitians say it tastes better.

Bernadette Nelson, a charcoal middleman, lives in Port-au-Prince, but she rents a house in the windblown Môle St.-Nicolas. The Môle —in French the word *môle* means breakwater—is a dusty town on the northernmost tip of the Northwest province, sixty miles across the Windward Passage from Cuba. Bernadette has a hands-on approach to her business. She doesn't delegate, because hiring people costs too much. So you find her one day on the top of a hill between Bombardopolis and the Môle, counting her bags, and another day she's right there at the port in the Môle, supervising the loading of her boat.

The hill near the Môle is her depot, a spot along the rutted road under a single tree (the only one visible in the near distance), where the ground below your feet is black and crunches from the charcoal that has fallen over the years from Bernadette's bags. She brings the bags themselves up from Port-au-Prince after their contents have been emptied. If you treat a bag well, she says, it can last for more than twenty trips.

"They're made of something strong," Bernadette says, pulling on the two ends of a bag to demonstrate their durability. Her hands are made of something strong, too: big, bony and muscular. Her palms are black from charcoal. Twice a month, Bernadette makes the long trip up to the Môle by tap-tap, alone. She distributes bags to her usual suppliers along the way up, along with gossip from the capital, and later returns to the depot to see what they will bring her. She pays half up front and half upon delivery. A bag of charcoal, or *chabon de bwa,* she says, costs her about three dollars, sometimes less, up here in the Northwest where everyone is desperate for anything they can get—money, food, water. For three days, or sometimes a week if things are slow and her suppliers are having trouble finding trees, Bernadette spends a daily fourteen hours at her depot, counting, paying, tying up the bags, chatting with her people. Afterward when her consignment is complete, she has the stuff taken down to the Môle by camionnette or tap-tap. There she rents one of the boats, or *batimen,* as they are called in Creole, that have come in from Port-au-Prince with a clairin or wheat or flour delivery.

For a few symbolic hours each week, the port at the Môle is stocked with incoming barrels of clairin and outgoing bags of charcoal. The charcoal bags are laid out on top of one another like corpses in a mass grave, and the rum sits in barrels protected from the sun by open-air lean-tos. Both are waiting to be picked up, the dry black fuel for cooking in town and the wet white fuel for dreaming in the countryside, for heating things up at the local cockfight, for passing the evening after not much of a meal, for making hard work in the hot sun bearable. At these moments when the paths of the two goods cross, you have the feeling that the peasants are bartering away what little remains of their agriculture for alcohol, trading trees for rum. It just looks that way; it isn't exactly or even more or less true. Yet there is power in the image, especially after you have watched skinny farmers and day workers all over the country pulling flasks out of their ripped pockets and gulping clairin while they rake and hoe, while they clear their fields; after you have watched clever lumberjacks chopping up tree trunks for planks, chopping, sawing, sanding, while they sing and drink; after you have watched a man spend two days on a steep hillside, cutting down the last tree there, his bottle beside him on the ground. Rum is what many peasants use to anesthetize themselves against the pain of their endless, fruitless work. They're not drunk, they're just numb enough to carry on.

On any day at the Môle's port, you may find as many as twelve batimen ready to be loaded with charcoal and sent down to Port-au-Prince. The boat Bernadette has rented this time is the *Poukipale*— Why Talk? Along with seven others, it is anchored about fifty feet out from the port, which is nothing more than a beach with plenty of space to stack deliveries, and a general store where you can buy peanuts and soap, concentrated milk and clairin. No dock. The Army headquarters are nearby; the three or four soldiers there have a view of the port. On weekdays, market women set up their charcoal stoves on the beach and cook goat with rice and beans or cornmeal for the boatmen. The *Poukipale* has been stuck in port for two days now because the winds between Cuba and Haiti are too strong to attempt the voyage around the tip of the island and down the coast.

The water is bluer than the skies, and the boatmen are taking down their sails because of the cutting wind. Men in a rowboat are bringing food out to the captain of the *Poukipale*. Their boat bounces wildly on the choppy waves, and then they send a small boy into the water to tie a line from the little boat to the *Poukipale*. I can see them all gesturing and shouting, and the boy disappears for so long I'm sure he's been pulled down by a current—the currents must be crazy in that place, with that wind—until finally his head appears and his whole body shoots out of the water. He's laughing and holding the rope in his teeth, and all the men are shouting at him. I can hear pieces of their shouting through the wind. They are saying the things I want to say to him: "How could you do that?" "We're going to skin you." "I thought you were drowned." "*Ti dezòd.*" Little mischief. Vagabond. And he's laughing at the men, who are all standing in the little boat and yelling at him and laughing, and, as he paddles to keep himself in one spot and afloat in the churning sea, the boy tosses the rope up to the captain of the *Poukipale,* and the captain grabs it and winds it around a hook, and up from the little boat come buckets of rice and beans and a bucket of grilled goat meat and some drinking water, not too clean, but drinkable, and a flask of clairin. The boy clambers aboard the *Poukipale,* and, in return for his valor and clowning, the captain gives him a swallow of the rum. The boy jumps back into the little boat, and the captain turns back to his crew of two sitting among Bernadette's hundred bags of charcoal, and they begin to eat.

I'm turning black as I stand there in the wind, watching. Not from the sun, but from the dust. The charcoal dust is swirling around me. The wind is hot, and black dust is sweeping along the beach. When I look into the rearview mirror later, my eyelashes are powdered with black dust, and cinder has smudged my forehead and my cheeks. Being in the Môle was like being on board a burning ship. No wonder the little boy felt so comfortable in the wild water. In the dust, on the beach, I felt as if I were suffocating, drowning. I wanted to swim. I wanted to get away from charcoal. But there is no escaping charcoal in Haiti.

A charcoal pit—that is, a pit for making charcoal—looks like the grave of a giant. You might not notice it at first: a low mound as you come around a bend in the road. But then you see the smoke escaping up from the fire under the earth. The charcoal-makers cut down trees, hundreds of them, usually small trees, since most of the big ones were chopped down years ago, and dig a pit at the side of the road. They chop up the trees and throw them in, and set a slow fire burning. Once it is cooking, they cover the burning wood with earth, leaving crevices near the ground where the smoke can escape. A charcoal mound can be more than thirty-five feet long, more than ten feet wide.

A long, burning charcoal pit lies just a hundred or so yards down the road from Bernadette's depot outside the Môle. It is the handiwork of the Almaneau family, one of Bernadette's suppliers. The family lives in a two-room house across from the pit, a little way down the side of the hill. You can't live too near the pit, because with the sun coming down from the sky and the heat coming up from the pit, you'd shrivel up, you'd broil. Chickens can't breathe near the pit. The Almaneau family has four chickens, scrawny animals, all leg and feet, not even worth thinking about eating, says Claudette Almaneau, though she and her family will eat them, and soon, or try to fatten them for market. The chickens peck across the yard among the dry brown millet shells, looking for stray kernels.

Claudette is watching the charcoal pit for her husband, who she says is out somewhere down the side of the hill, cutting down trees. I don't see any trees anywhere, except for the one in Claudette's yard; her husband must have gone a long way off in his search for wood. Sometimes he has to pay distant landowners a fee to cut down trees on their property. He sells his bags of charcoal to Bernadette for two or three dollars. Along with other charcoal-makers in his extended family of about twenty-five people including children, he sells about five sacks a month to Bernadette. Claudette says it takes about fifty small trees to make a bag of charcoal. It depends on the size of the tree, of course, she says, but they aren't very big these days. She herself uses brushwood for cooking; her younger son gathers it when he comes back from school. If he can't find enough, she'll use charcoal, but it cuts into the family's income.

The Almaneaus used to have three pigs, but they were shot by the chef de section's men a few years ago during the pig-eradication program, and were never replaced. Back then, before they came to kill all the pigs, Claudette's husband counted on his pigs for spare money. The pigs would root around, eat up the garbage, corncobs, mango skins, whatever they found lying around. When they needed to pay for the boys' school or if someone in the family had to go down to Port-au-Prince, the family would sell a piglet. Now, like other peasants in the same situation, they have intensified their tree-cutting because they need the cash.

Claudette is washing two small white shirts this afternoon. They are her sons', part of their school uniform. The two boys get up before sunrise and walk to school in the Môle. One is eight years old, the other ten. Today, they couldn't go to school because their shirts were dirty; Claudette hadn't been able to get to the water source to do laundry the other day. She had been too busy cooking food with her daughters for the men who were making the charcoal pit. The boys stand by the side of the road, naked, waiting for their shirts, watching the smoking mound.

Claudette sits on a flat black rock and pounds the shirts against another stone, using water from a bucket. She scoops the water out with a blue plastic cup, one cupful to wash each shirt, and two cupfuls to rinse them. She has to be sparing with the water, because it comes from so far away. It takes her a full day to get to the water source and back, she says. She goes twice a week with her two daughters, and they return with three buckets of water. Usually, she says, she does all her laundry at the source, which she describes as a deep well. The last time it rained here was more than a year ago, Claudette tells me. In some places in the Northwest, farmers say it's been more than three years.

In his posthumously published novel *Masters of the Dew* (*Gouverneurs de la rosée*), Jacques Roumain writes of the desolation of a village called Fonds Rouge (Red Land or Red Roots) where all the trees but the mapou have been destroyed for charcoal, where the peasants have no water for their exhausted fields, and only voodoo to fall back upon. Roumain, a wealthy mulatto educated in Zurich and Paris, was a major force in the indigenous literary movement in Haiti that began with novels and poems based on Haitian rather than French culture, and culminated later in the beginnings of a Creole literature. Roumain's earliest novels attacked his own elite mulatto class: parasitic, prejudiced, paralyzed, was his judgment. His later novels explored peasant life and the universe of voodoo, and there too he concluded that Haitians were trapped inside a corrupt society whose authoritarian leaders and beliefs would not allow them to take charge of their own destinies. Along with many other Caribbean writers of his day, he believed that only Marxism could provide the road out of his country's misery and stagnation.

When not in exile, Roumain, a founder of the Haitian Communist Party, was seldom absent from the political arena. He established the Bureau of Ethnology, of which François Duvalier and Dr. J. C. Dorsainvil later became members. In 1929 he led a series of successful student protests which turned into a long-lived violent national strike against the fourteen-year-old U.S. occupation, and which were the first in a series of disruptions that recalled the depths of discontent of the earlier, peasant-inspired revolts led by Charlemagne Péralte against the Americans. Though the strikes and protests Roumain supported initially caused the United States to reinstate martial law in Haiti, they were also responsible for establishing a climate of discontent that finally brought about the end of the Marines' reign. The moment the Marines set sail, the new President, Stenio Vincent, jailed Roumain on charges of subversion. The novelist remained imprisoned for almost three years. Upon Roumain's release, the President banned Communism and Communists, and Roumain headed for Paris and exile. In 1941 he returned to Haiti, only to be named chargé d'affaires and packed off to Mexico, where he died suddenly a scant three years later, at the age of thirty-six.

Manuel Délivrance, the hero of *Masters of the Dew*, which is generally considered Roumain's masterpiece, returns to Fonds

Rouge, his birthplace, after years spent cutting cane in Cuba. He is
startled by the change in his village and the land surrounding it
(translation from the French by Langston Hughes and Mercer
Cook):

> . . . what he saw was a grilled expanse of dirty rust color
> spotted by a scattering of moldy huts. He stared at the
> barren hill overlooking the village, ravaged by wide whitish
> gullies where erosion had bared its flanks to the rock. He
> tried to remember the tall oaks once animated with wood
> pigeons fond of blackberries, the mahogany trees bathed in
> the shadowy light, the Congo beans whose dry husks rus-
> tled in the wind, the long rows of sweet potato hills. But all
> that, the sun had licked up, effaced with a single stroke of
> its fiery tongue.
> . . . [A] familiar odor came up to meet him—the musty
> smell of stale charcoal smoke when all that is left of the pit
> is a circular mass of dirt.

Manuel, undefeated by the ravaged face of this landscape, decides
to find a water source for his village. He is a protagonist typical of
the heroes of Socialist Realism in the 1930s, strong, tall, direct, open
and honest, with a light that shines from his temples and an experience of labor organization in the Cuban canefields. When Manuel
returned to Fonds Rouge, the only water source the villagers knew
of was a place called Zombi Pool, "a pond of mosquitoes, water as
rotten as a dead adder, thick stagnant water too weak to flow." After
weeks of searching for a new source, Manuel notices a grove of trees
far from the village, and in the shade of a giant mapou he unearths a
buried spring. The next task he sets himself is to bring the water to
the village to irrigate the fields. He knows that to do this he will need
the help of many villagers organized into a *coumbite,* or traditional
Haitian work team, but Fonds Rouge is divided by a long-standing
feud—based on jealousy, violence and suspicion—and if Manuel's
side wants to bring the water down to the village, the other side will
refuse to work on the project. Against Manuel are also arrayed the
authorities, particularly Hilarion, the powerful local policeman, who
wants to wait until the peasants, totally dispirited by the unending
drought, decide to leave their lands, which he will take over; then
and only then will Hilarion see to it that the water comes to Fonds
Rouge.

Angered by Manuel's attempt to put an end to the feud, an enemy knifes him. On his deathbed, he tells his old mother, Délira, where the source is and begs her to ask the village to sing his funeral rites with the song of the work coumbite digging the irrigation canal, rather than the traditional funeral chants. Hilarion is furious that Manuel died before the authorities could torture the location of the source out of him, and the policeman vows to get his hands on whatever profit there is to be had from the water. If the peasants succeed in their plan, Hilarion swears, he will tax the water they bring to the village. The book ends with Délira on the top of a hill, listening to the singing of the coumbite and watching the newly dug canal fill with the water—"a thin blade of silver"—the peasants following alongside it, shouting with delight and throwing their straw hats into the air.

Roumain's book, published in 1946, could just as well have been written in 1987, with its triumphant sunlit finale overshadowed by the impending actions of Hilarion and the authorities. The massacre at the Northwest province's capital of Jean-Rabel, which effectively put an end to the cooperative ventures of the peasants there, was only the most dramatic of the attacks on the peasantry by Haitian authorities and large landholders toward the end of the 1980s. At Papaye, a small village outside Hinche, the capital of the Plateau-Central province, Chavannes Jean-Baptiste, a Catholic lay worker, had organized a large peasant movement with national ambitions. When Duvalier fell, movements like Chavannes', which had maintained a fairly low profile under Duvalier, burst out into the open and grew rapidly, only to discover that the network of power they thought had been undone by the Dechoukaj was still in place and ready to strike back at them when the time should prove fortuitous. After the Jean-Rabel massacre, open season was declared on the peasantry, and Papaye did not escape the hunters.

The local authorities started with Chavannes himself. A Communist, they said; the same charge had been leveled against the peasant groups of Jean-Rabel and their Church organizers. The chef de section told the peasants that Chavannes, who was in hiding, had gone to the Soviet Union and was living in a big house there, that he had sold out his movement, and now the authorities were going to kill everyone associated with him. At the beginning of 1988, the chef de section began issuing warrants for the arrest of members of

Chavannes' movement, and twenty-eight were thrown into prison. Later, the authorities attempted to sabotage the movement's credit system, which provided loans to *ti peyizan,* or smallholding peasants, at rates they could afford. Chavannes' people organized vigilance brigades to protect their stores of cereal; sometimes the groups numbered as many as a hundred peasants, armed with rocks, sticks and machetes. Unlike peasant silos in other areas, Chavannes' remained untouched.

The chef de section was also furious with Chavannes for encouraging the peasants to refuse to pay their market taxes, a refusal that peasant leaders nationwide had been supporting. A chef de section has to come up with the monthly market-tax revenues or explain his failure to do so to the national authorities. Sometimes he is forced to pay out of his own pocket what is lacking from his tax revenues. In addition, by inflating the authorized market tax, he makes a handsome profit for himself. Thus, the payment of the market tax can become a matter of some personal interest to the chef. When the chef of the Papaye region tried to arrest seven peasants for failure to pay their tax, which is collected at the weekly market, the entire community blocked his way, and no arrests were made.

One spring day in 1988, Chavannes and some twenty organizers of the Peasant Movement of Papaye (MPP) held an outdoor meeting, trying to avoid the sun while they discussed the expansion of the movement on a national level. They were sitting around on benches and market chairs under a large tree, facing a field of papayas that Chavannes had planted. It was hot, and drops of sweat fell onto the pads on which the men and two women, all of them in their mid-twenties to midthirties, were writing. Chavannes, at forty-one older than the others, with a boy's unlined face, sat silent in his tee shirt and shorts as the men read through lists and reports.

"Uh-huh," he said, appearing to listen, tipping his chair back so that some shade would fall across his face. "Yes, but how about the Northwest? What have we got there?" Chavannes always has energy to spare, and, even when he is just sitting around, his legs bounce incessantly, as if he's headed somewhere. He stays up each night until one or two in the morning, and always arises by five.

One of the men began to speak of organizers in the Northwest, then suddenly fell silent, looking over the heads of the others. A soldier was approaching. He came up to the circle, said hello to everyone individually, and shook hands with Chavannes. He handed Chavannes a letter, shook his hand again, and left. The letter said:

"The Commander invites Chavannes Jean-Baptiste to appear at Army headquarters upon receipt of this letter."

Chavannes passed the letter around, smiling drily. "I suppose I have to say yes to this charming invitation," he said. "I guess I'll change my clothes. If I'm not back in two hours, well, do whatever you think is appropriate."

Two hours were almost up when he returned. The commander and the chef de section had been waiting for him at headquarters, he told the movement organizers. The chef had told him to tell the peasants to pay their market taxes.

"I'm not the one who decides," Chavannes said he told the authorities. "The peasants decide themselves. It's not up to me. If you would provide them with services for the taxes they pay, they would be happy to hand over their money. But they have so little, and then you take their money in return for nothing. Well, what do you expect?"

"They must pay first," said the chef de section. "Then we will see about services. You are playing politics."

"Certainly," Chavannes said. "Everything is political in Haiti."

"Tell them to pay," Chavannes said the chef de section told him. "And if they do not pay, we will force them to pay, down to the last little market lady."

Soon after Chavannes delivered this report, the organizers went off on their mopeds and motorcycles and on foot to warn the peasants in their regions that a campaign to enforce the tax collection was about to begin. They could not know how soon.

That afternoon, I left Papaye for Port-au-Prince. The river outside Hinche was high, and a wind was driving rain clouds in over the plateau from the Dominican Republic. I took the rented jeep through the fast river water, flushing up mud and gravel. No one was out. The pale dirt road twisted down toward the west. That way lay the setting sun, a patch of light shining out into the darkness. A field next to the road was burning beneath the clouds, in preparation for the next planting. The red flames rose up and a chicken walked among them. The sky was lowering down.

Smoke ascended from lean-to kitchens along the way. A truck piled high with charcoal bags rumbled by, stirring up dust. A peasant sat on top of the gray load, holding his machete; a piece of plastic was wrapped around his head against the approaching rains. The road twisted on; for all my traveling, I had not left Papaye far behind. I passed down a hill and through a small stream, where a great white pig was lounging on a rock, waiting for rain. Farther on, more people seemed to be about. Peasant men were standing at their doors, while the women made smoke in the kitchens. Two boys squatted in a yard, playing marbles.

Then, around a bend, I seemed suddenly to have driven right back into the days of Papa Doc. Ahead of me, approaching on horseback, not fast but purposefully, were six men on well-fed chestnut horses. They were not peasants. Peasants ride burros, not horses. As I came upon them, I saw that they were wearing blue denim. A few wore straw hats, and others policemen's caps. Several wore sunglasses in this deepening gloom, and each carried a machete. Three had revolvers at their waists. They didn't look at me when I stopped the jeep to let their horses pass. They rode around me as if I weren't there. I watched their backs go on down the road, and continued on, wondering at this abrupt vision of the rural Tontons Macoute.

Who were *they,* I asked a group of peasants who were staring back down the road at the horsemen.

"I don't know," said one man, turning away quickly.

A woman beckoned me. "The chef de section," she said. "And his deputies. They are going to a little market near here. To collect the taxes." I thought of Hilarion and the tax he wanted to level on Manuel's water. The peasants stayed at the side of the road, watching the men's backs ride away.

I followed those men, at a safe distance. They went a long way down the main thoroughfare, and then turned up a red dirt road into the back country toward the market. I didn't want to follow them in because the road was too narrow for quick flight. I knew by now that I didn't like to be in small places with men with guns. So I drove farther down to another little road that the peasants told me led to the same market. I turned into the muddy route, more a path than a road really, driving slowly, in first gear. Children came to the side of the road to look at the jeep as it passed. Splashes of rain began to hit my windshield, a drizzle of fat drops. A short time, and I was at the market clearing. No one was manning the stalls. A few men hung around the entrance to the market.

"Where is everybody?" I asked them.

They looked over their shoulders. "Market's over," one of them said. I got out of the jeep and looked past them.

All the peasants from the market were gathered around the men on horseback, and one of the men was shouting and waving his gun.

"What is he talking about?" I asked.

"Oh, nothing," one man said to me. "They come here every Wednesday, like this."

"So he's not talking about taxes, is he?" I asked.

They all laughed, and looked over their shoulders.

"Now, why would he be talking about taxes?" asked a little wiry man in shorts, from under the brim of a broad straw hat. "Who told you he'd be talking about taxes, little girl? What do you know about taxes?" He looked me up and down. "Where are you coming from?"

I lied. "Port-au-Prince," I said.

"You're not coming from Papaye?"

"Papaye?" I said. "Where's that?"

"Where are you going, then?" the little man asked.

"To Hinche," I said. "I have friends there, in Hinche."

"What do these friends do?" the little man asked.

"They work for CARE," I said. I had no idea whether CARE had people in Hinche.

"Oh," he said. "I see."

He pushed forward as I tried to get closer to the crowd of peasants to hear what the men were saying.

"The rain is getting worse," the little man said to me, looking up at the mean sky from under his hat. "You'd better get on to Hinche, or you won't make it across the river. And it's getting dark. Little girls shouldn't travel in the dark." He smiled broadly at me.

I obeyed, stumbling up into the jeep, and I drove away, leaving the peasants to their taxes and their masters.

In those days before the bridges were completed, you needed a jeep to get to Hinche and Papaye; you could not ford the rivers without one, unless you had a horse or a donkey, like the people who live there. This out-of-the-way spot has long been a center of peasant resistance. Since before the Haitian Revolution, opposition to white domination and, later, to Port-au-Prince rule has traditionally located its redoubts in inaccessible fastnesses, often on the steep mountainsides; Henry Christophe's Citadelle is only the most spectacular example. Haitian guerrillas (like others in Latin America) have always understood that it is easier to organize when you are not under the watchful eye of the Army barracks in town, whether in Cap-Haïtien, Gonaïves or Port-au-Prince. During the days of French rule, unexplored mountain regions, unsuited for labor-intensive crops, were peopled by Maroons who had illegally established themselves on patches of land in the hills where their discovery and return by officers of the *maréchaussée,* or constabulary, was unlikely. Here in the mountains the Maroons lived virtually as had their ancestors in Africa, free men and women, subsistence farmers. Nor had they forgotten their hereditary role as warriors.

The colonial historian Moreau de Saint-Méry describes the continual depredations wreaked on the French planters, on their mulatto counterparts (freemen who often owned plantations and slaves themselves); and on their property by the Maroons, often abetted by France's rivals to the east, the Spaniards. Of an incident in 1761, in which the French and their mulatto troops attempted to quell a rebellion among slaves who had escaped to the mountains, Moreau de Saint-Méry writes: "Behind a hill, the negroes defied their adversaries, and danced. The attackers, furious, threw themselves across the ditch that separated them, but the bottom of the ditch was full of pine-wood spikes, and the top had been covered with vines and grasses. Fourteen mulattos, or about half of the force, were maimed. Many negroes were killed; others were taken with their arrows and their firearms."

When the planters tried to get at the rebellious slaves farther up in the hills, their campaigns were less successful. The Maroons' dogs barked during the night preceding the revenge attack, reports Moreau de Saint-Méry, and the slaves "fled into the woods, which were so dense that the troops could not penetrate them. The detachment, overcome with fatigue—men even being reduced to drinking their own urine—retreated to get provisions. More than 30 mulattos disbanded, and the detachment had to wait for another 15 grenadiers or hunters. A month's worth of provisions were also sent. So [the detachment] set out anew, and they did not find the slaves." This was a time when abundant trees provided protection for the mountain people.

The potential for revolt has always preoccupied Haiti's rulers, especially the French slavers and the U.S. Marines. Trying to convey to Napoleon the impossibility of winning his Haitian war, General Leclerc, who died of yellow fever in 1802, a year before the French lost Haiti to Dessalines, told the French Emperor that the only way to defeat the slaves was "to exterminate all the blacks in the mountains, women as well as men, except for children under twelve."

Not least among French concerns was the strategic inviolability of the runaway slaves' territory. The Marines had the same problem more than a hundred years later when the peasant groups known as Cacos rose up under Charlemagne Péralte against the occupation. In Heinl and Heinl's *Written in Blood,* the authors describe the location of Péralte's Hinche (now within Chavannes' purview) during the early days of the U.S. occupation. "Remote, forbidding, wild, the place bore . . . a sinister title: 'Hinche the Accursed.' Across the Cul-de-Sac, 3,000 feet up the face of Morne-à-Cabrit, . . . past Mirebalais, over the headwaters of the Artibonite, through Lascahobas and the Montagnes Noires, thence to Thomonde and onto the Plateau du Centre . . ."

But access to Péralte's Hinche soon was made easier. "Using rough-and-ready expedients, including a rival of [the] corvée," write the Heinls, "Marine district and subdistrict Gendarmerie commanders began the enormous job of creating roads, bridges, water supply, telegraph lines . . . in short, a national infrastructure, where only ruins had lain." The corvée, a brutal precursor of Food-for-Work projects, was a system of enforced labor that dated from the old Code Rural, in which peasants were conscripted into public works and were paid for their travails in food and rum. The corvée was reinstated by the Marines in 1916, "when occupation authorities began to think about roads and economic development, and also of routes of penetration into Caco fastnesses," according to the Heinls.

Workers on the corvée were often dragged into service, and sometimes rounded up from hiding and tied together at the ankles. Those who were able could pay off the local gendarme and were permitted to escape the exacting highway labors, but the less fortunate were beaten into service, thereby losing time they could ill afford to spend away from their own ungenerous fields. The Marines soon discovered, however, that the corvée was a two-edged policy instrument. On one hand, the new roads gave the Marines access to Caco regions; on the other, the enforced labor inflamed peasant resentment and brought hundreds of eager new guerrillas into Péralte's camp. Eventually, the Marines estimated that Péralte could claim some five thousand men as his soldiers; countless more believed in his cause of ousting the occupation.

In October 1919, Péralte and a hundred Cacos came down from the Plateau-Central to Source Matelas near Cabaret—later Duvalierville—and from this encampment thirty kilometers outside the capital began their attempt to overthrow the occupation's puppet President, Sudre Dartiguenave. This part of the strategy was not planned as a military or guerrilla attack, but as a destabilizing "ad-

vance-guard move," according to the Haitian historian Roger Gaillard in his book *Charlemagne Péralte, Le Caco.* Meanwhile, in the
Plaine de Cul-de-Sac and at Croix-des-Bouquets, just an hour or so
out of town, Péralte's armies lay waiting. At 4 A.M. on October 7,
his advance guard, mostly on foot, reached the Portail St.-Joseph at
La Saline—today the corner near St.-Jean-Bosco—and split into
two groups. One headed down Grande Rue, but was eventually
blocked in its progress by the police. Reversing its route, this group
of about thirty men headed toward the Bel-Air slums; again they
were cut off, this time by a Ford in which seven Marines were riding.
Gunfire was exchanged; the Cacos knocked out the Ford's radiator
with their bullets, and then fled into the corridors of Bel-Air. The
Marines pursued them on foot to no avail. The slums in the city
were the equivalent of the thick forests in which the runaway slaves
had hidden. The white man could not penetrate them.

    Conspiring with Jean-Baptiste Conzé, a spy in Péralte's inner cir-
cle, two Marines in blackface, armed with revolvers and a machine
gun, eventually ambushed Charlemagne at three in the morning on
November 1, 1919, less than a month after the descent on Port-au-
Prince, at his encampment three hours by foot from the village of
Mazère near Ste.-Suzanne. One of them, Captain Herman Hanneken, shot the Caco twice in the heart as Péralte sat talking with his
girlfriend by the light of a dinner fire. "The woman turned the pot
over on the grill," writes Gaillard, "and night fell." Hanneken
claimed he shot Péralte when the Caco tried to escape, but an illus-
tration of the event drawn for the U.S. military newspaper and
entitled "A Bullet for Charlemagne" shows Hanneken shooting the
armed guerrilla leader face to face, with the spilled dinner pot overturned in the fire, and a woman's hand at Péralte's falling knees.

On their way to get water in the early morning and then again at
sunset, the women and children of Bombardopolis, a small town in
the Northwest, pass the tree nursery, the *pepinyè.* It's a five-minute
walk from the center of Bombard and the borlette-lined main street.
At sunset, the men of Bombard are picking up their winnings at the
borlettes along the dusty street, or—more often—commiserating
about their losses and discussing future bets. Almost all of them are
farmers, *kiltivatè,* and they have spent a long day in the fields, trying
to convince their corn to grow, worrying about rain. In Bombardopolis, the rains are late as usual this year. They get later and later

every year, and old men will tell you that the rainy seasons they once knew have all folded together, and that every year another rainy season is lost. "We had five rains before the harvest in my day, or more," said one white-haired farmer sitting out in front of a pink borlette, his machete at his side, as a white sun went down behind the main street's houses. "Now sometimes we have to wait until September for the rains to come. Some years they just don't come. *Tout pye-bwa koupe, lapli pa tonbe.*" All the trees have been cut, the rain doesn't fall.

But as you walk down the steep hill to the nursery, it seems that rain—which is hope in rural Haiti—is in the air. The first thing you notice, before you set eyes on the nursery, is the dampness. Humidity is a rare commodity in the Northwest province. Near the nursery, your skin suddenly expands, your eyes blink more easily, you can feel the moisture in your hair. Seedlings from the nursery stand two feet high on the hill, valiantly holding back the topsoil, or what is left of it. Their little leaves hold the promise of showers.

The nursery, like a dozen or so similar ones in the Northwest, is administered by CARE and funded by USAID, as a part of the agency's Agroforestry Outreach Project. Seedlings for ten to fifteen different types of fast-growing, soil-retaining trees are nurtured here on row after row of wrought-iron racks. The delicate green seedlings are sheltered from the sun by a banana-leaf roof, and ten employees tend them every day, checking the soil, repairing the banana roof, planting new seeds and watering the tiny trees. The nursery has its own water source, which is locked up when it's not in use. Otherwise, peasants might steal the water. The water belongs to CARE because the source is on property CARE has rented. The coddled seedlings, with their water and roof and constant attention, are reminiscent of the white American pigs that have been imported through USAID to replace the black Haitian pigs killed in the swine-fever-eradication program. Those American pigs live in concrete houses with running water. They eat imported food.

But the pig program differs from the tree program. Piglets from the pig program are being sold to peasants for as much as fifty dollars (five times what a peasant used to pay for a Creole piglet)—sold not in the end by USAID (which supplied their parents) or by any other aid organization, but by the businessmen and large landowners and chefs de section who were entrusted by USAID with the care and raising of the new pigs. Only people of some wealth, it was thought, would have the means to keep the sensitive animals alive in the unfriendly Haitian climate. The seedlings, on the other hand, are distributed directly from the CARE nurseries, on demand and free of charge.

Peasants come frequently to the nursery to pick up seedlings, which they plant on their own land with their own labor. They are interested in trees, especially free trees, because the trees grow up, and then they can cut them down to sell as charcoal or, in the case of the harder, straighter species, as wood—planks or poles—for construction. The tree program gives them something for nothing, it seems. The peasants like the idea of soil retention, but that is a secondary concern for them. Their biggest worry is immediate: they need money, and the kind of trees that USAID and CARE have been providing are a cash crop. All over Haiti, peasants working with CARE and other distribution agencies' seedlings have been planting some seven million trees a year, according to USAID. Seven million is a lot. It sounds like a lot. But then there are other statistics: in spite of an old law, now repealed, that made it illegal to cut down trees in Haiti, Haitian peasants have been cutting down some twenty million trees a year. The law was never enforced. Often the Agroforestry Outreach Project is referred to as *reboisement,* reforesting. But, as one of the project managers points out, the program is inadequate even to replace the annual tree loss. "Peasants don't make as much as fast planting trees as they do cutting them down," he says. "Even if we had the resources to offer them twenty million seedlings a year, I don't think they would find it a reasonable investment."

A good project, most peasants will say, if you ask them about the AID agroforestry program. This is a high mark, since in general, if someone associated with a program isn't standing nearby, peasants are very critical of foreign-aid projects. Oddly enough, most will also say that they do not participate in reboisement. Joachim, a Bombard peasant whose field, like that of most Haitian peasants, is smaller than one *carreau,* or less than three acres, tells me that he doesn't have the space to grow trees that don't produce food. He feeds a family of five, plus an occasional member of his extended family, from his limited and depleted land, and he believes that he cannot afford to turn even a small section of his farm over to the production of a more long-term cash crop. "If they were fruit trees," Joachim says, "maybe I would consider it, because fruit you can eat as well as sell. Mangoes I might plant, or orange trees. But not these little things where I'll have to wait months and months, or maybe a year or two, and not be able to plant my little bit of corn or millet on the patch where they are growing. I just can't do it." Joachim knows he can plant beans and millet and other crops in among the trees, but he worries about rain. "Trees need so much water, and there is so little of it these days," he says. "I'm afraid that if I plant the trees and there isn't enough rain, then nothing at all will grow, because the trees will drink up all of my water. I can't afford to take risks."

Who does plant the trees? Peasants who are among the 30 percent of Haitian farmers who own two thirds of the country's arable land, peasants with more than three carreaux, peasants already doing well enough to dedicate a portion of their land to a solely cash crop—big peasants and middle peasants. The big peasants are usually families who have had large tracts of land almost since the time of the colony, virtual feudal lords in their regions. In many cases, they added to their already large holdings during the Duvalier years, when certain peasants in favor with the government were allowed to take over state lands at low or no rent, often evicting ti peyizan, who thought that after several generations of tilling the land it belonged to them. The middle peasants are people who have also added to their land in more recent years, by similar means. Frequently, these are low-ranking former or current state officials, chefs de section and their deputies, and former Tontons Macoute.

CARE does not ask the people who come for seedlings how much land they have, and CARE's aim, as its administrators will readily admit, is to get trees planted, not to provide a crop for poor peasants, although to get them planted CARE must make the trees in some way attractive to the peasants. As a World Bank policy recommendation stated recently, it was now time for foreign-aid donors to take advantage of the "emerging combination of traditional landowners and the new entrepreneurial class's managerial skills." If poor peasants benefit from the tree program, fine, but the goal of the program is simply to plant trees and retain soil. In a generation or two, all peasants will benefit, CARE agroforesters say.

While Duvalier was still in power, CARE's attitude did not harm the reforestation projects. Joachim was not going to complain if the Macoute who took his chickens and demanded protection money was getting a couple of dozen free seedlings from the CARE nursery. Nor was he going to complain if the big local landholder was using the CARE-administered Food-for-Work program to pay his day workers, or diverting water resources located by aid projects to his own uses. It was rare that peasants raised their voices against the system that kept them in the severest penury. The costs of protest were too high: imprisonment, hard labor, confiscation of property and land, torture, death.

Once Duvalier had fled and the Tontons Macoute were at least officially disbanded, however, the climate changed. Peasant groups like Chavannes' sprang up all over the countryside. Often encouraged by Catholic missionaries and progressive priests who had been working with the poorest of the peasants for years, they immediately began clamoring for basic rights: the right to retain the land they worked and the right to regain land taken illegally from them during the thirty years of the Duvalier dynasty. These protests were largely directed against the large local landholders, or *grandons,* and in their wake they generated protests about other abuses by the big peasants, which included their appropriation of benefits from foreign aid. The massacre at Jean-Rabel occurred after attempts by such peasant groups to retake land they felt was theirs.

The first targets of protests like these were the CARE food depots, where Food-for-Work staples were kept. In Port-au-Prince, Gonaïves, Cap-Haïtien and Jacmel, the depots were looted and dechouked. The depots were obvious targets for peasant and city-dweller alike, and though the depot dechoukaj had serious political overtones, it was also sparked by the knowledge that there was food in those depots, and that the forces of order which might have protected the warehouses were momentarily out of commission.

Not everyone who helped dechouke the warehouses was a little peasant taking cooking oil and rice for his family. Often, a truck would pull up and men would scramble to load it down with box upon box of foodstuffs. That cooking oil and flour and condensed milk would later appear in the markets, for sale, just as it always had. In the old days, however, it was Duvalier's people who got hold of the free food and then sold it in the markets. The Haitians call the foreign food aid *mange sinistre,* disaster food. The derivation of this Creole compound is simple: the biggest shipments of food aid for Haiti came in the wake of 1954's disastrous Hurricane Hazel, which ripped down hundreds of thousands of *pye-bwa,* or trees, and destroyed crops all over the country. Hurricane Hazel also gave a big boost to the already booming charcoal industry in Haiti: what else were starving peasants to do with the broken trees that littered their lands?

At the end of 1986, I began hearing about the American Plan for Haiti. Aristide talked about the American Plan, but I thought that that was just his way of defining the whole range of U.S. policies toward Haiti. Then I noticed that people in the street were talking about it, in just his words: the American Plan, *plan meriken*. Some document embarrassing to the Americans, I supposed, had been made public. The American Plan—it was a Machiavellian conspiracy to force Haiti to comply with U.S. economic and geopolitical needs in the region. That was as much as I gathered from the street talk.

A week or so later, I was talking with the Well-Placed Embassy Official. We were discussing the tension in town, how things seemed to be building toward some sort of crisis during the spring and the summer before the elections. He mentioned what he perceived as "growing anti-Americanism." I told him that I'd never been in a country where people were more unfailingly polite and friendly to Americans. Even when they were shouting in the streets against the American government, Haitians would turn to me and say, "Not the American people, the American government."

"No," said the Embassy Official, unsmiling. "A certain element is encouraging anti-Americanism. You know who they are. Just look at the so-called American Plan. It hasn't been easy for us to deal with it. That thing has really been our biggest p.r. headache to date. Completely fabricated, of course."

I asked him what it was, exactly.

"It's this sort of report with 'American Plan' as its title that purports to be what the Reagan Administration plans to do with Haiti." The Embassy Official told me that the document had been put together by Haitians, and that he didn't have a copy of it. He said he wasn't even sure it actually existed on paper. No Haitian newspaper ever reprinted a copy of the American Plan, although the leftist paper *Haïti Progrès* mentioned it in numerous articles.

The actual document, it turned out, was a collection of quotes from U.S. government documents, compiled by Ernst Verdieu, a member of the independent electoral council. As the months wore on, I heard more and more about it. The plan seemed to grow as it became a byword among Haitians. Verdieu's report alleged that the United States wanted to turn Haiti into an export-led economy that would feed American markets with coffee, fruit, processed foods and cheaply made manufactured goods, and that the U.S. was not interested in boosting Haitian domestic production. The U.S. goal in

Haiti, Verdieu said, was to reduce self-sufficient farming, thereby causing peasants to migrate to Port-au-Prince, where they would provide a useful and very cheap labor force to work in American assembly factories. Food aid would be used to lower the prices of Haitian crops, thereby providing a disincentive to further domestic production. Haiti would be dependent on U.S. food exports, and would in turn raise its revenues by exporting assembled goods and export crops, as well as agribusiness produce like tomato paste. Haiti would become an extension of the United States, an economic colony. In fact, although there may not have been a specific "American Plan" for Haiti, there were a number of U.S. development programs for the country that, taken together, would probably have had the effects that Verdieu cited.

In the Haitian imagination, however, the American Plan did not stop with economics. A wealthy mulatto woman went to the beach one weekend and returned with an itching rash and a fever. Many people had the same experience that weekend. Some of them blamed the illness on the jellyfish that occasionally invade the north coast of Haiti's southern peninsula. But this woman told me her rash came from toxic wastes that an American boat had dumped offshore. "It's part of the American Plan," she said. "You know there is that boat from the States looking for a place to dump its trash. I think that's what happened. It dumped it on Haiti, of course." (A few months later, in collusion with two brothers of the Casernes Dessalines' Colonel Paul, a U.S. boat called the *Khian Sea* did dump a haul of Philadelphia's toxic wastes outside Gonaïves.)

A young man, a student waiting for his AIDS test at the National Research Institute, told me that AIDS was a part of the plan.

"You get so many people to move into the city to work in your factories," he said, "and then suddenly you realize you can't give them all jobs. All those people together, without jobs and money— they're bound to stir up some kind of revolution, so you decide you're going to get rid of them. You can't do it with guns, though, because that would be inhumane. So you give them AIDS. It's part of the American Plan, people are saying. It makes sense, so I sort of believe it. People say that the CIA developed AIDS, and you know that the Americans are always saying there are too many Haitians."

It got to be a source of black humor. I drove past a messy car crash, and the Haitian sitting in my passenger seat said, "More evidence of the insidious American Plan." He laughed. Three people were killed in a rainstorm, and a journalist said, "The American

Plan." The rain came in through the roof of the Holiday Inn during a press conference held by opposition leaders, and splashed down on Victor Benoit's head. One of his supporters in the Group of Fifty-seven laughed, and said, "The American Plan." You'd see a white woman standing by as five Haitians fixed her flat tire, and the conclusion was inescapable: the American Plan.

It was funny, but not to the American Embassy. They took the thing very seriously. Their business was serious, after all. Early on, adding fuel to the controversy, Ambassador Brunson McKinley made a speech denying the existence of an American Plan. A copy of the speech was forwarded to all U.S. personnel with the following message from the U.S. public-affairs officer: "The speech is a clear statement of U.S. policy with respect to development and its relation to democracy. Please feel free to use it in conversations with Haitian friends and associates."

The first Haitian Constitution, written in 1805 under the auspices of Dessalines, forbade foreigners to purchase or own land in Haiti. Over the years, there was much debate among Haitians about this controversial section, which remained intact for more than a century through the rocky course of Haiti's constitutional history. Those who called for the section's repeal argued that Haiti needed to be able to sell land to certain foreigners in order to gain leverage with friendly nations and freeze out unfriendly ones. But the section stuck, an institutional reminder of how badly modern Haiti's ancestors had suffered under the French and the Spanish, and was not repealed until the Constitution of 1918 was adopted, three years into the U.S. occupation. Once the new constitution, which was in large measure the creation of Franklin D. Roosevelt, then Assistant Secretary of the U.S. Navy, was in place, American companies immediately set about buying large tracts of land for agrobusiness. The idea that there exists an American Plan for Haiti is not new.

In 1941, the United States and Haiti began a cooperative venture called the Société Haïtiano-Américaine de Développement Agricole (SHADA), the Haitian-American Company for Agricultural Development, a prototypical aid project run by Americans who ignored the protests of responsible Haitian experts. Financed by an Export-Import Bank loan of $5 million and later the recipient of another $7

million in U.S. credit, SHADA proposed to raise sisal and rubber
—products in short world supply at the time because of the growing
World War—in Haiti. SHADA was a bold project, and the Haitian
government, also ignoring the indigenous experts, did everything it
could to help implement the plans of the American agronomist who
had developed the idea, Thomas Fennell. This meant that the then
President, Elie Lescot (the man who had sent Roumain to Mexico
rather than keep the revolutionary writer at home), allowed Fennell
to do as he pleased with the peasants of the areas where the sisal and
the cryptostegia (vine rubber) were to be produced. (Lescot had also
offered Franklin Roosevelt the Môle St.-Nicolas as a U.S. naval
base.)

In *Written in Blood,* SHADA's methods are described: "Fennell
and SHADA ran roughshod over peasant proprietors, condemning
choice agricultural plots, bulldozing cailles [peasant houses], even
sacred houmforts [voodoo temples], . . . paying in pittances, and
rehiring as day laborers expropriated peasants who had been subsistence farmers."

In the end, according to the summary in *Written in Blood* and in
other reports of the SHADA debacle, some forty thousand families
were kicked off their property, although the project never cultivated
even half of that land. For four years, SHADA had managed more
than 5 percent of Haiti's finest agricultural lands, yet when the project was over, only five tons of rubber—a scandalously low return—
had been harvested. After the project was abandoned, the few peasants who returned to their plots were at a loss as to how to start their
cultivation up again, so badly had their land been treated. In some
cases, they could not even recognize their own fields, because the
identifying trees, hills and bushes had all been bulldozed away.

Haitian objections to U.S. aid projects sound paranoid. "It's as if
your grandfather handed you a check for twenty-five thousand dollars," said the Well-Placed Embassy Official, "and your first response
was to say, 'You're trying to run my life.' " But it is undeniably true
that individuals who give money do expect something in return for
that generosity. So do institutions. So do governments. In this re-
gard, it is instructive to look at the World Bank's 1985 report, entitled "Haiti: Policy Proposals for Growth." This report is unusually
frank about the policy goals that foreign-aid givers would like to see
instituted by the Haitian government. Perhaps this is because the

report had a restricted distribution and was intended for use "only in the performance of official duties."

"Haiti is close to the North American market," the report begins, in a statement of its overall policy outlook.

> It has large untapped agricultural possibilities that could result from concentrating on farm enterprises with high productive potential. Haiti has a comparative advantage in a number of crops like bananas, coffee, rice, maize and sugarcane if they are grown with modern techniques. Agro-industry presents sizeable opportunities that could be exploited by the emerging combination of traditional land-owners and the new entrepreneurial class's managerial skills. Industry as a whole can take advantage of the factors that have so attracted largely foreign assembly firms: productive low-cost labor, proximity to the United States, functioning basic infrastructure, liberal economic outlook and political stability.
>
> The development strategy must be export-oriented . . . [Domestic] consumption . . . will have to be markedly restrained in order to shift the required share of output increases into exports . . . More emphasis will have to be put on development projects that support the expansion of private enterprises in agriculture, industry and services. Private projects with high economic returns should be strongly supported with accordingly less relative emphasis on public expenditures in the social sectors.

The recommendations of an institution like the World Bank are not mere recommendations, and this is one reason that policies that were for the most part adopted by the Haitian government have nonetheless been characterized as "the American Plan." As Josh DeWind and David Kinley point out in their report "Aiding Migration: The Impact of International Development Assistance on Haiti," the World Bank and other international development agencies virtually forced the Haitian government into accepting their export-led proposals for growth. DeWind and Kinley cite a 1983 World Bank Country Program paper on Haiti, which states: "Under strong pressure from the international financial community and from governments of traditional donor agencies, the President of Haiti and the group surrounding him were made to understand that continued aid to Haiti would require major policy corrections."

The authors of the 1985 World Bank report advise the Haitian government—and, by extension, foreign-aid donors—to cut back on social and health programs and use the monies thus saved to build up infrastructure. In a chapter called "The Way Forward," the World Bank suggests that "capital expenditure not essential to increasing output . . . should be reduced and should be stabilized in the case of health and the social components within rural development projects. . . . Part of the resources earned or saved through the preceding measures could be allocated to complete the physical infrastructure which export-oriented businesses need to operate efficiently and competitively."

In a more specific passage, the World Bank authors write that "temporarily, less emphasis should be placed on social objectives which increase consumption, since the urgent need is to free a major share of GDP [gross domestic product] growth for export." What is a "social objective that increases consumption"? The things that consume in an economy are people, and a social objective that increases consumption in a country like Haiti is a social objective that keeps people, or consumers, alive. Thus, infant-mortality programs, health-care programs, free clinics and the like might be included in programs that have social objectives that increase consumption.

On the subject of education, the World Bank report continues in the same vein. "Education," it states, "is essential to long-term development. In the short-term, however, it is a cost. This cost is necessary but should be minimized. . . . Thus, social objectives should be more strictly related to economic growth . . . and private sector participation in the achievement of social objectives should be pursued where possible." In other words, get the Haitian private sector to pay for education as far as possible.

The report goes on: "The private sector already makes a substantial contribution, as evidenced by the numerous schools . . . found in Port-au-Prince, and the provision of health services on a private basis, even in rural areas." The World Bank is content to encourage such private-sector endeavors, but if you visit a number of these schools and clinics throughout the country, you quickly become aware that they don't come near providing adequate services. Most of the schools resemble the one in Passe-Reine at the Baptist mission. The school across from Lucy's house in Duverger is run by a twenty-one-year-old teacher who teaches his Creole-speaking students in

French, even though they can't speak it and his own French is negligible. The schoolbooks date from early in Papa Doc's rule. Most teachers in the Haitian countryside, and many in town, are subliterate. Health clinics from Milot in the north down to Carrefour and out to Jérémie on the tip of the southern peninsula are often filthy, always undersupplied. Of course, the health and education of the Haitian slum-dweller and the Haitian peasant were not the first priority of the public policies that the World Bank wanted to see instituted in Haiti, and thus they could be left to the care of the Haitian private sector. The goal of the policies, rather, was fast growth that might have a trickle-down effect in the future.

Yet people like Lucy, out in Duverger, were affected by U.S. policy. In their small and unwitting way, they went along with what people were calling the American Plan. They had heard about the assembly factories in the capital; they saw in them hope for employment. Lucy herself came to Port-au-Prince and looked for factory work for a month. She left her son Ariole with the family. But she couldn't find anything, she said. She had no connections, no family member who worked for the assembly industry. These jobs, where women sew dozens of dresses or stuffed animals or baseballs in crowded warehouses for $3.50 a day and spend as much as a dollar a day on transportation and lunch—these jobs are plums, and hard to find. The export-led policy wasn't working for Lucy, nor for thousands like her.

"Of course, the U.S. has its own agenda here," says Aristide. "That's natural. If you are a rich man, and you have money to spend, you like to make investments. Then, once you've made the investment, well, you want to make sure the operation works the way you envisioned it. You want to make sure it gives you the best rate of return: stability and profit, in the case of the U.S. in Haiti. This is normal, capitalist behavior, and I don't care if the U.S. wants to do it at home. You can do whatever you want in your own home, right? But it is monstrous to come down here and impose your will on another people. Why should we advance the way you want us to advance? I understand the reality of the geographical situation, and the geopolitical situation, but I cannot accept that Haiti should be whatever the United States wants it to be. And it won't be, I can assure you of that. I don't know what Haiti will become in the future—I know what I'd like it to become, what many would like it to become—but one thing Haitians have made clear, from Dessalines to Duvalier, good and bad alike, is that we do not bow to the will of other nations. We may pretend to, but we don't. We've never been a client state."

"We are trying to do what we think is best for Haiti, without losing sight of our interests here," says the Well-Placed Embassy Official. It is late July 1987. "Our interests would be best protected by a stable, democratic government, healthy agriculture, an educated, healthy population. We tried to do this during the occupation, and it worked fairly well. But once we left, the Haitians went about doing business the way they always have—they stole from their own people, they lined their own pockets, they deprived the population of anything like liberty. There was no government for the people, the government was against the people, as it almost invariably has been here. Sometimes, the U.S. supported that government, Papa Doc's government—maybe that was wrong, but at the time, and now too, we needed a stable government here, so near Cuba. Today, we are supporting Namphy, because we feel that, however unwillingly, he will help bring about a process that will further Haiti's democratic aims.

"People say that the Haitians don't know how to govern themselves. I wouldn't say that, but I would say that the Haitians who have governed this country didn't know how to do it, or didn't care to. Since Jean-Claude came to power, and things loosened up a bit, the U.S. has seen a window of opportunity for change in Haiti, and we have tried to exploit it. We want democratic progress for Haiti. That seems simple. All our aid programs are geared in one way or another to this democratic end, and that includes tree-planting, food aid, road-building, everything they talk about in the American Plan. The real American Plan for Haiti is democracy. I can't understand why any Haitian would object to our providing the money and means for them to work their way toward this goal. It's all beyond me: what are they complaining about?"

When you are driving past Haiti's naked mountains, it is easy to like USAID's Agroforestry Outreach Project. You're at the CARE nursery at Bombardopolis. Women with their heads wrapped in bandanas and men in broad straw hats are carefully watering the slender seedlings while other peasants come by to pick up a batch for planting. All around you, people are working in harmony; a kind of rural community reigns, filled with sunlight and cool water. When you feel this rare pastoral peace, and watch the dedicated nursery workers laboring over the little trees, you think that here—maybe just in this one place—nature might for once provide. When you see a sloping hillside nearby planted with CARE trees, and beans among them, you begin to think maybe this is the foreign-aid project that can work, maybe it is the one useful one, the one that is sincerely well-intentioned and not exploitive. You think, What are they complaining about?

But as the spring of 1987 wore on, rumblings against the project sprang up all over the Northwest. In Passe-Catabois, a market village near Beau Champ where Benito treats his patients, the CARE nursery on an American missionary's land was dechouked. Three others in the Northwest met the same fate. A nursery run by the World Bank in Jean-Rabel was destroyed, the seedlings flung from their seedbeds and left to shrivel up. A progressive Haitian priest who had worked with peasants for years had gotten it into his head that the American trees were being planted in order to sap the ground of the few nutrients left in it. (In fact the trees help create more nutrients, although they require watering with scarce water.) CARE people claimed that this priest and other progressive Church workers were in part responsible for the nursery dechoukajs, and that the nurseries and the project itself still had the full support of most peasants. Nonetheless, they were careful to put up "a 5-strand barbed wire fence and two locked gates" around one rebuilt nursery.

The destruction seemed senseless, a tragic example of peasants unwittingly working against their own best interests. But in fact, according to their own logic, their actions were reasonable: the peasants weren't complaining, as the Well-Placed Embassy Official would say, about the trees themselves, they were complaining about the policy, the larger U.S.-aid policy that informed the tree-planting project and other projects in the country. The CARE nurseries had fallen into a category that was anathema to the newly politicized and organized peasants in the Northwest. As the spring 1987 CARE quarterly report from that province stated:

> CARE is seen in the NW as a front for the U.S. government, and as implementers of the "American Plan." The image of CARE is negative in the NW because of the un-

wanted dependency on [CARE-supplied] food aid. As the
biggest employer in the NW and with a 35–40 year presence, CARE is a natural target of resentment among the
"have-nots." People in the NW still want the trees, but the
leaders of the leftists tell them that taking trees is only a
way for CARE to get them into CARE's confidence.

Against the background of a series of moves against foreign aid,
the attacks on the CARE nurseries seemed the logical next step. As
the CARE report notes, the most important program to suffer during the months and years after Duvalier's fall was Food-for-Work, a
program implemented by CARE and other relief agencies using
U.S.-government-supplied surplus food. When analyzed as a part of
"the American Plan," U.S. food aid no longer looked much like a
humanitarian donation. If in exchange for your labor you ate a free
Food-for-Work meal or received three pails of wheat, you would
have to buy that much less corn and beans at the market, or you
could sell it at the market for less than the going rate for similar
staples. Food aid, whether distributed at a work project or sold more
cheaply than local staples at market, lowered demand for local produce, thus forcing down prices for Haitian food and cutting down
the farmer's income. The farmer's inability to compete successfully
with this alternative food source encouraged him to leave his land
for the city, where he would not only cease to put a consumption
burden on the overworked Haitian land, but also become a potential
worker in the assembly factories. There, living in La Saline or Cité
Soleil, he and his family could eat mange sinistre, if they were lucky,
until Haiti, with its income from assembly exports, became a net
importer of U.S. food, sending its exotic fruits and coffee and as-
sembly-factory goods to American markets, while its people ate
American wheat and rice. Meanwhile, the peasant's land in the countryside could be annexed by large landholders for future agribusiness
ventures. According to Haitians who believed that there was an
American Plan for their country, these future agribusiness ventures
would be run by Americans and the "traditional landowners" of the
World Bank report. The American Plan would reinforce the status
quo in Haiti and allow for greater U.S. penetration of the Haitian
economy.

Reacting to such potential effects of food aid, progressive groups,
some of them sponsored by the Catholic Church's foreign-aid branch
CARITAS, had been developing programs whereby peasant pro-

duce was bought at market prices and then distributed free to needy peasants. The CARITAS food programs supported Haitian agriculture and at the same time provided humanitarian relief. Unlike Food-for-Work and other foreign food aid, this method of food distribution did not force down the price of Haitian produce, and thus did not encourage farmers to reduce their production.

The peasant groups that managed CARITAS and other similar distribution centers—or canteens—sometimes built silos to stockpile grains like rice and corn that would otherwise have gone to waste, since there are few places where you can effectively store food in the Haitian countryside. The silos and warehouses were run by cooperatives, and proved marginally effective on a local level in meeting the food demands of the hungry. The canteens were particularly successful in the dry and famished Northwest. In such areas, as another CARE report points out, foreign food aid was not accepted. Even in places like the La Saline slum, where food aid is a vital part of everyday life, you would see graffiti on the walls that read: *"La Saline pa vle mange sinistre."* La Saline does not want food aid.

Gen. Namphy and the junta exacerbated the anger over food aid when they opened up Haiti's provincial ports, and contraband food, especially surplus rice from Miami, began flooding the country. Miami rice, it was called. Up until then, rice had not been a part of the U.S. food-aid program. At market, the contraband rice cost far less than Haitian rice. When the contraband started flowing into the port town of Gonaïves, many farmers from the fertile Artibonite valley that feeds that city had to stop harvesting, because they were not going to be able to sell at competitive prices and make back their investment. The shipments created a political division between city-dwellers, whose misery was eased by the lower rice price, and the farmer whose way of life was threatened by it. Where formerly the people of Gonaïves and the Artibonite had presented a more or less unified progressive block, contraband turned the region into a battlefield. During the unrest of the spring and summer of 1987, progressives in Haiti saw Miami rice as a logical parallel—whether intended or not—of the American Plan: U.S. food producers, in tandem with the Haitian junta, attempting to defuse a Third World political and economic crisis with that oldest of tools, food. Gonaïves, which not long before had proudly called itself the birthplace of the Dechoukaj, grew bustling and complacent on the profits from Miami rice.

Soon, small wars between contrabanders and rice farmers broke out. You would hear every morning about farmers who had hijacked a truck of Miami rice and spilled its contents over the highway. Groups of fifty or more farmers and their friends would set up a roadblock and then attack the trucks with machetes. Sometimes, the truck driver, fearful for his life, simply would not stop, and a few peasants would be run down. The Army was reported to be deeply involved in contraband trafficking; eventually, the rice trucks were provided with Army escorts in order to make the run from Gonaïves to Port-au-Prince without incident.

Because some of the people of Gonaïves profited so handily from foreign food aid and from contraband, it was difficult for those who opposed such distributions to organize effectively against them. But in some sections of the Northwest—those surrounding Beau Champ, for example—food aid was blocked. "That vicinity," read a CARE report, "doesn't want any food aid, any CARE people or CARE programs. They had tossed out Food for Work in 1986, as a result of CARITAS pressure, and have previously burned down a house of one of the CARE employees. They threatened to do it again if CARE returns. CARE has agreed to stay out and to dismiss the monitors in that section."

Peter Welle, a young CARE agroforester responsible for the Northwest, was distraught during the dechoukajs of the CARE nurseries. "We've really been trying to help these people," he said, "and it just doesn't work. Our help is not the help they want, I guess. Sometimes I feel like I'm just a U.S.-government employee. Before the troubles began, I felt like I was doing good, helping Haiti, helping Haitians, just planting trees, you know, making the place green again, making it a little livable, or something. Now I feel like I'm the bad guy. And maybe I am.

"You know," Peter says, "you get into this thing where you think you know better than they do what is good for them, this sort of paternalistic thing. You say, Oh, they think the trees are bad, they think the trees are taking away their land, but they're wrong, these trees will help them. But then, the more you hear their arguments and see the way they live and imagine what would happen if all their hillside fields were planted with trees, the more you have to think, maybe they know best what they need. You can't make a project work against the people who are supposed to be its beneficiaries." Peter still continued to believe strongly in the project, however.

The CARE report also acknowledged that there were substantive issues at work in the precipitous decline in popularity of the CARE nurseries. "The objections to tree planting are general ones, as related to Rick Scott [a CARE agroforestry administrator] by the priest [one of the progressive priests in the Northwest]. It is claimed that trees dry out the soil and that farmers should be planting crops, not trees. Trees reduce the area of agricultural land. . . . The local priests are convinced that there is an 'American Plan,' whereby the farmers are enrolled to plant trees on their land."

The local priests may have gotten their agroforestry wrong, but they were not much mistaken about the ultimate goals of U.S. reforestation projects. "The potential for productivity and growth rests much more with the better rainfed and irrigated flatlands than with the mountainous areas . . ." reads the World Bank report.

> Ongoing activities [on hillside farms] to conserve the soils and plant large areas with trees should be intensified with continued external aid on very concessional terms. These measures are fundamental to the viability of investments in the flatter areas, especially when they concern the protection of watersheds that feed the irrigation systems. A strategy of incentives toward planting improved varieties of coffee trees [an export-crop tree] . . . should also be actively pursued. It is inescapable that, in the long term, the problems of deforestation and erosion must be addressed by measures to encourage migration from the mountains. This means expansion of agricultural employment in the plains and industrial employment in the cities.

The tableau painted by the World Bank is appealing: green hills, displaced peasants gainfully employed in factories in town, rolling plains for agrobusiness that give forth tons of tomatoes and other produce each year; well-paid farm workers. It hasn't worked that way, however. Each year by the thousands, Haitians do indeed move from the countryside to Port-au-Prince or Gonaïves or Cap-Haïtien: migration from the mountains, as the World Bank says. But they don't find jobs, nor do the hills they have abandoned become green. Sometimes squatters take over the property, sometimes it is left alone, but always it is stripped of its trees by the departing peasant, who sells the wood for charcoal to get cash for the trip to town.

Meanwhile, it has become more difficult for those peasants who do remain behind in the countryside to organize land-reform movements and other opposition to the government in isolation from the forces of order. Roads have been built (many of them using Food-for-Work to pay the employees), and the peasants themselves have cut down much of their protective forest. You can drive to Hinche now in two and a half hours in the dry season, and Army trucks and armored cars can make the trip in less time, even during the rainy season, although before the newest bridges were completed they could not make it when the rivers were at their height. Still, the best way to ensure that the peasants do not again revolt is to move them into more controllable areas, ideally to the cities, where they would have to contend with hundreds of troops trained for the terrain, and where they can be watched and bought. This is one of the perhaps unintended effects of the "American Plan."

As a 1984 USAID Country Development strategy assessment stated, "The existence of a non-hostile government and populace in Haiti is a fundamental security interest." The plan to reforest mountain and hillside fields, thus relocating the peasants who currently live in such areas, is one method that helps guarantee "a non-hostile populace," or at least one less able to mount an armed guerrilla offensive. DeWind and Kinley point out that in its 1982 Country Development Strategy Statement, USAID

> anticipates that such a drastic reorientation of agriculture will cause a decline in income and nutritional status, especially for small farmers and peasants. . . . Even if transition to export agriculture is successful, AID anticipates a "massive" displacement of peasant farmers and migration to urban centers.

The American strategy for developing Haiti, then, achieves two strategic U.S. goals—one, a restructured and dependent agriculture that exports to U.S. markets and is open to American exploitation, and the other, a displaced rural population that not only can be employed in offshore U.S. industries in the towns, but is more susceptible to Army control.

In all foreign-aid programs, donors, no matter their ultimate strategic and political goals, are trying to cure immediate ills, the ones they can identify and quantify, with long-term projects. No doubt the U.S. government would be pleased if tomorrow Haiti became a prosperous nation capable of adequately feeding its people: prosperous nations are rarely revolutionary. But once a donor nation has accepted the reality of a starving, depleted country, it has many choices about the aid policies it will implement.

On the question of food aid, for example, the United States, like CARITAS, might have chosen to support Haitian farmers with food-distribution programs that used local produce, rather than to undermine them by providing American staples at low cost. Part of the reason for choosing to dump food rather than to work with farmers to help encourage production is bureaucratic: Title 1 of Public Law 480 (P.L. 480, in foreign-aid parlance) provides low-interest loans to certain countries to purchase surplus American food, and this law has been on the books since 1954. It was created to get rid of U.S. surplus food, as a part of an American agricultural-relief program. The mechanism for such food aid, thus, is already in place; it's a known quantity, and easy to implement. (The law was modified in 1977 to force governments that receive P.L. 480 food to require that its sale not undercut the prices of local producers. The amendment, however, had little effect. According to Frances Moore Lappé, Rachel Schurman and Kevin Danaher, the authors of *Betraying the National Interest,* no country has ever been denied a P.L. 480 loan on such a basis.) The U.S. food policy and many of the other American, French and Canadian aid projects are also politically useful abroad. P.L. 480 is a quick-fix solution to the explosive conditions in Third World cities. Put a wheat biscuit in the mouth of a hungry man clamoring for land reform and dechou-kaj, and he'll shut up and chew.

If one believes that USAID's programs are sincere, that is, if one believes that the agency actually wishes to help solve Haiti's problems and to ensure a viable future for the country, one still must conclude that misinformation and arrogance dictate much of the agency's policy decisions. To use the Well-Placed Embassy Official's metaphor, it is as though your grandfather gave you $25,000, but stipulated that you could have the money only if you agreed to go to law school or to medical school or join the family business, in spite of the fact that he knew you wanted to be a painter or a social worker. Even under Jean-Claude Duvalier, the Haitian government had to be coerced into the Americans' export-led economic model. Perhaps someday, a U.S. plan for Haiti will work to the good of Haitians. Anything is possible. For the present, U.S. aid policies are contributing to dislocation, hunger and massive urban unemployment.

In the end, people like Peter Welle get caught in a trap they never devised. Peter believes that the policy aims of the program he works for are questionable, but he still feels happy when he sees a small farm that has topsoil because of the trees his nursery provided. Similarly, people who administer P.L. 480 projects are often satisfied with the immediate results of their efforts—hungry children being fed—and try not to think about the detrimental effects on production. Low-level development workers, who spend most of their time out "in the field"—as anthropologists and aid people call the countryside—live in a painful limbo: often the good advice they give to the bureaucrats in the capital is ignored or pooh-poohed or characterized as radical; then they have to go back into the field and tell the Haitians they work with that an idea they have all agreed upon—much higher numbers of fruit trees for planting, say—is not considered viable by the people who run the program. When their ideas are ignored and their input is scorned by the white bureaucracy that they had hoped would help them begin to change their country, Haitians even in the farthest reaches of the provinces begin to talk about the American Plan.

At lunch at the Oloffson one afternoon, an AID worker based in Port-au-Prince was talking about widening the road through Carrefour. It is a project that needs doing; the road is a major market-access route, and it is almost always stopped dead by traffic. But the people who live in Carrefour in houses that come right up to the road don't support the project. Too often, they know, foreign-aid projects—like the pig-eradication program—do not make good on their promises of monetary or in-kind restitution. I brought up this problem with the AID worker.

"I know, I know," he said. "But at a certain point, who cares if they want it? They need it, and they're going to have it. They don't understand. What Haiti needs is infrastructure, and we are going to make sure they get it whether they want it or not."

A Haitian at the table excused himself at this moment, and we could hear him get into his car and drive off. Peter might have done the same thing.

Duverger Dancing

The twins chased the tarantula out of the shallow river-bed and up the hard dirt bank. They were running fast, but the spider knew that mortal enemies pursued him, and he moved quickly along under the sparse grasses near the water, hauling his fat hairy body along the land with the same lumbering grace he had shown in the mud near the water. Just as the twins closed on him, they crashed into each other, and the spider edged under the mosses that covered the heavy roots of the tree that grows out over the river, and disappeared.

"*Kote krab arenyen-an?*" one of the twins shouted to the other. Where's the tarantula?

"*M pa we-l.* I don't see it," said the other boy, who was crouched over and peering into the tree's gnarled roots. "It's dark under there. I'm not going in there."

The spider, meanwhile, was scaling the mosses at the tree's back, silently climbing, almost invisible, like a piece of the tree's bark moving. He came to rest in the crook of a branch, and the boys never found him.

"*Krab-la pèdi,*" one of them said to his little sister Adeline as he descended toward the river. The spider is lost.

"Ou pèdi-l," she corrected him. You lost him.

Adeline was on the other side of the river, filling up her calabash with water from the *source,* one of the two watering holes in the riverbank. The children bathed in the river at sunset, with the women of Duverger. Sometimes the women and the girls did laundry at the same time. The men bathed upriver, for privacy.

Clouds were building above the banana trees. Across the river, the sun hung low over the dry bean fields. The smell of charcoal floated on the air, someone was making fritay. A few thin farmers stood leaning on their hoes in the fields above the river, waiting for dark. The river grew pink, then gold, in the fading sun. Drums came from the mountains, faint. Adeline tripped across the gold river with a filled calabash on her head. The hem of her white dress was wet. As the twins started to play and bathe, she began the steep ascent toward home. She walked to the rhythm of the boys' water games; they were beating the gold water like a drum with their open palms. Gold droplets rose around them. Their laughter went up to join the sound of splashing and drums.

Back at the house, Lucy was making fritay. Even in the cool of sunset, her fever brought out a sweat on her forehead. The whites of her eyes were blue through the charcoal smoke. Sonya, her little cousin, was sitting nearby, chopping beef. Sonya was fat, and slow. Miss said that Sonya was *egare,* which means lost, or strayed. Her mind strays, was what Miss meant. But Sonya knew how to chop beef, and she knew how to look up from under batting eyelids and get what she wanted out of Miss, me, Lucy. Of all the children, Sonya was never hit. Then again, Sonya never did anything wrong. Sonya never did anything except what she was told to do. Lucy handed her a mixture of scallions, thyme, garlic and a chicken-and-tomato bouillon cube that had all been pounded together. This mixture they called *epis,* spices. Sonya mixed it in with the chopped beef.

Lucy, bent over the pot of bubbling oil, was talking about Ti Djo, her boyfriend from Carrefour, the great wild red-light district outside Port-au-Prince. "Ti Djo, he was sweet," she said. *Li dous.* She wiped a lock of straightened hair from her forehead and looked up at me. "Oh, he was sweet, *ma chère.* But not for long, no. He turned bad. You know why? He turned bad because some lowlife girl here, she told him I had another man, here in Duverger. You know what Ti Djo did then? Oh, ma chère, it was terrible, a crime. First, he hits me. That's bad enough, you'll say. Well, yes, bad enough. Then he starts smashing everything. I ran away. We didn't know what to do, he was crazy, he says he'll kill me. He's a tough one, he's seen all the bad life in Carrefour, all the vagabonds, the cheap girls. Well, I ran off and stayed with Miss for the night. Ma chère, what a story."

Lucy wiped her temples with the back of a banana frond. With a stick, she poked at the fritay frying in the oil. She shook her head, maybe over Djo, maybe over the fritay. Two white chickens I had bought went walking into the house, behind Lucy's back.

"And the worst was, he stole my bed. That very night. Poor Djo, as if that would change anything. But he stole that bed right out from under my back. I've never seen him since. You wouldn't believe how sweet that man could be." She shook her head again. *"Dous, dous, dous."*

"But Lucy," I asked her, *"did* you have another man in Duverger?"

She looked up at me, and smiled.

"These are ready," she said. She turned to Yvette, a teenaged girl who worked in the house for Lucy. Yvette was sitting on a small chair, looking dreamily into the banana trees. She pretended not to have heard. Yvette had spent the afternoon having her hair braided.

"Yvette, I said these are ready." Lucy made a clucking, angry noise with her lips. She looked at me and shrugged.

After a good long wait, Yvette came forward, and Lucy dumped the fritay into the upturned front of her dress.

Tonight we were going to have a party, a little one, not a proper bamboche, with everyone from the village, but this night just the family. Yvette's hair was corn-rowed for tonight, and Jetta, a friend of Lucy's, had tucked bought rayon hair from market into her own braids to make them fat and thick and shining. Abner was working on the cassette machine. Tonight we would have music. Jetta stood under a banana tree in the field, watching Abner work, moving to a song she had in her head. Bernier, a brother of Abner and Lucy, watched Jetta and tapped his foot. Bernier's wife watched him watching. The cassette player was an old pink thing, secondhand. I gave Abner the batteries of my flashlight to make it work again, but then the tape broke. It started and stopped, like that, and when we pulled it out we saw that it had come undone, a mesh of brown filament like the roots the tarantula had hidden in. Abner gave the cassette a scientific look. He held it up against the moon, turning it in the bright light.

"Banm plim-ou-an," he said. Give me your pen.

I handed it over, and he started twirling. The muscles in his wide forearms rose under the surface of his skin, reflecting the blue moonlight. The tape was flattened and crinkled and folded. It was going to take a little time, unwinding and rewinding, but no one doubted that Abner could do it. I went over to Miss's house with Bernier to buy clairin. We didn't buy a lot, but we bought what Bern said would be enough. It seemed to cost nothing, what we bought, maybe a dollar. Bern poured it from Miss's container into his own, both old Barbancourt bottles.

We walked back to Lucy's in the moonlight. The light bulb in the chef de section's house, away down the curving road, right at the bend, was burning strong. His pigs were sleeping.

"Will you do something for me?" Bern asked, turning to me, serious.

"Depends," I said. I moved away from him.

He watched me for a second, then burst out laughing.

"I want you to read something for me," he said, laughing some more, his eyes, his teeth, his white shirt bright in the moonlight. "That's all."

"Oh, okay," I said, moving back. "Sure"

When we got back to the house, Bern disappeared. Abner was still winding the cassette. Jetta and Yvette whispered in the courtyard in blue dresses. Feverish in the candlelight, Lucy was lying on her new secondhand mattress, a thin item laid unsentimentally on the hard dirt floor. I gave her aspirin to take down the fever. She coughed, and coughed again. I remembered that in Haiti tuberculosis is one of the diseases that accompanies AIDS. Carrefour is a dirty place. I thought about Lucy's boyfriend Ti Djo, and about Nina and Olga, the Dominican prostitutes at El Caribeño.

When I went back outside, Bern was there, watching Abner's progress. He had a letter in his hand.

"Read this," he said. "My cousin Erick sent it to me three years ago. I had someone read it for me then, but I've forgotten some of it. He went to French Guiana, that's where he wrote it from. He was supposed to send for me once he got the money together. They have jobs in French Guiana."

I opened the carefully folded paper, white with blue ruling. Bern stood two candles next to me.

" 'It has been so long since we were separated,' " I read. Bern nodded. The letter was written in a formal broken French.

"Today, I take up my pen to write you these lines in order to give you a little news. Well, dear brother, for my part, things are going almost okay, thank God. Yes, my dear Bernier, excuse me because you have never received a letter from me, but it's not for no reason. It's from another kind of negligence, so think nothing of it, please. Erick is always Bern's, and Bern is always Erick's. Bernier, my dear, I think of you a lot. It's because I haven't found anything for you yet that I'm sending you an empty letter, but don't think that during my voyage I have forgotten all that we have shared together. So, dear brother, have patience. One day you will have something from me."

Bern nodded. "Go on," he said. The candles waved in a brief breeze.

" 'Bernier,' " I read, " 'you must write me and let me know how the 24th of December was, and you must write me right away. Talk to me on a cassette. I'd like to hear your voice. Yours forever, Erick to Bernier.' "

"Thanks," said Bern, taking back the letter. He put it into his shorts pocket. The pigs up at the chef de section's house snorted in the midst of their dreams, and the guinea fowl's weird sound, a low screech, came through the night sky.

"You ever write back to him?" I asked.

"Sure, sure," Bern said. He stood up to take the precious document back home for safekeeping.

"We wrote back right away," said Abner. "The schoolteacher wrote the letter."

"Well?" I asked, looking up at Bern.

"Oh, well," said Bern. He shrugged.

"I guess Erick's letters must have gotten lost," said Abner as Bern disappeared among the banana trees. "We waited. Yes, we waited. Erick. But I'll tell you, ma chère, it's not easy for anyone, this life."

The moon was high. In their concrete house up the road, the American pigs were still dreaming, their heads filled with visions of their forebears' sunny wheatfields and dry Iowa air. In their sleep, they pushed the round hulk of their backs up against the cold, damp concrete walls of the sty. A rat made its careful way down the center aisle, darting into one pig's cell, then another's, until a dreaming pig stuck the flat of his snout into the puddle of slop the rat was sniffing. The rat ran away, making rat sounds, a high chirrup, but the pig did not wake from his dreaming. In Iowa, the rat was a pretty bird, singing above the wheatfields. In Iowa, the slop was the mudhole. The man who guarded the pigs was asleep on the sty stair. He was snorting, too. Abner listened to the low snorts as he tried to make the cassette work.

"*Kochon-yo kontan,*" he said, smiling. The pigs are happy. "*Men, moun-yo pa kontan,*" he continued, "*paske kasèt-sa-a pa mache.*" But the people aren't happy, because this cassette isn't working.

"*Sa wap fè la, mon cher?*" asked Ludovic, the day worker from Gustave's fields, as he entered the family courtyard. What are you doing there?

Abner told him we were going to have dancing tonight.

Ludovic sat down and looked at Jetta. "Have you got any clairin?" he asked Abner.

Lucy was guarding the clairin. "It's for later," Abner said to Ludovic. "When the music starts."

Ludovic nodded. He had already been drinking all day in the field.

When the music began, Sonya drew near the house, her head tilted. The sky was papered with stars. Abner watched the cassette player, nodding as the tape continued to go forward. The music was thin, tinny, but recognizable still as Port-au-Prince *compas.* Attracted by the sound, the twins and Adeline emerged from their house in back. Slowly, couples rose and began to dance. They danced one step only, the bolero, Haiti's most popular dance, where you hardly move and you press yourselves as close together as possible, holding on tight. Unsteadily, Ludovic came over to Lucy, and she stood, coughing, and put her elbows on his hips and danced with her head back. Jetta and Bernier danced in the shadows of the banana trees, almost out of sight. A slender young man walked into the yard, smoking a cigarette. He drank off two capfuls of clairin, and began dancing with Yvette. They stood locked together there in the middle of the group, immobile. The young man kept his cigarette in his mouth. The twins danced together. They giggled and pulled at Adeline's dress. She chased them behind the house, her white dress flying out behind her. She was fast, and you could hear the boys laughing and gasping behind the house. The candles were getting low, but the moonlight was strong. Abner sat quietly on the narrow porch, drinking, having a smoke, watching the dancers.

The lyrics of the song ran on. "*Fòk nou mete tèt ansanm, fòk nou plante."* We've got to get together; we've got to plant. Like so much of the music in Haiti now, it was about everyday life and about the political situation at the same time. The next song came on—it was a tape someone, had made that mixed songs from all of the most popular groups. Even I knew the lyrics of this song. It was all over the radio. *"Cheri, ou twompe mwen."* Baby, you're cheating on me. Baby, you've betrayed me. It was about the junta.

Abner put out his cigarette. He stood up and walked over to sad Sonya, who was sitting in her usual chair, playing with the beads she was wearing around her neck. Abner leaned down to her; he had to lean far, because she was just a child. She didn't notice him at first. That was Sonya, it took her longer than most to see things, to understand. Finally she looked up and saw his face almost against her own. He took her two hands away from the beads and lifted her from her chair. Her smile was enormous. When she was standing, her head reached just above Abner's belly. He bowed a small bow to her, and she put her arms around his waist. They started to dance the bolero.

Ruelle Vaillant

Djo was still running cocaine. He had moved to La Saline from Cité Soleil, now, and set up business, and his two cousins who had never found work in the capital had volunteered to help organize the November 1987 elections, billed in the foreign press as the first free and fair elections in Haiti since the advent of François Duvalier. Djo's cousins were going to be poll watchers, but Djo wanted no part of the thing. Djo was interested in money. He watched in disgust as his cousins headed off to the electoral council's offices; he pulled his reflector sunglasses down on his nose to indicate his disdain. Not enough money in elections, he said. Djo has sharp shoes and wears stone-washed blue jeans, very cool.

Mimette's uncle wasn't interested in elections, either. He lives near Marie-Hélène and the kids in another section of La Saline, not far from Djo, but more run-down because Mimette's uncle makes hats and he doesn't earn as much as Djo does at his job. Mimette's uncle objected to the elections. He wove the green and brown straw in his lap, twisting, twisting, pulling, first the top, then the roll, finally the brim, a hat in a half an hour. He didn't need to look at what he was doing. He watched the market traffic passing, shouted greetings to his friends and acquaintances. From under their various burdens, they nodded and laughed at his joking and teasing. He sent Mimette out to the fritay ladies over at the corner to fetch him a *pat,* a bit of dough filled with a bit of meat and peppers, fried over charcoal.

"What are we supposed to think of these elections?" he said, licking the end of a strip of straw. "I mean, we, the people of La Saline. It's all a big joke. They say *lib e onèt,* free and fair. But how can we expect free and fair under the CNG? Look at what Namphy has done. You've seen it as well as I have. You think a murderer like that, a killer of people, is going to allow us to have free and fair elections? Big joke. He wants to stay in power like all Haitian politicians, all Haitian generals. He says he's sick of being President, wants to go home and drink his tafia. I say it's all a big joke. *Mèsi, cheri.*" Mimette hands him his *pat.* He puts the hat he has just finished on her head. It's too big, only her nose and mouth peep out from under the brim. She laughs, and watches her uncle pop the *pat* into his mouth. We all enjoy the silence while he chews. Mimette's uncle is quiet only when he's eating. Mimette lifts her chin from beneath the hat's broad brim to see what's happening. She looks like a miniature peasant woman; all she needs is a pipe and a burro. She comes and stands behind me, and I feel her begin to braid my hair.

"These elections will bring more violence," her uncle says. The *pat* is finished and the monologue continues. "You hear what Father Aristide says about them, and he is right. They are *eleksyon pèpè-yo.* Secondhand elections." *Pèpè* is the word for the secondhand clothing that is sold in the bidonville markets. Most of it comes in from Miami, and it is the reason why so many Haitians wear tee shirts advertising garages on the New Jersey shore, or running teams from Atlanta, or sexy vacations in Virginia, or California universities. Sometimes pèpè is called *kenedi,* because the big shipments began arriving from the States when John F. Kennedy was in the White House. "The elections come from *lòt bò dlo,*" Mimette's uncle says. The other side of the water. "An American import, these elections. Namphy won't tolerate it, and even if he did, I'm not sure that's what we want here in La Saline, here in Haiti. Do we want an American President? I don't think so. We've already had one or two or three, Jean-Claude, for example. They didn't do me much good. Still weaving hats for nothing, you see."

He puts the next hat on my head, and Mimette whines.

"You're ruining her braids," she tells her uncle.

"She looks better when you can't see what you've done to her hair, *cheri*." He picks up another batch of straw.

"Tonton?" Mimette asks.

"Wi, cheri," he says, patiently.

"Map vote nan eleksyon-sa-yo?" Am I going to vote in these elections?

"Cheri, if they are anything like the elections we have had in Haiti so far, you'll be able to vote, too. *Pa okipe w."* Don't worry. He laughs, reaches into his pocket and sends her off for another *pat*.

I should have introduced Mimette's uncle to Harry. As usual, he was one of the first foreign journalists to arrive back in Haiti for the big news story, this time the November elections. He got there early to watch the whole story unfold. Harry had antennae for Haitian drama.

"My editors," he said. "You know what they want?" He looked up from the manila envelope on which he was scribbling notes for an interview. "They say 'C'mon, Harry. What is Fred Voodoo saying?' You know who Fred Voodoo is? The Haitian man in the street. They always want a fucking interview with this Fred Voodoo chap. I never do that stuff.

"You want to do something smart?" he asked me. "Go interview Leslie Manigat. He's a very intelligent man, he's running for President, and who knows, maybe one day he will have the high honor of being the fattest President Haiti has ever had. I like Leslie, known him for years, wonderful cracked voice, always wagging his finger like the teacher he is."

But Manigat didn't stand a chance. Everyone agreed that the battle was among four candidates. There was Louis Déjoie, Jr., the mulatto son of one of the candidates who ran against François Duvalier in 1957. There was Sylvio Claude, the pastor who was once imprisoned by Jean-Claude. There was Marc Bazin, a former World Bank official and a former Finance Minister under Jean-Claude, well-spoken and well-dressed, known as "Mr. Clean," an anti-Communist who was thought to be the favorite candidate of the Reagan Administration. He seemed almost as American as Bill Cosby. And then there was Gérard Gourgue, a schoolteacher and human-rights activist with impeccable Parisian French and a habit of looking down at the ground while he turned the baroque phrases that 85 percent of Haitians could not understand. When he was angry, however, he spoke bitter Creole and looked straight at you. When they first took power, Namphy's junta was made up of six men, one of them Gourgue, as Justice Minister. He was the leaven that made the junta attractive to foreign aid donors, the token democrat among Duvalierists and soldiers. After lending the weight of his legitimacy to the new junta, Gourgue rapidly arrived at the politic and principled decision to resign. Now he was the candidate of the Unity Front (Front de Concertation), a spinoff of the summer's Group of Fifty-seven; with the Front behind him, he was plausibly the most popular candidate. The Front comprised many center and left-of-center associations, including Victor Benoit's Konakom, the group he and others had formed during the memorable National Congress of Democratic Movements. Benoit's people were known laughingly as the Konacommunists, and Benoit himself was a senatorial candidate for the Front in the Artibonite Valley. The Front was strong in the highly mobilized and populous Artibonite, and once Gourgue was chosen as its candidate, the Front looked formidable, the biggest threat to Bazin's candidacy.

Peasants and the urban poor loved Gourgue because he had championed human rights and been beaten by Jean-Claude Duvalier's thugs. They remembered the incident: a human-rights conference in November 1979, held at what would later be Aristide's church, St.-Jean-Bosco. (The Haitian Salesians have a history of making their meeting halls available to democratic and human-rights groups; another example was the 1987 Congress where Konakom was formed.) While the human-rights meeting was in session, a band of Tontons Macoute descended on the church complex and briefly clubbed everyone in sight, including Gourgue. The people also respected Gourgue because he had quit the diabolical junta instead of staying on and enjoying the fruits of corruption, although they resented him for participating in the first place. In Bombardopolis, sitting by the side of their fields in the evening, farmers would listen to Gourgue's French on the radio, and turn to each other afterward, nodding, and say, *"Min Mèt Goug."* That's Master Gourgue. (*Mèt* is the honorific for a lawyer.)

Peasants and the poor also loved Pastor Claude, because he had been imprisoned for speaking against the regime, and he was a riveting preacher and a man of God. People in the southern peninsula loved Déjoie because his family was from the southern peninsula. No one loved Bazin, but the Port-au-Prince business community supported his candidacy. You could tell who Bazin's people were by the placement of his biggest campaign sign. To anyone who came down the hill from Pétionville to town, as the bourgeoisie did each day, the big black-and-white sign read: VOTEZ MARC BAZIN. In French. On the way up, the trip that maids and gardiens made each day, it read: NIZAB CRAM ZETOV.

If you described the election in these terms, as the Well-Placed Embassy Official did, as the American media did, as some Haitians tried to, it sounded almost normal, a battle among four respectable candidates with large or powerful voting blocs, and a hoard of other, lesser men. In the foreign press, the Haitian democratic process was moving toward its logical finale: elections. But this was not what was really happening in Haiti.

What was happening was a panic among those in power, a panic about keeping that power in the right hands. The junta—the Army—panicked because they saw that this time around they would not be able to install their own man. The Front was a threat. Gourgue was a threat. Any candidate elected with an actual popular mandate was a threat. You could see their panic; they were not shy about providing evidence. Two lesser candidates, Athis and Volel, had already been assassinated in the months before the elections, and the others had hired bodyguards and had virtually stopped campaigning, in spite of the cynical advice they received from the junta to go out and hit the trail. Déjoie kept a pistol on his desk. Bazin said he had taken "all necessary precautions." All had walkie-talkies. The massacre at Jean-Rabel had silenced the voice of the peasantry, and most organizing for the elections in the countryside was semiclandestine. Every night in Port-au-Prince, gunfire spattered the city. Erstwhile candidates like retired General Claude Raymond, François Duvalier's former minister Clovis Désinor—the man none of the foreign journalists had been able to identify back when Duvalier was falling—and former Port-au-Prince Mayor Franck Romain, excluded from the elections on the constitutional grounds that they had been avid Duvalierists, set up camp in their homes, and Raymond's and Romain's supporters' big Mitsubishi jeeps left their residences every evening before the street shooting began. At Raymond's, the lights stayed on well into the night. Hundreds of men came and went; they were in constant conference. The jeeps shot out from under the purple bougainvillea. Later, gunfire. Like a sudden and hard Haitian rain, it could wake you out of a deep sleep, even though the next morning, when you got up before seven to make sure to catch the detailed Creole news on Radio Soleil, you would hear that the killings had happened all the way across town. Gunfire echoes across the valley in which Port-au-Prince lies.

There was no way around the quandary. Any election worth having in Haiti would have to be stopped, while a sham election would happily be permitted. What eventually happened to the November elections in Haiti was the final testimony to their potential worth. A massacre as a stamp of democratic approval.

The inevitable confrontation between the junta and the voters on election day was grounded in the 1987 Constitution, which provided for a provisional electoral council, the Conseil Electoral Provisoire, or CEP, to organize the upcoming elections that the United States had insisted on as a quid pro quo for continuing its aid to Haiti. Although Article 289 of the Constitution clearly stated that "the National Council of Government [CNG] shall form a Provisional Electoral Council made up of nine members, charged with promulgating the electoral law that will regulate the upcoming elections," it was widely assumed that the CEP would function outside of the junta's control. This assumption was based on the fact that of the nine members to sit on the council, only one by law was to be selected by the junta, and he or she was not to be a government functionary. The others were to be appointed by organizations of varying independence—for example, the Catholic Church, the Protestant churches, the journalists' association, human-rights groups, the university council, the Supreme Court. The armed forces were conspicuously excluded.

Namphy quickly perceived that this liberal institution, if permitted to function on its own, would be able—and likely—to thwart attempts by the junta to control the outcome of the voting. Like a good, if blunt, military man, he also understood the strategic corollary: in order to select a candidate acceptable to the Army on election day, he would have to take control of the council. He had attempted to do so as far back as June 1987, but was immediately rebuffed by a popular strike which over the summer became the rache manyok movement. Namphy always maintained that the summer and fall problems were caused by a "constitutional crisis," brought on by a faulty Constitution that in and of itself pitted the Army against the electoral process. His analysis was not incorrect, but, of course, the Army was against the electoral process before the Constitution was ever written.

When the CEP refused to validate the candidacies of the Duvalierists on constitutional grounds (the famous Article 291), the junta
recognized the possibility for an alliance: the Duvalierist Army and
the so-called Macoutes—Raymond, Romain and Désinor were all
excluded from running—against the elections. Afterward, any violence caused by this alliance could be foisted off on the Tontons
Macoute, the junta hoped. Thus, when the violence turned against
the CEP, against the ballots, and finally against the voters, the Army
participated or did nothing. The junta refused to provide guards to
protect the council's headquarters. The junta refused to provide
helicopters to the council in order to distribute ballots safely across
the country. No police arrived after the attacks, no firefighters were
sent while polling places burned, and no one was ever arrested,
much less prosecuted. In fact, the junta that Elliott Abrams had
called Haiti's best chance for democracy was pleased by the attacks
on the electoral process, and doubtless encouraged them; it was
beyond question that the Army had struck a deal with the Macoutes.
Every morning, new corpses turned up on the capital's streets.

Everyone in Claude Raymond's neighborhood in Debussy near
Pacot was nervous. On the wall opposite his house, supporters had
written *"Votez Claude Raymond P."* They must have been about to
write *"Président"* when they were interrupted by a rival faction.
Sometimes, however, the gunfire in the neighborhood had nothing
to do with Raymond. A frightened gardien heard a noise, and discharged his revolver to scare off whatever lurked in the night. A
homeowner suspected that his place was targeted; he went out into
the garden at midnight and shot off a few rounds from his rifle, just
in case. It was seldom clear how the night's victims had been selected. Usually they were nobodies knocked off at random, perhaps
killed to settle small scores. Sometimes, however, they were young
members of opposition organizations, and the nightly murders, the
daily cadavers in the street, the randomness, the unknown killers,
the whole setup was a warning to everyone associated with the elections and with the opposition, and that included voters. No one went
out at night in Port-au-Prince. The only sound of traffic came from
Raymond's and Romain's jeeps and the Army's trucks. The clubs in
Pétionville were silent. The restaurants were shuttered by nine
o'clock.

As election day drew near, the violence became more specific. One
night in early November, after the CEP had announced that twelve
Duvalierist candidates would not be permitted to participate in the

elections, six men with machine guns broke into the council's offices downtown and ransacked the place, smashing to pieces the council's computers, the motorcycles used by volunteers like Djo's two cousins, the typewriters and the printers. They tore apart the posters that read: "ELEKSYON 87. M'AP VOTE." ('87 Election. I'm voting.) At the same time, only a few blocks away, men set fire to the store of council member Emmanuel Ambroise, whose brother and sister-in-law had been tortured and killed in 1966 by François Duvalier's men, and who was the human-rights official on the council, a white-haired man of furious dedication. In front of Téléco, the phone company they were guarding down the street from Ambroise's, Army sentinels remained stoically unmoved by the conflagration. Sylvio Claude's headquarters were raked by gunfire the same night, and armed men also shot up the residence of a former member of the assembly that had put together the anti-Duvalierist Constitution. A few nights later, the printing house that was running off the ballots for the elections was burned, and the headquarters of Bazin, Manigat and Grégoire Eugène were stoned and shot up.

All over Pacot there was new, overnight graffiti: *"A bas CEP, Vive l'Armée."* Down with the CEP, Long Live the Army. The junta and the Macoutes were going to protect their turf, *kout ke kout,* cost what it might cost. And all of Haiti, they felt, was theirs to protect. By tradition, the country was the private property of whoever ruled it; its coffers and customs were their source of revenue; its airstrips, ports, boats and planes theirs to use to ship whatever was most profitable: in our day, cocaine. No one was going to take this honey pot away from them, not Gérard Gourgue, not the Well-Placed Embassy Official, not Emmanuel Ambroise, and not Elliott Abrams. The Dechoukaj of 1986 had failed, and the whole society was still too sick with corruption to permit valid elections. All the money that the United States and other nations finally funneled into the CEP, some $8 million, could not put the elections together against this concerted attack by all of the armed forces in the land. But the job the council did was good enough to warrant a blitzkrieg in the days preceding the elections, and on election day.

Catlike, Raymond remained silent. But the occasionally garrulous Désinor, whose heavy lids gave him a narcotized aura belied by his easy and well-known viciousness, held a press conference after the two nights of terror. "The independent electoral council, the Church, and foreign powers," he said, "want to direct these elections in order to put a minority class into power." A true Duvalierist,

Désinor was using old noirist scapegoats—*mulatrisme* ("a minority class") and the white man (foreign powers, the Church)—to drum up popular revulsion against the elections. The Americans and the mulatto elite, he was telling the people, are using the council to impose these elections on you. "You are a Duvalierist, are you not?" he was asked at around the same time on CBS's *60 Minutes*. He looked at the interviewer from under his sarcastic, reptilian lids. "Who . . . who . . . who . . . told you that?" he replied, but finally admitted, "Yes. I am proud of it."

Désinor's response echoed one made years before by his mentor, François Duvalier. When Dr. Duvalier was interviewed on CBS's *Face the Nation* in late June 1966, panelist Martin Agronsky asked him what national-security reasons compelled him to imprison and execute his fellow Haitians. Seated in a gold and blue throne in the National Palace, Duvalier looked away from his interviewers, and, with his odd, habitual half-smile, he responded in English, "What . . . what . . . what . . . what . . . what . . . what . . . what . . . did you get that?"

"What did you get that?" It wasn't a badly phrased question, given Haitian realities at the time—and now. It had an absurd ring. If you tripped over a body in the street one morning, what better question to ask him than "What did you get that?" If you were stopped by a man in civilian clothes waving a machine gun, perhaps the best thing to say—as he took your money and examined your driver's license and swung his gun perilously close to your head—was, "What did you get that?" Maybe he would ask you the same thing, in turn. When I drove past Sylvio Claude's headquarters later and saw the bullet holes and the shattered windows, and the broken glass sparkling up from the street a few meters from the Holiday Inn, and all of the pastor's lost boys wandering through the debris, I thought, Well, what did they get that? It seemed to make sense.

The Oloffson was full again. On Thanksgiving night, three days before the election, I drove down from my house in Pacot to see my old friends from the days of Duvalier's downfall. Many of them had already ensconced themselves at the hotel, and were listening to Radio Havana and the BBC on their nine-band Sony radios out on the veranda. Although the hotel had closed for a year, it had reopened under new management just in time for the journalists' deluge. Suzanne, the former proprietor, and Keith, the former manager, were both gone, and the alcoholic haze of the place had lifted somewhat. Europeans loved the new Oloffson as they had the old, but most of the big-time American reporters and television crews had moved their business permanently down to the Holiday Inn or up to the modern hotels in Pétionville. The *New York Times* had a suite at the Holiday Inn, the *Washington Post* was there, *Time* magazine—as well as the usual international election observers. Now, instead of coming to the Oloffson, Harry would head down the Rue Capois to the Holiday Inn to find out what the U.S. Embassy was telling the *New York Times,* and the *New York Times* would come to the Oloffson for drinks or dinner to find out what the French, West German and Canadian embassies were saying. Faithful Harry was staying once again at the run-down Palace, midway between the Oloffson and the Holiday Inn, and was already lecturing newcomers on its authenticity.

The endless gunfire made the journalists edgy, especially the Americans and the first-timers. The Americans were nervous because, as one reporter put it, "The elections are our fault." The newcomers were frightened for obvious reasons. And the gunfire was not far from the Oloffson.

In fact, on Thanksgiving night, as we ate turkey on the terrace, the focus of the night's violence was in our neighborhood, Carrefour Feuilles. At St.-Gérard Church just up the hill, the liberation priest had been raising his congregation's political consciousness for more than a year, and, like every other neighborhood in Port-au-Prince, Carrefour Feuilles was filled with young and jobless men and women eager for a change in Haiti. Now the Macoutes and the junta were attacking Carrefour Feuilles. Each taste of turkey that night was interrupted by a blast, and when finally several rounds went off in a place that sounded as though it must be just around the corner, six of us left in two cars to see what was happening.

Everyone in the neighborhood was outside. The night was black, but candles and single bulbs inside people's homes lit up their little yards. Whole families stood at attention, waiting for the next shots. This—all these hundreds, maybe thousands, of people—was the Carrefour Feuilles *brigade de vigilance,* one of the neighborhood vigilance committees organized around the country to protect the electoral offices, the ballots and the volunteers who were helping to organize the elections locally. The brigades had started up recently, in response to the preelection violence.

A young woman in a pink dress, standing outside a pink house and holding her machete under her arm in the light of a streetlamp, told me that she was out that night to defend Haiti against what she called *"eskago lanmò,"* by which she meant the death squads (in proper Creole, *eskadwon lanmò*). She didn't really know what an eskadwon was, not literally, anyway, and she got it confused with another, more common word. She called the death squads the "snails of death." She knew what the snails were up to, however, and, like others in the brigade, she was not going to let them have their way with her people. Not tonight, anyway.

The brigades had erected barricades throughout her neighborhood to stop the Macoutes and the Army from driving through at unsnail-like top speed and spraying the houses with machine-gun fire, as they had done in other neighborhoods and in other towns. We got to one barricade, and I couldn't go around it. Worse, I was suddenly unable, in my panic, to put the car into reverse. It was a new car. My colleagues in the backseat were screaming, *"Jounalis! Jounalis!"* at the boys at the barricade, but the boys had seen a car where there should have been no cars, and they came around the barricade with their rocks, and it was only by seconds that I found reverse and got us out of there.

My colleagues were not pleased.

"Learn to drive," said the *Chicago Tribune*.

We went back in the opposite direction, passing by the hotel again, and then passing below the steep hill of St.-Gérard. Again, people were lining the streets, machetes in hand. Some of them seemed to be trying to see down the hill, around a bend, and I guessed that this was where something had happened.

When we got to the main intersection leading out of Carrefour Feuilles and into the bidonville called Fifth Avenue, we saw, only vaguely at first, what was the matter. A car was stopped in the middle of the intersection, directly under a streetlight. A crowd had gathered, and was teeming through the area with machetes and sticks. It looked as though this car had been unluckier than ours. Its windows were shattered. No passengers were to be seen.

We got out of our cars, and people surrounded us to tell us what had happened.

"They came," said one young man in peasant shorts, "and we stopped them, here, with stones and a small barricade. They were Macoutes. When we told them to get out of the car, one guy pulled a revolver out of his pocket and started shooting. We grabbed him, and disarmed him. The other Macoute got away."

"Where is this guy?" asked one of the reporters I was with. "I want to talk to him."

"He's over there," said the young man, gesturing toward the car. "But I don't think he's giving interviews."

The photographers started to make their way over to the car, and the reporters followed, more slowly. When I looked at the car again, the photographers were standing on its roof, shooting something. I approached the car. Yes, there was the alleged Macoute, what was left of him, stretched across the top of the car. His clothes were slit almost off, his face was sliced up, his stomach had been ripped open, and his feet and hands had been chopped off. It wasn't something I wanted to look at long.

And if his passenger had gotten away, it wasn't something that was safe to look at long. Word spreads quickly in Port-au-Prince; I knew that the minute the fleeing passenger got to a telephone, almost all his friends would know what had happened. Revenge would follow swiftly. No matter who the man had been, if he had had a gun, his friends would have guns, too. I wanted to get out of there.

The photographers wanted to stay.

"Who's going to publish that picture?" I yelled at them. They were still on the roof. "*Time? Newsweek?*"

They didn't respond.

"Hey, guys," shouted the reporter for *Newsweek*. "This man has friends. Let's get out of here. No one will ever use that picture, anyway."

They kept shooting.

"*Paris-Match* might use it," one of them shouted. "Leave us a car, if you're worried. We'll leave soon."

I drove the writers away.

It turned out that the man did have friends. But the reprisals did not come that night. The photographers got their extra frames, but no U.S. publication ever ran any of their pictures.

That night, the night the Macoute was murdered, I heard a ringing clamor in the streets. It was a sound that I had heard before, but never so insistent. The noise kept me up all night, that night. An endless beating of iron on iron, a din, I imagined, not too different from the sound of Irishwomen beating on their pots and pans in protest. In Haiti it is called a *teneb,* from the French for "darkness," because it is an anonymous protest or celebration. Haitian women make the noise with pots and pans and kitchen knives, and Haitian men make it by hitting any piece of metal, and most often, their machetes, against telephone poles, streetlights and wrought-iron gates and fences. There had been an impromptu, celebratory tenèb in town after Aristide made his triumphant reappearance at the cathedral. Every once in a while, during the summer of protests, the opposition would call for a tenèb, and downtown all traffic would come to a halt for ten minutes while the streets rang with noise. Horn-honking is a big part of the daytime tenèb. But this one—the one that was keeping me awake as I lay on a daybed in the Irving Stone Suite at the Oloffson, too frightened to return home through those streets—came out of the night, and its iron strength made my heart stir with fear and with hope. Above the slam of the machetes and the kitchen knives, you could hear the somber, still notes of men blowing the *lambi,* or conch shell, the same instrument that drew the slaves together for battle during the revolution, and that had been blown in every demonstration during the summer. Each time a gun went off somewhere in town, the tenèb began again, a warning sent out from men with machetes to men with machine guns, and the noise stopped only with the dawn.

A warning from machetes to machine guns is a curious exercise, and one that in the long run rarely impresses the men with the machine guns. What the photographers should have waited to see—not that night, but the next day and night—were the Army trucks that came into Carrefour Feuilles, barreling from house to house, rounding up young people from the neighborhood.

The dead man on top of the car was reported to have been an off-duty officer from Recherches Criminelles, the same police unit associated with the assassination of presidential candidate Yves Volel. The Army did not take the officer's murder lightly, unlike Volel's death. On the verge of elections that it did not wish to take place, the junta could not tolerate a successful maneuver by a vigilance brigade. There were similar brigades in every town, all with the same goal: protecting the opposition and the electoral process, and keeping the vote clean. The junta wanted to make sure the people in the brigades understood that their actions would be swiftly and severely punished. It was rumored, and in fact reported in the United States, that some forty young people from Carrefour Feuilles were taken to Fort Dimanche, the police prison near La Saline, and executed in a cell. Sources within the military verified the story secondhand. In any case, many young men disappeared from Carrefour Feuilles at the time, although many may have simply fled to the hills. The rumor rested on the testimony of one of the young women picked up that night, and it was not clear whether she had actually seen what she said had taken place. She herself was spared, she said, because an officer in charge of the massacre recognized her as the niece of a friend, and took her away. Isidore Pongnon, the swaggering commander of Fort Dimanche, denied the story, but that didn't mean much.

Although the photographs of the dead Macoute were not published in the United States, some equally horrifying pictures did appear, most notably a series depicting a man with a machete in the act of murdering a Macoute. Another photograph also made an impact, one of a charred, castrated torso that reporters named "Smokey Joe." Smokey Joe, another Macoute, became something of a landmark the day his remains were discovered; as each wave of photographers returned from shooting him, another set out from their hotels to take his picture down on Grande Rue. He had been stoned and macheted to death, his arms and legs chopped off. Then they set him on fire.

Smokey Joe was a gruesome sight, as are all victims of stonings and knifings. Mobs get carried away when they get violent. Nonetheless, when I saw these pictures in the American newsmagazines later, what shocked me most was the fact that killings by gunfire look so much less vicious than killings by people without guns. A shot body lies in repose with its arms and legs more or less intact, but it is no less dead than Smokey Joe. Yet it is natural that photo editors in New York, when given a choice—as they so often were in the days before the elections—between pictures of the numerous bodies shot dead by the Army or the Duvalierists and those of a couple of smoking, decapitated remains, would choose to publish photographs of the latter. The weight of the coverage, and thus of public revulsion in the United States and elsewhere, goes against the perpetrators of the more dramatic violence—"the people"—but these pictures do not tell the real story. The violence of the Duvalierist and junta forces at the time was purely aggressive, the violence of the people mostly defensive. Three slum-dwellers lying in small, decorous puddles of blood, however, look much less offensive than poor Smokey Joe, and thus the people look much more brutal than the armed forces. The reverse is true.

• • • •

It wasn't long before Aubelin Jolicoeur showed up on the veranda of the Oloffson, in his white suit. He was less of a celebrity now than he had been as Duvalier fell. The thin veneer of anti-Duvalierism which he had worn then with such panache had been sanded away by his continued collaboration and support of the junta. He was no longer perceived as a democrat by the international press corps, not that he had ever deserved the honor. If Gérard Gourgue and the Unity Front should win the elections, everyone realized, Jolicoeur would have few friends in power.

He invited me to his house in Pacot for drinks, and I went. As the sun set amid his bougainvillea, we sipped champagne and ate caviar. Caviar in Haiti. Jolicoeur toyed with his flamboyant ascot and told me how the junta's strongman, General Williams Régala (only recently promoted by Namphy from the rank of colonel), had asked him over to his office a few weeks before.

"He wanted me to do profiles of the candidates for my paper, *Le Nouvelliste,* you see," Jolicoeur said. "Because he is a democrat, and he wanted people to see that these candidates are candidates in a democratic election. He was appalled that these men who call themselves democrats were not campaigning, he felt that this did not give the elections the proper image of democracy."

Aubelin clapped his hands, and his houseboy appeared.

"More champagne? Canada, another bottle," he said to the young man.

"You know, Bill and I are very good friends, old friends. We see each other every week or so, every two weeks. He trusts me, of course. Aubelin Jolicoeur is a reliable man. François Duvalier called me his son, he trusted me, too. 'Aubelin Jolicoeur is my son,' he would tell people. We were close. Bill and I are close, too. Would you like to meet Bill?" he asked me.

I sipped my champagne.

"Sure," I said.

"It can be arranged. It can be arranged."

No doubt such a meeting would have had its price. With Jolicoeur, everything had a price.

Other meetings were taking place, some of them with Bill. Rumors about meetings between various heads of the armed forces, old-time Duvalierists and U.S. Embassy officials cropped up each day. On the Wednesday before the election, according to several sources, there was such a meeting but those involved were unable to come to an agreement concerning the election. Some were said to have argued for dissolving the electoral council and calling off the elections before the day itself dawned. The Army had already warned the United States that election day would be violent, that the elections might well be canceled. On Thursday the same meeting allegedly reconvened, and was visited briefly by embassy personnel. The day before the elections, Régala reportedly visited Washington. The embassy would neither confirm nor deny Régala's visit, and Jeffrey Lite, the U.S. Information Services officer, refused to speculate on what the General's purpose might have been, if indeed he had gone to Washington. Certainly preelection violence, possible U.S. intervention and election cancellation must have been discussed at any meeting between Régala and the State Department.

I tried to reach Aristide. Like so many others, like the candidates themselves, he had gone into hiding. No one was home. Phones rang and rang, but no one picked up after seven at night, even though you would learn later that they had been there, listening to the ringing, wondering who was calling, a friend or an enemy. Members of the Unity Front slept in a different place each night. A tall light-skinned, white-bearded human-rights advocate laughed when he told me he was in hiding.

"I'm in hiding, sure," he said. "But where can a man who looks like this hide in Haiti? I hate going out in my car; I'm trying to stay inside."

The director of the Catholic Church's literacy program was squirreled away, all the progressive priests were underground, the presidential candidates set up press conferences and then did not appear, calling reporters at night in their rooms to apologize. Nor were the phones considered secure. Most of those who were in hiding would call you at about seven o'clock, just before they were to leave wherever it was they were, and head for their night's shelter. It was not a comfortable feeling, all these voices coming out of the night, disembodied.

The following evening, Clovis Désinor appeared on government-controlled Télévision Nationale. We watched on the small black-and-white TV in the Oloffson bar.

"There are foreigners in the kitchen of the Haitian elections," Désinor said. He was wearing a white suit, and his heavy eyelids flitted nervously. "We denounce the complicity of all these foreign countries in trying to control our elections."

A dog barked somewhere near Désinor, you could hear the same dog on the television and outside the hotel.

"The CEP is plotting the end of your sovereignty," said the aging Duvalierist. "Do not fall for these elections. Join our battle, which is your battle." He paused dramatically, and the dog barked again.

"What I am calling for, make no mistake," Désinor continued, "is total abstention. Stay calm."

"At last," remarked one British reporter. "A Haitian politician promotes the cure for AIDS."

We were foolish. We didn't quite see what was coming. We should have known better, after the summer. The signs were all there, the murders, the attacks on the electoral offices, the writing on the walls. The evidence was already in. But we kept hoping. As the violence grew more intense, the elections seemed more and more worth saving.

And then, there was also Jeffrey Lite, the man who had given a press conference from the bushes of the U.S. Embassy the night Duvalier left. He came over to the Holiday Inn's brisk, air-conditioned dining room each morning in his blue safari suit to brief the *Los Angeles Times,* the *Miami Herald,* the *New York Times, Time* magazine and the *Washington Post.*

Lite acted as if a normal election were taking place.

"Well, we've tried to give them helicopters," he said, "but Namphy doesn't seem to think they are necessary. After all, the electoral council has trucks. The ballots are going to the countryside by truck, right now, apparently. I believe they are arriving safely."

Note-taking by the journalists.

"Does the U.S. have anything to say about the preelection violence?" asked the *Miami Herald.*

"Of course we abhor all violence, especially violence that is aimed at destabilizing a democratic election. But we are confident that the CNG will guarantee the safety of the voters and the honesty of the elections."

"Who do you think is behind the violence?"

"That would be speculation, wouldn't it?" A smile. "But obviously there are certain forces who have not been permitted to participate in the elections who may not be happy with that decision."

"You mean the Duvalierists?"

"I mean what I said."

"Then you don't think Namphy is involved in these activities?"

"As I said, we believe that the CNG will guarantee the safety of these elections."

"What about the graffiti that says, you know, 'Up with the Army, down with the CEP'? Doesn't that seem to be emanating from sources close to the CNG?"

"Come on, guys," Lite said. "You're starting to think like Haitians. You know as well as I do that anyone can scrawl up a sign on the street. Some people have told me it's a campaign by the Front to implicate the Army in the violence. Who knows? But certainly I'm not going to speculate on what that graffiti might or might not mean. You guys speculate." A smile. "It's your job."

The day before the elections, I left town at around five in the morning with a convoy of journalists. Three cars. We were going to meet the ballot truck for Gonaïves and the Artibonite at Arcahaie, the dusty little town where Dessalines had ripped the white from the French *tricolore* and made it Haitian. We followed close behind the big white truck. The day seemed normal. All along Route Nationale there were signs that barricades had been built the night before: burned branches and smoldering tires. These were the barricades of the vigilance brigades. We drove right over them. No one was building new ones; it was too early in the morning.

We met the ballot truck at Arcahaie and arrived at Gonaïves a few hours later without incident. The photographers were depressed. No action. I went upstairs into the half-completed building that housed the Artibonite province's central electoral bureau, down the street from the Gonaïves Army barracks. On the side of the building was written: *"Aba tout divalyeris."* Down with all Duvalierists. Ballots were stacked everywhere. They had been produced to be used in a country where the voters were illiterate, and so pictures of Grégoire Eugène and Marc Bazin and Louis Déjoie and Leslie Manigat and the sour-faced Gourgue peered up from the floor like head shots from their own obituaries. The illiterate voters would never know these faces, of course, though they might recognize the senatorial candidates, who were usually well known in their areas. Radio was the only way the peasants knew the presidential candidates, if they knew them at all. They know voices; this is one reason why all democratic elections in illiterate nations are suspect. In some countries, they use color codes to represent the different parties, and rely on word of mouth and radio to educate the people about which color represents whom. But the CEP didn't have enough time for such fine points.

After Gonaïves, the ballot truck continued on to Verrettes, and two of our cars followed. We had decided to go out to Verrettes and then return to Gonaïves for the night; we would watch the voting there in the capital of the Artibonite, and then return down Route Nationale to Port-au-Prince, checking in on other voting places along the way. Somehow, we thought election day was going to be normal. We had listened to the rational voice of Jeffrey Lite. We had made a big mistake. The other carload of journalists returned to Port-au-Prince later in the day, following the ballot truck back. They made a mistake, too. At a roadblock, the ballot truck driver was forced out of his cab and chased into the bushes by a band of men with machetes. The journalists never saw him again. They themselves were threatened by members of the same armed group, and then allowed to pass. Out in Verrettes, with two radios whose batteries had run down, we had no idea what our colleagues had experienced, and little forewarning of what tomorrow might bring for us.

Just as we were about to leave Gonaïves for Verrettes that morning, I saw a familiar figure, gray-haired, straight-backed, riding a bicycle down Route Nationale. It was my friend the Senatorial Candidate. He dismounted.

"Well, what do you think of our little election?" he asked. "Have the ballots arrived?"

I said yes.

"We'll see how long they last," he said. "They're only made of paper." Then he paraphrased a famous proverb supposedly coined by Dessalines. *"Bilten se papye, bayonèt se fè,"* he said. The ballot is made of paper, but the bayonet is made of iron.

"What are you doing out on a bicycle?" I asked him. It seemed imprudent. But then, he and Aristide were among the few people I knew who did not try to puff themselves up by talking about how much time they were spending in hiding, how they were targets of the Army, how high up their names were on the Duvalierists' death lists.

"What are you doing in Haiti?" he asked me back, laughing. "We're both doing our jobs, kout ke kout. Anyway, I'm safe in

Gonaïves. Here, everyone knows everyone else. There is no anonymous violence in Gonaïves."

"It doesn't have to be anonymous to be effective," I told him.

He nodded. "No, I know," he said. "I'm being careful."

I told him we were going to Verrettes, and he wished us luck, got back up on his old bicycle and pedaled away.

In Verrettes, local CEP members had to beg the captain of the little barracks to protect the ballots that came in on the truck and were being stacked in a warehouse not far from the church. We arrived there at about nine in the morning. As our cars pulled in, I glimpsed a priest I knew driving his jeep at full speed out of town. I later found out that the church had been shot up the night before by men whom the priests suspected were from the barracks. My friend waved at me from his jeep, but he wasn't stopping. He was going into hiding in the hills.

People from Verrettes stood around, watching the men unload the ballots. Three young men leaned against the warehouse, hiding in its shadows from the hot morning sun. A tap-tap called Love Is Love was circling the town, blasting a disco version of "Auld Lang Syne" from its outside speakers. The people of Port-au-Prince had sung "Auld Lang Syne" outside the palace the day Duvalier fled. Each time Love Is Love passed by the ballot building, the three young men broke into a dance called skoo-bee-doo, a sort of Caribbean break dance. They showed me their wash jeans. *"Fashion,"* one of them said to me, preening.

"Ou koul," I said to him. You're cool.

He was pleased.

"Nap vote?" I asked. You all going to vote?

"Yes, yes," they all said. "Kout ke kout."

"For whom?" I asked.

"Oh, no," they responded

"We're not telling you that," the cool one said. "After all, the ballot is secret."

"Mèt Goug," one of them whispered to me, under the cover of "Auld Lang Syne." "We're all going to vote for Gourgue. But we don't want the Army to know."

"Why are you voting for Gourgue?"

"Because he is the only worthwhile candidate."

The young man looked over his shoulder to make sure neither his friends nor anyone else was listening. "And we know the people who are working for him in the Artibonite. They're good friends of ours."

"Why are you whispering?" I asked him.

"Listen," he said to me, behind his hand. "Last night they rounded up some young guys who work for the Front. They took them, and they beat them. They say we are Communists. They let some of the guys go, but we haven't accounted for everyone. This is a dangerous situation. They don't even want to see me talking to a journalist, much less a foreign journalist. They are afraid I will tell you the truth. This is the truth: The Army in the Artibonite is trying to stop the elections. They are working with the old Tontons Macoute, the chef de section, all the same old guys. Namphy is against elections. You tell the Americans that, okay? The Americans know it already, but tell them we know it, too."

I promised I would.

"I'm going to tell you one more thing," he said as I started to walk away. *"Eleksyon-sa-yo, yo pap janm fèt."* These elections will never take place. *"Pa bliye sa map di w."* Don't forget what I'm telling you.

Love Is Love sped by, and the young men started to skoo-bee-doo.

Victor Benoit, the leader of Konakom and a senatorial candidate for the Front, has a house in Borel, a small village on the road from Route Nationale to Verrettes. A few days before the election, a group of soldiers came into Borel saying they were searching for a bus driver who was feuding with the wife of the Verrettes Army commander. They went house to house, ostensibly looking for the man. When they tried to impose a curfew on Borel, the people refused. That evening, a group of bare-chested men with rifles came into town at about eight o'clock and opened fire. Again they went house to house. They tried to burn down the church. When a bus from the Verrettes barracks came through to Borel that night, the people of Borel burned it.

The next morning at around nine, two truckloads of armed civilians and soldiers from Verrettes came into Borel and opened fire for three hours, with machine guns and rifles. Three men were killed, one shot by the side of his house, another shot as he hid under his bed, another as he tried to flee into the back country. The invaders burned down two houses, including the one where the electoral bureau operated. They killed the peasants' few pigs. They broke down Benoit's door and arrested two of the people who were in the house. Benoit had hidden, and later he fled, along with the rest of the men of Borel who were not captured or killed.

. . .

When we got back to Gonaïves from Verrettes, the town was silent.
The usual bicyclists, riding their secondhand bikes from Miami,
were not out this evening, flirting and driving their girlfriends
around town. The schoolgirls who play jump rope on the porch of
the general store across from the Senatorial Candidate's house before
dinner were nowhere to be seen. Our two cars seemed to be the only
ones in town. The houses and the stores were all shuttered. The
Senatorial Candidate, I was told when I stopped by to see him, was
out at a meeting. But he had left a message. Benoit, who was in
hiding, was upstairs, and would talk to us.

Benoit was sitting on the upstairs balcony, with his shirt open, in
a rocking chair. The night was hot and still. No matter the heat,
though, he buttoned up his guayabera over his round belly and
moved the interview inside. The four of us sat on a bed under a light
bulb. Benoit moved the rocking chair inside and carefully closed the
shutters behind him. He sat down, folded his hands. He kept his
eyes half closed as he spoke.

"I was saved by the peasants of Borel," he told us. "During the
attack, they made me a raft of banana leaves and floated me down
the Artibonite. I lost my wallet and walked for four hours, but here
I am. Safe for the moment.

"You know, of course, that the CEP announced tonight that it
was postponing the elections in the Artibonite? Too much violence,
they said, although Gonaïves is still scheduled to vote. A few days
ago they burned down the electoral office opposite the barracks in
Verrettes, and they have repeatedly attacked the offices here in Gonaïves. Even if it's not the Army doing this, whoever is attacking us
certainly has the okay of the Army. The reason it's been worst in the
Artibonite is because this is a traditionally Macoute-controlled area.
The Port-au-Prince chief of police comes from St.-Marc. The captain of St.-Marc is Namphy's old chauffeur. All of this violence was
organized in Port-au-Prince by Namphy, Régala and the chief of
police. It's a battle between the Macoutes and the democrats.

"Obviously, if we had a clean election the democratic sector would
win hands down. And if the Macoutes perturb the elections, we'll
win anyway. In any case, what they may consider a victory is not
one. But I don't want to take any more rides in banana rafts, thank
you."

. . .

My bed was shaking from the grenades going off outside. It was two in the morning, and the shooting wouldn't let up. The electricity had been cut, and the mosquitoes were descending through the breezeless air. There was no light. Gonaïves that night was a blind man's nightmare: a universe filled only with noise, but not the kind of noise that gave you a clue where you stood in the world. There was no way to tell where the sounds were coming from. You only knew, each time a grenade didn't hit your room, that it probably hadn't touched the hotel. All you could tell was that each time a shot didn't shatter your window, each time a grenade didn't land on you, it had shattered someone else's pane, had landed near someone somewhere else. It sounded as though we were caught in the middle of fireworks. Pistol reports, rifle bursts, machine-gun fire and grenades —fireworks without the light, without the color. I was sharing a room with the dark-haired photographer from the days of Duvalier's departure, the woman Aubelin loved so deeply. We had the radio on —new batteries—but the only Haitian station we could get was Radio Nationale, more noise with no meaning. They were playing a recording of an old voodoo ceremony. All night the hounsis on the radio kept up their chants about Legba, Damballah, Guinée, while outside Chez Frantz, the little inn where we were staying in Gonaïves, Legba's country was blowing up. The drums came over shallow on my radio. Every time we thought the shooting was over, it began again.

We woke up before sunrise the next morning—if you could call it waking up, since we had not slept—and went out into the streets of Gonaïves. The shooting had come to an end about half an hour earlier. It was five-thirty now, and people in Raboteau, Gonaïves' wide, dry shantytown, were already lined up at the polling places, with their registration cards in their hands. By the cutoff date in October, some 2.2 million Haitians out of the three million old enough to vote had legally registered for the elections, an unprecedented event in the nation's history.

But no ballots had so far been distributed in Raboteau. A volunteer I talked to, a young man, said that when they had discussed distribution the day before, they had felt the situation was too volatile to distribute the ballots, that the ballots and, more important, the people would be less vulnerable if the ballots remained overnight at the electoral office near the town's center and were distributed in the early morning.

"But after last night," the young man said, "you're not going to see people running to pick up the ballots. Last night, man, it was serious."

All the people standing in line at the school where they were to vote nodded.

"But if people are too scared to go get the ballots, why are you here, standing like targets in front of a polling place?" I asked them, in a general sort of way.

Much yelling and shouting came back to me from those in line.

"Because we want the Macoutes to know that we are willing to die to bring their rule to an end," cried one woman.

"Because we cannot be deprived of our human right to vote. Haitians have rights, too, they just never knew it before." This from a serious older man who had put on a felt hat and a Sunday suit and tie to come vote.

"Paske bilten-yo pi fo pase bal-yo," shouted a young man. Because ballots are stronger than bullets.

"Because someone has to be willing to die to change Haiti," said a woman carrying a child in her arms. "I despise their guns. I spit on their guns. We have had enough of them, too much. It's over for them."

The young election volunteer came up to me. "My motorcycle is out of gas. Can you take me over to the electoral office?" He climbed in the back, and we rode around Raboteau. In each zone of the slum —which looks more like Soweto than any other Haitian bidonville— a line of people had formed at the polling place. At some intersections, the barricades of the vigilance brigades were still burning. Armed men had come into Raboteau the night before and shot at the shanties of election volunteers and at any other shanties nearby.

"Were they in uniform?" I asked the young man in the backseat.

"We weren't really looking," he said, laughing. "I was under the bed with my little sister."

At the electoral office, things were getting into shape. Scores of boys who had come on bicycle were running in and out of the building—which was now more shot up than yesterday—with boxes of ballots on their heads. Their bikes lined the street in front of the office, along with the motorcycles of the more important organizers. Another hundred or so bike-riders had stopped by just to see what was going on. The ballot-runners would emerge from the office, balancing boxes carefully on their heads, get on their bikes, and drive away over the pebbly road.

Back at Chez Frantz, we tried to get Radio Soleil or Radio Haïti-

Inter, but we couldn't find anything. A few minutes later, I called the Senatorial Candidate. He wasn't at home, but the man who answered the phone at his house explained to me that last night in Port-au-Prince the antenna of Radio Soleil had been exploded, Radio Haïti-Inter had been seriously shot up, two other stations had been hit, and no one was broadcasting. Nationale was playing music.

"Will you be there for a while?" I asked him.

"Sure," he said. "Call back if you have any questions—or information."

I hung up and told the assembled journalists, five of us in all, that the radio stations had been shut down.

"Sounds like a coup d'état," said the *Chicago Tribune*. "First you take out the radio stations, then you close the airport. Is the airport closed?" He speared another piece of ham from his Chez Frantz breakfast.

"I didn't ask," I said. I tried to call back the Senatorial Candidate's man to find out about the airport, but no one answered, and then a burst of gunfire blasted out from the center of town like a confirmation of the *Tribune*'s speculations. We leaped up as if the fire had been aimed in our direction.

When we got to the electoral office, about five minutes later, there was no one. Abandoned bikes lay scattered across the street. All up the street toward the mountains, all down the street toward the Army headquarters, there was no one. The air was still. I had the sudden, vertiginous feeling that we were the only people left here. In the middle of the street, like a pyre lit in sacrifice to the bicycle gods, thousands of ballots burned. You could still see those poor faces looking up at you from the cinders: Manigat, Bazin, Gourgue, Benoit, Eugène. Their ashes were floating over the neighborhood.

The photographers were shooting the funeral pyre because they couldn't think of anything else to shoot. The writers sort of shuffled around, looking aimlessly through the debris. I heard a noise, and looked up. Through the rising heat, I saw a big black car coming down the street at us through the flames like a vision sent by the Immaterial Being. We backed away to give the big old sedan some room. It could have been wearing sunglasses over its headlights, its intent was so obviously malevolent. A white sky, a dusty road, fire, and a big black car. It seemed to be coming from far, far away. Even before it was upon us, I heard gunfire, and saw those little pockets of dust appear in the street, the ones that you see in the movies when the bad guys shoot wild and miss the hero cop or the sheriff or the American terminator.

We started to run for cover, and I found myself behind a post, the kind I like best, a wide white one. But it didn't feel secure the way it used to during the demonstrations in Port-au-Prince. The shooting was aimed at us specifically, and no post is wide enough to stop you from feeling fear in your throat and heart when you know you are the target. The men in the car were shooting all over the place toward our scant shelter. They didn't stop, they just slowed and shot, twelve or fifteen rounds, and continued on. We watched the black and chrome disappear through the dust.

Timidly, we ventured forth once more. The photographers again gravitated toward the burning ballots. I kept gravitating back toward the post—it felt almost magnetic to me—and the *Tribune* went looking for spent cartridges amid the bikes. I have noticed about reporters that they like to know the caliber of guns, the make of cars, the type of airplane. I will never forget that it was a U.S. Air Force C-141 that carried Duvalier out of Haiti, though I could never understand why it mattered or who but an aircraft specialist would understand what C-141 meant. I was thinking to myself, I should have noticed what kind of car that was, when shots started smashing against the ground again. I moved behind the post, only a few steps away this time, and everyone else hid, too. The shots kept coming, from a building opposite the electoral office. A sniper.

"I think they want us to leave," said the *Tribune*.

"I think I want us to leave," I said.

"Let's try and get out of here," said the *Tribune*.

One photographer was hiding behind a car, the rest of us were behind posts. It is amazing how the movies come back to you in these situations.

"Okay," said the *Tribune*. "Alex and I will run to our car, and then you guys follow us. We'll draw their fire." Draw their fire, I thought. *What* does it mean? But I didn't have time to brood about it. Alex and the *Tribune* ran, keeping low, as though we could give them cover. And the sniper fired some more. Then we followed, jumped into our cars and sped away, gunfire chasing us up the street.

We drove over to Raboteau. A few young men were standing near one of the entrances to the slum, but otherwise everyone was indoors. They beckoned to us.

"No elections here," they told us.

We told them we were going to leave town. They looked forlorn.

"Once you leave, they can do whatever they want," one man said.

"What can we do?" asked a photographer. "If we stay, all they'll

do is shoot at us." We started our cars again, and one young man
leaned over to us.

"Hey, listen. We've heard that there are roadblocks all the way to
Port-au-Prince. Army roadblocks. Be careful."

But the highway was quiet. We were the only traffic. At L'Estère, a
town where the rice wars had been violent during the spring and
summer, hundreds of people were lined up at a church, voting.
From either side of the enclosed churchyard, over the walls, came
gunfire. Each time the guns went off I flinched, and the voters
laughed.

"Don't worry. They're just trying to scare us," said one woman.

Inside the polling place, people were choosing their candidates.
There was nothing secret about the vote, because the people could
neither read the ballots nor recognize their candidates.

"M vle Pastè Clod," said an old man who was voting. I want
Pastor Claude. He was handed a Sylvio Claude ballot, which he
stuffed into the ballot box. Each time a voter selected his candidate
from among the piles for all the candidates, the election workers
ripped up a set of the other ballots, to prevent ballot stuffing. These
people voted Claude or Gourgue, no one else, and, each time, the
election workers ripped up Manigat, ripped up Eugène, ripped up
everyone who had not been selected, and threw them into the waste-
basket. The shooting continued over our heads.

We went through a number of Army checkpoints as we headed
south, and at each one the soldiers nodded at us and let us pass.
From the side of the road, people shouted at us.

"Jounalis vanyan!" they cried. "Brave journalists!" The dark-
haired photographer and I laughed, remembering our precipitous
departure from Gonaïves.

The only other traffic we saw the whole way down to St.-Marc
was an ambulance, carrying a man who had been shot in the shoulder
as he tried to vote that morning. We all stopped in the middle of
Route Nationale to exchange information. They were afraid to head
north, we were afraid to head south. Neither could help the other
much. We told them the road seemed safe; they said the same, but
warned us that they had come from north of St.-Marc and did not
know what was happening in that Macoute bastion.

At the infamous checkpoint at St.-Marc—where during the summer Aristide and the other priests had been stopped and searched,

then sent on to a more aggressive barricade a little farther south—
we had no problem.

"*Ou mèt pase, ou mèt pase,*" said a soldier, glancing briefly at our
press passes. "Go on, go on."

We were relieved. We had passed the last checkpoint before Port-
au-Prince. The dark-haired photographer turned to me and smiled.
She exhaled a breath to calm herself.

"Maybe we'll make it," she said.

"I think so," I said.

Then we came around the bend, the bend at Freycineau, and
there was the barricade, just as it had been when I pictured it in my
head, the big concrete-and-tree-trunk barricade that had stopped the
priests. Our convoy came up sharp, all two of us. We tried to back
away from the huge structure—made more impressive by the trailer
of a ballot truck half overturned amid the banana trees at the side of
the road. We saw the men emerging from around the trailer with
their machetes drawn, but they were upon us before we could get
away, and, out of the dust from the north, *CBS News,* in its great
black car that looked like the car from Gonaïves, pulled up behind
us and put an effective end to any ideas of retreat.

"*Desann,*" a man in peasant shorts shouted at me as he slammed
the side of his machete up against the car door. "Get out." I didn't
want to get out, but I got out. The blades of their machetes seemed
caricaturishly long, like something made to scare children in a car-
toon. The dark-haired photographer was forced from the car, too.
Four or five men gathered around us, there were about twenty in all,
maybe more. They shouted orders and questions at us: Get
out, Open the trunk, Get back in, Where are you going, Communists, Get out. Each man thrust his blade at you when he spoke.
A little way behind us, CBS was filming while its driver, who was
famous for getting CBS reporters out of impossible jams, tried to
negotiate our way out. He wasn't having much success.

"*Ouvri sak-ou.*" Open your bag. I did. The man peered into it;
he seemed confused by its contents. No wallet. "*Ouvri sa-a.*" Open
that. It was my makeup bag. He looked into it. I tried to explain
that it was just makeup, but my Creole failed me, and I found myself
speaking something that sounded like part Spanish, part French. He
looked up at me as if I was crazy. He threw the makeup kit back into
my bag and scooped out the wad of singles that I kept handy, and
visible, in a side pocket.

"*Banm radyo-a.*" Give me the radio. I handed him Alex's big

Sony; Alex had lent us his radio for the trip because our car didn't have one. I wondered how many Sonys these men had picked up in the last two days. Meanwhile, I was trying to look at the barricade to see if there was any way to drive through it. There didn't seem to be, although I noticed a white pickup truck in its midst, parked in the direction of the north, that didn't seem to have been there a moment before. Then I saw someone new among us. This one had no machete, and he was talking to the leader of the vagabonds. He had his arm around the leader's naked shoulders. He was a portly little man, wearing white pants and a white guayabera. He must have been a gwo nèg from the area.

"Ou pa bezwen kenbe moun-sa-yo," he said to the leader. You don't need to hold these people.

My legs were feeling weak, and I couldn't seem to see anything except a sort of frieze with the two men fixed in the center in a luminescent light and then dozens of black figures in different positions placed decoratively around the central scene like angels in a depiction of Christ. The glinting of the machetes I caught, too. I kept thinking how easy and how stupid it would be to die here.

"Men se kominis yo ye." But they are Communists.

"Yo se jounalis. Pa okipe w." They're journalists. Don't worry about it.

Everything else was in stop time while the gwo nèg talked to the men. I felt as though he had been sent to save us. At the same time, I thought perhaps he was responsible for the barricade's being here in the first place. He kept talking, very friendly, very calm.

"Okay, okay," the vagabonds' leader finally said. He didn't look at us.

"Vous pouvez partir maintenant," said the man in white, offhand, in French. You can go now. He didn't look at us, either.

We got back into our cars, shut up our windows tight, and sped through the hole the man in white made for us when he moved his pickup truck and headed north. It was about nine o'clock. On the right-hand side of the highway, as we flew away from Freycineau, I saw the rusted skeleton of the little Charade that they had burned the summer before, thinking it was Aristide's.

"Looks as though the *Times* is going to have to report that the elections were 'marred by violence,' " I said to the dark-haired photographer when I recovered my powers of speech. CBS had quickly overtaken us and was no longer visible down the long highway. It was hard enough to drive after the scene at the barricade, but speaking and driving at the same time took all my concentration. The little Charade had really thrown me.

"Marred by violence? Would you even think of noting—I mean voting, I'm still nervous—under these conditions?" She was going through her camera bag. "We're crazy to be here. I think I'm going to go back to Texas and live with my mama." She examined one of her Leicas. She was very happy not to have lost her equipment to the men at the barricade. "After all, what would they do with a light meter?" she wanted to know.

"Next time," I said, "we definitely die."

"Look." She pointed to the car ahead of us. "They want us to stop." The reporters in the car ahead of us were slowing down. We were just outside Port-au-Prince, at Cazeau.

We pulled up next to the other car.

"I think you should know," said the *Tribune,* "that we just heard on the radio that there's been a massacre in town—we think at a polling place—and the elections have been canceled. Something like thirty people are dead. Guys came in with machine guns, something like that."

We were trying to take in the information, and to figure out how dangerous the capital was going to be when we got there.

"Hey!" We heard a joyous cry of recognition coming from the side of the road, and in the midst of all the news Waldeck appeared, holding a small kitchen knife. He set up immediately between the two cars and started begging.

"Hey, mister," he said to the *Tribune* in English, "give me five dollars."

"Hey, what is this?" said the *Tribune,* looking at us accusingly.

"Just some kid we know," said the dark-haired photographer. "Not now, Waldeck."

He came over to my window while the others were discussing strategy.

"Legliz-la fèmen," he said to me. The church is closed. *"Pè-a pa ka ba-nou lajan."* The priest can't give us any money. *"Mwen grangou."* I'm hungry.

"What are you doing with that knife?" I asked him.

"It's to kill all the Macoutes if they try to come and get us. If they try to kill Titid, it's to cut out their eyes."

"I see," I said.

"Banm di dola, souple," he said urgently. Give me ten dollars, please.

"Robbers at Freycineau took all my money," I told him.

Waldeck's eyes got wide. *"Pa vre."* Not true, he said, meaning, How awful. *"Map touye yo pou ou."* I'm going to kill them for you.

"When I see you later in town, tomorrow or something, I'll have some money, okay?" I said.

"Okay," he said. "I understand."

"Now go home and stay put," I said.

He smiled, and I knew he never would. We left him standing in the road, admiring his knife, waiting for the next car full of journalists.

Port-au-Prince was as silent as a graveyard. We saw only one person, a body lying in front of the old boarded-up cathedral. He had been shot. The photographers jumped out to take his picture, but the *Tribune* said, "Are you guys insane? Let's go." As he pointed out later, there would certainly be enough bodies to photograph this week; now was not the time to be standing around in the street.

Every foreign journalist in Port-au-Prince was at the Holiday Inn, except a few of those who had been present at the massacre and had been chased away by the attackers up John Brown and into hiding. The panic even among the most professional was alarming. Those who had been cornered at the polling place inside the school on Ruelle Vaillant where the massacre had just occurred did not want to be cornered at the Holiday Inn. Each time a big black car sped past the hotel, the journalists who were hanging out in front would run inside. In the press office that the CEP had set up with U.S. funding to facilitate the reporting of election returns, journalists were lining up to call their mothers on the AT&T USA Direct phones. Long sheets of printout paper had been hastily taped to the press-office windows, which faced the street. No one wanted to be blasted away while assuring his mother that he was okay.

Some journalists had gathered in the dining room at the back of the hotel to try to relax and amass the details of the massacre over a beer or a sandwich. When another black car sped past the hotel, a large group of reporters outside ran into the hotel, people just inside ran toward the dining room, and a stampede began. The journalists turned over tables and shattered the back window of the restaurant, fleeing to the roof. Several were injured in the panic.

"Who knew?" said the dark-haired photographer later as she

hunted for her camera bag amid the wrecked room. "We thought the Tontons Macoute were about to rush the restaurant at the Holiday Inn. Anything could happen today, I guess."

The stories from the massacre were incredible, and clearly accounted for the *kouri jounalis,* the journalists' panic, as the Haitians began laughingly to call the Holiday Inn stampede. The voters at Ruelle Vaillant had done their civic duty: they had lined up at the Ecole Nationale Argentine Bellegarde, off Avenue John Brown, and they were waiting to vote, about a hundred or so, calm in spite of the sporadic shooting that had been heard throughout the morning. Quite a few journalists were watching them, the way we had watched the voting in L'Estère. A few of these later said they had seen General Namphy drive by Ruelle Vaillant earlier in the day, perhaps just out to inspect the progress of the vote. After all, almost everyone drives past Ruelle Vaillant once or twice a day—it is just another small street that intersects John Brown. Journalists driving up a street had seen and videotaped a horde of men carrying machetes and guns running down Martin Luther King toward Ruelle Vaillant.

When the band of men with machetes and machine guns charged the place, the orderly, peaceable schoolyard was transformed in an instant into a chaos of screaming and blood. The men went chopping and shooting through the panicked crowd, showing no emotion other than enthusiasm. The Ecole Argentine was a good place for a bloodbath, because there was no way out of the enclosed schoolyard except the entrance through which the attackers had come. The voters tried to escape, fleeing into the playground, into empty classrooms, overturning chairs and school benches, hunkering down in the bathroom, trying to scale the compound's back wall, tearing their hands and legs on the cemented broken glass that topped the barrier, a disincentive to trespassers. At least seventeen of the voters were killed, and a television journalist from the Dominican Republic was gunned down after he put his hands up over his head. Under an almond tree in the school's front yard, the attackers hacked a screaming woman to death. Two more women were killed in the bathroom. One family who came to vote, grandmother, daughter and granddaughter, were all killed. Voters who piled up in a corner of a classroom were massacred. The attackers left, then returned and bore down on the journalists who had come to record the results of the massacre. Journalists' cars, parked on Ruelle Vaillant and recognizable by their *location,* or rental, license plates, had their back windows and windshields shattered. The reporters were fired on as they left the scene.

"There were soldiers there, definitely," said one *Time* magazine photographer familiar with Haiti. "Guys from the Casernes Dessalines, Jean-Claude Paul's men." According to Haitians who were present, two of Claude Raymond's sons were also involved. One was visible in a corner, they said, with his machine gun. They said he had been seen earlier in the morning shooting it off farther up John Brown.

The layout of the Ecole Argentine was perfect for a massacre, and its location was also strategic. In a fast jeep on a day with no traffic —a volatile election-day Sunday, for example—it's not far from Clovis Désinor's house, nor from Franck Romain's City Hall. At most, it's a two-minute drive from the Raymonds' house to the Ecole Argentine. You make a right as you come out from under Raymond's bougainvillea-shrouded driveway, turn left on Martin Luther King, drive straight to John Brown, turn left, and Ruelle Vaillant is your first right. On foot, at a run, it might take ten minutes. The getaway is equally simple, not that there was anyone for the murderers to get away from. By the time the attackers were finished with their work, everyone was dead or had run away, and the journalists who remained on the scene were busy comforting the dying. No one was in any shape to chase the assassins. Of course neither the police nor the Army attempted to stop the killing.

The State Department, or at least its representatives in Port-au-Prince, seem to have been frazzled all the way up to the end. They had believed—or had seemed to believe—that they could stop Namphy from becoming another obvious dictator like Panama's Noriega, at the time another prominent case of our man gone publicly bad. They had believed that Namphy was well-intentioned, or so they had said.

All along, as the United States was well aware, Namphy was a tool of old Duvalierist-military forces, the willing instrument of Colonel Prosper Avril, a U.S.-trained military man and a member of the original junta who had been forced out of office by popular outcry. Avril was no democrat; for years he had been a trusted adviser of the Duvaliers, a behind-the-scenes operator. Kicked out of the junta, he still could pull many strings, and did. The prospect of any of the four leading candidates, especially Gourgue, running the country was not one that pleased Avril. It wasn't so much that Gourgue himself was a threat. After all, like many other Haitian politicians, Gourgue himself was a known quantity, he had spoken freely with U.S. Embassy officials on occasion, and since the junta had come to power he had rarely taken the lead among opposition figures. Rather, it was the fact that Gourgue represented the Front, and the Front was not just another freewheeling Haitian political party whose sole raison d'être was the promotion of one man. The Front was an anomaly in Haiti, an organization with actual democratic goals. Because it was so big and comprised so many groups, it was not easily susceptible to corruption, or to control.

Among the leading candidates, Gourgue would have been the most likely to prosecute at least some of those government, military and paramilitary officials and quasi-officials accused of crimes under the Duvaliers. Many of Avril's friends, many of Namphy's friends, and even the two men themselves might have been included in this category. Certainly Claude Raymond, a godson of François Duvalier, who early in Papa Doc's reign had commanded the prestigious Presidential Guard, would eventually have been hauled before a judge, if he did not flee beforehand. In other words, there was a substantial—and well-armed—old guard who stood to lose everything, both personally and politically, if Gourgue were elected, and it looked toward the end as though he would be.

The election debacle proved what everyone had always known. Without arms, you cannot force an army to change. There are only two ways to push a military dictatorship aside without arms. On the one hand, you can try to divide the Army up against itself and gain a strong faction that favors change. Or (a strategy whose success is much less likely), along with the middle class, you can attempt to convince the Army that change is inevitable, and that it would benefit the Army to help with and thereby guide the change, rather than to stand in its way.

This latter was the strategy that the United States, along with much of the Haitian opposition, adopted. Throughout the two years of the junta's rule, there were also sporadic attempts to destabilize the Army, but none was particularly successful. Namphy pretended to go along with the plan for the elections, although even in masquerade he was a reluctant democrat, one the Haitians, at least, saw through quickly. Even after the massacre, it was possible to argue that Namphy would have gone along with elections in which the Army and the Duvalierists had been allowed to play a bigger role. Though such elections could never really be considered free and fair, it was argued, they might provide a small window of opportunity for democratic progress. Events were to prove that Namphy, Avril, and the Duvalierist-military apparatus were not capable of tolerating even such a small step.

During the bloody summer that preceded the elections, the Well-Placed Embassy Official had justified U.S. military aid to Namphy by asserting that the aid helped the Army quell popular disturbances without violence. He was not swayed when it was pointed out that all summer there had been only one instance of crowd control that did not include fatal attacks on unarmed demonstrators. After the massacre at Ruelle Vaillant, however, even the embassy could no longer swallow its own sugar pill. On election day, in the evening, the exhausted press corps along with a number of election observers flocked to a press conference at the Holiday Inn, given by Jeffrey Lite.

"Do you think Namphy's government has upheld its promises to protect human rights?" one journalist asked.

"I leave that to you to decide," said Lite.

"Do you think," asked another reporter, "that U.S. military aid to the junta has been used for peacekeeping purposes, as the State Department has maintained?"

Lite hesitated, and into the small space of his hesitation burst forth the sound of a dozen rounds of pistol fire and a spray of automatic weapons, not far from the hotel. The journalists broke into loud and nervous laughter, and then began to applaud. By the end of the day, the United States had finally suspended military aid —though more than 95 percent of the 1987 monies had already been distributed—and had revoked at least another $70 million in non-humanitarian assistance.

"Now that we've seen how these elections have ended up, do you think the American policy toward the CNG was correct?"

Lite: "Personally, I believe the U.S. acted in a way that was likely to guarantee free and fair elections."

"Clearly, the CNG fooled the Americans, wouldn't you say?"

Lite: "They never gave us any reason to doubt their sincerity. Up until now, that is."

"You just didn't have a clue about what was going to happen?"

Lite: "Well, as you all know, there was supposed to be an election today."

"Does the U.S. have any plans for a military intervention?"
Lite: "No."

A Democratic Congressman who was in touch daily with the U.S.
Embassy in the weeks leading up to the elections later told me that
Ambassador McKinley was already giving out the same line Namphy
would later spout: The electoral council was being run by foreign
leftists, and Gourgue was at least a Communist front man, if not a
Communist himself.

The night of the attack at Ruelle Vailtant, Namphy appeared on
television. By decree, he had already dissolved the CEP.

"The electoral council," he told the people in French, "deserves
its failure. It was a menace to national security. The CEP allowed
itself to be manipulated, and deliberately cut off dialogue with the
CNG. The CEP knowingly violated principles of both the Constitution and the electoral law, which the council itself devised. The
CEP invited foreign powers to interfere in the domestic affairs of the
country . . . and thus attacked our dignity as a free and sovereign
people. . . . The CNG," he concluded, "is untainted by special interest or partisan politics, and renews its determination to pursue an
electoral calendar."

As so often, Namphy's reasoning was not too different from that
of his predecessor François Duvalier. The specter of the long arm of
the United States, the major "foreign power" of which Namphy was
speaking, was one that Papa Doc knew how to summon and manipulate. In 1962, after the United States had made it clear to Duvalier
that it did not consider his most recent election valid, and withdrew
its ambassador to Washington just before Haitian "National Sovereignty Day" was to be celebrated, Duvalier had given a long speech.
In conclusion he asked his people whether a Haitian democracy of
which the United States approved would be "democracy or mas-
queraded colonialism." Namphy's speech was no different.

As always in times of crisis, rumors of an American intervention
washed over the city.

"I've heard from our Washington bureau that there are two U.S.
battleships steaming for Port-au-Prince harbor right now," said one
American journalist.

"This time, the Marines will definitely come," many Haitians told me. (In quite recent years, in fact, the Americans had come. When François Duvalier died in 1971, the United States sent several naval units into waters off Haiti to "assure order and to discourage exile infiltration," according to the State Department.) After the massacre at Ruelle Vaillant, some Haitians said they supported the idea of an intervention: they were so sick of their own military, they said, that the presence of another armed force would be a relief. In a radio broadcast, Sylvio Claude said he would not oppose a multinational interventionary force. But most Haitians, left and right, are fiercely nationalistic and since the time of the revolution have deeply resented the idea of foreign occupation. Namphy was playing on this when he talked of the CEP's sins against the national sovereignty. When the enemy is within, he knew, it can be useful to behave as though the threat comes from abroad. In this fashion, all members of the opposition are quickly relegated to the category of foreign agents.

In the days that followed the massacre, the following phrase kept appearing on Télévision Nationale: " 'You will return to this city only after I have reduced it to ashes. And even upon those ashes, I will continue to fight you.' " Thus Henry Christophe had threatened the French when they were trying to retake Cap-Haïtien (Cap-François at the time). He made good on his word, and now Namphy was taking up his cry, as though those two apocryphal U.S. battleships were actually anchored offshore.

Grégoire Eugène managed to get in his two cents, as well. For weeks before the election, he had been accusing the CEP of colluding with the Front to elect Gourgue. Now, on the Oloffson's little TV, we could listen to Eugène's analysis of Haitian politics on the government station. He read from his notes, with his eyeglasses down on his nose and the pages flickering up white under the studio lights.

"We are living," he read, "through a democratic transition during which we need a clairvoyant, honest leader, one who is balanced. All radical attitudes lead to confrontations. The left is ready to do anything to stop a right-wing government from making Communism illegal."

"What?" said Harry, looking up briefly from his own notes. "What the bloody hell's Grégoire talking about now?"

"But the centrist parties," Eugène continued, "are dedicated to preventing a Communist government, because it would make life impossible for anything other than the Communist alternative."

On the one hand Télévision Nationale was telling the Haitians to beware of the Americans from lòt bò dlo, on the other to watch out for the Communists within.

"I think it's time for us all to play dead," said a priest from Carrefour Feuilles.

News was traveling fast, as it always travels in times of crisis, although not always accurately. Families that had television sets gathered around them at night, with the servants standing in the background, watching, and the next morning when the servants went home to the slums they would describe what they had seen. Their friends and neighbors from the slums would use this visual information to embellish what they had heard on the radio, if they had radios.

Meanwhile, Haitian journalists were constantly on the telephone, spreading the news they had heard among other journalists or had gotten from Army sources or sources within the Macoutes, but could not confirm. Neighbors of Claude Raymond called friends, who called friends, who called journalists to talk about the late-night meetings at Raymond's, and how they had seen a hoard of Macoutes, armed with clubs and machetes, descend from Raymond's driveway that election morning. Eventually, such word-of-mouth information, or teledyòl, as it is called in Creole, would make it into the local radio reports.

Once the radio reports were out, people would add bits of folklore to them: a black-magic ritual peformed at Raymond's on election-day eve, the sightings of a huge black moth over Raymond's bougainvillea that night, or the insane screaming fit of one of Raymond's son's mistresses during the election-day massacre. These were akin to the reports, later quoted without qualification in some American newspapers, that before Jean-Claude and Michèle Duvalier left Haiti they murdered two unbaptized babies on their big bed in the palace, in order to ensure that no future President would ever sleep soundly within its walls. Sometimes these stories, even the ones from the palace, came directly from servants in the households of those involved, but that didn't make them any truer. Nonetheless, they became subjects of heated discussion in the slums, and were frequently mulled over even in the homes of people who had television sets and servants who liked to tell tall stories. No one knew the exact source of these anecdotes, and the teledyòl took several days to appear in the Haitian newspapers or on the radio. But the stories would race through town. After a day, everyone had heard them.

I finally found Aristide. He was all wound up, almost skittish, animated by an anger he reserved for crimes against humanity and that went beyond his usual fire into a sort of cindery, ashen heat. He was above the scene, beyond it, he had predicted it all, he already knew the end of the story.

"The people of Ruelle Vaillant were sent to die a brutal, criminal death," he said, sitting in a rocking chair in his living quarters, not rocking. "Who is responsible? First and foremost, the butchers who came with their machine guns and machetes. But not only these Macoutes. No, not only. The candidates too must accept their share of the blame. Who encouraged these people, these poor, innocent victims, to believe in false prophets, false elections? The candidates, the CEP, the Americans. We have said all along that there is no possibility for free elections under this criminal, Namphy. The Haitian people should never have been led into this trap, this electoral trap from which there was finally no exit but a bloody death. No election can be held until the people have thrown off the yoke of the Macoutes and the military. Haitian history will never happen the way the U.S. envisions it. The Americans' plan for Haiti is a dream for the U.S., and now we we have the proof, which we have always known, that it is a nightmare for the Haitian people."

He hated being underground, and was busy making a tape for circulation. It was called "Two of the Living Dead," and in it he took on the persona of a voter killed at Ruelle Vaillant, speaking from the dead, and addressing his listeners by the diminutive Creole names for little boys and little girls, Ti Roro and Ti Choune. You could hear the lambi sounding in the background as he begged them not to be discouraged, and warned them of the perils that lay ahead.

"If the criminal CNG does not go," he said on the tape, in a voice like syrup, "what will happen? Tell me what you think, Ti Roro. Yes, Ti Choune, I understand you, I agree with you, I'm with you. Let me tell you what I think, here's what I think. I think that if the CNG stays it will organize a new CEP, another electoral council—which it has already begun to do today, with so many lies in its mouth—so that the Macoute CNG can plot with the similarly Macoute CEP to allow all Macoute candidates to run, Désinor, Raymond, Romain . . . and all the other Macoutes like them who are crazy to become President, or senator, or deputy.

"So . . . and what if by chance the Macoute CNG should remain in power and if by chance the other, new CEP that is coming should not be filled with Macoutes? Does this mean that we will have elections? No. There will be an election, but you won't be able to call it an election in the proper sense of the word.

"Because in reality this election will be a sham election that the CNG has organized in order to put a Macoute like themselves in power. This Macoute will give them protection because they are well aware of all the crimes they've commited. The other day, we saw the kinds of crimes they commit. Further back, at Jean-Rabel, we saw the kinds of crimes they commit. And today, on the twenty-ninth of November, the reason we're talking like this is because we've just seen again the kinds of crimes they are still committing.

"Sham elections with a new CEP will plunge us into blood, into death, into massacre. The Macoutes, they must be dechouked. Since February 7, 1986, they have shown that they have not converted, they say they will not convert. They are still sanguinary. If they're used to drinking blood, it's blood they'll drink; they've shown that they are lice. We're not going to give them wine if it's blood they want. They'll keep drinking blood, the way they drank blood today."

The day after the massacre, the faces on the street were downcast. They had that remarkable dead look of zombis, the living dead. You got no reading from those faces. When I nodded at people, the customary greeting between strangers, they would shrug and shake their heads. Fred Voodoo was not giving interviews.

Ruelle Vaillant was too quiet for me. As I walked up the short sunny street, I was afraid that the men from yesterday were going to return. The sun on the curb glinted off glass from the journalists' shattered windshields, and the wrought-iron gates of the Ecole Argentine hung open, like the entryway to a haunted place. Inside, Haitians were wandering silently, downcast and shrugging. Like all places in Haiti where history is made, the school had already become a museum. People were sitting on the low cement walls in the schoolyard, holding their heads and sobbing noiselessly. A boy was pointing to a woman's blue vinyl purse, left behind in the shade of the almond tree. He didn't speak. The bodies had all been trucked away.

Blood had spurted in delicate arabesques over the upturned tables in the voting room. A few loose shoes lost in the panic protruded from beneath the chaos. A ballot box was wedged in a corner, and ballots were scattered everywhere, thick as a carpet in some places and like a flurry of confetti in others. The blood was heavier in the bathroom, near the toilet, and a woman's black bag stood open near the door. Two women died here, I remembered. Down in back, at the foot of the retaining wall that had been scaled by those lucky and strong enough to escape, I found a broken briefcase, a cheap thing with no clasps. Part of a pants leg was flopped over it.

The worst killings had come in the classroom opposite the voting place. A few benches were still askew, but many had been moved and stacked up to facilitate the removal of the bodies of the voters who had fled into a corner and then could not get away. Puddles of coagulated blood stained the cement floor, and walking was still a sticky business. A peasant's straw hat, half dyed with blood, gave a jaunty look to one brown pool, and a stray yellow thong dipped its toe into another. Faint footprints from soldiers' boots made a dance pattern on the floor. The sun was pounding through the open walls of the school; the place smelled bad, like death, like La Saline. Two boys sat on the side of the classroom, their thin legs pointing toward the sun. They were wearing blue school uniforms, and behind them were splashes of old blood and the spidery rivulets where it had dripped down the wall. On the floor near the corner, still purplish and fresh, lay a human brain. You could trace the story of the massacre in the design of blood on the floor and walls. You could see them run, fall, rise, and stumble to their end. Shoes and bags and briefcases and hats stood like landmarks at the important twists and turns of futile paths. Between the lakes of blood were thin trails, drying rivers of deep red that marked the last, short movements of the dead, and then the bloody tributaries winding away. It was like a map of Haiti.

The Flood

Gangan Pierre has left off drinking. "My heart," he says, hitting himself on the chest to show why. Still, he takes the bottle of rum I offer him and puts it in the green room on a shelf lined with similar bottles. One of his fifteen children, a son about forty years old, is wandering barefoot in the courtyard, feeding the chickens. The son is as toothless as the father.

"Since Duvalier," Gangan Pierre says, "I pay no attention to politics. Namphy? I've seen him on the television, but I don't listen to what he says. I watch them all, but I don't listen. Politics is the affair of men. They go back and forth, these politicians, creating nothing, nothing but death. I serve the spirits, who are above man, who created life, which is magic. Man sees only money, all men can be bought. Look at these elections. Man loves the fruit but not the tree. Man betrays man. Wife betrays husband. War comes and destroys all. Only the spirits are pure."

Today, the painting on his easel is of Damballah, the greatest of the voodoo gods, whose vèvè is the double serpent. In green and red, Gangan Pierre has painted Damballah emerging from a thick forest onto a Haitian coast. The god is wearing the miter of a bishop, and he is pouring water into the sea. Behind him in the sky are two rainbows.

"Damballah is putting water on the world," Pierre says, explaining the painting. "The rainbows are his witness. Two rainbows," he says, "signify a deluge, a tempest that is coming, *lavalas*." The flood.

He pushes himself back in his rocking chair. "I don't drink. For three months, I haven't had a sip. But I still take remèd." A remèd is folk medicine of any kind, herbs, teas, infusions. Gangan Pierre disappears into the green room for a moment, and shuffles back with a bottle of clairin filled with curative leaves. He proffers it, but I refuse. He takes a sip. "This is what saves me," he says.

The chickens are pecking in the dust outside. Gangan Pierre watches them with his lips to the bottle's rim, then turns his gaze back to me. He takes his sip, wipes his mouth against his sleeve, and smiles for longer than usual.

"When I say lavalas," he says, then stops. Another sip. "When I say lavalas, that does not mean the flood is bad. No. You wash dirty clothes in God's clean water. You soak beans in God's clean water and when the bad ones float to the top, you get rid of them. The flood is to rid the world of man's corruption and make it new. That is Damballah's flood."

Namphy called a second election, and, as Harry had predicted, the bulging historian and university professor Leslie Manigat became President. Haitians did not like Manigat, and they tried to ignore him, but it wasn't easy. First of all, he talked too much, hours of hectoring Creole on radio and television, talking too loudly, badgering, wagging his head and pointing at the viewer. It was a habit he had developed as a teacher.

And then there was the matter of how Le Professeur, as French journalists derisively called him, had gained proprietorship of what Haitians always refer to as the Presidential Chair: le Fauteuil Présidentiel. A second attempt at "democracy," organized by the new electoral council appointed by Namphy's junta after the massacre at Ruelle Vaillant, had been scheduled for January 17, 1988. None of the major candidates from the November elections had agreed to participate; they did not want to lend their prestige to an illegitimate process. Bazin, Déjoie, Gourgue and Claude believed that anyone who ran in the January election would lose his political legitimacy and the chance to run later when more palatable elections might take place. Although they were all almost visibly salivating at the idea of a shortcut to the Presidential Chair, they managed to control themselves and sat out the January election.

Manigat had no such concerns. He felt, it seemed, that he could turn a prostituted election into an honest presidency. He quickly emerged from a field of nobodies, including Grégoire Eugène, to become the principal candidate. Like Duvalier before him, he had reportedly made the most attractive concessions to the Army. As a historian, he ought to have remembered an old Haitian maxim: *Si lame fè, se lame kap defè*. If the Army makes you, it's the Army that will undo you. But the thing Manigat found hardest to see was his own weakness. "He's so smart," said a Haitian who had studied under Le Professeur, "he can't see how dumb he is."

The January election had been one big joke. Manigat's voters were given rum and money; "campaign workers" doled out dollars to voters from the back of a big black car outside Cité Soleil. A foreign journalist, a white man, was paid five dollars to vote for Manigat. The voters, ragtag groups in most places, toured the towns by tap-tap, voting—and then voting again. In Cité Soleil and in the coastal town of St.-Marc, just north of the spot where thugs had twice erected the Freycineau barricade, teams of young men used lime and lye and boric acid to remove the magenta ink that was used to stain the fingers of those who had already voted. Ballot boxes arrived already stuffed at many polling places. Children voted. Mimette was definitely eligible in this election, but her family stayed home with the doors firmly shut. Hundreds of slum-dwellers like Mimette's family left town the week before the election, filling up tap-taps and trucks. They wanted to avoid being forced to vote. At least 75 percent of eligible Haitians did not participate. *"Se te youn seleksyon, se pat youn eleksyon,"* dozens told me in the days after the vote. It was a selection, not an election.

Unlike Dr. Duvalier, Manigat remained imprisoned by the deals he had made with the Army. In a desperate and ill-considered attempt to escape his powerless predicament, he formed what he thought was an alliance with Colonel Jean-Claude Paul, one of the reported instigators of the November massacre. With Paul apparently in his camp—and Paul's men, the well-armed and dog-loyal soldiers of the Casernes Dessalines—Manigat thought he could end Namphy's control as well as that of Colonel Prosper Avril, the head of the Presidential Guard and the brains behind Namphy. The Professor played out his hand far too quickly. By mid-June 1988, four and a half months into his presidency, he was in the midst of a full-fledged fight with the Army.

In the first of the maneuvers that eventually led to his overthrow, Manigat retired General Namphy, who had remained at the head of the Haitian armed forces, and put him under house arrest. In rapid succession, he steamrolled other prominent military figures, perhaps hoping that speed and surprise would win the day. He demoted Avril, a fatal mistake. In dealing with master tacticians like Avril, Manigat would soon learn, you have to be subtle and slow. The Army did not react calmly to Manigat's moves.

The men of the Presidential Guard, who dealt with Namphy and the new President every day, were disgruntled. As far as they were concerned, Manigat was a civilian and had no business deciding who was to be retired from the Army, nor who was to head which unit. In fact, the popular 1987 Constitution declared that the elected President was the "nominal" head of the Army, but specified that he was under no circumstances to "command the Army in person." Aside from the legal arguments, which did not particularly interest the lower ranks of the Guard, Namphy and the officers around him had always treated their men well; the men, almost all of whom were from poor families, lived off their generosity and were grateful to them. In a futile and premature attempt to end corruption in the armed forces, Manigat had reportedly cut off the flow of gifts. The Presidential Guard also resented the increasing powers of Colonel Paul's Casernes, located only yards away from the Guard's barracks in the National Palace. Dissatisfied, angry, the sergeants in the Presidential Guard organized a coup, backed by Colonel Avril. Two days after Ennui Namphy was retired by Manigat, they brought Namphy back to the palace as President.

Ennui, accompanied by his wife and young daughter, was driven back to his old haunt in an armored vehicle on the night of June 19 while gunfire exploded near the National Palace. The coup was not contested and no one was injured, no one died. The gunfire had been merely a warning to the other units of the Haitian Army not to interfere. Manigat was quickly taken out of the country and went to the Concorde Hotel in Santo Domingo.

It was said that Namphy was a reluctant returnee, but by one in the morning, a few hours after the coup began, he seemed pleased enough. Port-au-Princiens who kept their televisions on throughout the ordeal saw the General on Télévision Nationale live from the palace, and surrounded by his men, all in uniform. Next to him stood Colonel Avril, who had been promoted that evening and was already wearing a general's silver star. Namphy held a machine gun aloft as he told the Haitian people that they and the Army were one. "The Army will now run the country as it should be run—with order and discipline. . . . Trust me! Trust the Army!"

Namphy was back, the light-skinned, twinkly-eyed villain of Haiti's latest nightmare. As I watched him make tough speech after speech in the weeks that followed, speeches about the unchallenged might of the Army, I kept remembering the time, a few days after Jean-Claude Duvalier left, when the General, laughing and smiling and cracking jokes, had chucked me under the chin in the Presidential Hall at the National Palace. "The problems have been solved, sweetheart," he had said to me then. A few weeks after his coup, Namphy moved from his walled house outside Port-au-Prince into the National Palace, last inhabited by Jean-Claude and his wife. During his earlier regime and that of Manigat, such a move would have seemed symbolically inappropriate. Perhaps Manigat was afraid also to live so near the Presidential Guard. But now that democratic pretense had been dropped, it seemed proper to enjoy the fruits of power.

Doubtless Namphy believed that his presence in the palace was in the national interest. He must also have believed in all his talk of national reconciliation; how else to explain his motivation, two weeks later, when he invited Aristide, his most vocal detractor, to attend a ceremony at which he announced the revocation of the Constitution? Among those who came and who were given places in the front row in the Presidential Hall were Grégoire Eugène, Clovis Désinor, and Claude Raymond. Aristide, of course, did not go, but I almost wished he had. I wanted to know whether Namphy had drunk as much after he revoked the Constitution as he had drunk at the party in the document's honor that I had attended more than a year before, when he swore to uphold it.

Namphy's new regime picked up quickly where his junta had left off. The return to Duvalierist tactics was swift. On Rue Pavée, which intersects Grande Rue, an unknown man was shot at noon by officers from Recherches Criminelles, and no one knew why. In the Artibonite near Verrettes, the chef de section and his men descended on a gathering of young activists who were getting ready for a soccer game and shot four dead, wounding many others. Chavannes, the boyish peasant leader from Papaye, who had been threatened so many times before, was arrested, held for six hours, and released. During the same period, René Poirier, a Canadian priest who coincidentally bears the surname of one of the first foreign priests exiled by Dr. Duvalier, was summarily kicked out of the country for refusing to provide names of his congregants to the authorities and for failing to participate in the festivities welcoming General (and once again President) Henri Namphy to Poirier's southern parish. Mani-

gat, in exile, told the foreign press that Namphy was mentally un-
balanced. In Haiti, people began talking hopefully about the
General's cirrhotic decline.

Manigat had made the mistake of relying on an unpredictable force:
Colonel Paul. Paul was a loyal officer, certainly, but loyal to one
ideal only, and that ideal was a strong and united Casernes Dessalines, under his command. Ever since his ascension to the commander's post at the Casernes in the final days of Jean-Claude
Duvalier's regime, Paul had worked hard toward that goal, and the
battalion was by all accounts the strongest and best organized in the
Haitian armed forces.

  Under Paul's command, the Casernes' men had taken numerous
Tontons Macoute into protective custody during the 1986 Dechoukaj. Soliders from Paul's garrison had guarded Paul Véricain's headquarters in Pétionville on the day when the people were ready to
take it apart, and it was under the Casernes' protection that Véricain
had been taken to the penitentiary "to relax."

  Realizing that such frightened men, along with their arms, could
prove useful to him at the Casernes, Paul soon began a process of
recruitment. The Tontons Macoute, orphaned without their organization, were looking for a foster home, and Paul welcomed them
by the tens, then by the hundreds, and eventually, according to later
reports, by the thousands. Among the enlisted men, the recruited
Macoutes were called "attachés." Paul was building a strong battalion into a private army.

  No one knew for sure where he had gotten the money to pay all
these new men, but it was presumed that cocaine-trafficking and
involvement in the contraband food trade were the cornerstones of
Paul's fortune. The Colonel was emboldened by his growing influence. During the days of demonstrations in the summer of 1987, he
gave his men pep talks on crowd control, and when there was violence against unarmed demonstrators the gunfire usually came from
the Casernes' men. The Casernes was the Army unit most in evidence at the massacre at Ruelle Vaillant; some witnesses said they
saw truckloads of Paul's soldiers sitting near the end of the short
street as the massacre took place.

  In March 1988, a month after Manigat was inaugurated, a Miami
grand jury had indicted Paul on charges of conspiring to export
narcotics to the United States. The indictment came as the U.S.

government was moving, with limited success, against General Manuel Antonio Noriega of Panama on similar charges, and three months after it had cut off aid to Haiti in the wake of the election-day massacre. Haiti desperately needed that aid restored; already the Treasury was running low, and soon the barest essentials, such as monthly gasoline imports, would become unaffordable. The State Department quickly made it clear to the Haitian government that Paul's removal from power was one of the conditions on which restoration of aid depended.

This put Paul in an extremely delicate position. As the head of the country's foremost military unit, he would have to be depended on by any Haitian government for its stability. Yet to ensure that same stability, any Haitian government would need the large financial infusion that only the American government could provide, which was contingent on Paul's extradition. From the moment of the indictment, Paul became a pivotal figure in political maneuvering and military jockeying.

When Paul found out that Namphy was back in the palace and that the Guard had control of the Haitian armed forces' armored vehicles, he realized it was time for negotiations. In order to avoid a pitched battle between the Guard and the Casernes, Paul would have to make deals with the just promoted General Avril. It was obvious to any Army man that someone as high in the military as Avril must have participated in the coup. How else would twenty or so rank-and-file members of the Guard have gotten their hands on those jealously protected armored vehicles? By six that morning, Paul had convinced Avril to come over from the palace to the Casernes to negotiate. A few hours later, the Colonel appeared on the front steps of the palace with Namphy and Avril for a public ceremony announcing the formation of a new government. It was the first time that armed men from the Casernes were allowed to participate in security measures on the palace grounds alongside the Presidential Guard. Paul had insisted on their presence for his own protection.

Things were back to normal. Paul Véricain was released from the penitentiary, and Max Beauvoir, the houngan who cures AIDS, was thoroughly rehabilitated. He had appeared at Manigat's inauguration in a white suit, but was hardly discommoded when his latest patron fell. Jolicoeur was not surprised by the latest coup, but lay low for a

while. Hérard Simon, the voodoo priest who danced for the National
Congress of Democratic Movements in January 1987, was allegedly
bought off soon afterward by the junta for $2,000, and was report-
edly loyal to the reincarnated Namphy. Soon after the Namphy
coup, Marc Bazin, the U.S. government's favorite son in the November elections, began asking for constructive dialogue with the
military dictatorship.

In the middle of a night at the beginning of July, four men wearing black hoods and carrying machine guns burst into the home of
Laënnec Hurbon—the historian who had written books about Haitian culture and its relation to dictatorship, and the *éminence grise*
behind the National Congress—and ripped apart his notes and his
library. In the middle of another night a week later, on July 10 or
11, Lafontant Joseph, a human-rights activist, one of the country's
few uncorrupted lawyers and another participant in the Congress,
was knifed to death and left in his jeep near the airport road, one of
Dr. Duvalier's favorite places for dumping his victims' bodies.

The penis boys had returned to the Barbancourt Castle , but there
were still no tourists. Perhaps the missionaries continued to provide
the market; I had seen another troupe there on a recent trip up the
mountain. The black clouds still weighed down on the peak, and the
National Palace still gleamed like a vision of purity, even with Namphy living there. I drove down before nightfall, and nothing had
changed. The boys at the barricades were gone now, of course, but
the Macoutes were all still there, back behind their iron gates and
their clusters of bougainvillea. Claude Raymond was at home, conspiring in his cavernous living room with Grégoire Eugène and other
politicians. Sylvain and Jeanne were vacationing in France and planning a dinner party on their return. They were not certain how long
their friend Namphy would last this time around, and even they
were growing tired of his military regime. For this dinner, they
wanted to invite some of the people from the National Congress:
perhaps Victor Benoit.

Radio Nationale was playing tapes of voodoo ceremonies, and on
the Protestant station you could still tune in to English lessons:
"Sally va à l'école avec sa boîte à déjeuner." Sally goes to school
with her lunchbox. *"Aujourd'hui, Sally et les autres élèves vont
patiner."* Today, Sally and the other students are going ice-staking.
The Haitian spring was over. *"Nap suiv,"* was what most people
said when you asked them about Namphy's new regime. We're following the situation. They shrugged. *"Peyi-a ap fè bak,"* they said.

The country's in reverse. "I'm sick of it," one Haitian opposition leader told me. "From now on, I'm spending my days at the beach in the company of beautiful women."

Soon, perhaps, the United States would restore the aid it had cut off earlier after the November elections. The U.S. government would find a way. Perhaps Namphy would offer up Jean-Claude Paul in exchange; perhaps he wouldn't have to. Aside from a few initial expressions of shock, the United States showed little displeasure at the return of Namphy to the palace. They had always liked the General. "Haiti's best chance for democracy"—it was hard to forget the words of the then Assistant Secretary of State for Inter-American Affairs.

Aristide went on as though nothing had changed. *"Ça avance,"* he would always respond when I asked him how things were going. It's moving forward. His residence at St.-Jean-Bosco was guarded by dogs and alarms now, but he had a relaxed attitude about his own safety. "If they want me, they'll get me," he said. "I can't stop living my life because of that." He had opened up a house for Lafanmi Selavi and a clinic in the same building for the sick of La Saline right in the heart of my middle-class neighborhood, next to a nursery school, not far from Claude Raymond's. Every day, he drove the patients who assembled at St.-Jean-Bosco over to the clinic across town in his jeep so they wouldn't have to pay for transportation. On the outside wall of the new house, in cheerful letters, was written the motto "M RENMEN W," on a blue and red background that looked like the Haitian flag. I Love You. And next to it, "CLINIC FOR THE POOR."

Others started taking on a new character after the coup. Gangan Pierre stopped drinking. The Well-Placed Embassy Official dropped his habitual pretense of innocent surprise. "It's so calm here, you could almost call it tranquil," he said. "Haiti needs a long period of calm." Sylvain told me he was thinking of contributing to Aristide's projects. The Senatorial Candidate grew more pessimistic about his country's future; he shook his head often, and regretted the day he had begun to support elections. Ayiti blackened and straightened his hair, and he and Waldeck and Ti Bernard began smoking marijuana and crack, and when they ran out of money they would sniff turpentine. The courtyard at St.-Jean-Bosco always smelled from the stuff.

In spite of the public message of love inscribed on the boys' new house, many of their new neighbors were not happy with the setup. "They are dirty, they have lice," said a woman who lived across the street, "and now they're doing drugs. I'm all for Aristide's preachings, and I'm glad that he works with these poor children, but he doesn't know how wild they are." He did know, however. He could feel the atmosphere changing at the church and among the boys. It was as though someone were turning the boys against their protector. One day he had to send a boy who had picked a fight into a basement room to think about his sins. Another week, Waldeck and Ayiti were forbidden to come into the churchyard or into the new house; Aristide had caught them sniffing turpentine, again. Outside the church, on Grande Rue, Ayiti and Waldeck, high on turpentine and angry over their expulsion, threatened Aristide's visitors with rocks and sticks. Waldeck's fights were growing more vicious. One day I found him proudly showing off three fresh razor wounds across his cheek to a bunch of fascinated boys. Another boy I'd seen around the church was banned because he kept trying to seduce the younger boys. Ti Bernard was in and out, accepted and refused. He too was sniffing turpentine, and no one could tell what other mischief he was up to. He was definitely selling something. One day he had new *tennis,* or sneakers, and the next a whole new outfit. Ti Bernard always had access to marijuana. At first, no one knew how he got it.

The situation was tense, but Aristide never let up. He was enjoying the excitement, the fear. It was a heady sensation, being the only one left in public opposition. He celebrated a funeral mass for the assassinated lawyer Lafontant Joseph, he celebrated a mass in commemoration of the massacre at Jean-Rabel, he celebrated a mass marking the anniversary of the landing of the U.S. Marines on Haitian soil in 1915. He kept on talking when everyone else was silent. His continuing jeremiads may not have been wise, given the increasingly repressive situation, but they were, he felt, an important part of his mission, which, he once said, was "to continue to deliver the message I have been called upon to deliver." Though a wider and wider section of the population was coming to respect his courage, Aristide and his congregation were increasingly isolated. Nonetheless, on the walls in Gonaïves you could still read a scrawled *"Nou vle Titid"* here and there: We want Titid. Farther south, however, the little Charade had vanished completely from the side of the Route Nationale; somehow, scavengers had found a use for every part of its charred body.

· · ·

The Americans were leaving Haiti by the dozens. The cutoff in U.S. aid had meant that many development workers were now out of a job. Many others were leaving because, as one said to me, "We just can't hack it with Namphy. Not again. Somehow, it's worse than Jean-Claude." In Pacot and Pétionville, scores of big houses with broad terraces and swimming pools were coming on the market, but there was no market. No one much wanted to stay on in "these depressing conditions," as one U.S. development worker described the unfolding Namphy regime. The Well-Placed Embassy Official was on his way out, too, packing up his big house, spending his days orienting his successor and supervising his seven Haitian movers.

The signs and portents were not favorable. The most significant was the return of the Lully shark. Off the fishing village of Lully on the western coast, a shark that had not been seen in eight years made an appearance. After his last visit, a hurricane had blown into the country. This time around, the shark came right up to a small child who was fishing near the water's edge, and tugged on his little line. The fishermen of Lully said the storm would come soon. The meteorologists agreed with the shark: an onde tropicale, if not something bigger, was on its way. A friend of mine from Cité Soleil, whose fisherman father had been killed in a boating accident and who had a tempestuous relationship with Agwe, the voodoo god of the sea, wouldn't go near the water this season. She said she could feel Agwe's pull again. Peasants in the Artibonite said the next time the Army came into their village shooting, they would run all the way to the sea and drown themselves. *"Peyi-a ap fini nan lanmè."* The country is going to end up in the sea, they said.

The week before the Embassy Official left, the days were overcast and the evenings stormy. One evening, American Airlines had to land a flight in the Dominican Republic; Haiti's climate was too uncertain. Except for the fishermen of Lully, no one knew when the storm would break. And the fishermen of Lully were not giving out dates. The heat was unendurable; the tropical air was lying in wait, ready to slap you with sweat each time you moved. Everything seemed ominous: the three bloody slashes on Waldeck's face, the gaping potholes on the street outside the shining new Téléco building, the gold signet ring of a driver whose face you couldn't see behind his smoke-tinted jeep windows.

One Sunday morning, half the city was blacked out. The night before, a two-hour gun battle had raged up near Pétionville, and someone in the heat of the fight had thrown two grenades into a nearby power station. That same Sunday, the Feast of the Ascen-

sion, Aristide preached against evil-doing foreigners in Haiti. When
I went to visit the dressmaker a few days later, Radio Soleil was
broadcasting his sermon. "The good and decent foreigners may remain, but the exploiters," he said, "the evil blan, they must leave
our country." Radio Soleil segued from Aristide's sermon to announce that Jeffrey Lite's tour of duty had ended.

While the rest of the opposition had been quashed or was regroup-
ing in secret, Aristide's raised voice was becoming more and more
annoying to the new Namphy regime. The people who had been
clamoring for his blood were growing more influential within the
walls of the palace. Namphy had once been reported to dismiss their
ideas with a firm, dismissive shake of the head. "Let the little priest
talk," he would say. But that apparently was no longer the case. On
the first Sunday in September 1988, a man walked into St.-Jean-
Bosco during Aristide's mass, started making his way toward the
altar in the communion line, and took out his .38 revolver. As had
happened in the past, the youths from the church disarmed him,
but the assailant somehow escaped with two of his accomplices.
There were five bullets in the .38's chamber. The following Tuesday, September 6, after Aristide's evening mass, a crowd of men
gathered around the walls of the church and began shooting and
throwing rocks against its windows. The siege lasted for three or
four hours, and, as they left, the attackers shouted that they would
return the following Sunday.

It wasn't hard to understand why certain elements wanted Aristide
dead. As the regime became more violent, his preaching became less
veiled. At the mass when the attacker was disarmed, Aristide had
preached: "We are telling you today that we have anger in our veins,
in our guts, but one day—we don't know when that day will arrive
—one day we will put that anger into action. From one moment to
the next, anything can happen, because when the winds of vicissi-
tude blow, when the winds of hunger blow, when the storm of
injustice is raging, one fine day a people weighed down by all this
human and inhuman suffering—this people will become a people
marching toward justice. One day, they will establish their own
tribunals."

Talking to Aristide, though, I sensed something new. He seemed
almost frightened. "What is going to happen now, in the next few
days, will be worse than anyone can imagine," he told me, "worse
than Ruelle Vaillant." As usual, his vision of the future had less to
do with prophecy than with facts. Every day now, he was receiving

death threats. He had been warned by friends in the military that another attack on the church was planned. Everyone in town had heard the rumor. It was accepted that something else was going to happen at St.-Jean-Bosco.

The dark-haired photographer was driving past City Hall near the port two days after the attack on Aristide's evening mass, when she noticed an unusual number of government cars and jeeps and Army trucks parked outside. As the Lully shark had foretold, Hurricane Gilbert was on his way toward Haiti, and the somber green afternoon light was good for shooting. She stopped in front of City Hall and tried to get into the big white colonnaded building, but the guard at the door refused.

"No one enters," he told her.

She objected, but he would not budge from his post. She heard a whistle from an upstairs balcony. Someone inside had seen her and was motioning to the guard to let her in.

"Go ahead," he told her.

She went upstairs. In a wide salon, General Namphy and Franck Romain, the mayor of Port-au-Prince, were seated side by side on a sofa. This was Romain's turf. He knew City Hall well. After his years in François Duvalier's Presidential Guard, Romain had been mayor under Jean-Claude, and in the Manigat election he had managed to take the seat again. His nickname was Pa Ka Pa La. It was an old intimidating campaign slogan that had stuck: "I can't not be there." Romain was a construction engineer as well as a politician, and over the years he had made a lot of money in the two businesses. He had jeeps at his disposal and plenty of men to whom he had given jobs and favors over the years. Those men had reportedly participated with enthusiasm in the election-day massacre. Romain and his men were famous for their ruthlessness and brutality, but the dark-haired photographer didn't know that.

A group of civil servants in their best clothes were waiting in line to talk with these important officials. One after another, the men would approach the sofa timidly and tell the dignitaries what they needed. The photographer could not quite make out the Creole, but it was clear that the civil servants were asking for favors. Something was being planned, and they were requesting payment for whatever it was they were going to do for the General and the mayor. After a while, the photographer, bored, sidled over to a window to take a look at the view. A soldier holding an Uzi was standing out on the balcony, looking quietly at something, mesmerized. She followed his gaze. It was an astonishing sight: there were two rainbows, complete from end to end, arching over the city. Even Namphy's attention had been attracted. He was looking out the window from his soft seat on the couch, not quite listening to his latest supplicant.

After the last civil servant finished asking for his payment, Namphy and Mayor Romain went into a small office off the main hall. The dark-haired photographer had started putting her equipment in order when an officer standing outside the door to the office beckoned her, and she was ushered into the inner sanctum. Namphy leaned back in his chair and began lecturing her. First he talked about the Church, how the priests were stirring up trouble, how there were Communist infiltrators within the Church. Then he got onto the Americans. The U.S. government, he told her, wanted Communism in Haiti; that was why they had cut off aid—what else could an aid cutoff do but destabilize the nation and help the Communist cause? He proceeded to foreign journalists: Why did they always write bad stories about Haiti, about General Namphy (as he called himself)? Why did they always go to Marc Bazin or Gérard Gourgue for their interviews? These foreign journalists, they were probably in league with the Communists and the American government. As a rational man, he could not understand their behavior.

He was very angry, almost rude. Mayor Romain was different. A tough, strong man, bulky, with long sideburns and eyes that showed too much white, Romain sat off to the side, saying nothing, while the General let loose. He watched and fiddled with his cuffs, his lapel. After Namphy finished and the photographer was about to leave, Romain called her over.

"I'm Franck Romain," he told her. "Mayor of Port-au-Prince. What is your name?"

She told him.

"Have you been coming to Haiti for a long time?" he asked.

She said yes. He was polite, interested, gentlemanly.

"So you must be very familiar with the city," he said, smiling.

"Oh, yes," she said.

"And where do you stay when you come to Haiti?" the mayor wanted to know.

"At the Hotel Oloffson," she told him.

"Oh, that's a very nice place," he said, nodding. "I know it well. They just reopened, isn't that so?"

"Yes," she said. "A little while ago. It's very nice."

"Well, I hope you have a good stay here in Port-au-Prince," he said to her, smiling again.

"Thank you, Mr. Mayor," she said.

It was late at night on Saturday, September 10, 1988, and Aristide and the youths from St.-Jean-Bosco still had not decided whether or not to hold the usual nine-o'clock Sunday-morning mass the next day. The priest's telephone had not stopped ringing for the last two days, and the callers all had bad news to report: rumors of a pending attack against the church, rumors of a planned blitzkrieg against the priests' residence, rumors of a meeting two days earlier between Namphy and Romain and the killers they had hired. The coming Sunday had been declared a day of commemoration for the now abrogated 1987 Constitution, and those who wished to show their support for the document were supposed to wear white. Aristide had planned to talk about the Constitution in his sermon.

The pressure on Aristide was increasing, and he had stopped eating the day before. Finally, he and the youths came to a decision. If the congregation showed up in reasonable numbers in spite of the rumors, Aristide would say a brief mass. But the front gate to the courtyard would be locked the moment the priest entered the church, and young men would be posted at the gate and at each window of the church and at the doors.

The dark-haired photographer arrived early for mass, and parked her car out on Grande Rue rather than inside the church courtyard, as had been her custom. She wanted to be sure to be able to make a fast getaway if people started shooting. The night before and that morning, she kept remembering the long blades of the san manmans at the barricade on election day. She didn't want to see any more like those.

The church began to fill up, although many of the congregants had been frightened off by the rumors, and the pews were not as crowded as they usually were. Many among the eight hundred or so faithful were wearing white. Latecomers, of whom there were usually about a hundred, were scared away by a crowd they had seen coming down Grande Rue. A friend of Aristide's who had attended the six-o'clock Sunday mass (because he had basketball practice at nine that morning) later saw several hundred young men marching down Grande Rue, armed with spikes, kitchen knives, machetes,

long, pointed steel poles called *fwen,* and all kinds of guns. He tried
to telephone the church to warn Aristide, but the phone was busy.
The armed men were marching toward the church. Some of them
had been loaded into Franck Romain's City Hall trucks. The men
wore red armbands and were coming from the direction of Fort
Dimanche—where demonstrators had been killed in 1986 and where
members of the vigilance brigades from the November election had
allegedly been taken and then executed—and from Cité Soleil,
whose mayor was a friend of Romain's. They sang a simple song:
"Jodi-a, se jou malè." Today is an accursed day. According to eye-
witnesses, Mayor Romain was outside the church in a white car on
Grande Rue, watching the procession and smoking a cigar. Inside
the church, the photographer was up near the altar, waiting for
Aristide to enter. Once the priest was inside, the youths standing
guard clanged shut the wrought-iron church gates through which he
had entered, and locked them.

Aristide had read the day's text, and was about to pronounce a short
sermon when the men in red armbands surrounded thè church complex. From inside the church, it seemed at first just like the attack
on the preceding Tuesday. A rain of rocks poured against the sides
of the church. Windows broke. A panic began, but the priest calmed
the congregation, and they began to sing a Ti Legliz standard: "Let
the Holy Spirit descend upon us. We have a single mission for
Haiti." They held hands in their pews as the rocks continued to fall
and gunfire exploded. "Blessed be the Eternal," Aristide shouted
over and over from the pulpit. "Hallelujah." The congregation repeated his words. Youths in the outer courtyard started throwing
rocks back at the assailants over the church complex's walls, but they
were forced to retreat beneath the blasts from the attackers' machine
guns. As the men in armbands approached the locked gate, they
fired on a fresco vendor who was waiting outside to sell his ices to a
thirsty congregation. The vendor fell next to his red cart and bled to
death on Grande Rue.

The men, still singing their little song, began sawing off the gate's
padlock while they continued to shoot into the courtyard. Men in
the olive-green uniforms of the Haitian Army stood by, watching the
proceedings. Inside the church, the congregation kept up its singing
and chanting. The youths who had been protecting the gate fled,
but not before a few among the assailants were wounded by their

rocks and Molotov cocktails. Suddenly, the men were within the gates. Through the locked wrought-iron doors of the church, Aristide and the dark-haired photographer could see them hurling rocks into the cars parked in the courtyard. "Everyone who wants to go, go now," Aristide shouted to his congregation. "Those who want to stay, stay." He held on to the microphone, his eyes wide with shock, as the men continued to batter the cars.

In seconds, about thirty of them had entered the church. People fled in all directions. Those who were wearing white were the first victims. The dark-haired photographer tried to take pictures, but she was also trying to get away. She couldn't see any escape route, though. The door to the sacristy was blocked with people trying to flee, and the killers were coming in from the main door.

People were screaming and bleeding. Gunfire rang inside the building. Chavannes, who had scheduled a meeting with Aristide for after the mass, ran down the main aisle. The man who was ahead of him and the woman behind were both gunned down. The men in the red armbands were approaching the altar, looking for the priest. The dark-haired photographer began to run, but a congregant grabbed her by the ankle and tried to use her as a shield. He wouldn't let her go. Finally she turned and hit him, and his grasp loosened. She ran toward the sacristy door, but it was still plugged up with people. She couldn't think of anything else to do but try the front door. That meant running down the center aisle, where she could see the attackers holding their victims and stabbing them.

Antoine, the blind beggar, was cowering in a corner. Another man, a young newlywed and a friend of Aristide's, was slashed across the skull with a machete by one attacker, then beaten severely by another as he lay on the floor, and finally shot twice in the chest by a third man. A woman seven months pregnant was repeatedly stabbed in the stomach. The attackers shouted "Give me your purse, give me your purse," as they cut their victims. They stole the chalice, the ciborium that holds the Host and the cloths that cover the altar.

The photographer was able to get only halfway down the center aisle when she was grabbed by a big young man who pulled back his machete to stab her. She wrenched away, and her dress ripped down the back. Realizing there was no escape possible by this route, she fled back to the sacristy door, and pushed against the backs of those who were trying to get through. She and some others finally pushed so hard that the bottleneck popped open, and they all fell into the sacristy, and then fell again, out through the door near Aristide's office. Chavannes was nearly trampled to death in the melee. Finally, they all ran and stumbled into the inner courtyard.

Meanwhile, a group of assailants were being taken down Grande Rue in the mayor's trucks to look for gasoline. The Army and the police had by now surrounded the church complex, but were not interfering. The men with the red armbands drove down to the Esso station at the corner of Rue St.-Martin, picked up about ten containers of gasoline, returned to the church and set it on fire. In the outer courtyard they poured gas on the congregants' cars and jeeps and lit them. As the church began to burn, a group of killers, still looking for Aristide, attempted to get into the inner courtyard. But the youths hiding within fought back with a hail of rocks, and the attackers retreated. No one from the Military Airport or the Traffic Police, both of which face the intersection where St.-Jean-Bosco stands, interceded during the attack.

The siege had gone on for more than an hour now. The cars were burning. The church was burning. Black smoke fanned out of its windows. Suddenly, the attackers withdrew. The Army and the police were gathering outside the complex. Quiet descended, interspersed by gunfire, sometimes from nearby and sometimes from far off. In the heat of the attack, the killers had failed to find their principal target. Just before the men entered the church, Aristide's bodyguards had surrounded him at the altar and pushed and pulled him forcibly out through the sacristy and back into the inner courtyard. Since then, no one else had seen him.

The police arrived, but again Aristide's youths would not let them into the inner courtyard. A few minutes later, about twenty policemen climbed the walls of the residence courtyard and jumped inside, pushing and shoving the parishioners assembled there. Hurriedly, Father Jacques Mésidor, who was the local director of Aristide's order, and another Salesian priest began negotiating with the men, who told the priests that they had come for security reasons. Finally the priests agreed to allow the entire police squadron in. The men in blue immediately began shooting into the air, causing a panic among the already terrified parishioners, who were soon evacuated.

Upstairs in the residence, Aristide was sitting alone in a room that was not his own. Only two friends among the close circle of clergy and laypeople inside the residence knew which room he was in.

By now, down in the courtyard there were some fifty high-ranking soldiers and another hundred or so men from Recherches Criminelles, in plainclothes. One of the high-ranking officers, a colonel, came to the door of the residence and asked that everyone leave. "We have orders," he said, "to evacuate St.-Jean-Bosco completely." Meanwhile, Mésidor was on the phone to the Papal Nuncio, asking him to come down to the church. The Nuncio reportedly refused, saying that the Red Cross would take care of their evacuation.

Taking the Colonel at his word, those who were inside the residence, including Aristide, decided to leave. With Chavannes at the front of the line, they filed down the stairs to the locked door, but as Chavannes opened it, the Colonel, still standing there, said, "No one may leave this building. We have just received an order to search it and its occupants." Chavannes and the six people who had followed him downstairs turned and retreated back up the stairs. The officers followed them, accompanied by fifteen or so of the men from Recherches Criminelles. They forced Aristide to remove his shirt so that they could check for weapons. He had none.

In his undershirt, Aristide lay down on the sofa in the residence's reception room, not speaking, his eyes closed. Chavannes sat beside him. The search went on, with Mésidor and another priest following the officers to make sure that no arms were planted in any of the priests' rooms. Meanwhile, through the open downstairs door, a procession of the armed men from Recherches Criminelles was filing into the building. Up the stairs they tramped, all two hundred of them, one after another, and circled around the sofa where Aristide was lying, the chair Chavannes was seated in. They insulted the two men.

"Look at you," said one to Aristide, who did not open his eyes. "Now you're pretending you can't talk, but before your voice was loud enough. I bet you're afraid now."

"You used to talk all the time, didn't you?" said another, addressing both of the men. "Now you're as quiet as two frightened sheep."

"We're looking at you," said another. "We won't forget your faces. No matter where you go, we'll be able to find you. You'll never be safe again."

At one point, a young man stood in front of the priest with the snout of his revolver aimed at the priest's heart. An older man stood behind Aristide with a gun also pointed vaguely in his direction. Their disjointed conversation wore on.

The young man was hotheaded, and wanted to shoot. That's why we're here, he reportedly said, shoving his gun toward the priest.

What do you think is going to happen to us after we pull the trigger and then try to walk out of here? another asked the young man.

This did not frighten the young man and those who agreed with him.

We've got the guns, the young man said. If they try anything, we'll kill them all.

But no one wanted to finish off Aristide alone.

Cowards, the young man said. He braced himself, aiming.

At that moment, Aristide felt movement behind him. There was some kind of commotion, and the older man who had been at his back stepped out from behind Aristide and moved in front of the priest, between him and the younger man.

"Nou pa ka fè sa," he said to the young man. "We can't do this."

Why not? asked the young man.

"Because I know him," the man said. "We went to school together. He is a friend."

The young man and his supporters backed off, as if they had been looking for an excuse the whole time. "A friend?"

Aristide opened his eyes briefly to take a look at his defender. He had never seen the man before. And it seemed to him that they could not have been in school together. The man was much older than he.

At four o'clock, the officers came up to Mésidor and said, "We're finished. You are free to go." Although Namphy's men were always claiming that Aristide had an arms cache, that Chavannes had one, they had found no guns in their search, but they didn't care. Whatever they found, they took: all of Aristide's audio and video cassettes, other priests' radios, tape machines, anything of value, papers. They made a list of all the people who were inside the residence with Aristide. Mésidor asked if the people there could be assured of protection upon leaving the church complex, and was told that security could not be guaranteed. "We just cannot promise you full security," said one of the colonels. "I really regret it, but how can we?"

A little while later, a young Salesian teacher who had been with the priests and Chavannes before the search began pulled an old car right up to the door of the residence, and amid a huddle of those present Chavannes got into the front seat between the driver and another priest, and Aristide got in back between two nuns. With no protection for himself or his fugitive passengers, the driver floored the car out of the courtyard and onto Grande Rue without stopping, and they were almost hit by a truck that Chavannes remembers as

bigger than any truck he had ever seen before, barreling down
Grande Rue like another vision of death.

At least thirteen people had been killed at St.-Jean-Bosco, and at
least seventy-seven wounded. According to all accounts, the men
with red armbands were paid seven dollars each plus a bottle of
Barbancourt rum worth three dollars to do their damage. When
hours after the attack began, the police came in and evacuated the
congregants who were still hiding inside the inner courtyard, the
body of a man dressed in white for the Constitution lay face down
in a puddle of blood halfway across the inner courtyard. Wounded
in the attack, he had managed to make it out of the church and
through the sacristy. He had wandered, bleeding, across the courtyard, and then collapsed.

An hour or so before the evacuation, the dark-haired photographer, noticing a lull in the shooting, had broken through a window
in a classroom that faced the outer courtyard, and escaped. She ran
onto Grande Rue with her car keys in her hand, but all that remained
of her rented Charade was a charred heap. There were other cars
parked on Grande Rue, but hers was the only one on the street that
had been burned by Mayor Romain's men. She turned away from it
and ran to the Delmas road, holding her dress together with her
hand. She flagged down a taxi and climbed into the back.

It was reported that toward the end of the siege the Papal Nuncio
had come down from his imposing residence near Boutilliers on the
top of Calvary Mountain. A week before, after the initial attack
against Aristide, the Nuncio's secretary had reportedly refused to
make a statement or to intercede in any way, saying that the assassination attempt was purely political and had nothing to do with the
Church. During the siege and after, the Nuncio and a Haitian bishop
reportedly stayed across the street from St.-Jean-Bosco at the residence of the Salesian Sisters. The Nuncio didn't feel comfortable at
St.-Jean-Bosco even on a normal day. He had never liked Aristide,
and probably did not relish the task of protecting him.

The same afternoon, men wearing red armbands went to two radio
stations, including Radio Soleil, and attacked the buildings with
rocks and gunfire. The next day, September 12, armed men who
had participated in the attack at St.-Jean-Bosco broke into the ma-
ternity ward at University Hospital and forced all the women there
to lift their robes to see whether they had any knife wounds on

their bellies; the men were looking for the pregnant woman whom they had knifed at the church. They wanted to kill her. It was their way of sending the message that nothing was sacred, just in case that message had not already been sent. Fortunately, the woman had been taken to a private hospital up above Pacot, where a cesarean was performed. Both the mother and her baby, a girl, survived, although the child also had multiple injuries from the attack.

The night after the massacre, a group of attackers arrived at the studios of the government-run television station, eager to talk about what they had done and what they planned to do next. They also appeared on Télé-Haïti, the independent station, to repeat what they had said at Télévision Nationale.

They were young people, eighteen to twenty years old. At Télé-Haïti, they sat in comfortable chairs. The attackers looked like a lot of people I had been used to seeing at St.-Jean-Bosco: the big, muscular young man in his sleeveless tee shirt with a bold Chinese design, the young woman with crimped hair and a churchgoing blue dress. As it turned out, many of the men who had organized and participated in the massacre were former congregants. They knew the layout of the church complex. No woman had been noticed among the attackers at the church. Perhaps the girl was brought along to the television studio on a lark, or to get sympathy.

"The battle has just begun," said the big young man in the Chinese tee shirt. This big young man, people from St.-Jean-Bosco later told me, was Gwo Schiller, Big Schiller. He looked familiar; I was fairly certain I had seen him on several occasions in the church courtyard, and at Aristide's masses, too. I noticed that Gwo Schiller had a gold chain around his neck, and a gold watch, both indications that his services might have been bought with gifts.

"We want to put an end to Aristide," Gwo Schiller said. "Listen," he said, fingering his gold medallion. "Any parish that allows Aristide to celebrate a mass, only a bunch of corpses will attend it. It's Father Aristide that makes us do this. As long as we have to hear from this guy, there won't be a place in Port-au-Prince where he can be. He is not worthy to be in the country. . . .

"We're telling Father Aristide, even if he is not scared, we're here at this station to let him know our plans. He may not want to understand us, but our work will be done in this country. He can hide wherever he wants to. We'll find him so we can get our work done. Wherever Aristide appears, there we will kill, we will burn down the church. Whatever church he goes to, only a bunch of corpses will hear him speak. *Nou vle Aristid.* We want Aristide."

Télé-Haïti's interviewer remained silent throughout this speech, which seemed to have been rehearsed, and then turned to the young woman.

"You are a woman," the interviewer said. "As a woman, how can you condone the stabbing of a pregnant woman and the innocent child she was carrying?"

The young woman stared at the interviewer. "That pregnant woman, her baby, they are not innocent," she said. "They were there to hear Aristide. That makes them guilty. Anyone who listens to this Aristide, they deserve what they get. If you were innocent, you'd stay home."

Mayor Romain also had his say. He admitted that among the attackers were many men who worked for him at City Hall, but he denied all responsibility. "They did it for political reasons," he said, "for reasons of conviction." Like the young woman, Romain felt that Aristide deserved what he had gotten. "He preaches violence," the mayor said on Radio Métropole. *"Qui seme le vent,"* he added, *"récolte la tempête."* Who sows the whirlwind reaps the storm.

Aristide, shuttled in the dark and the rain from one hiding place to another that night, was lying restless on a bed in a church residence in Delmas. Chavannes was sleeping on an iron cot next to him. The rain was coming down. The Valium the sisters had given Aristide wasn't working well enough; he dozed and then awoke with a start. He kept seeing the smoke pouring from his church.

At about one in the morning, an urgent whisper awoke Chavannes.

"Chavannes, Chavannes," Aristide said.

"Yes?"

"Was the church burned down completely?"

"Yes."

A few moments of silence. Chavannes dozed off again.

"Chavannes."

"Yes."

"How many are dead?"

"Mésidor said five, but I saw others he didn't. About twelve, I think."

Another silence.

"Do you know their names?"
"No," Chavannes said.
"Oh, my God."

The night of the massacre, Hurricane Gilbert descended on Haiti.
It hit hardest along the coast of the southern peninsula, but its
sweeping winds and dark clouds, green at first, then black as the
storm came in, blew rain down on the capital as well, extinguishing
the embers of St.-Jean-Bosco and putting an end to any further
rampage. Single-handedly, Gilbert averted the burning of Aristide's
boys' new house. The hurricane lay down a slippery floor of water
on the road up to St.-Gérard Church in Carrefour Feuilles near the
Oloffson, and thwarted those who had schemed to attack the chapel.
Gilbert quashed a plan for a night search of the hospital. It slammed
down houses in the slums, and beat against the doors of the National
Palace and City Hall. It shoved boulders off Boutilliers and down
the mountainside, halting the progress of jeeps and trucks and even
armored cars. Up on Calvary Mountain, the storm pelted the Nuncio's residence with bullets of rain, and jolted it with gusts of wind,
but could not get it to budge. Gilbert wrapped himself around the
building where Aristide was trying to sleep, and battered the place,
guarding the door with sheets of Damballah's clean water.

For Aristide, the massacre was just the start of a prolonged crisis.
The afternoon of the attack, some members of the Church hierarchy
—echoing Mayor Romain—had already begun to blame the priest
for the massacre that had taken place at his church, and in his
strained emotional state Aristide worried that in fact he might have
been responsible. All the questions that for years others had posed
about his tactics, his preachings, his passionate relationship with his
parishioners, he began suddenly to ask himself, with a vision before
his eyes of his people screaming and fleeing and of shattered glass
outside the wrought-iron doors of the church. He cried over the
deaths of the congregants—no one yet knew how many. He was not
always in command of his faculties, and to calm him the priests and
nuns around him gave him Valium and other drugs. But the drugs
sometimes brought on delirium. He begged to see his personal doctor, but his request was denied for reasons, he was told, of security.
The afternoon after the attack, he had had presented to him for his

signature a formal letter sent by the regional Salesian order, based in the Dominican Republic, stating that he agreed to be transferred from Haiti. Traumatized and on the verge of nervous collapse, he signed it. Chavannes left him alone in his hiding place on the morning after the massacre. For almost a week, no visits were permitted. He was not allowed to watch television or listen to the radio—again, he was told, for his own sake: the news was too disturbing. Isolated and incommunicado, alone for the most part in his small room, unable to eat or sleep, his head full of the sights and sounds of the bloody siege, Aristide was living in a hell that was, he thought, at least in part of his own devising.

Namphy and Romain had not yet finished their work. They had big plans. They wanted to burn down the cathedral at Cap-Haïtien, burn down the independent radio stations, burn down the independent newspapers. They had a plan to round up journalists and put them in front of a firing squad along with members of the democratic opposition. Exile, they decided, would be the best fate that any progressive priest or nun—Haitian or foreign—could expect. Aristide was still on their hit list. They couldn't believe he had escaped death once again.

Hurricane Gilbert left Haiti as quickly as it had come, heading for Jamaica, and the dark-haired photographer flew out of the country as soon as Gilbert had lifted its dark mantle. She didn't like the idea that Franck Romain knew where she was staying, that her car had been a particular target of his Macoutes. On a sunny Saturday almost a week after the attack on St.-Jean-Bosco, Frank Romain and Namphy—surrounded by photographers and accompanied by his Minister of Information, Colonel Acédius Saint-Louis—paid a visit to Lakou Breya, a bidonville where the General was greeted by his supporters, among them Gwo Schiller, wearing an open-necked shirt to show off his medallion. The President shook Schiller's hand, and someone snapped a picture. In the background a young man was pouring tafia for the President and his men. Schiller and his young friends encircled Namphy, put their arms around him. Jean-Claude, Colachatte, Ti Guito, Elysée, Ti Claude—many of these smiling young men had been there for the attack on the church. Someone snapped another picture. The young men were flattered by the visit of their powerful friend. The General laughed with them, and called them his *"équipe solide,"* his solid team. He congratulated them on "the great service they were going to do for the nation." The visit was broadcast on Télévision Nationale.

A year after the Jean-Rabel massacre and a month before the attack on St.-Jean-Bosco, Brunson McKinley, the American ambassador to Haiti, reluctantly gave an interview to two U.S. human-rights organizations. "Human-rights violations," he said, "are endemic to the Haitian tradition." He was explaining why the embassy so often failed to protest when abuses were committed by the Haitian government and its agents. "It's part of the culture. The way Haitians deal with robbers is stoning them to death. We may not like it, but it's their tradition." Members of the human-rights groups went on to ask him whether repeated attacks on union offices and peasant groups in the countryside were not evidence of a pattern of human-rights abuses on the part of the Haitian government and military.

"Most things that are done by the Haitian government are done by gosh and by golly," he said, "and often by hazard. I don't see any evidence of a policy against human rights, any more than they have a policy about anything else." In any case, he added, "the countryside is out of the control of the Haitian government. It's pretty primitive out there . . . [Since the U.S. Occupation] it's been the law of the jungle out there." Although he said that the embassy was "the biggest human-rights organization in Haiti," he defended its failure to protest numerous abuses by saying, "Anyone can make a statement about human rights. You can't accomplish anything sitting around the Foreign Minister's office. . . . Repetition becomes boring."

Every working day at four-thirty or five o'clock, Ambassador McKinley goes horseback riding at the stables at Delmas 33, in breeches, boots and riding cap.

The week before Namphy paid his visit to Lakou Breya, it had seemed as though the entire country was in hiding. No one went out; travel during the day had become as dangerous as it was at night. Colonel Paul reportedly sent his men to protect St.-Gérard Church against another rumored attack by the san manmans, as the St.-Jean-Bosco attackers had come to be called. On the telephone, even Aristide's closest associates would not pronounce his name. His friends developed a series of nicknames to refer to him; the most popular among them was Ti Kabrit, Little Goat. Very few besides his colleagues and his superiors knew where the Little Goat was hidden.

Rumors of a coup d'état swirled over Port-au-Prince. No one could believe that an attack like the one that had occurred, unparalleled even in Papa Doc's time for its cruelty and bravura, would fail to bring down the regime. If Namphy did not fall, people were saying, his new regime would be the bloodiest yet in Haitian history. General Prosper Avril, the Duvalier adviser who had helped bring Namphy back to power, made a brief visit to Washington that week. He later claimed that he took the trip to bring his children back to school in the States after their summer vacation, but many believed that the General had gone for an emergency consultation with the State Department. By Saturday he had returned. He got back in plenty of time to see Namphy and Gwo Schiller slapping each other on the back on Télévision Nationale.

"Turn your ass in whatever direction you like," Schiller and his friends told Namphy on Télévision Nationale. "The country is yours." Namphy gave the cameras the V-for-victory sign, with a big smile spread across his face. Viewers watched in shock. No one knew what would happen next, but everyone expected some kind of explosion. From one moment to the next, as the Little Goat had said in his sermon, anything could happen.

After he finished accepting the praise of his colleagues at Lakou Breya, Namphy got into his Mercedes and headed back toward the palace. It was almost five o'clock on September 17, 1988. Information Minister Saint-Louis was riding back to the palace in the presidential motorcade, and he reportedly knew something Namphy didn't, which was that the General's welcome back there was not going to be as warm as the one his boys had accorded him at Lakou Breya. When they got to the palace, Namphy was arrested, Romain fled, and heavy-arms fire started to sound in the street surrounding the presidential residence. Coup d'état, as simple as it could be. Several hours later, an armored vehicle pulled up to the palace grounds, and Namphy and his wife and daughter were hurried on board and driven to the airport. Government television and radio continued to broadcast scenes from Lakou Breya as the gunfire roared. There was the General, again and again, giving the V sign.

The coup of September 17 was officially credited to the noncommissioned officers and enlisted men of the Army, in particular those same sergeants from the Presidential Guard who had been responsible for overthrowing Manigat in June. Rumor had it that at one point Sergeant Joseph Hébreux, reportedly a leader of the noncoms, was selected as the next head of state. Hébreux, a small young man, twenty-seven years old, was reported to have burst into tears several minutes after being chosen, and to have sobbed that he was not capable of such a task. Later, it was assumed that these rumors were deliberately fabricated by the man who finally became President. At two in the morning, with sporadic bursts of gunfire going off in the background, Hébreux made the first statement from the new government. "We, the noncommissioned officers of the Presidential Guard who organized this coup d'état, have chosen Lieutenant General Prosper Avril as President." Avril, Hébreux continued, was "the most honest officer in the Haitian armed forces."

Avril then took the microphone. "The soldiers of the Presidential Guard," he said in French, addressing the international community rather than the Haitian people, "sick and tired of the way in which the country has been governed since February 7, 1988 [the date of Leslie Manigat's inauguration], were forced once again to take action." At their request, he declared, he found himself "forced to accept the presidency of the military government." At ten that morning, Avril, Hébreux, Colonel Jean-Claude Paul and Carl-Michel Nicolas, chief of staff of the Army, appeared on the steps of the palace and stood at attention as they were given a twenty-one-gun salute. A photograph taken at the event shows Paul swaggering a bit in front of the rest. A tighter shot shows Avril and Hébreux saluting. Avril's elbow is in Hébreux's face, and the sergeant's helmet is so big it makes his head and neck look like a mushroom on a stick.

The entire nation was flabbergasted, confused. Prosper Avril? That old Duvalierist? The soldiers of the Presidential Guard? What was this coup? Where did it really come from, the men or their military masters? What did it mean? When Namphy came back to power, the people had had an idea of what it would mean for them: nothing good. But this was different, and the demands of the men who had supposedly directed this coup, the *ti soldats*—little soldiers, as they were quickly dubbed by the people—were not what Haitians had come to expect from the Army.

There were many surprises among the nineteen demands released by the ti soldats in the hours following the coup. They wanted all officers who were serving past retirement age to be retired immediately; that meant all of François Duvalier's men. They wanted all paramilitary groups abolished; they asked for an end to the recent practice of bringing former Tontons Macoute and other hangers-on into the Army as armed "attachés." The ti soldats also demanded that the Casernes Dessalines discontinue its practice of arming civilians, a clear reference to Colonel Paul's recent habit of enlisting attachés in his corps. They demanded the separation of the Army and the police, and the elimination of inhumane police practices.

But they did not stop with the Army and the police. They sought to uproot corruption in the various agencies of the government, and asked for the appointment of able ministers who would not simply sit behind their desks and collect their paychecks. They called for the restoration of the 1987 Constitution, complete with the famous Article 291 barring Duvalierists from seeking public office for ten years. They sought a draft for the Army that would eliminate the practice of recruiting Macoutes into the ranks. They asked that all cars be forced to keep the driver's window down, so that Army patrols could see who was at the wheel and not be shot at unawares. And they demanded an end to the harassment of three Air Force enlisted men who were members of Aristide's congregation.

One ti soldat went to Radio Soleil's headquarters to elaborate on the nineteen demands. "The movement of the seventeenth of September," he said in Creole, referring to the coup, "is a people's movement. The little soldiers are on the people's side, we are men of the people, we live in the bidonvilles with the people. The hierarchy of the Army is corrupt. They have enriched themselves at our expense, at the expense of the people. They live in big villas, they have several houses, they take trips to foreign countries, while we the enlisted men live in shanties and can't even have a refectory in our barracks.

"The last straw, really, was the attack on St.-Jean-Bosco," he continued. "This we could not accept, that the Haitian people would perceive the Haitian Army as accomplices in such an act. It was intolerable, we could not hold our heads up in front of our brothers. To attack a church while the priest is saying mass: no, we could not accept this. We were already ready to move, we knew we had to move, and after St.-Jean-Bosco we moved. Namphy could not defy us. We are the majority. The armed majority. We are on the people's side."

Unlike the pronouncements of Gwo Schiller on Télévision Nationale the week before, this little soldier's speech was obviously unrehearsed, and it heartened the Haitians who heard it. And almost everyone heard it. "This," said the Senatorial Candidate, "is what was supposed to happen in the days after Duvalier left. This is what we wanted to hear from the Army: that they wouldn't shoot their brothers anymore."

One of the few Haitians who did not hear the little soldier on Radio Soleil was Aristide, still not permitted to listen to the radio. It was not until two days after it happened that he heard of the coup d'état that had, in all likelihood, saved his life. By the time he heard about it, crowds from La Saline had already dechouked several of the men who had participated in the attack against St.-Jean-Bosco. *"Viv Titid!"* they shouted as they burned the bodies of Gwo Schiller and Colachatte—the man who had reportedly stabbed the pregnant woman. They burned the bodies out in front of the church, on Grande Rue, next to the skeleton of the dark-haired photographer's car, on a pyre of wood and old tires. Long live Aristide, they yelled. Two days after the coup, seven of the men with red armbands had been killed, and their bodies subsequently burned in front of the church. Little red fires in tires, as Aristide had said in that controversial speech in the summer of 1987 at the reopening of the CATH labor union's headquarters.

As usual, the Little Goat had accurately foretold the future.

The foreign journalists descended once again. Like the Haitian people, they could not figure out what was going on. They were expecting a countercoup; the U.S. State Department, publicly quite cautious on the subject of Avril and the ti soldats, was telling journalists that a countercoup might follow swiftly on the heels of this last upset. The journalists thought that Colonel Paul might launch an attack against Avril. After all, in the hours after the coup, the government's spokesman had announced that Paul was to be the new head of the Haitian armed forces, but this appointment, which caused panic in the State Department, had never come to pass. The State Department could not believe that a new Haitian government, desperate for the restoration of U.S. aid, would name as head of the Army a man wanted by the U.S. on drug-trafficking charges. The journalists thought that Paul had demanded the position in return for his support of the coup, and that now, realizing that he was not going to be given the job, he would strike back.

Haitians, on the other hand, speculated that the ti soldats, perhaps unhappy with the choice of Avril as President, might bestir themselves once again to get rid of him. The Army was still in turmoil, they reasoned, and Avril—with his long Duvalierist record and his palatial house up near Pétionville in Juvenat—was certainly an unlikely choice for a people's movement within the ranks. But the countercoup, if it was to come, failed to materialize quickly enough for the foreign journalists to catch it. Instead, within the week, Avril had retired fifty-seven of the Army's top-ranking officers, including former Information Minister Saint-Louis and Chief of Staff Carl-Michel Nicolas. Sometimes the retirement was achieved by presidential decree; but on other occasions there were mutinies within the ranks against commanders, and pitched battles, and scenes of men bringing their officers handcuffed to the central military headquarters across from the palace. All over the country, barracks full of sergeants were kicking out their commanders and throwing them into jail. For a few days, it felt as though the country were in the midst of a revolution.

Franck Romain and his men and his family were holed up at the residence of the Dominican ambassador. Two of the mayor's homes had been dechouked by the people. Namphy's properties had received similar treatment. Namphy and his wife and daughter had arrived in Santo Domingo and were staying at the modern Dominican Concorde Hotel in the same suite Leslie Manigat had occupied when he was deposed. Haitians called it the Presidential Suite. According to an account in *Haïti Observateur,* while Namphy wept over his lost power upstairs, Dominican journalists picketed the hotel, asking for the arrest of the man they held responsible for the killing of Dominican cameraman Carlos Grullon at Ruelle Vaillant. In Port-au-Prince, a joke was making the rounds: Namphy arrives at the Concorde and runs into Manigat in the lobby. The two men embrace, and Manigat says, "Well? Did you bring my toothbrush?" Namphy responds, "Damn. No. I forgot. You know what else? I forgot mine too." And Manigat says, "Well, never mind. We'll just have to wait for Prosper."

Prosper Avril. It was a beautiful name, and he was a clever man, a survivor. A few years after he graduated from the Military Academy, one of the officers who was in his class had said, watching Avril's upward progress, "There are three things I fear: God, François Duvalier and Prosper Avril." Jean-Claude Duvalier felt much the same way. Ever since Papa Doc, Avril had managed the finances of the Duvalier family; he knew where every penny was, according to some in his circle. During Jean-Claude's rule, the young Duvalier was always trying to squeeze out from under Prosper's thumb, but Prosper made a friend out of Michèle Bennett (she thought he was "classy"), and after that his continued position was more or less assured. After Duvalier fell, the deposed dictator was reported to have spoken to Namphy from his exile in France. "Watch Avril," Duvalier told him. "He's your biggest threat." One of Manigat's many mistakes had been his order demoting Avril.

So it was not easy to imagine that Prosper Avril was the useful tool of the ti soldats. It was not easy to imagine Prosper struggling for democratic reform. It was not easy to imagine Prosper "deduvalierizing" the country. Yet the image we saw every day in the newspapers, every night on Télévision Nationale and on Télé-Haïti, was that of Avril and Hébreux, the President and the ti soldat, attending all public functions together, having discussions with opposition figures and religious leaders, together. When the New York Times, the Miami Herald and the Los Angeles Times went to Avril's house up in Juvenat for his first big interview with the foreign press, Hébreux came, too. Some said that Hébreux was there to keep an eye on Avril for the ti soldats. Others said that Hébreux was virtually Avril's bodyguard, his servant. "Is Avril Hébreux's Hostage, or is Hébreux Avril's?" read the headline in Haïti en Marche. The foreign press dubbed the odd couple "the Prez and the Sarge," and made jokes about the two men trying to sleep together. "Do you think," one American journalist asked me, "that Hébreux wears that helmet to bed?" The Haitian and French press created a new nickname for the President: Poisson d'Avril. In French it means April Fool. Avril and the sergeants: it looked like the old Haitian politique de doublure, understudy politics. But there was one problem. You couldn't tell who was the understudy and who was the star.

There were no more masses at St.-Jean-Bosco. No one was around. I had to beg a boy to let me through the locked gates. The courtyard was desolate, littered with spent shells. The burned-out cars of the parishioners lay like old dead oxen in a heap in front of the yellow church, now blackened and showing some of its former pink facade. The roof of St.-Jean-Bosco had fallen in, all of the pews had burned, as well as the altar. Those windows that hadn't been shattered by rocks had burst from the heat. The fire had hollowed out the church.

Cinders crunched beneath my shoes. The men with red armbands had chopped to bits the statue of Saint John Bosco that had stood to the right of the altar. His well-combed head, solemn face and black robes were gone, and all that remained were his black shoes and the shoes of the figure of the orphan boy who had stood next to him, looking up. They were like the shoes left behind in the street after a panic, a *kouri*.

The sacristy was destroyed as well, and the cabinet where Waldeck had stored that big old manioc. I remembered Aristide turning this way and that in the sacristy among the crowd of his congregants, after mass; the turbulent throng that encircled him, and the sound of the women's shiny polyester dresses as they pushed to get near enough to him to say hello. The doorway where the three priests had once stood, waiting for him with their inexhaustible patience, was now barricaded with cinderblocks.

Although he was finally in communication with a few of his friends, and had heard the news of the coup, Aristide was still hidden, and the order that he had signed still stood: He was to leave Haiti. On September 25, the Sunday after Namphy fell, youths from St.-Jean-Bosco and St.-Gérard held a morning mass at St.-Gérard. On the walls near the church, fresh graffiti had been painted: *"Aristid ou lanmò."* Aristide or death. *"Aba tout monsenyè makout."* Down with all Macoute monsignors. *"Nons-lan pou Wom, Titid pou Lasalin."* The Nuncio belongs in Rome, Titid belongs in La Saline. The mood was jubilant, as though the youths had done the coup themselves. Everyone was thankful not to be dead. They were hoping, some of the St.-Jean-Bosco kids told me, that Aristide would show up—they had invited him to the mass through an intermediary. During the sermon, the priest used the image of a child who was leading a bull by a rope. The child, he said, was the ti soldat, and the bull was the hierarchy of the Army. In front of the altar stood an empty chair with a white cassock draped over it. This was Aristide's chair.

When the mass ended, the youths, disappointed that Aristide had not come and concerned over rumors they had heard about his deteriorating condition, announced that they were going to lead a march to his hiding place. They had planned this tactic in the event that the priest did not come. They invited all present to join them; it would be a long march, all the way from St.-Gérard to Pétionville. It was a hot day, but it was always a hot day in Haiti. The road was long, but then the road is always long in Haiti. I was used to it by

now. I drank Pepsis and ate bites of the sandwiches offered to me
by the foreign journalists who led the march in their cars. Behind
them, at the front of the long, snaking parade, a young seminarian
carried a cross, and the two young women flanking him held the
Bible up and open to the Gospels. The crowd of about three thousand knelt at St.-Jean-Bosco for their fallen friends, and then again
at Ruelle Vaillant, in memory of the victims of election day. Every
once in a while, priests who were in contact with Aristide would
drive down to the march in their jeeps to note our progress. They
were trying to make sure that Aristide would be wherever it was we
were going, whenever it was we got there. They did not want a riot
on their hands. It took us three and a half hours to get to Pétionville,
with people from the streets joining us as we went. The whole time,
we were terrified that somehow the Tontons Macoute would make a
reappearance and attack the march. Later it was reported that Colonel Paul had told the organizers of the march that he would ensure
their security. The Colonel was trying to make new friends wherever
he could. And there were no incidents along our way. Only Waldeck,
sucking on a cherry fresco, made a scene, shouting at all the foreign
journalists, begging for *tennis.*

The crowd surged through the Pétionville market and into the
courtyard of the Salesian residence. *"Ba-nou Titid!"* they screamed.
Give us Aristide! Among the crowd there were Aristide's youths,
but there were also market women, simple commerçantes, tailors
and handymen, ironworkers, employees of the flour mill, charcoal
vendors, cane cutters, men who pulled brouettes, mechanics, maids
and hatmakers, borlette boys and soldiers out of uniform—Aristide's
congregation, all of whom had walked the whole way on the hot
asphalt of John Brown, some of them barefoot, like Waldeck.

Then Aristide appeared, on a third-story balcony. *"Min pwo-
fet-la!"* shouted an older woman in black. There's the prophet! And
she fell in a faint into the crowd. Aristide was supported on either
side by priests. He walked shakily. His white guayabera hung from
his shoulders as though a wire hanger were all that was holding it
up. His cheeks were hollow, and his eyes closed. When he raised a
hand to salute the crowd, his arm had to be held at the elbow. He
had no strength. He stood at the edge of the balcony, holding on to
a ledge, and the crowd fell to its knees. "Let the Holy Spirit descend
on us," they sang, "we have one mission for Haiti." Tears dropped
from his closed eyes.

I had seen him like this before, traumatized, but never so badly.
I watched, thinking it must be some kind of act. Either he was dying

of some heartbreak, or some poison, or it must be an act. Everyone knew by now that he had signed the document authorizing his own departure from Haiti. That would be enough of a heartbreak to make him sick, I thought. But still, his extreme frailty as he made his way across the balcony seemed inconceivable. Someone else might be broken by such an ordeal, but not this man. Any second now, I told myself, he'll open his eyes and speak, and it will be as if nothing had happened. Even if his body is weak, his voice will be strong. That was how it always had been. After all, it had been two weeks since the massacre. He had had time to collect his wits.

But his friends in the Ti Legliz told me that Aristide wasn't ready for this emotional scene, all those people—it all reminded him of the last time he had said mass. That wasn't something he wanted to remember, they said, and it wasn't something he could forget. And, later, he told me that he hadn't wanted to appear at all; apparently he did not want to do the Church the favor of calming his people. He looked like a life-sized puppet up there, being held on either side by priests, his arm held up in the air to salute the crowd. And that was, perhaps, how he meant it to look, to send a message that this was not the real Aristide.

He spoke, and we couldn't hear his words. Even on the tapes that the radio stations made from close up, his voice was faint, full of tears, tremulous. "The Lord be with you," he told the crowd, who could not hear him, but who listened in silence nevertheless. "Those who have fallen are with us, too. Don't be discouraged. The day will come when we will all advance together. Our work has just begun. The cleanup has just begun. I can't talk now, but later I will be able to say more."

In the crowd, women sobbed. After listening to the statement on their tape recorders, journalists turned to one another.

"What does he mean, 'I can't talk now'?" asked a Haitian reporter. "Does he mean he isn't physically able to, or that they won't let him, or that some problem he has stops him from saying everything he has in mind?"

I shook my head. It had been a discouraging sight.

"I think he means all of those things," the reporter said. "That boy's in trouble."

But we couldn't get near him. He was in deep hiding. Minutes after the crowd dispersed, his guardians whisked him away.

· · ·

Later that day, the Bishops' Conference released a message on the coup d'état and its implications. In the message, Haiti's ten bishops gave their support to the coup and to General Avril, and called for the *"déracinement du Macoutisme,"* the uprooting of Macoutism. *Déracinement* is French for dechoukaj, and most Haitians were pleasantly surprised to hear the Church, which in 1986 had called for a halt to the Dechoukaj, now supporting it. As is usual with the bishops, however, there were nuances of phrasing. Uprooting of Macoutism is not the same as uprooting Macoutes. The policy that the bishops' message recommended included

> the disarming of the Macoutes and the exclusion from government service of all who in any guise contributed actively to the consolidation and perpetuation of the dictatorial system during the past thirty years. . . .
>
> But we cannot be content only to disarm the Macoutes, we must also establish adequate judicial structures. To avoid violence, the people must be able to achieve their demands for justice.
>
> Is not this the best method to ensure that their demands for justice are not transformed into demands for vengeance, a vengeance which is being sought today in a manner strangely similar to that of the torturers of yesterday? . . .

The message—which also included a long-awaited condemnation of the attack on the Sunday mass celebration at St.-Jean-Bosco, without mentioning the name either of the church or of the priest who was celebrating the mass—ended with a call to foreign aid organizations to step up their donations to Haiti. On first reading, the message seemed to be an admission from the hierarchy that the principles of Ti Legliz had triumphed in Haiti: Dechoukaj, a restatement of the anti-Duvalierist Article 291 of the Constitution, a demand for justice for the people. It was like reading an expurgated passage from one of Aristide's sermons. Still, it was hard to take the message seriously. As the French news agency Agence France-Presse pointed out in its dispatch that day, "Nonetheless, the fate reserved by the Catholic hierarchy for the leader of the Ti Legliz, Father Jean-Bertrand Aristide, reveals the increasing depths of the contradictions between the Church's progressive and conservative factions." It was certainly odd, as everyone including Agence France-Presse noted, that it had taken the hierarchy two weeks to condemn the attack on St.-Jean-Bosco. Of course, the reasons for the delay were obvious. It was difficult to condemn such an attack on a priest if at the same time you were planning to kick him out of the country.

I was going to meet a friend who lived on Martin Luther King, and I was running into the usual dilemma. The shortcut to her house ran right in front of Claude Raymond's. It was always dangerous driving past there; people walking and driving by had been shot at. On November 29 a passerby had been badly wounded by a bullet from Raymond's. The Tontons Macoute were always predictable, in a way. In victory they used their guns; in defeat, as now, they used their guns. On the other hand, the shortcut was fast and I was eager to see my friend. She'd spent the whole day on another long march, walking from St.-Jean-Bosco up to the Papal Nuncio's house near Boutilliers with thousands of other young people. *"Sa pa fè-m anyen si Ligonde ale,"* they sang as they marched. *"Aleluya, Aristid kenbe."* I don't care if Ligondé leaves, they were saying. Hallelujah, Aristide must stay. Ligondé, the Duvalierist Archbishop of Port-au-Prince, was no friend of Aristide's.

Soldiers defending the Nuncio's residence had met the marchers up in front of its courtyard on Calvary Mountain, but the Nuncio had refused to see the youths. *"Viv Legliz Popilè,"* shouted the crowd kneeling outside the Nuncio's house, loudly enough so that anyone in the neighborhood could hear. Long live the People's Church. After that long day, my friend wasn't feeling well—blisters, fever, sunstroke. It was five o'clock. The storm would start soon; for hours already, the clouds coming over dark and fast from above the Nuncio's had looked as though they intended to put on a dramatic performance. I wanted to get out to my friend's house and then I wanted to get back. The shortcut was fast, and I took it.

Raymond's house is around a bend, and I slowed down as I came around the curve so that I could see whatever was to be seen before I was in its midst. There wasn't much; just an Army truck, and three soldiers out in front of Raymond's barrière, which was uncharacteristically shut. One of the soldiers watched me go by, while the others peeped timidly around the barrière. A gun went off inside, a warning to the soldiers. I sped up.

I came home early that night, and then the rains started up. At around ten, I heard gunfire coming from near Raymond's. Heavy arms, machine guns, a grenade. I called the Disco Doctor, whose house sits right behind Raymond's.

"Did you hear that?" I asked him.

"It's my neighbor," he said, laughing.

"What's happening?"

"I just got home," he told me. The Disco Doctor still kept fairly late hours, in spite of the dangers. It was a habit he had acquired in the old days. On this night, however, he had been held up by the rain.

"I had the usual debate with myself after it stopped raining," he said, "you know, whether to go past Raymond's? But I did, I was driving pretty fast, naturally, and suddenly there were two soldiers in my path with their rifles out. I stopped, and they made me get out and identify myself. I was terrified. You know, the Army hasn't had such a good reputation until the last couple of weeks. They were terrified, too. They thought I was one of Raymond's guys, I guess they thought I was going to mow them down or something. But when they saw who I was, just me, you know, little and inoffensive, they said, 'Okay, Doc, we have no problem with you. Go home, fast. *Nous essayons de mettre de l'ordre dans le pays.* We are trying to enforce order in the country.' Well, I split, fast, and now war has broken out over there."

While the gunfire continued over at Raymond's, a friend who lived in Delmas called to say that a shootout between the Army and Jean-Claude Paul's attachés was going on at Delmas 19, where the Duvalierists had the headquarters of their party, the Rassemblement des Démocrates pour la République, Democrats for the Republic. My friend called it a pitched battle. "Lots of gunfire, lots," he said.

Then the Disco Doctor called back. "Have you heard? Avril just retired Jean-Claude Paul. Incredible, *n'est-ce pas?*" He laughed. "And not only retired him, but announced the terms of his pension. Nine hundred eighty dollars a month. Can you believe it? For a man who runs our cocaine business? Ah, the long arm of the State Department. Maybe now that Paul is out of the Army, Avril can hand the poor thing over to the Americans. Avril is really going for that U.S. aid. I bet Reagan is happy tonight."

But although Paul was now retired, he still posed a thorny problem for the Americans and Avril. First, Haiti has no extradition treaty with the United States. Second, since the latest coup, Paul had seemed to be gaining some measure of popular support. In the big demonstration in support of the ti soldats that had taken place just a few days earlier, the crowd had passed by the Casernes Dessalines and chanted Colonel Paul's praise. Waldeck was there, working the crowd, singing along with them, trying to sell a roll of film he had just begged from a French photographer. He was sniffing turpentine. *"Ba-nou Polo,"* sang the crowd. *"Nap boule Meriken-yo."* Give us Polo; we're going to burn the Americans. Waldeck sang along with them, happily.

No one knew why this sudden diversion of the crowd had occurred, although it was presumed that Polo had infiltrated the throng with his men. Until a few weeks before, Paul had been considered one of the people's greatest enemies, and no one would have sung his praises outside the Casernes or anywhere else. No one had forgotten his suspected role in the massacre at Ruelle Vaillant. On the other hand, his protection of St.-Gerard and the youths' march for Aristide had helped somewhat to begin his rehabilitation in the eyes of the people. That, plus the U.S. government's continuing demand that Paul be neutralized before any talks on aid resumption could begin, had increased Paul's stature in the eyes of many of his fellow Haitians. They simply did not like the idea of the Americans indicting a Haitian and demanding that he be brought to justice. After all, Paul's alleged crimes had been committed in Haiti, not in the United States.

It was suspected that some of Paul's men in civilian clothes, perhaps with the support of the Communist Party, which had recently issued a statement in Paul's favor, had led the crowd to the Casernes that day, and begun the chanting. Paul and the Haitian Communists: another odd coupling. At any rate, Polo had agreed to his own retirement, perhaps because it was presented as preferable to extradition, or execution. It was said that he cried when he signed the papers. These were tough times; all of Haiti's strong men were crying.

Some of the Macoutes were gone. General Williams Régala, the number-two man in Namphy's first government, had fled to Miami. Franck Romain was still in the Dominican ambassador's residence, the subject of a feigned battle between the Dominican Republic, which wanted to give him asylum, and Avril, who at first refused to grant Romain a safe conduct out of the country because the General feared a huge popular outcry. Except for his brief appearance at Namphy's reinstallation, Clovis Désinor had been silent since Manigat's election, and his house and his person had so far been spared the indignities of dechoukaj. Every day, journalists drove past Désinor's house on Rue Rivière to see whether it was still there. Claude

Raymond, people said, was in Seoul for the Olympics. A Haitian, Dieudonné Lamothe, was participating in the marathon competition. At any rate, Raymond was nowhere to be seen. Jean-Claude Paul had retreated up to his ex-wife's house above Boutilliers, in Fermathe, near the Baptist mission. Paul's ex-wife, who had also been indicted in Florida for conspiring with her ex-husband and his brother Antonio to bring cocaine into the United States, had fled to Haiti months before.

General Avril had announced that his government would welcome back René Poirier, the stubborn Canadian priest who had refused to participate in the parades and celebrations during Namphy's summer tour of the southern peninsula, and who had been brusquely exiled by Namphy a month before his fall. It was a wise move from General Avril, conciliatory to both the hierarchy, who had never objected to Father Poirier's gentle progressivism, and to Ti Legliz, who had made him into a symbol after his exile. Still, it came at an awkward time for the hierarchy. While the government was welcoming back one priest, the Church was trying to exile another. Aristide was already the most important figure in Ti Legliz; he was fast becoming a symbol of all the newly outspoken progressive movements throughout the country. The Church was dragging its feet in setting a public deadline for his departure. Both the civil and ecclesiastical authorities were concerned that any deadline would set off a wave of popular protest and destabilize the new government.

The stability of the Avril government, as all Haitians were aware, was fragile. As an institution, the Army had proven over the past two years to be full of fissures—it was a collection of gangs run by a collection of individual gwo neg. Within each gang there were divisions, as well. Faced with popular protest, the whole lacy network could come apart.

If it did, the Church, that other grand Haitian institution, would not be able to come to the aid of the Army as a healthy, united front, the way it had during the 1986 Dechoukaj. The hierarchy and the Ti Legliz were now farther apart than ever, and the bishops' two-week delay in commenting on the St.-Jean-Bosco massacre had not helped heal the wounds. Equally, the conditions of Aristide's hiding, which had been dictated by certain members of the hierarchy—his isolation, the pressure that was put on him to sign the letter of removal, the blame that had been heaped upon him—had shocked his youthful parishioners and his friends among the priests and nuns of Ti Legliz.

Since the coup, Legliz Popilè, or the People's Church, had become more vocal. Using Aristide as their symbol, its young activists, most of them lay people, had initiated a series of protests that disturbed even the fiery priest. The youths could not be reconciled to the idea that men like Archbishop Ligondé, a *sou-sou diktatè,* as the youths called him—a suck-up to dictators—was allowed to continue in his august position while Aristide, who spoke, the youths said, on behalf of the people, who had almost been killed on behalf of the people, was being forced out of the country. To these youths, this seeming contradiction was proof of the Church's corruption, its participation in the corrupt system that made Haiti such a bad place to live in.

They were lay people, and, unlike Aristide, they did not see the use of quiet diplomacy within the Church. They did not have to weigh the same variables that were part of a priest's formula; they did not have to think, What will happen to me as a priest if I do this, if I do that? The lay people were free to act as they chose, and they did. Learning that Ligondé was to say the first Sunday mass of October at Ste.-Thérèse Church in Pétionville, a group of young people went to protest his presence; a few of them had told me that if they could get their hands on him, they would remove the Archbishop's cassock and miter, since he was not worthy to wear those garments. But Ligondé, who for months had not shown his face for fear of such protests, did not appear, and in his stead came the Papal Nuncio, who was even less popular than Ligondé with the young people within the Church, because he was not Haitian, and because he was so powerful and so conservative, and a representative of a foreign power, the Vatican. As the Nuncio began to say the mass, the lay people started shouting, *"Viv Legliz Popilè!"* The disruption was successful enough to stop the mass until an Army unit arrived and put an end to the protest. The Nuncio was furious, and so was Madame Prosper Avril, who was in Ste.-Thérèse's congregation that day.

The night after Colonel Paul was retired, I went to a party for USAID's agroforestry project up at the end of a long road near my house. The hostess' place was just a few blocks up from the place where Aristide was being hidden. The anthropologists and agroforesters were playing loud soul music; I wondered whether the priest could hear it down where he was. We had vegetable lasagna because agroforesters tend to be vegetarians, and people told stories. Everyone was white and American except for a Haitian secretary. Someone told a story about the night he was out on his lawn with his little son during Namphy's second regime and a soldier came by and pointed a gun at them. Another told about the time he was arrested for driving without his license and put into the Pétionville prison for eight hours. Peter Welle, who ran the nurseries in the Northwest province, was there, too, listening to the chat. He seemed depressed, and kept asking people whether Avril was any good. Who is in charge of this government? Peter wanted to know. Are the ti soldats any good? What is Aristide up to? No one could respond to Peter's satisfaction.

They were all figuring out what they would do after Haiti, as if Haiti were, somehow, finished. One was going to teach in the States, others were heading for Africa or Washington. They all shook their heads when we heard gunfire, and made jokes about Namphy's eventual return to the palace. Peter was quiet that night. He wanted to stay in Haiti, and he was moving up in the ranks at CARE. But he was finding his new situation disturbing. CARE had rented him a house in town, moved him and his wife and their three kids out of Passe-Reine, where they had lived next to Joyce and Eldon at the Baptist mission. Now they had a big place up on Calvary Mountain near the Nuncio's. More and more, Peter's was a desk job, but what he loved was what they all called "the field." He didn't know how to handle the situation. He didn't want to become one of those arrogant bureaucrats who doesn't know what is happening in the countryside.

"Come on, you understand what they're doing with Peter," another agroforestry worker said to me. "When you get too good at something, they pull you out. Peter really understood the Northwest, the project, CARE's position. He was getting too into it, and they want to pull him away—they see his potential for CARE, but they also see that anyone that bright and committed and, above all, involved, might get radicalized. They want to spare him that fate, and also keep making use of him. They think maybe if he becomes a big shot, he'll forget about Jean-Rabel and the rest of the mess." He looked over at Peter, who was standing next to his wife and looking out over the city in the direction of the gunfire. "That's the way all these bureaucrats think, you know? I think they're wrong about Peter, though," he said.

. . .

The Little Goat was still under wraps. Although goats are famous in Haiti for talking almost all the time (hence the nickname), this one did not want to speak until he had a definite word from the Church as to his future in Haiti or elsewhere. He was hoping that pressure from Ti Legliz as well as from other sectors would work to invalidate the order he had signed on the day of the massacre, and he was asking for a new document, one that would specify the terms of his continuing work at St.-Jean-Bosco. He couldn't bear to live any longer knowing that at any moment he might be moved. He wanted assurances, and the historical moment—the fall of Namphy and the rise of the progressive ti soldats—seemed to have strengthened his hand considerably.

On October 3, the Little Goat got what he wanted, more or less. Radio Soleil announced that Father Jacques Mésidor, head of the Salesian order in Haiti, had sent Father Jean-Bertrand Aristide— "now known as The Prophet," commented Radio Soleil—a letter authorizing his return to St.-Jean-Bosco "to continue his work there." For how long? *"Mystè,"* Aristide said. A mystery. In any case, at the moment there was no "there" there, but already Ti Legliz and the fund-raising arm of Aristide's Lafanmi Selavi were planning the reconstruction of the church. Father Mésidor's message seemed to put an end to Aristide's long nightmare. Encouraged, the Little Goat set about becoming, once again, Aristide.

Two days later, Radio Soleil played an extraordinary tape over the airwaves. It rocked the country and caused extreme consternation in Avril's circle. No one talked about another thing in the days that followed. It was Aristide, and this time it sounded like him. Bitter, brilliant Creole that also made people laugh at its cleverness, its wordplay, its riddles and rhymes.

"The victims of the massacre of St.-Jean-Bosco," Aristide said, "were bathed in love, and they fell like Jesus in order to liberate the country. There is no greater proof of love than accepting to die for those you love. In prayer, I continue to kneel before the courage of all of those victims, who live in my heart, my blood, my memory. On Sunday, the eleventh of September, our prayers rose up. Seven days later, grace descended. On the eighteenth of September, grace appeared like the morning light of an Easter Sunday: the Work of God. God is light. His light is rising up, and the cleanup has begun. . . ."

He congratulated the "valiant soldiers" on the coup, and reminded Avril that because of his Duvalierist past the people did not trust him. He asked the General and the ti soldats to carry on with the

"cleanup" and suggested that before the anniversary of Dessalines'
death on the seventeenth of October—"one month exactly after the
seventeenth of September"—Avril close Fort Dimanche, bring
Franck Romain to justice, and remove the Duvalierist director of the
government's television and radio stations. "General-President,"
Aristide said, "it's your turn." He added that if trials of those who
had already been dechouked did not begin soon, "we will have to say
that we have been taken for April Fools." *Nou met di nou pran nan
Poisson d'Avril,* the same pun people all over the country were using
to refer to the likelihood of Avril's duplicity.

"I am here to cry out to you," Aristide said in conclusion, "that
we have come from far away in order to arrive at a remote destination. We have left the ravine of death in order to arrive at the top of
the mountain of life. Are we there yet? No. Do we want to get there?
Yes. Can we get there? Yes. . . . When we get there, we will sow
the will of the people. The will of the people is the will of God.
When we get to that distant point, we will have made a worthy
revolution; we will have upset the table of privilege so that we too
will be welcome to sit and eat. We want to get there, we can get
there, we will get there, in the name of Jesus who has helped us
come all that great distance to arrive at our rightful destination,
amen."

Aristide's speech was a public pronouncement of what the people of La Saline had been telling me ever since the coup: *"Nap
gade-yo."* We're watching them. Immediately after the speech was
aired, some people said that although it was brilliant and moving,
the priest had made a huge mistake. He had set a deadline for Avril:
October 17, Dessalines Day. "In Haiti," these people said, "priests
do not set deadlines for generals. He is asking to be rebuffed," they
said. "And if Avril fails to meet his deadline, Aristide is the one who
will look like an April Fool. He'll be finished."

But there was more to the speech than that. Those people thought
that Aristide's characteristic intransigence was meant to menace and
threaten Avril. Indeed, in a way, the speech was a warning, but
what Aristide was asking for was what the people of La Saline—and
everyone else—had been asking for in the past weeks. A clarification.
Was Avril in charge of this government, or was it being run by
progressive soldiers? Let's not sit around and wait to find out, the
priest was saying. We'll give them a deadline to do certain specific
things, to show their goodwill. The demands he put forth in the
speech were demands that had been voiced ever since Duvalier had

left: Close Fort Dimanche. Judge the criminals. Get rid of the Macoutes in government. A President who wanted to achieve those
goals could begin quite rapidly. Aristide's threat was implicit: If you
do not show your goodwill by Dessalines Day, who knows what will
happen?

A few days after the cassette was broadcast, the bishops delivered
two messages. One message stated that they themselves were united
and that they supported the Nuncio, an unprecedented statement
that merely made most people believe that deep divisions existed
among the ten bishops and between the bishops and the Nuncio.
The other message was a frontal attack on the People's Church,
which, the bishops said, was made up of a bunch of agitators who
wanted a church with no hierarchy, no bishops, no Pope. We are in
a period of deep crisis for the Church, the bishops said. Referring to
the bishops' attack on Legliz Popilè, *Haïti en Marche* commented
later: "The Church has committed suicide."

The bishops were not content to leave it at that. Their ultimate
response to Aristide's message was broadcast on October 11, when
Radio Soleil announced that Aristide had received another letter,
this one from his superiors in Rome, ordering him to leave Haiti by
October 17 at the latest, "a date," as Aristide said laconically in a
brief press release concerning the new order, "that is not like all
other dates, because it is the seventeenth of October." Father Edward Capelletti, a spokesman for the Salesian order, said that the
Salesians would never have issued such a directive without prompt-
ing from the Haitian bishops.

For four days after this last announcement, protesters took to the
streets of Port-au-Prince in some of the largest demonstrations since
Jean-Claude Duvalier's departure. They blocked the road to the
airport, burned tires along the main thoroughfares, and generally
disrupted the life of the city to such an extent that on Dessalines
Day itself Radio Soleil announced that Aristide was still in Haiti. *"Il
se trouve dans l'impossibilité matériel de partir,"* Radio Soleil's announcer said. It is physically impossible for him to leave. Meanwhile, General Avril had announced the closing of Fort Dimanche,
had indicated his intention to try Romain, and had fired the head of
the government-run radio and television stations. Aristide had won
his first round with the new regime, it seemed. But he was still in
hiding.

· · ·

Avril had given in to a few of Aristide's demands, or so it appeared. The General's tenure in the palace, however, was still far from certain. In the game Avril was playing, there were plenty of elements besides Aristide. On the night of October 15, amid rumors of a coup d'état, Avril had had fifteen noncommissioned officers arrested, charging them with an attempted coup. Among those arrested was Sergeant Patrick Beauchard of the Presidential Guard, a man who, according to most reports, had been one of the leaders of the coup d'état of September 17, and who was among the most progressive of the noncommissioned officers. Beauchard, it was said, had led the siege against Raymond's house and the Tontons Macoute headquarters in Delmas the night Colonel Paul was retired. Beauchard, it was said, had organized the daily meetings that had been taking place among the progressive noncommissioned officers who were trying to push Avril into meeting the original nineteen demands of the ti soldats, the progressive demands that had attracted wide popular support for the coup in the days just after Namphy was ousted. Suddenly, Beauchard became the embodiment of the ti soldats' movement, though few had heard of him before. Poor little Sergeant Hébreux was left standing at Avril's side, looking more than ever like the General's right-hand man.

It seemed as though Avril had preempted any coup on Beauchard's part by arresting him along with various noncommissioned officers who had friends among the democratic opposition. But the presidential candidates and other factions in the democratic opposition were not the only ones attempting to seduce or link themselves with one or another bloc within the Army. The fifty-seven and more officers retired by Avril, the Duvalierists and the big Tontons Macoute—everyone in the political class of Port-au-Prince was trying to push someone in the Army forward. No other route to power was available. Elections had failed, the Church was crumbling, the Tontons Macoute organization no longer existed. "The Army has both its feet in politics," wrote *Haïti en Marche* after Avril made his arrests. "Diverse political currents are running through the institution, and until it is proven otherwise, the Army has the only visa stamped for the palace." With all other political and extrapolitical means to power blocked, the Army became the focus of every infight, every ideological battle, every personal vendetta, every power struggle, little or big. It was the kind of situation that often leads to coups and countercoups.

The fact that Avril had remained in power for more than a month in such a chaotic and back-stabbing environment was testimony to his powers of survival. During his long service to the Duvaliers *père et fils* he had apparently learned a few useful lessons. One: Have no pity for weak friends—they will pull you down with them. That may have been one reason Avril got rid of Namphy. Two: Before you dump him, let your predecessor do your dirty work and eliminate as many future enemies as possible. That may have been why Avril waited for the attack on St.-Jean-Bosco and, he may have hoped, Aristide's assassination, before he moved with the ti soldats to kick Namphy out. Three: Get rid of your strongest enemies quickly, effectively, definitively and, if possible, secretly. In this category there were already many examples of how well Avril had learned his catechism, and there would be more. Jean-Claude Paul, for example, though retired, was still in Haiti, capable of creating serious trouble for Avril. His case needed Avril's immediate attention. Four: Get rid of those who brought you to power; they did it once, they will do it again, and the next time not for you. This, perhaps, was the best explanation for Avril's arrests of Sergeant Beauchard and the other noncommissioned officers.

One further explanation of the Beauchard affair existed. Prosper Avril was a Duvalierist; many of his friends and associates were Duvalierists or members of the Haitian elite, or both; he had a strong relationship with the U.S. Embassy. Neither the Duvalierists, the elite, nor the embassy had been particularly pleased with the first pronouncements of the noncommissioned officers after Namphy was deposed. Maybe Avril was following the Duvaliers' fifth lesson: Eliminate your ideological foes. The Duvaliers targeted democrats, and it seemed that Avril, too, was directing his fire in that direction, perhaps under pressure from the Duvalierists who remained in his military entourage.

"Wait till we get hold of Ti Bernard," said Waldeck, showing me the razor blade he had in his hand, dragging it meaningfully across his throat.

"What?" I said. "Why? Where is Ti Bernard, anyway?"

"I don't know," said Ayiti. "We haven't seen him. He's scared."

"But why?" I asked. "You're all safe now."

"Not Ti Bernard," said Waldeck. "Don't you know?"

"No," I said, "Tell me."

"He was a spy for Gwo Schiller," Ayiti said. *"Li se ti san maman."* He's a little bastard.

"We used to see him riding in one of Franck Romain's cars, with

Gwo Schiller," Waldeck said. "Schiller bought him *tennis,* he gave him marijuana." Waldeck looked wistful. His feet were still bare.

"So Ti Bernard told Schiller everything," said Ayiti. "He told him which guys were closest to Titid, who were his bodyguards, everybody's name. Your name, too."

"My name?" I said.

"Yeah," said Waldeck. He looked down at the razor blade, and told me that Schiller knew about me and about the dark-haired photographer.

"What do you mean, he knew about us?" I asked.

"She's lucky to be alive," Waldeck said. "If you had been there, he would have gotten you, too. He knew there were two foreign journalists who were always around."

"He knew your faces, anyway," said Ayiti. "But Ti Bernard told him names. Our names, too. *Si nou jwen ti sanmaman-an, nap boule-l.*" If we find the little bastard, we'll burn him.

"We could have gone along with Schiller, too, for the money, and all those presents," said Waldeck. "But we didn't. We wouldn't do that to Titid."

Like Aristide, poor Ti Bernard was in hiding. He was living in a house near a friend of mine, and she said he cried every day. He hadn't understood what Gwo Schiller was up too. "I don't care about my *tennis* anymore," he told her, pointing to the sneakers that he had stuck in a corner. He was barefoot.

"I didn't know Schiller was going to try to kill Titid and everyone else. I didn't know. *Kounye-a, yap touye-m,*" he said. Now they're going to kill me.

On Christmas and New Year's Day, and on Sundays in the mountains as the weather gets a little cooler—in autumn and in winter—Haitians traditionally eat pumpkin soup for their big midday meal. It's a comforting holiday meal, a thick pumpkin base with chunks of spicy marinated beef and pieces of carrot, potato, manioc and cabbage.

Like any good Haitian, Jean-Claude Paul liked his pumpkin soup, and, driving back to his ex-wife's mountain home one Sunday in early November 1988, he was probably looking forward to the meal. He had just come from visiting his father out in Thomazeau, his hometown and the hometown of General Avril and Sergeant Hébreux. These days, the Colonel had to think of new ways to fill his hours. He missed the Casernes. It was a long ride from Thomazeau to the house up in Fermathe. By the time he arrived home, the Colonel was hungry.

He sat down at the table with his ex-wife, and the maid brought in the steaming pumpkin soup. Halfway through, Polo started feeling ill. He called up his brother Antonio (who had been cited as a co-conspirator in the Miami indictment) and asked him to come over immediately, according to one version of the story. Soon after, the Colonel began to go into convulsions. He turned to Antonio and said, "Your brother is going to die." Less than two hours later, Colonel Paul was dead in Antonio's arms. The doctors arrived too late, and so did the police.

The first official version was a heart attack. Even the government, however, conceded that the death was suspicious, and began an investigation. They sent the remains of the soup to Miami for analysis. They performed an autopsy, then refused to release the results. The maid and the gardien from the house at Fermathe were arrested. Cyanide, the people said, and assumed that the Avril government was responsible. *Poison d'Avril,* was the new joke: Avril's Poison—a play on the earlier April Fool pun. Paul's twelve-year-old son went on the radio a few days after his father died and announced that he too had eaten the famous soup, but hadn't been hurt. He said the family thought it was a heart attack. Some said Paul's brothers had arranged his death in order to get their hands on his fortune; others said his ex-wife killed him at the behest of the CIA, and some said the Colonel died after doing too much cocaine.

It didn't really matter what had killed Paul; the fact was, he was gone. No one was particularly sad to say goodbye to Polo—he and his men had killed too many people. But on *Libre Tribune,* the call-in radio program, many Haitians pointed out that, one way or another, the Colonel had probably been a victim of the U.S. policy seeking his trial in return for resumption of aid. It was, they said, politically and legally impossible for the Avril regime to bring Polo to justice or to allow him to be extradited. Retired but still in Haiti, he would continue to destabilize the situation. Hence, assassination was the only solution. At least it would put Paul out of the way. Ever since the Miami grand jury indicted Paul, each Haitian leader —Manigat, Namphy and now Avril—had been participating in a game that was the military and political equivalent of playing hot potato with a grenade. When a grenade blows up, it takes many things along with it. The soup, on the other hand, had gotten only Colonel Paul.

Not immediately, but a few months later, the United States, which was eager to restore aid to Haiti under Avril (a man the State Department could live with), would be able to do so without having to admit defeat on the Paul situation. The pumpkin soup would save the State Department's face. Under the *New York Times* story on Colonel Paul's suspicious death, the editors ran a short item:

> U.S. Still Balks on Aid
> Washington, Nov. 7 (Reuters) — A State Department spokesman said today that the United States was not ready to resume aid to Haiti despite the death of Colonel Paul. Asked if Washington would resume $70 million in aid suspended after the failed election, the spokesman, Charles E. Redman, said: "Colonel Paul had been part of the problem but not the entire problem."

On the night of November 11, six days after the Colonel's demise, two cars forced the jeep of Prosper Avril's brother-in-law off a downtown street and opened fire. The man's body, riddled with bullets, was found the next morning. Perhaps the President's brother-in-law had some personal enemies. He had reportedly been an honest immigration official at a time when many armed men who feared for their lives in Haiti were trying to flee the country with falsified visas. But to most Haitians his death looked like a revenge killing. It was Colonel Paul's men who did it, they said. The murder made it easier to believe that Polo's pumpkin soup had been poisoned. More than a month later, the autopsy made it official. The cause of Colonel Paul's death, it said, was poison.

"I suspect," said a woman I knew who worked at the embassy, "those young soldiers who did the coup, the guys Avril arrested in October. I think they were Communists. That's what my Haitian friends tell me, and it sounds right. You heard their nineteen demands." She leaned forward and almost whispered. "I heard a crazy rumor at the embassy, you won't believe it." She paused and laughed. "They're saying that Father Aristide was behind those little soldiers. They say he ordered the first coup, the one against Namphy, and that he ordered this last attempt too." As *Haïti en Marche* wrote about such rumors: "It's the special dish of the day—Father Aristide is the spice in every sauce." The disinformation campaign against him was continuing.

You could get crazy thinking about Haiti; eventually even the crazy rumors sounded as if they might be true, or at least not entirely false. If you merely presumed for one second that the people you knew were nothing like what they seemed to be—if you thought of them as comedians, as Graham Greene had—anything could be true. Faced day after day with a Duvalierist talking about democracy, and with such *sincerity,* you began to think, Well, maybe the Duvalierists are democrats, maybe Avril means it.

From there, for the fragile mind, it was only a small, shaky step to Aristide masterminding a coup d'état. Hey, I thought, why not? I hadn't spoken to him for weeks. Maybe he had changed. I was tired. A coup d'état. Why not? He could do it. Ambition, self-confidence—he had those things. I mused. Titid's coup d'état: it didn't sound bad in concept, although the bishops wouldn't like the idea. I mused more. The Pope would be annoyed. But it was true that Aristide knew some people in the Army—I had discovered this over time. Perhaps they were not the highest-ranking men, but they were people with decent reputations, respectable soldiers, some of them with records of long service, most of them, as far as could be ascertained, untainted. Maybe Aristide and Sergeant Beauchard . . .

History had been happening so fast in Haiti that anything seemed possible, especially after a long day. Maybe the attack on St.-Jean-Bosco had been intended to preempt a coup that was to be led by the priest and Beauchard. Namphy found out that Aristide was planning a coup d'état, and he went after him. Anything's possible. Anything's possible. What was it Aristide had said? From one moment to the next, anything can happen. To me, that was beginning to sound like a national motto.

I was tired. The night was gathering around the house. The barrière clanked as the watchman let himself in. He was late because of the rain. A dog barked across the street, and a giant black moth—night butterflies, the Haitians call them—was trying to get at the light above the driveway. His wings made a noise like erasers being clapped together.

I sat down on the sofa in the living room and listened to the rain come down on the jalousies. There was an old *Vanity Fair* on the coffee table, with an actress on the cover dressed as a jungle savage; there was an old *Nation* and some old Haitian papers showing the smoking church. I let myself keep thinking. Maybe the United States had finally found out who was really backing the September 17 coup, and the CIA had sent Agent Avril in to control the noncommissioned officers and thwart Aristide's mad dictatorial plans. Maybe Aristide then turned to Colonel Paul—shadowy kingpin of the world's narcotics industry—to form an unholy Communist alliance to take power back for the KGB-funded ti soldats. Could that be why the demonstrators had come to the Casernes to shout their praise of Paul? That was it: those demonstrators who sang for Paul were Aristide's kids, the Communists that the bishops said had infiltrated Legliz Popilè. Hey, this was all the beginning to make sense. . . .

Your mind—what was left of it after four hours of demonstrations and five hours of gossip-filled radio broadcasts and two hours of phone calls, one after another, filled with news and contradictions and contracontradictions—could run away with you. In those confusing days, I tried to shut down by eleven at night, tried to block out the day's clutter and commotion, tried to remember those things I had seen in the last three years that had meant something, events that were clear-cut, times without coups, times when the people and the regime confronted each other face to face. I wanted to remember things that would steer me through the confusion.

I lay down with the rain still falling, but just a drizzle now. Guard dogs barked in the neighborhood and farther off. The electricity was out. We were in blackness. A jeep drove by down on Rue Trois. I tried to remember what I had seen of Haiti and what it had meant, but I couldn't do the intellectual work. My head was heavy, I was too tired, there were blisters on my feet, and they hurt and the latest rumors had sent my head spinning. Instead of remembering, I just saw.

I saw soccer players running backward in orange shorts up a hill in Cap-Haïtien in a rainstorm. A long time ago, it seemed. And Crazy Emilia in the market at Jean-Rabel, toothless and bewigged, preaching to the market crowd from a book of metric tables which she could not read, and dousing herself with clairin. A boy in Port-au-Prince, higher than high on marijuana, playing marbles alone in the middle of the street behind the Iron Market. A soldier at the gates of a northern town, taking down my passport number on the inside cover of a cheap French novel he was reading.

The phone was ringing, but I didn't pick it up. I was afraid of more confusion, or bad news. What if it was someone from New

York? The phone was too far away, New York was too far away, and it must be late, and it rang and stopped ringing and I heard instead two young students reciting the narrative of the death of Dessalines in the cool, echoing chambers of Fort-Liberté's ruined colonial fortress. Heard other students whispering their biology lessons under the streetlights of Port-au-Prince. An old blind man playing music on a set of tin cans in the National Cemetery. The drunkard at a cockfight in Bombardopolis who wanted me to marry him and take him to New York. "Marry me," he said in English. "Marry me." Now, how could he speak English? In Bombard. My mind came back to me for a second, but I drifted off again. English? No sense, no sense to it.

Ten hungry boys were break-dancing in the middle of the night on a run-down terrace in Jean-Rabel. The dark-haired photographer was taking their picture, wasn't she? What was that flash? Lightning over the horizon, and a dozen black baby coffins floating above the heads of a huge demonstration. They meant something, those baby coffins. Yes, now, what was it? Tear gas and the crowd's back, fleeing down the corridors of Bel-Air, a dusty labyrinth. The rain coming down through the Holiday Inn onto Victor Benoit's head. A man slipping down my hill, wrapped in cellophane against the rain; the gleaming guts of the Macoute whose stomach had been cut open; the brain on the floor at Ruelle Vaillant. Aristide dancing to the drums in the churchyard, Waldeck and his kitchen knife, Mimette and her eternal kite.

From remembering, I fell into a dream. Claude Raymond was chasing a presidential candidate across the courtyard at St.-Jean-Bosco while Waldeck watched, a vanilla ice-cream cone dripping in his hand. Aristide came out of the burning church and shot the two men down. They were both wearing white, and they fell into pools of blood. A jeep drove up with the Senatorial Candidate at the wheel. Aristide jumped in. They were going to meet Colonel Paul at the Casernes for lunch. Each time the jeep came to a burning barricade on Grande Rue, it flew over the fires. "Auld Lang Syne" was playing on the jeep's radio, and then the "Dessalinienne," then "New York State of Mind."

Aristide sang along in English. English? It made no sense. Colonel Paul met the jeep at the gates of the yellow Casernes. The gates were locked, and the Colonel had to ask Waldeck to open them. Two long tables were set in the Casernes courtyard; all of Paul's men were there, each one wearing a three-cornered hat, satin epaulets, and sunglasses. Aristide sat down at the head of one table, the Senatorial Candidate at the other. Aristide said grace, the men bowed their heads and said amen. Girls served them pumpkin soup. The steam from the bowls turned into tear gas, everyone was running. I couldn't get out. Colonel Paul climbed onto a table to try to calm the crowd, and fell down dead. Amid the panicked throng, Aristide stood over Polo's body, and when the Colonel came back to life he was Prosper Avril. Under his khaki cap, Avril had a jack-o'-lantern for a face.

Change did not come easily to Haiti. At Delmas 19, where the Tontons Macoute had been rounded up on the night of Polo's retirement, the downstairs hallway and bathroom were stained with blood. At Claude Raymond's dechouked house, ballots from the elections in which he was not allowed to participate—the November elections whose cancellation he had helped arrange—had been scattered everywhere. They paved the street in front of his house and floated in the bougainvillea like Christmas ornaments. "Claude Raymond, President," they read. No one could say that tomorrow, or the day after, or next year, such a man would not have such a job.

In the countryside a few things had happened. In Port-de-Paix, the soldiers had removed their commander on charges of corruption. In Côtes-de-Fer in the south, the people had set up a popular tribunal and were judging former government employees, Tontons Macoute and Army officers. Other similar episodes had occurred all over the country. But most were short-lived. In Port-de-Paix, the Army and the Macoutes struck back, broke up demonstrations, and returned to their posts. This was called *rechoukaj*. In Côtes-de-Fer one day, soldiers arrived and dispersed the popular tribunal. In St.-Marc and the lower Artibonite Valley, the san manmans had returned after a brief flight into the hills. Avril's Army took no steps to disarm this band of robbers and killers, the men who were responsible for setting up the Freycineau barricade, among other outrages. Soon that barricade was up again, and people on Route Nationale were being stopped and robbed by men with machetes and guns. The peasants from the groups up in Jean-Rabel that had been attacked in July 1987 had just released a record: "Nou Se Lavalas." We Are the Flood. In the title song, which was not played on Haitian radio, the peasants sang, *"Nap file manchet. Nou se lavalas. Nap pòte ale."* We are sharpening our machetes. We are the flood. We are sweeping everything away. In these days of returning Tontons Macoute and san mamans, the peasants' optimism seemed premature. Every once in a while, I had the evil thought that Avril had only dechouked enough Tontons Macoute to isolate and eliminate Colonel Paul and get that American money flowing. Once Paul was gone, the Army's role in the Dechoukaj ended, and soon the cleanup came to a halt.

Sometimes it was hard for me to distinguish my dreams from reality. On the way out to the airport to greet Father René Poirier, who was returning in triumph from the exile into which Namphy had shoved him, three girls in the backseat of my car kept chanting, "Viv Legliz Popilè." We stopped at the traffic light at Delmas and Martin Luther King, and they kept singing. On Radio Haïti, I heard Lyliane Pierre-Paul begin her news broadcast with the usual sign-on: "Li fè katrè." It's four o'clock. Suddenly, a man jumped out of a tap-tap that was waiting at the corner to pick up passengers. He was running, and he whipped out what I thought was a sunglass case from his pocket, but the sunglasses turned out to be a pistol, and he fired. His victim fell, the girls in the backseat shouted, "Attaché!" the light changed, and I drove through the intersection toward the airport road.

Father Poirier arrived. A kindly-looking white man, he seemed surprised by the enthusiasm of the greeting that awaited him at the airport. The young people from his parish out in Grand Goâve had come by the dozens to welcome him back, and they lifted him first onto their shoulders and then onto the back of a flatbed truck. They surrounded him. A Haitian flag had been attached to the truck's antenna, and it fluttered in Poirier's face while he was giving a live interview to Radio Métropole's reporter, who smelled of rum. In the middle of the interview, two of my girls started shouting, "Viv Legliz Popilè!" into the microphone.

On the way back to town, we got caught in a traffic jam in Bel-Air, the old slum that sits behind the cathedral. The heat was painful, but I was afraid my car would collapse if I kept the air-conditioning on, so I turned it off. We rolled down the windows. Outside in the street, people were listening to a rebroadcast of Métropole's interview with Father Poirier. Someone in a tailor's shop was playing that song by System Band—"Cheri ou twompe mwen." Baby, you're cheating on me. In the backseat, the girls were gossiping about the Papal Nuncio. They had nothing nice to say about him.

The spires of the cathedral rose in the distance, and down a precipitous hill, crowded with market women and men carrying all kinds of burdens, you could see the palace. Finally we inched down Sans-Fil onto Borgella, and there was a white car coming fast in the opposite direction. *"La petite Charade!"* shouted one of the girls, pointing. I looked, expecting for no reason other than the little car's speed to see Aristide at the wheel. But no, the driver was the daughter of the family to whom the priest had given his car after Freycineau, where their green Charade, mistaken for his car, had been burned. In my rearview mirror I watched her zipping up Sans-Fil. The little Charade disappeared around the bend. A tap-tap called Esclave was following her. Slave. One of the girls pointed again and shouted *"Esclave—gade!"* Slave—look!

The traffic jam ended abruptly at Rue Lamarre, and we kept on descending toward the palace. We passed Radio Soleil and the ice-cream stand where I had bought Waldeck his vanilla cones, and then we were at the Champ-de-Mars, the big green space where downtown ends and the residential sections begin. *"Général-Président,"* cried one of the girls as we passed the palace, *"jwet pou ou."* She was quoting Aristide: General-President, it's your turn. The girls laughed. As we approached the palace sentry box, she shouted it again. I was glad the air-conditioning was back on and the windows were rolled up. On the radio, I listened to Father Poirier saying diplomatic things about the new regime. The sky was darkening with nightfall, but the day had been clear, the evening was rosy. Pink clouds were blowing by us as the sun set. The palace sentry, I noticed, seemed to be asleep at his post, his head resting on his folded arms. Across from the palace, the National Museum was having an exhibition of works by Philomé Obin, the artist from Cap-Haïtien who had painted the famous crucifixion of Charlemagne Péralte.

Wisps of pink haze were blowing out to sea, and the dark clouds seemed to have stalled up above Boutilliers. No rain this evening. I could drive the girls home in peace. Far above our heads, on their exalted pedestals in the Champ-de-Mars, a bronze Dessalines and a bronze Christophe were riding their horses toward liberty. I dropped the giggling girls at a meeting off Martin Luther King. Even at this late hour, bulldozers were repairing the potholes that had been deepening for a year now in front of the new Téléco building, and I had to drive through the rubble that had been spread over the street by recent storms and the big yellow machines. I got a flat, of course, just above Claude Raymond's house. Immediately, three young men emerged from nowhere to fix my tire. I wondered what they were doing hanging out in the neighborhood. Now was the hour when everyone was at home, or headed there.

I leaned against the wall outside a bottle depot and watched them work. Working in the evening is better than working in the day; it's so much cooler. Women and their small children were making their way up to the bidonvilles from the nearby water fountain, carrying buckets on their heads. Two goats were foraging in the bushes. Down a street, two more young men were busy dismantling one of Raymond's cars, an old jalopy that had always been parked in his courtyard. They had picked it almost clean already. One rusty bumper was left, and they were using a crowbar to pull it away from the chassis. A fresco vendor was pushing his cart home up the street; I stopped him and bought a cherry ice. It took no time for the three young men to fix my flat, and they wouldn't take my money. As I drove off, I saw them head back toward Raymond's car. That was where they had come from.

Pulling Away:
January 1989

Aristide was ordered to leave Haiti, but he never left. This must have been a disappointment to the U.S. ambassador, who, in Washington two weeks after Avril's coup d'état, reportedly boasted, "We've finally gotten rid of him." The last time I saw Aristide, he arrived at our meeting place hidden on the floor of a jeep. He said he was more resigned than ever to his fate, and laughingly called himself one of the walking dead. "Ever since Freycineau," he said, "what I have left of life has been a gift. I'm grateful for it." Then he vanished into hiding again. All over town, even on Henry Christophe's pedestal, were scrawled the words *"Aristid kanpe, pale, sikile ak pèp-la."* Aristide, stand up, speak, circulate among the people.

Little by little, the priest began to do what those signs urged him to. Other progressive priests were thinking about inviting him to say mass in their parishes, but it was a risky proposition. Here and there, Aristide was seen, but for the most part he lay low, waiting for some final dispensation on his case from the Church. He continued sending cassettes to the radio stations, with messages for those who were begging for his presence. Each time one of his messages was broadcast, the outcry against the government was renewed. Aristide upbraided the hierarchy of the Church, mocked General Avril. "One coup d'état. Another coup d'état," he said in one cassette. "A general leaves. A general returns. And then? And then, nothing. . . . General Avril, don't you see that the train that derailed Namphy is going to carry you away even faster? . . . Alone, we are weak; together, we are strong. Together, we are the flood. The blessing of the Lord is upon the people. Let his grace descend until the flood itself brings down all Duvalierists, all Macoutes, all criminals from this day forth and forever more, amen." There were persistent rumors that he would soon be defrocked. "I think all this is going to end badly for me," he told a friend.

In New York, the Haitian exile community, sick of the succession of military governments, and convinced by now that no peaceful means could bring about change in Haiti, was talking about armed struggle. They seemed sincere, but who was going to lead this armed struggle? Perhaps they themselves intended to. It had happened before in Haiti, under Dr. Duvalier, when small groups of exiles trying to topple the regime regularly infiltrated the country and were captured, disarmed and executed.

"Remember that anyone who talks about armed struggle," the Senatorial Candidate had told me years before, "is not doing it or is a fool. When you're doing it, preparing it, you don't talk about it." In Haiti, no one was talking about it. Opposition activists mentioned the need for "strategy and infrastructure." Strategy I could understand. But infrastructure?

"Infrastructure?" I would ask them. "It sounds like a code word."

"Infrastructure," they would respond, looking at me significantly. I had to presume they meant organization and arms, not roads and bridges. There were constant rumors of illicit arms shipments to Haiti, and I had heard that they were not all going to the Tontons Macoute and the attachés. Some had been distributed among the people of the bidonvilles, I heard. But when you recalled that the attackers at St.-Jean-Bosco were from the bidonvilles, paid in rum and chump change, this thought was not comforting. I had begun to think that it was money to buy men and women, and not ideas to move them, that made Haitian history. Perhaps it was both. When the opposition activists said "strategy," they meant ideas. Maybe when they said "infrastructure," they meant money.

The election masquerade had begun yet again. On November 3, 1988, Avril issued a provisional electoral decree outlining a proposal for establishing yet another electoral council that would set a timetable for elections. Like Namphy before him, he "pledged to lead Haiti to democracy," as the *New York Times* put it. He was sounding all the proper notes: he had rid himself of Colonel Paul, now he was talking about elections. The truth of the matter was that his government was broke, and if the U.S. did not renew aid soon, Avril would be unable to pay for gas and wheat. There would be instability. Although after the aborted election of 1987 the American Congress had banned almost any kind of aid to Haiti, the U.S. Administration soon released some $30 million to Avril, on technicalities. "We are encouraged by what the Avril government is doing," the *New York Times* quoted a U.S. official as saying.

But what was the Avril government doing? The most one could say about the General's first months in power was that he had dealt with Colonel Paul, who had become an impediment in resecuring American aid, and had taken apart Paul's attaché system. And then? And then, nothing. No one had been arrested in connection with the massacres at Jean-Rabel, Ruelle Vaillant or St.-Jean-Bosco. No one had been arrested in the wake of government investigations of the murders of two presidential candidates and the progressive lawyer Lafontant Joseph. This was not because no one knew who the suspects were, but because the Avril government, like Namphy's governments before it, did not want to bring to the witness stand anyone who might testify about the complicity of members of the regime. Though there had been much talk of reparations for victims of political violence, Avril's government made no move to recompense either the families of people killed in the recent massacres or those of the Duvaliers' victims.

With considerably more finesse than Namphy, Avril was maintaining the status quo. As the *New York Times* put it, Avril "has continued to offer assurances that his objectives are in line with those of the United States." In renewing some aid to Haiti, the United States showed what its objectives were. The way in which the aid was restored revealed a concern for the stability of the Haitian government, and not for any democratic intentions. According to U.S. Embassy sources, two thirds of the $30 million released to Avril had been scheduled to be issued quietly to Namphy in the middle of September, quietly because the massacre at Ruelle Vaillant had turned Namphy into an embarrassment to the United States. The signing of the document releasing the aid, planned for September 12 or 13, had had to be postponed in the aftermath of the attack on St.-Jean-Bosco. According to the same embassy sources, the document was finally signed by the U.S. government at the beginning of October, a few weeks before Avril issued his electoral decree on November 3. Yet a month later, after it added another $10 million to the initial aid package, the U.S. government trumpeted the release and portrayed its action as an incentive to Avril to continue on the path toward democracy.

What Third World democracy means to the U.S. government is best expressed in an article written by former Secretaries of State Henry A. Kissinger and Cyrus Vance in *Foreign Affairs* (Summer 1988), entitled "Bipartisan Objectives for American Foreign Policy." "Preventive diplomacy and preemptive reform," the two men wrote, "can reduce the risks of extremist political infection and radical contamination." Perhaps "preemptive reform" includes elections ("preventive diplomacy" in Haiti might include working with those in the Church hierarchy who want to "get rid" of Aristide). U.S. support for elections, Vance and Kissinger's vocabulary implies, should be based not so much on a people's right to self-determination as on preventing unfriendly governments from establishing themselves.

Some Haitians, like the Senatorial Candidate, used to think that even an election devised by a military dictatorship might have some value. "It can give you a space to work in," he said in the days leading up to the November 1987 election. "It can allow you to organize your people to work for real democracy." But he agrees now that Haiti's last two elections—one aborted, and the other, a sham —do not prove his theory.

Haiti is a special case. In countries like Chile, Pakistan, Argentina, the ruling class can sometimes be persuaded that even in a state where some form of law is respected they will be able to maintain their place in society. But the Haitian ruling class is so small and has been corrupt and criminal for so long that its members are certain that the rule of law would destroy them; thus the attack on Ruelle Vaillant. They are so few and have so much that they remind you of the frightened French planters, who had to be cruel to their slaves in proportion to how greatly they were outnumbered. They are like the planter beating his slave on the eve of Boukman's descent. Perhaps they are becoming more desperate because they know that their reign is nearing its end. They are certainly getting ready to leave when the moment comes. A common saying in Port-au-Prince is, *Boujwa-a ap mache avek viza-l nan pòch li*. The bourgeois goes around with his visa in his pocket.

A scion of one of Haiti's wealthiest families was electrocuted in the middle of the night recently when he went out in a rainstorm to turn off electricity that he was siphoning from one of Electricité d'Haïti's lines. He had been warned by an Electricité d'Haïti employee that a rare inspection was planned. He was stealing from the government, and he was so cheap—or so impulsive—that he didn't think to pay some lackey two dollars to hide the fact for him. Rather than spend a couple of dollars paying someone else to sever the illicit connection, he died. Jeanne thought he deserved what he got. It was ill-bred of him, she said, to have done it himself. Especially in the rain. Other Haitians say that his fate will eventually be the fate of the entire ruling class. The elite will kill itself off, they say, because of its obsessive need to steal from the nation. Reacting to such greed, people like Gangan Pierre call for divine retribution. Others, like the girls from the People's Church, call for revolution. At the end of 1988, one of the dead man's relatives, planning for the latter, was building a house with a fake wall in it where he could hide his "hunting guns." Prosper Avril was smarter. He reportedly sold his house to the Haitian government for $1.5 million. In the event of a revolution, another coup, another dechoukaj, he would be liquid.

Someday soon in Haiti, another round of elections will go forth. Maybe Marc Bazin will be the Americans' candidate once more, maybe not; in any case, a field of familiar faces will join him in the run for the presidency. Once again, these elections will be run by a military dictatorship, under Avril or under whatever general or colonel may have replaced him by then. Perhaps there will be a new electoral council. The result of the elections will be ambiguous. As Namphy once said, democracy in Haiti is not for tomorrow. He was in a position to know.

After Namphy deposed Manigat, a friend of mine analyzed the prospects for Haiti's future. "Well, it will be like this," he said with a wicked smile. "One day, Namphy will gather his men around him at the palace and say, 'Look, guys, the Americans are on my back again. The fools still want elections. We want their money. So I figure, let's give them elections. What the hell. Can't hurt.'

"His ministers nod.

" 'Yeah,' they say to him. 'No big deal.'

"He sits back in his chair, ruminating.

" 'The problem is,' he tells them, 'who's going to be our man?'

"They knit their brows, he knits his. You know these Army fellows, it takes them a while to come up with an idea. So, okay, after a few minutes of deep thought, Namphy's face lights up.

" 'Hey,' he says. 'There is this one guy. I remember him from back a little while ago. This guy, man, he'd do anything to be President. Fat guy . . . talks too much . . . what's his name?'

"His ministers think back, heads in hands, poor things.

" 'Ah,' says one, after long reflection, 'I think I know who you mean. Um . . . Manigat, right? Fat Leslie.' The minister laughs.

"Namphy nods. 'Right, right,' he says. 'That's the one. Let's run him.'

"And so," my friend predicted, laughing, "we will have an endless round of Manigat elections and Namphy coups. It doesn't matter which actor is playing the role, but it is still always Namphy and Manigat, the Army and the corrupt politician. Until we change things for real. Until the people move. One day they will, you know. That revolution has been boiling in our blood for too long now. It will come." My friend was not morally indignant at this bleak prediction for Haiti's immediate future. Rather, he was faintly disgusted, amused, finally optimistic. A philosopher. A Haitian.

I hadn't known Haiti long enough to adopt his long view, though I could see that it had its merits. The long view kept discouragement at bay. Those who believed that Haiti was capable of change could see beyond the endless Namphys and Manigats; they could see beyond the perpetual dance of the Port-au-Prince politicians and take solace in small victories: Aristide's cassettes, twelve pigs distributed free to peasants, the continuing work of Chavannes' peasant movement out in Hinche. Someday, they believed, all those small victories would add up to a larger triumph.

But I had arrived in Haiti at a moment when change seemed imminent. I had seen strikes and protests and men and women who stood up and took charge of their lives and spoke out against dictatorship. I had seen Lucy who didn't have time for the long view. I believed then that it would all happen now. When it didn't, I was no longer consoled by peasant collectives, by neighborhood committees, by breathtaking sermons. I was still an outsider, and an American. Like the U.S. government which pretended to believe that Haiti's problems could be solved by the miracle of an election, I had believed that real change could be accomplished quickly. After Duvalier fell, I wanted the people to rise as one and bring liberty, equality, fraternity—and democracy—to Haiti. But I learned that it was more complicated than that.

"Ou twò prese," a Haitian woman told me. You're in too much of a hurry.

Of course she was right. The Senatorial Candidate had told me the same thing after the massacre at Ruelle Vaillant, in different words: *"Se lè koulèv mouri, ou konn longè-l."* He smiled. "Do you know what that means?"

I told him I hadn't quite understood.

He repeated the sentence, a Haitian proverb.

"What's *koulèv?*" I asked him.

"Snake," he said in English. "Serpent." He translated: "Only when the serpent dies can you take its measure." He looked away. "It was a long serpent."

Back in Manhattan, I tried to learn the long view. I wanted to be a philosopher like my Haitian friends, raise my eyebrows, let a wicked smile play around my mouth, tell jokes, and continue to believe. If only I could see Haiti as it had been years ago, I thought, if only I could see the endless procession of Namphys and Manigats, of Bazins and Aristides, of Well-Placed Embassy Officials and Chavannes, of Duvaliers and Péraltes parading before me while the people in the background grew restive, perhaps I would come to believe again that change would one day come to what U.S. magazines like to call "our troubled island neighbor."

I decided to teach myself a lesson. Down on West Fifty-seventh Street, a technician named Iksang Junne led me into a room in the CBS archives, a beige air-conditioned room lit with fluorescent bulbs. Iksang runs the tapes for people like me who are trying to get the long view on a subject. He is not a talkative man.

"These are from the early days of Duvalier's reign," he said. "They will be silent, black-and-white. Negative." Iksang's back was to me; he was fitting a tape through the complicated mechanism.

The tape started to run. An election, 1957; it was a negative, blacks and whites reversed. The voters stood in line, silently, their white faces topped with shocking white hair. Soldiers stood around in gray uniforms, holding white guns. Dr. Duvalier came onto the screen, emerging from a long white car. He was running for President. He looked uncharacteristically flashy in his white suit, white bowler hat and white bow tie. Overshadowed by his tall wife, Simone, Dr. Duvalier cast his vote, for himself no doubt, since in an interview he gave CBS six years later he had said, "I have always been the most popular presidential candidate in Haiti."

Then the inauguration. The cars pulled up at the palace, disgorging ministers in white suits. Black priests in black soutanes bowed their heads to the new President; these were the European bishops of Haiti, and soon Duvalier would be rid of them—doubtless one of them was Monsignor Poirier, the Archbishop of Port-au-Prince who in a few years would be exiled, like his namesake under Namphy. The new President shook hands with a series of men in civilian clothes, diplomats from the United States and France. He raised a glass of champagne to the assembled and began to speak. Iksang and I heard silence, and the tape machine.

Now it was Carnival, 1963. The deepest days of Duvalier's terror were beginning. Shipped in from the countryside, the people descended from big buses to join in the street festivities. It was noon-time in Port-au-Prince, but on our negative film it was night. The sky was black, the road was white. We were on Grande Rue. Bands were playing silent tin drums and blowing noiselessly through long sticks of bamboo. A float drifted across the screen; on it was a saxophone player and a trio of voodoo drummers. Costumed men came into the picture in close-up, dressed like apparitions from the last days of the French monarchy, sequins and crinoline, silk and feathers and high hairdos. Their faces were painted like African tribesmen. A truck sailed behind them. "Vive Duvalier" was written across its side.

Next, La Saline; the slum was bigger then, before Dr. Duvalier had completed his housing project, Cité-Simone (named after his wife and later renamed Cité Soleil after the Catholic station Radio Soleil), and razed part of La Saline in order to beautify the port area of the capital. Our car drove down Boulevard de La Saline past gleaming tin shanties that seemed to give off their own light. The sky was black; it was always night in this Haiti. We entered the slum, driving over glistening puddles of white slime that shone amid the black dust. Now we were walking through La Saline. Down one bright narrow passageway, we found another band, playing music at a cockfight. They were blowing the bamboo, and playing their silent notes through a huge tin funnel. The funnel blower wore a high dunce cap, and everyone was dancing to the inaudible drums. I got bored at the cockfight; it was too much like an election. I asked Iksang to speed through it, and we watched the two furious animals quickly peck each other into a macédoine of feathers and blood while the spectators shouted and placed their bets soundlessly.

We headed through downtown up to Boutilliers. On the gray street the cars made white shadows, like pools of gold chasing behind them. The sky was still pitch-black; it would be hours before the storm clouds descended and the night sky grew white. The houses up above Pacot were the color of charcoal in the bright afternoon sunshine, and their windows were glowing with an incandescent light that made me think of Sylvain and Jeanne, and of chandeliers and dinner parties, or of people waiting up through the night for bad news.

Finally we arrived. Up here, we would get the long view. Our cameraman panned back and forth across the valley of Port-au-Prince, showing us a field of white trees with here and there a black spot—the rooftops of gingerbread houses. Far in the distance rose the towering black spires of the cathedral; the cameraman contemplated them for a few seconds, but then something else caught his attentive eye: a large black three-humped structure stretched out like a tropical monster. It was Duvalier's palace; he was in there now, getting a few last hours of the day's business attended to before night set in and other business was undertaken.

There was something about it, that palace. Our cameraman couldn't get away from it. Each time he pulled back to show us the long view, the whole range of the city—the black waters of the bay, the tin shanties and cardboard shacks of La Saline, the bright foliage that covered much of the capital, the hills of Bel-Air—he zoomed back to the palace. Look at this over here, he would say, pointing his lens at the graveyard. But only for a moment, and then back to the monolith. Look at this new hotel, he said, panning up to a point above the cemetery; that cross up on the hill, the mountains in the distance, that little road you can see winding over there—but then, each time, back to the black palace.

This obsession with the seat of power was an outsider's obsession, the obsession of the U.S. government, the obsession of foreign correspondents; that was the lesson I learned from the cameraman's failure to keep his eye on the long view. The palace exerted a singular attraction for him, the way Dr. Duvalier had for Graham Greene, the way elections have for the State Department and the *New York Times,* the way the zombi has for foreign anthropologists. Most Haitians try to look away from the palace, try to avoid it. They know that Haiti is bigger than that. The evil power is not the only thing. Of course the chef de section still rides through the Haitian hills with his revolver at his hip, and the President still travels in a twenty-car motorcade, armed to the teeth. But the long view sees more than a trail of Mercedes limousines twisting through mountains of misery, more than Dr. Duvalier riding through town and tossing bright coins to the children of La Saline.

The long view sees those children, not the dictator. It takes into account the villages and the slums and the pretty houses of Pacot, as well as the palace and the Casernes Dessalines. If you cast your eyes wider than the palace grounds, you can see dozens of small churches, with their paper flowers hanging behind the altar, and their broken fans, their makeshift seating arrangements and slatted windows. You'll see rifles too, and revolvers, grenades and tear gas, but there are also tailors' sewing machines and beauticians' hair dryers, doctors' stethoscopes and accountants' computers. Besides the Macoutes and the Police and the Army, there are the car salesmen, the dry cleaners, the jewelry-store owners, and the poor relations who work for free in the homes of their wealthier aunts or uncles or cousins. Duvalier is present, certainly, or Namphy, or Avril now, or the colonel or general who is next in line. There are the people who profit from power, but also the people who take a loss.

Gangan Pierre is sitting in his studio thinking about rum and rainbows, and the Senatorial Candidate is teaching new students about Dessalines. Dockworkers are unloading Miami rice and bicycles, and towels and washrags from the People's Republic of China. Restaurateurs are minding their dwindling registers, and waiters are serving grilled pork and salted fish. Marianne is doing Jeanne's laundry; Djo's girlfriend has found a job in a factory near the Parc Industriel, stuffing dolls for export to the U.S.A. X-ray technicians and opthalmologists and specialists in tropical disease are seeing patients at Aristide's Clinic for the Poor, looking for developments in Lucy's tuberculosis, in Waldeck's Vitamin-B deficiency, in the sores, scabs, rashes, wounds and other complaints of the people who have managed to get across town now that it is too dangerous for Aristide himself to run the jitney service from the slums. The Disco Doctor is helping rich men and kids like Djo to stop taking drugs, stop drinking. Bernadette is getting ready to board the tap-tap for the Northwest province and her charcoal pickup; and the workers at the nursery in Bombard are watering a new batch of seedlings in the sun. In Jean-Rabel, the peasants are still organizing, and undertakers are putting the finishing touches on silver-painted coffins. Musicians are writing songs about the new regime, and a band of blind men is singing a song called "Chemen Viktwa (Li Long)." The Road to Victory (It's Long). A painter is painting a portrait of a Tonton Macoute in post-postcolonial dress: a satin blue-and-red uniform, and reflector sunglasses overshadowed by a three-cornered hat. It is called "The New Familiar."

These people do not want anything to do with the palace. They are working on other projects; their politics are practical. All, in their various ways, are thinking about change, about strategy—and infrastructure. Marianne, beating Jeanne's cotton shirts between two rocks; the Disco Doctor, listening to the story of how his latest patient from Pétionville or La Saline became involved in the cocaine trade; even Bernadette, wondering whether there will be enough charcoal next year to keep her supplied. The CBS camerman had the same problem that plagues U.S. policy-makers; he needed a wider-angle lens.

For months, each time the phone rang late at night in my Manhattan apartment, I panicked. I was always certain that the call would bring news of Aristide's death. Nothing seemed more likely. The elite still sensed a threat from his corner. The new government would surely be happier without him, and the Church hierarchy was still adamantly, publicly silent about his fate. In fact the attack on St.-Jean-Bosco had momentarily strengthened Aristide's position, as had all previous attempts against him. The elite understood this. One wealthy woman who had just arrived in New York for a vacation told me that Aristide was "issuing ultimatums." I asked her what she meant.

"Those radio broadcasts," she said.

"Those are ultimatums?" I asked.

"His tone of voice is too strong, it's threatening," she said. "He is frightening people off the streets."

More likely, I thought, it was the armed robberies and late-night street murders that were keeping people at home. But her perception of Aristide, and that of others like her, was what made me frightened each time the phone rang. When such people feel threatened, there is no assurance that their response will not be stark. After so many unsuccessful attempts to maneuver the priest out of the political arena, his detractors clearly felt by now that the only workable solution to the Affaire Aristide was assassination. Otherwise, he would simply continue on. Past experience showed that he was not easily diverted. He would keep on talking, undaunted.

Aristide turned the logic of his enemies on its head. "My best protection," he told me, "is to keep on doing exactly what I have always done." If the people continued to support him, he felt, no one would risk killing him, because of the chaos that would ensue. The people were Aristide's bodyguards, another progressive priest told me. "Sometimes," Aristide said, "if you let a man live, he is less dangerous than if you kill him. If you kill him, you will never be rid of him."

The Church finally used its weapon of last resort against Aristide. On December 15, the Salesian order expelled him, with the approval of the Vatican. The communiqué, issued from Rome and released to the Associated Press before Aristide received it in Haiti, cited the priest's refusal to disengage himself from politics as the reason for his expulsion. The Salesians claimed that Aristide's preachings "exalted violence and class struggle" and were "in contrast with his Salesian and priestly vocation." Within the Church, the communiqué was seen as the culmination of the long campaign against Aristide and Ti Legliz. Rumor had it that the Papal Nuncio and the Archbishop of Cap-Haïtien were in Rome advising the Vatican and the Salesian order in the weeks during which the Salesians were putting together the four-page directive.

"The type of political commitment Aristide has assumed," the communiqué stated, "is in serious contrast with the clear will of the founder [of the Salesian order, Saint John Bosco]. . . . In addition, the incitement to hate and violence, the exaltation of class struggle, go directly against that fidelity to the [teachings] of the Church that forms a living part of the Salesian spirit." The communiqué further accused Aristide of encouraging the "destabilization" of the Church in Haiti. The Salesians hastened to add, however, that Aristide remained a Roman Catholic priest.

Progressive priests in Haiti laughed at the idea. "That thing about being a priest, it's meaningless," said one. "You're not really a priest if you have nowhere to perform the sacraments, and now Titid has really nowhere to go. He can't say mass in Haiti, that's for sure. One of the bishops would have to agree to allow Aristide to say mass in his diocese, and there is no bishop in Haiti, not even Romélus, who will allow that to happen after such a communiqué, with its Vatican stamp of approval. Titid has been banned."

Aristide was now a priest without a parish and, more important, without a pulpit. The Salesians' directive expelling him from the order was the nonsecular equivalent of burning down his church, but its effect was more far-reaching. Now, even if St.-Jean-Bosco were rebuilt, Aristide would not be allowed to preach there. His

friends in Ti Legliz, who issued a Christmas protest against the
expulsion, wondered whether he would rise from the ashes of his
priesthood as quickly as he had from those of St.-Jean-Bosco. "Right
now, he is in great danger if he shows himself," one priest said to
me. "Remember, so many times it has been his vestments that have
saved his skin." For the moment, Aristide himself remained silent.
He had been with the Salesians for twenty years, and even though
he had long expected the expulsion, it still came as a shock. His
family had rejected him. He was back in deep hiding.

During the week when the Salesians expelled Aristide, General
Avril was busy discharging noncommissioned officers throughout
the country. Many of the discharged men were the soldiers who had
purged their barracks of corrupt officers in the days following the
September 17 coup. Now they were being replaced by the very men
they had eliminated. Two weeks later, on New Year's Eve, in the
dead of night, Franck Romain was issued a safe-conduct and escorted across the border to the Dominican Republic by Haitian
troops. "THEY CRUCIFY CHRIST," read a headline in *Haïti en
Marche,* "AND LIBERATE BARABBAS."

It was a stuffy little apartment on 123rd Street in Manhattan, nine
blocks from my own. I walked there through the dark streets.

"Welcome," Ginette said as she stood in the kitchen frying pork.
The place smelled of pork fat. Ginette was a large woman with hair
that stood out from her face in all directions. She was a mambo, a
voodoo priestess. Ginette served many spirits, but Baron Samedi,
the Lord of the Dead, was her familiar.

Chairs lined the narrow corridor from the kitchen to the living
room. Drums and bamboo were playing on the stereo, and on the
plastic-covered sofa men were drinking beer from cans and talking
about the American elections.

"Bush," said an older man, *"se mem bagay avek Reagan."* Bush
is the same thing as Reagan.

"CIA," said a younger man. *"Li pi rèd pase Reagan, si sa posib."*
CIA. He's worse than Reagan, if that's possible.

On the floor across from them was a vèvè etched in cornmeal. A
smiling skull and bones, with stars like asterisks floating around it.
A little boy running back and forth across the linoleum kept stepping
in the vèvè.

"Be careful," said his mother in English, pointing at the skull.
"You'll ruin it."

A table behind the vèvè served as an altar to Baron. Cookies and candies were piled high on plates, and a sweet mash was solidifying in a glass bowl. Placed randomly around these offerings were white porcelain skulls and bottles of clairin, cheap perfume, and siwo, the powerfully sweet syrup used to flavor frescoes and desserts in Haiti. Two middle-aged women dressed in white were seated in front of the altar on either side of the vèvè, holding ritual rattles in their laps, waiting for the ceremony to begin.

At around eleven-thirty, Ginette entered at the head of a procession of young girls, each bearing upon her head another platter for the altar. She and the women with rattles began the ritual chants that start any voodoo ceremony, saluting first all the Catholic saints and then all the voodoo spirits. The worshipers, about twenty of them, sang along when they knew the words. The older people knew them. The younger people clapped in time to the beat of the rattles.

Then Ginette rose and began to flail and fall, and Damballah came down into her, and she sank to the floor in a snakelike writhe. As she lay there, the worshipers fed her sweets, stuffed them into her mouth. She slithered around the room and down the corridor, greeting each participant, hugging their legs and feet. She demanded presents and food without pronouncing a real word. Damballah does not speak the language of man—he talks in a birdlike twitter. An hour later, Erzulie Freda came to possess Ginette, and she sprayed perfume over her favorites and ordered an older man to marry her. They performed a wedding, complete with a written marriage certificate.

"He has to buy a ring tomorrow, to show that he is married to Erzulie," a friend of mine told me. "You do, too, because she kissed you and asked where was your ring." I said okay. The smell of Erzulie's bad perfume was in my hair.

It was getting late, time for Baron Samedi. The participants began calling for him.

"Ginette, Ginette," said a man with a belly. *"Kote Baron?"* Where's Baron?

"Tann li, tann li," she replied in the midst of a chant. "Wait for him, wait for him."

And he came, ripping Ginette across the room and sending her eyes back in her head. She was riveted to the center of the room, but the two other women hastily pulled her away back into a smaller room, where some of the young people had been flirting and giggling. A few minutes later she emerged. Her face had been powdered white, and she was wearing a black jacket over her white dress, a pair of black pants under it. On her head was a high fur hat, black also. She was wearing sunglasses, and swearing. She had a queer half-smile on her face. The Baron always swears. He talks dirty and dances close, the dance of copulation.

Baron lit a big cigar. "Hey, little girl," he said to one of the women sitting on the sofa. His voice was odd, nasal. It reminded me of something. "So your mother let you out of the house, eh? I guess she knows." He laughed. I kept thinking I had heard him before, but this was the first time I had seen Baron. All Barons, like all Damballahs, talk in the same voice, no matter whom they have possessed.

"Little girl," he continued, leering at her. "I guess your mother knows you need a big hard cock inside you, right?" Everyone laughed nervously. Baron, he was uncontrollable, a vakabon.

"I bet your mother knows." He grabbed the girl by the arm and started doing the dance of copulation with her. It was a little difficult for Baron to manage this, his stomach was too big, and the girl was reluctant, even though she knew she had to go along. He curled over the girl and pushed against her. "A big hard cock," he repeated, laughing. The girl laughed a little, and coughed because of the smoke from Baron's cigar. "Pretty girl," he said, letting her go abruptly.

He sat down and called for food. The women started distributing fried chicken and fried pork to the assembled, and we ate along with Baron.

I left at about two in the morning, and Baron was still eating. I went over to him, and shook his hand to thank him for the ceremony. *"M kontan wè w isit,"* he said to me. "I'm happy to see you here."

I was sure I knew that high-pitched, nasal voice, and, walking home, it came to me. It was the voice of Dr. Duvalier. "What, what, what . . . did you get that?" I remembered the phrase, the *Face the Nation* interview, with CBS's Martin Agronsky trying to get a straight answer out of Papa Doc. I remembered the voice, odd, nasal, and the queer half-smile.

On my last visit to Haiti, I stayed at the Oloffson. All my American friends had left the country, and my Haitian friends' houses weren't big enough for guests. I was in the Chambre Lillian Hellman, next door to the new Chambre Mick Jagger. Mick would have been happy. His name plate had been reassigned to a bigger room, just off the pool.

The Oloffson was quiet. Avril was in the palace, and the U.S. government was supporting him. After the initial cleanup in which Colonel Paul was swept from power, there had been little dramatic public action, and the foreign journalists stayed away. Avril eventually released the ti soldats he had imprisoned, but that wasn't much of a story. You couldn't really cover the nighttime murders and robberies, and the countryside was still too dangerous to explore. The Oloffson had a few guests, though. Two adventurous American tourists, a Dominican from the United Nations' High Commission on Refugees, a Frenchman who, he said, stayed at the hotel when he "did business" in Port-au-Prince, but otherwise lived in a house in Petit Goâve on the southern peninsula and was writing a novel. There were visitors in the evening, too. A group of Mormon missionary women who came to see the Monday-night voodoo show, a cousin of Franck Romain's who had supposedly been composing a new menu for the hotel for the last three months, Dieudonné Lamothe, the Olympic marathoner, and of course Aubelin Jolicoeur, in his white suit.

Out in the countryside, the Army was doubling its forces to begin a massive repression against Chavannes' peasant movement and Benoit's Konakom, a repression ordered by Avril and his Minister of Information. They had also published a list of five opposition leaders whose arrest was being sought. They arrested two others on trumped-up charges. The Avril regime was shaky, nothing new.

It was a Monday night, voodoo night. I went down to the pool. I had seen Aristide that morning, and I kept thinking of him traveling around town hidden on the floor of a jeep. It was dramatic, but it seemed humiliating, somehow. I took a swim; afterward, the night air was cool. The voodoo troupe was playing loud drums up on the veranda, and an occasional patter of applause filtered down. Bats flew low over the blue pool, and then back into the palm and banana trees. A dozen orange and white striped deck chairs lounged like lazy bathers around the deep end. Outside the Oloffson's grounds, tap-taps went screaming by, their music blaring and then fading into the distance. A near-accident seemed to occur every few minutes; tires would screech, and horns would erupt, and shouting, and then a momentary silence. There were two bright stars in the sky and a waxing moon, and gunfire.

I sat by the side of the pool with my feet in the water and the drums going and the bats swooping down, and thought about the struggles I had seen in Haiti, the long years that seemed to have accomplished so little. I had ended up where I'd begun, and that wasn't so bad. Some of the Haitians I had known had ended up there, too, Avril in the palace, the presidential candidates waiting for the next election, Mimette in La Saline. Duvalier and Namphy and Manigat had moved on, but that wasn't so bad. Manigat could probably come back soon, if he wanted to. Franck Romain had finally gone the way of Namphy and the rest. Others—their victims —had not been so lucky.

On the plane home, it wasn't easy to imagine returning to Manhattan, although Manhattan is just another island of corruption. For a long time, I used to see those old Haitian scenes whenever I shut my eyes to try to fall asleep. For a long time, back in New York, the attaché with his gun out, the man coming down my street wrapped in cellophane against the rain, Dessalines on horseback, the ballots outside Raymond's, the women of Duverger carrying their water back from the river, Waldeck with his vanilla ice-cream cones, and the coffins and all the faces and colors of the crowds in the markets and the demonstrations would come dazzling before my closed eyes.

Only after long struggle had I begun to understand the simple meaning of those scenes. This much I learned: the women walking down the road with water on their heads, the man coming down my hill wrapped in cellophane—these are not icons from the Third World, or mysteries, but rather women walking down the road with water on their heads, a man wrapped in cellophane against the rain. To the farmers watching the women return from the river, they are not objects for wonder and reflection, just as to your husband or your children or your guests you are not miraculous when you turn on the water faucet at the kitchen sink. The women are getting water; you are getting water. To another Haitian, the man wrapped in cellophane is as full of mystery as you in your raincoat are to me.

Still, to a foreigner the country was amazing, even when you knew it well. Misery walked around the place like a live being, with filth under its nails, garbage trailing around its ankles and nothing in its stomach, breathing foulness into rusted airless shacks, and sucking away life. Fires burned down the airless shacks and rains swept them away, and then the residents set up house under the shards of tin roofs for a month, while with no help from the outside they built the whole rotten place up again so that they could wait again for it to be wrecked again. And still my Mimette flew her ragged kite, and still the Senatorial Candidate rode bravely down the street on his rickety bike, dodging potholes. This was more than hope amid wretched-ness, the tiresome cliché of missionaries and development workers. This was energy, a force that, if channeled into something greater than endurance—which is already a great thing—could move a na-tion. I had seen that force begin to move, although it had been blocked and stymied, and finally turned back—with help from the outside. Supported by their friends on the other side of the water, the masters of misery were still in control. Sometimes, Haiti made me think of the laughter of slaves.

I knew that while I slept that night in my apartment in Manhat-tan, waiting for the old Haitian scenes to play before my shut eyes, the men of Bel-Air would be out on the street as usual, playing dominoes, waiting for their turn to sleep. The tireless corner women would be making fritay and selling cigarettes and candy. A knot of young men would be standing around, teasing a pretty girl. The morning I left, the Senatorial Candidate had taken a tap-tap back to Gonaïves, sitting stooped over on a hard seat, talking to a bunch of market women whose legs were stretched out next to him over their baskets. When he got to Gonaïves that afternoon, he would hurry home, and Josette the housegirl would give him lunch. After the sun went down, he would go visiting. He'd sit in a circle, discussing politics with the soft-drink distributor and the judge and the valiant accountant. Change would come, they would decide. It was taking too long, though, they would say. When the sun came up the next day in Manhattan and Port-au-Prince, Marianne would fix coffee for Sylvain and Jeanne, and tune into Radio Soleil at seven. I would miss the news, miss my regular chat with Marianne. She always had something to say about each item.

My plane was flying over the coast at Cap Haïtien, flying past Christophe's vain Citadelle. Waldeck had come halfway to the air-port with me that afternoon, without Ayiti. He had turned on the radio and the air-conditioning full blast, and begun chattering about himself. He needed money, he said. I smiled at him. Ayiti was cutting cane in the Dominican Republic, Waldeck told me. Maybe it was true. A few weeks before, he said, he and Ayiti had been taken across the border for a "vacation," and then sold to a cane plantation. In Waldeck's version, Waldeck had escaped. "I don't like that place," he said. He had grown a little since I last had seen him, but his legs were covered with sores. Aristide had taken Waldeck back into the family—with conditions. No drugs. Behave. I wondered how long that would last.

I left Waldeck off at the corner of Delmas and the airport road. In the rearview mirror, I saw him hail a tap-tap to take him down to St.-Jean-Bosco. He would spend the afternoon begging from the nuns and priests who might come by, and from foreign journalists who happened along to check out the ruins of the church. As I flew out over the Windward Passage, I thought of Aristide, living a straitened life, knowing that from one moment to the next, anything can happen. I thought about the last words of the note that he had sent me the night before, my last night in Haiti: *"Bon kouraj. Yo vin cheke-m. Fò-m ale."* Courage. They've come to check on me. I must go.

Bibliography

Alexis, Jacques Stephen. *L'Espace d'un cillement*. Paris: Gallimard, 1959.
———. *Compère Général Soleil*. Paris: Gallimard, 1955.
Anglade, Georges. *Atlas critique d'Haïti*. Montreal: ERCE & CRC, 1982.
Aristide, Jean-Bertrand. *Leve tab-la*. Port-au-Prince: J.-B. Aristide, 1986.
Archer, Marie-Thérèse. *La Créolologie haïtienne*. Port-au-Prince: Le Natal, 1987.
Balch, Emily Green. *Occupied Haiti*. New York: The Writers Publishing Company, Inc., 1927.
Banks, Russell. *Continental Drift*. New York: Ballantine Books, 1985.
Bastien, Rémy. *Le Paysan haïtien et sa famille*. Paris: KARTHALA, 1985.
Castor, Suzy. *Les Origines de la structure agraire en Haïti*. Port-au-Prince: Le Natal, 1987.
Cauna, Jacques. *Au Temps des isles à sucre: Histoire d'une plantation de Saint-Domingue au XVIIIè siècle*. Paris: KARTHALA, 1987.
Cone, James H. *God of the Oppressed*. New York: Seabury Press, 1975.
Corvington, Georges. *Port-au-Prince au cours des ans*. Port-au-Prince: Henri Deschamps, 1987.
Courlander, Harold. *Haiti Singing*. Chapel Hill: University of North Carolina Press, 1939.
Davis, Wade. *The Serpent and the Rainbow*. New York: Simon and Schuster, 1985.
Dejean, Paul. *Prélude à la liberté*. Port-au-Prince: M. Rodríguez, 1987.
Delince, Kern. *Armée et politique en Haïti*. Paris: L'Harmattan, 1979.
Denning, Melita, with Osborne Phillips. *Voudoun Fire: The Living Reality of Mystical Religion*. St. Paul: Llewellyn Publications, 1979.
Deren, Maya. *Divine Horsemen: The Living Gods of Haiti*. London: Thames and Hudson, 1953.

Désinor, Carlo A. *L'Affaire Jumelle*. Port-au-Prince: L'Imprimeur II, 1987.

————. *Daniel Fignolé: Un espoir vain*. Port-au-Prince: L'Imprimeur II, 1986.

Diederich, Bernard, and Al Burt. *Papa Doc and the Tonton Macoutes: The Truth About Haiti Today*. New York: McGraw Hill, 1969.

Dorsinville, Roger. *Mourir pour Haïti, ou Les Croisés d'Esther*. Paris: L'Harmattan, Collection Encres Noires, 1980.

————. *Toussaint Louverture*. Montreal: CIDIHCA, 1987.

Duvalier, François. *Mémoires d'un leader du Tiers Monde*. Paris: Hachette, 1969.

————, with Lorimer Denis, *Problèmes des classes à travers l'histoire d'Haïti*. Port-au-Prince: Les Griots, 1958.

Etienne, Frank. *Les Affres d'un défi*. Port-au-Prince: Henri Deschamps, 1979.

————. *Bobomasouri*. Port-au-Prince: F. Etienne, 1984.

————. *Troufoban*. Port-au-Prince: Les Presses Port-au-Princiennes, 1978.

Fass, Simon M. *Political Economy in Haiti: The Drama of Survival*. New Brunswick, N.J.: Transaction Books, 1988.

Ferguson, James. *Papa Doc, Baby Doc: Haiti and the Duvaliers*. Oxford: Basil Blackwell, 1987.

Fignolé, Jean-Claude. *Les Possédés de la pleine lune*. Paris: Editions du Seuil, 1987.

Fombrun, Odette Roy. *Le Drapeau et les armes de la République d'Haïti*. Port-au-Prince: Henri Deschamps, 1987.

Fouchard, Jean. *Les Marrons de la liberté*. Port-au-Prince: Henri Deschamps, 1988.

Gaillard, Roger. *Les Blancs débarquent: Hinche mise en croix*. Port-au-Prince: Le Natal, 1982.

————. *Les Blancs débarquent: Charlemagne Péralte, Le Caco*. Port-au-Prince: Le Natal, 1982.

————. *Les Blancs débarquent: La guérilla de Batraville*. Port-au-Prince: Le Natal, 1983.

————. *Charades haïtiennes*. Port-au-Prince: Editions de l'An 2000, 1972.

Greene, Graham. *The Comedians*. New York: Viking Press, 1965.

Gutiérrez, Gustavo. *Hablar de Dios desde el sufrimento del inocente: Una reflexión sobre el libro de Job*. Lima, Peru: CEP—Instituto Bartolomé de las Casas, 1985.

Haiti: Duvalierism Since Duvalier. New York: Americas Watch and the National Coalition for Haitian Refugees, 1986.

Heinl, Robert and Nancy. *Written in Blood: The Story of the Haitian People, 1492–1971*. Boston: Houghton Mifflin, 1978.

Herman, Edward S., and Frank Brodhead. *Demonstration Elections: U.S.-staged Elections in the Dominican Republic, Vietnam, and El Salvador*. Boston: South End Press, 1984.

Hobsbawm, E. J. *The Age of Revolution: 1789–1848*. London: Weidenfeld and Nicolson, 1962.

Hurbon, Laënnec. *Le Barbare imaginaire*. Port-au-Prince: Henri Deschamps, 1987.

————. *Comprendre Haïti: Essai sur l'etat, la nation, la culture*. Port-au-Prince: Henri Deschamps, 1987.

————. *Culture et dictature en Haïti: L'imaginaire sous controle*. Port-au-Prince: Henri Deschamps, 1987.

————. *Dieu dans le vaudou haïtien*. Port-au-Prince: Henri Deschamps, 1987.

Hyppolite, Michelson Paul. *Contes dramatiques haïtiens,* Tome I. Port-au-Prince: Imprimerie de l'Etat, 1951.

James, C. L. R. *The Black Jacobins: Toussaint L'Ouverture and the San Domingo Revolution*. New York: Random House, 1963.

Jonassaint, Jean. *Le Pouvoir des mots, les maux du pouvoir: Des romanciers haïtiens de l'exil*. Paris and Montreal: Arcantere/PUM, 1986.

Korngold, Ralph. *Citizen Toussaint*. Boston: Little, Brown, 1944.

Laguerre, Michel S. *Urban Life in the Caribbean*. Cambridge: Schenkman Publishing Co., 1982.

Lappé, Frances Moore, with Rachel Schurman and Kevin Danaher. *Betraying the National Interest*. New York: Grove Press, 1987.

Lemoine, Maurice. *Bitter Sugar: Slaves Today in the Caribbean*. Chicago: Banner Press, 1985.

Leyburn, James G. *The Haitian People*. New Haven: Yale University Press, 1941.

Lowenthal, Ira P. *Ritual Performance and Religious Experience: A Service for the Gods in Southern Haiti*. Albuquerque: University of New Mexico, 1978.

Luc, Jean. *Structures économiques et lutte nationale populaire en Haïti*. Montreal: Les Éditions Nouvelle Optique, 1976.

Madiou, Thomas. *Histoire d'Haïti*, Tome IV, *1807–1811*. Port-au-Prince: Henri Deschamps, 1987.

———. *Histoire d'Haïti*, Tome V, *1811–1818*. Port-au-Prince: Henri Deschamps, 1987.

Métraux, Alfred. *Voodoo in Haiti*. New York: Schocken Books, 1972.

Moise, Claude. *Constitutions et luttes de pouvoir en Haïti, 1804–1987*, Tome I, *La Faillite des classes dirigeantes*. Montreal: CIDIHCA, 1988.

Moral, Paul. *Le Paysan haïtien: Etude sur la vie rurale en Haïti*. Port-au-Prince: Fardin, 1978.

Moreau de Saint-Méry, Médéric-Louis-Elie. *Description de la partie française de l'isle Saint-Domingue*, Tomes I, II, III. Paris: Société Française d'Histoire d'Outre-Mer, 1984.

Nerée, Bob. *Duvalier: Le Pouvoir sur les autres, de père en fils*. Port-au-Prince: Henri Deschamps, 1988.

Nicholls, David. *From Dessalines to Duvalier: Race, Colour and National Independence in Haiti*. Cambridge, Eng.: Cambridge University Press, 1979.

Ott, Thomas O. *The Haitian Revolution, 1789–1804*. Knoxville: The University of Tennessee Press, 1973.

Pamphile, Léon Denius. *L'Education en Haïti sous l'occupation américaine 1915–1934*. Port-au-Prince: Antilles, 1988.

Paquin, Lyonel. *Classes sociales en Haïti: Classe moyenne et super classe*. New York: L. Paquin, 1986.

———. *The Haitians: Class and Color Politics*. Brooklyn, N.Y.: Multi-Type, 1983.

Perkins, Dexter. *The United States and the Caribbean*. Cambridge, Mass.: Harvard University Press, 1947.

Philippe, Jeanne. *Les Causes des maladies mentales en Haïti*. Port-au-Prince: Editions Fardin, 1968.

Pierre-Charles, Gérard. *Radiographie d'une dictature*. Port-au-Prince: Le Natal, 1987.

Price, Richard, ed. *Maroon Societies: Rebel Slave Communities in the Americas*. Baltimore: The Johns Hopkins University Press, 1979.

Price-Mars, Jean. *La Vocation de l'élite*. Port-au-Prince: Edmond Chenet, 1919.

———. *Ainsi parla l'oncle*. Paris: Imprimerie de Compiègne, 1928.

Prince, Rod. *Haiti: Family Business*. London: Latin America Bureau, 1985.

Report on the Situation of Human Rights in Haiti. Washington, D.C.: Organization of American States, 1988.

Rigaud, Milo. *Vè-vè: Diagrammes rituels du voudou*. New York: French and European Publications, 1974.

Roberts, Kenneth. *Lydia Bailey*. Garden City, N.Y.: Doubleday, 1947.

Rodman, Selden. *Haiti: The Black Republic*. New York: Devin-Adair, 1954.

Rotberg, Robert I., with Christopher K. Clague. *Haiti: The Politics of Squalor*. Boston: Houghton Mifflin, 1971.

Roumain, Jacques. *Gouverneurs de la rosée*. Paris: Messidor, 1944.

Seabrook, William B. *The Magic Island*. New York: Harcourt, Brace, 1929.

Soukar, Michel. *Un Général parle*. Port-au-Prince: Le Natal, 1987.

Thoby-Marcelin, Philippe, and Pierre Marcelin. *La Bête de Musseau*. New York: Éditions de la Maison Française, Inc., 1946.

Thompson, Robert Farris. *Flash of the Spirit*. New York: Vintage, 1984.

Trouillot, Michel-Rolph. *Les Racines historiques de l'état Duvalierien*. Port-au-Prince: Henri Deschamps, 1986.

Vandercook, John W. *Black Majesty: The Life of Christophe, King of Haiti*. New York and London: Harper & Brothers, 1928.

Vissière, Isabelle and Jean-Louis. *La Traite des noirs au Siècle des Lumières: Témoignages des négriers*. Paris: A. M. Métalié, 1982.

Index

DATE DUE		8/89
AUG 1 0 2020		